THE
SACRED
NETWORK

"Few among us are willing to follow our thoughts and intuitions until they bloom with discovery. Chris Hardy has devoted her life to finding out what lies beyond the veil and bringing it back to us so that we might share in her vision. *The Sacred Network* is nothing less than fascinating."

LINDA DENNARD, PH.D.,
ASSOCIATE PROFESSOR OF POLITICAL SCIENCE AND
PUBLIC ADMINISTRATION AT AUBURN UNIVERSITY
AND AUTHOR OF *COMPLEXITY AND POLICY ANALYSIS*

"Chris Hardy has been exploring the complex relationship between mind and matter over her entire career as a researcher and consciousness explorer. Now, with *The Sacred Network,* she's provided the definitive work on ley lines and other physical locations of power and their relationship to the psyche."

ROBIN ROBERTSON, PH.D.,
CLINICAL PSYCHOLOGIST, ASSOCIATE PROFESSOR AT THE
CALIFORNIA INSTITUTE OF INTEGRAL STUDIES,
AND AUTHOR OF *MINING THE SOUL*

THE
SACRED
NETWORK

Megaliths, Cathedrals, Ley Lines, and the Power of Shared Consciousness

CHRIS H. HARDY

Inner Traditions
Rochester, Vermont • Toronto, Canada

Inner Traditions
One Park Street
Rochester, Vermont 05767
www.InnerTraditions.com

Text paper is SFI certified

Library of Congress Cataloging-in-Publication Data
Hardy, Christine, 1949–
  [Decoding the sacred network]
  The sacred network : megaliths, cathedrals, ley lines, and the power of shared consciousness / Chris H. Hardy.
      p. cm.
  "Originally published in 2008 by Terra Futura under the title Decoding the sacred network"—T.p. verso.
  Includes bibliographical references and index.
  Summary: "How sacred sites amplify the energies of consciousness, the earth, and the universe"—Provided by publisher.
  ISBN 978-1-59477-381-5
  1. Consciousness—Miscellanea. 2. Sacred space—Miscellanea. I. Title.
  BF1999.H373 2011
  203'.5—dc22
                                                              2010046607

Printed and bound in the United States by Lake Book Manufacturing
The text paper is SFI certified. The Sustainable Forestry Initiative program promotes sustainable forest management.

10 9 8 7 6 5 4 3 2 1

Text design by Jon Desautels and layout by Priscilla Baker
This book was typeset in Garamond Premier Pro with Gill Sans and Augustea used as display typefaces

To send correspondence to the author of this book, mail a first-class letter to the author c/o Inner Traditions • Bear & Company, One Park Street, Rochester, VT 05767, and we will forward the communication, or visit the author's website at **www.sacrednetwork.net**.

This book is dedicated to the questers
who have explored the unknown
with magnificent skill and courage,
especially the ones who have taken on the difficult task
of harmonizing a scientist's mind and a natural talent
for sensing the semantic dimension.

In special homage to Carl Jung and Wolfgang Pauli
for their breathtaking pioneering work and
inspirational presence in the semantic dimension.

In homage to Linda Dennard, Stanley Krippner,
Tobi Zausner, Pille Bunnel, Jacques Donnars, Martine Le Coz,
Eric Pigani, Stéphane Grès, Gabriela Garcialuna, and
Nicole Bartolucci for the sacred enthusiasm motivating them
and their oeuvre; my heartfelt thanks to them for
our inspiring and stimulating exchanges.

CONTENTS

Acknowledgments   x

Foreword by Stanley Krippner, Ph.D.   xi

Introduction   1

PART 1

TELHAR FIELDS AND HARMONY FIELDS

1   A Quester's Direct Path   14

2   Music and Harmonic Rapture   50

3   The Secret of Shared Prayer   61

4   Inheriting Sacred Places   73

5   Weaving the Collective Consciousness   90

6   Consciousness as Energy   100

PART 2

THE SACRED NETWORK

7   Cathedral Builders and Megaliths   134

8   Unveiling the Christian-Druidic Grid   185

9   The Sacred Network of Paris: The Obelisk Node   197

10   St. John the Baptist's Pyramid and the
Châtelet Node   247

PART 3

EXCEPTIONAL TELHAR FIELDS
Space and Time Singularities

11	Annulling Space	267
12	Time Singularities	296
13	Toward a Planetary Consciousness	315

| | Conclusion | 331 |

APPENDIX 1	Sacred Lines in Paris: Major Axes and Leys	333
APPENDIX 2	Circle Drawn on the Apexes of the Obelisk Hexagon	346
APPENDIX 3	Grand Ten-pointed Star on Châtelet Node	348

	Notes	352
	Bibliography	357
	Index	362
	About the Author	369

LIST OF ILLUSTRATIONS

BLACK-AND-WHITE FIGURES

7.1	The St-Michel line in Brittany	145
7.2	Vertical cosmo-telluric lines	159
7.3	The crossing of two sacred lines to form a 3-D Sri Yantra	174
7.4	The Magdalene of Pilar	179
9.1	The heart chakra as a Sri Yantra	204
9.2	The Maltese cross or St. John cross, also called St. John the Baptist's cross	207
9.3	Golden rectangle, golden spiral, and the golden proportion	215
9.4	Paris golden rectangle and mandorle	219
9.5	Sri Yantra (Star of David)	224
9.6	A hexagon grid	225
11.1	Annulling space: rod and funnel in a telhar field in Brazil	274

COLOR PLATES

1	Main axes and leys in Paris
2	A Spot and G Spot at two crossings of cosmo-telluric lines
3	Flow of sacred lines around an obelisk and a cave
4	Obelisk: golden rectangle and hexagon
5	Obelisk: Sri Yantra
6	Châtelet: two small pentagrams
7	Châtelet: two embedded ten-pointed stars
8	St. John the Baptist's pyramid

ACKNOWLEDGMENTS

I'm grateful to Philip Thomas for showing me the circle routes he was unraveling and for his work on Paris's symbolic sculptures.

My friendly gratitude to Fred Tristant, who has given me his support in many ways in the process of collecting data.

My appreciation for their collaboration in designing the maps and figures to Ravi Saha, Fred Tristant, and Hemant Kumar Goswami.

To Jean-Paul Rouffignac, with whom I used to relish discussing these subjects, I send my thoughts in the semantic dimension.

I would like also to thank the team at Inner Traditions, especially Jon Graham who enthusiastically welcomed this book on board, and Chanc VanWinkle-Orzell, who gave me her relentless support and without whose patience, humor, and dedication (above and beyond her professional talents) this book wouldn't have reached completion.

I'm grateful to Joseph Rowe and Catherine Braslavski at Natural Chant for their early support for this book; but I would especially like to thank them for their astounding musical talent that enriched the marvelous times we shared in jam sessions with a group of friends along the years.

FOREWORD

Chris Hardy, Ph.D., is one of the most intrepid explorers of the frontiers of consciousness. Her books and articles have provided original insights into the human mind and its capacities. *The Sacred Network* follows in this tradition, providing its readers with a blueprint for their development both as individuals and as members of the human species.

In the first part of this book, Chris Hardy proposes that "collective consciousness" will be the next step in the evolution of humanity and points to the signs of its development. Perhaps the most positive indication is the increasing concern for the environment; more and more people are becoming more efficient in their use of energy sources and in preserving the natural world. She writes about a "collective harmony field" and how to attain it through meditation, prayer, and visiting sacred places.

In the literature on collective consciousness, there is a "weak" version and a "strong" version. The weak version consists of reports of shared attitudes and beliefs, a social group's agreement on moral, ethical, and political issues. The strong version is more profound; people have the experience of being entangled with others so deeply that their identity shifts from the person to the group.

I have witnessed this phenomenon myself in Bali, Indonesia where the Hindu Kecak chanters sit in a circle and begin their repetition of spiritual words and phrases. Gradually, the chant increases in rapidity and volume until it actually sounds like a single voice. Many participants told me that they lost their sense of personal identity and felt as if they were a part of a larger whole. Similar reports come from the Bushman shamans in Namibia whose mental technology allows them to "merge" with their ancestors to receive knowledge and healing power. In the Western world, the "gathered" meetings of the Quakers are spiritual occasions marked by collective consciousness. Chris Hardy provides a number of other examples including meditators, monks, musicians, and prayer groups.

All of these examples are reminiscent of Carl Jung's notion of the "collective unconscious" and Pierre Teilhard de Chardin's concept of the "noosphere," both of which were sources for the development of the Global Consciousness Project. This project involves an international collaboration of some 100 scientists who have recorded continuous data from electronic devices placed at dozens of networks around the globe. The data collected at these sites consist of electronically generated signals that are usually random. The exceptions show times of unexpected coherence in the signals that typically correspond with events involving a communal focus, generally implying a worldwide, or at least large scale, interest. These events are sometimes great celebrations, such as the World Cup or New Year's Eve. At other times, they are awful tragedies, such as the death of Princess Diana or the September 11th terrorist attacks in New York City and Washington D.C. Data from the Global Consciousness Project has been published in peer-reviewed journals and provides evidence for a "collective unconscious" that operates at an unconscious level.*

The second part of Chris Hardy's remarkable book discusses sacred edifices and the ley lines and arcs of energy that seem to be associated with them. She provides numerous examples ranging from the Egyptian pyramids and Chartres Cathedral to the "Sacred Network," a hypothetical grid that connects sites of different religions and eras all over the planet. Chris Hardy recounts her own experiences in several parts of the world including India where she

*See pages 24–25 and note 1 in chapter 1, page 351 and also: R. D. Nelson,. "Coherent Consciousness and Reduced Randomness: Correlations on September 11, 2001," *Journal of Scientific Exploration* 16 (2002): 549–70.

made the exceptional discovery of a "telepathic-harmonic field" in Nasik, one of the four towns that host, in turn, a gathering of ascetics, gurus, and savants known as the Kumba Mela. She discloses her immersion in a harmonious collective state in which she experienced "mental interconnectedness" that lasted even as she strolled through temples and gardens. Throughout the recounting of her encounters with "energy fields," Chris Hardy provides phenomenological descriptions, and hopes that her readers will explore similar states as they engage in exceptional experiences.

I once participated in an experiment in Great Britain, where thirty-five volunteers spent one or more nights in sacred sites in England and Wales.* They were accompanied by a partner who observed their eye movements as they slept, awakening them when the eyes darted back and forth, an indication that they were dreaming. The volunteers' dreams were duly recorded and compared to dreams they recalled while at home. Several significant differences emerged. Site dreams were more aggressive, home dreams were friendlier; site dreams had more male characters in them than home dreams, as well as more strangers. Whether these differences were due to the sites' strangeness and lack of comfort or to some intrinsic properties of the sites themselves is unknown. However, the study could be repeated elsewhere and, in the meantime, provides an example of how Chris Hardy's conjectures about "telepathic-harmonic fields" could be investigated.

In *The Sacred Network*'s chapter 1, "A Quester's Direct Path," Chris Hardy gives readers directions as to how they can plan, record, and learn from their own inner and outer voyages. Her knowledge-base spans Jungian psychology, parapsychology, systems theory, chaos theory,

---

*This study was conceptualized and executed by Paul Devereux and the statistical analysis was carried out by Stanley Krippner and Robert Tartz; Adam Fish provided an archeological context for the discussion of the results. For details, see: P. Devereux, S. Krippner, R. Tartz, and A. Fish, "A Preliminary Study on English and Welsh 'Sacred Sites' and Home Dream Reports," *Anthropology of Consciousness* 18 (2007): 2–28.

and Semantic Fields Theory (her original contribution). She sees a shift in human consciousness sweeping the world in a decade or two. If she is right, *The Sacred Network* will have played a role in this collective transformation of human consciousness.

STANLEY KRIPPNER, PH.D.

Stanley Krippner, Ph.D., is internationally known for his pioneering work in the scientific investigation of human consciousness, especially such areas as dreams, creativity, parapsychological phenomena, altered states of consciousness, shamanic cultures, and chaos theory. A professor of psychology at Saybrook University, San Francisco, Krippner previously directed the Dream Laboratory at Maimonides Medical Center in New York and was Director of the Child Study Center at Kent State University. His many awards include the 2002 American Psychological Association (APA) Award for Distinguished Contributions to the International Advancement of Psychology. He is also author or coauthor of 20 books and articles including *Personal Mythology, Extraordinary Dreams and How to Work with Them, The Mythic Path,* and *Haunted by Combat: Understanding PTSD in War Veterans.*

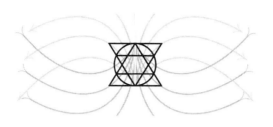

INTRODUCTION

This book stands at the crossroad of two eras: the future era already in the making and a very ancient past in which our ancestors left sacred markings on Earth that all religious currents passing with the ages were bound to respect.

This book stands at the very point where two pyramids touch at their tips and the field lines fan out in both directions: the far past and the far future. Indeed, my subject matter is twofold: on the one hand, I discuss collective states of harmony that point toward a leap in human consciousness in the near future, and on the other hand, I unveil a sacred network of monuments and sites located around the globe and built by our ancestors, the enigmatic people who erected the megaliths. Each facet of my subject matter sheds light on the other; indeed, I came to understand that our ancestors' very aim in building the prehistoric sacred network was to prod the emergence of a higher consciousness in humanity. I believe this is the reason why this sacred network has been not only protected but also beautifully expanded through the centuries, even in our modern world.

The first part of this text thus deals with the emergence of collective consciousness. Rather than viewing it in an abstract way, this part covers a very specific set of phenomena, namely energetic structures linked to consciousness. When several individuals are assembled for a common purpose, such as meditating or playing music, they might achieve a very extraordinary state of collective harmony and deep sharing. Sometimes this group attunement is so strong that it literally and discernibly results in the formation of a telepathic field, as if all participating minds have fused into one group mind.

If the experience is in itself puzzling, the physical anomalies it entails are even more bewildering. These states of attunement present precise energy structures—such as a circling torus of light or bipolar fields—that clearly suggest they are energy fields created by the energy of consciousness.

Thus, among my very first observations were large consciousness fields, permanent and stable, that existed in two sacred places: a church adjoining a monastery in Brittany and the holy city of Nasik in India. In these two instances, all people within the field were in deep telepathic or harmonic attunement within a collective mind. To my utter amazement, these two fields showed identical energetic features: a clear delineation in space marked by a precise boundary on the ground as well as a grid high up in the sky, forming a dome above. Such consciousness fields can be created in a variety of settings—for example, when people meditate or improvise music together. Because these fields are, at the psychological level, based on a deep harmonization of minds and they trigger a telepathic exchange, I call them *telhar fields* (telepathic-harmonic fields).

Suppose you were asked, "Have you ever experienced a state of harmony, or fusion, with another person (or with a group) such that you felt you were sharing and communicating beyond language?" Most of us would answer in the affirmative. The sharing of thoughts and feelings with another person would get the highest score, but fusion within a group would be far less uncommon than we would expect. Whether at a concert, during a collective prayer, or in extreme conditions (extreme sports and adventures, war, collective disaster, etc.), many of us have reached a state of silent communion far from the ordinary. Yet we generally have not fully grasped how remote this experience is from an ordinary exchange, implying words, images, or just context and body language. What stops us from doing so is our belief that consciousness is only a feeling, a quality—at best, a process. Yet to those of us who can actually see the energy of consciousness or thoughts, a whole new dimension of reality reveals itself. A state of deep harmony within a group literally creates a field of energy that encompasses the whole group—a field that is most commonly of a spherical shape. Sometimes, however, astounding energy structures will appear. A doughnut shape, or torus, seems to accompany extremely harmonized states of consciousness (a state of oneness or fusion, several minds blending into one group mind). As far as large collective fields are concerned, they are sometimes created around two distant centers—two people acting as *nodes,* linked by a powerful two-way stream of energy. While this peculiar structure may look like an electromagnetic dipole (a rod with one positive end and one negative end), there is, however, ample experimental evidence indicating that telepathy does not imply electromagnetic energies, even as a carrier wave for information.

We will thus explore consciousness—the fields of consciousness— with a totally new paradigm in mind: viewing consciousness-as-energy and tracking any occurrence in which it clearly appears this way, such as forming regular structures or having spatial boundaries. More exciting still, consciousness as energy defies the space and time of our good old Newtonian physics. It tinkers with space in annulling distance, and it tinkers with time in annulling timespan.

We are definitely entering a new dimension of reality in which past, present, and future coexist. "No big deal!" the smart ones say. "This was already proposed by general relativity." Agreed. But we are now talking about events, occurrences—something you may experience tomorrow!

My second theme, developed in the second part of this book, has to do with amazing arcs of light that spring out of churches and temples, steeples and domes, and that reach down toward other buildings, only to rebound again, thus creating magnificent webs of light linking monuments: the sacred network.

The sacred network, however, is not a recent configuration, nor is it specific to a country or a religion. In fact, the blueprint for the complex network we can observe today is, at least in Europe, a network of megaliths erected between 6000 and 2000 BCE.

Researchers studying megaliths have always been puzzled by their extremely precise configurations (such as ellipses, circles, or alignments), which in many instances point to clear-cut astronomical events.

Alfred Watkins, the discoverer of alignments, or *leys,* noted that these alignments include a great variety of prehistoric artwork that sometimes belongs to widely different periods. The fact that some additional standing stones, cairns, and the like have been erected centuries later right within the line of a previous alignment shows how much these alignments were held sacred through the millennia. More recent constructions, such as Roman ruins and churches, are also precisely integrated into the prehistoric leys, and, conversely, straight lines connecting churches and monuments often run through megaliths. More puzzling yet, sacred monuments are often built over ancient ones— as if preserving their exact position was of crucial importance—and we will discover why. Many cathedrals and churches have thus been erected over megalithic sacred sites—the most striking example is Chartres cathedral, which was intentionally built over a prominent Druidic shrine and is said to hide an arc of menhirs underground. In other places, ruins of Gallo-Roman or Egyptian temples are found beneath Christian edifices—such as the cathedral of Notre-Dame de Paris or Saint-Sulpice Church. Thus, despite the destruction of particular standing stones, the Christian network was superimposed on the megaliths' blueprint network—or arch-network—adding complexity, but nevertheless preserving the ancient grid.

A hypothesis developed in this book is that giant telluric waves, undulating vertically and linked to the geomagnetic field of Earth, create a network of crisscrossing lines all around the planet. The megalith builders understood that the points at which these waves crisscross each other had a paramount effect on consciousness. They marked these crossing points with standing stones, which became the open-air temples of the Celts until the Roman and Christian eras. Because, however, any elongated or pointed vertical shape (such as a menhir, steeple, or tower) acts as an antenna attracting cosmic energies, the waves flowing through a network of standing stones or churches are in fact cosmotelluric waves. Megaliths and prehistoric artwork are widely distributed on Earth, and we know that they were deemed highly sacred by many ancient civilizations, such as those of the Native Americans and the Dogons in Africa.

The megaliths people must have had the gift of seeing and sensing these cosmo-telluric lines—a gift that enabled them to gather a whole body of knowledge about the influence their flows and crossings had on human consciousness: they trigger a shift to a heightened and more spiritual state of consciousness. Furthermore, because these cosmo-telluric lines are naturally oscillating, an added benefit to erecting a standing stone or a temple at their crossings was to fix them. Once fixed, their energizing power was constantly reinforced by the people who gathered there to pray—that is, by the energy of consciousness, called *semantic energy*.

The sacred network in France, especially in Paris, unveils geoarchitectural planning that has respected the arch-network and these energetic laws over the two millennia of the Gallo-Roman and Christian eras at the very least. The building of larger Gothic churches to replace Roman-style churches, on top of Gallo-Roman temples, themselves on top of Druidic cult places, which in turn were set at the very spot where megaliths had been erected—all this kept charging sacred sites that were resonant with the earth with ever more spiritual energy. In the viewpoint of Semantic Fields Theory (SFT), such building continuously expanded and empowered the same semantic field (consciousness field) by concentrating spiritual energy on places that are naturally beneficial to soul and body.* With the elevation and refining of the Gothic style, the magnificent spiritual ships that were the Gothic cathedrals—the main rectangular part of which is called a *nave*—took to an even higher state of consciousness the spirits of people assembled there.

Through the ages, the sacred network of each religion had thus been precisely and respectfully embedded within all previous networks, weaving an architectural masterpiece, an alchemical Great Work dedicated to the elevation of consciousness—not only in space, but also in time. The *sacred nave of initiates*—a symbolic representation found in many

---

*A semantic field is the consciousness of an individual viewed as a dynamic mind-body-psyche system. I call the semantic fields on objects and places *eco-fields* (they are in effect eco-semantic fields). SFT uses the word *semantic* in its etymological sense—from the Greek *semantikos,* a signification, an act of signifying. See Hardy, *Networks of Meaning.*

religions—superbly crossed time toward its luminous Omega Point: the dawn of a harmonized collective consciousness.

In Paris, the outstanding geo-architecture of the sacred network creates a constant bouncing of meaning among geometry, names, symbolic forms, and nature's beauty, such as the Seine and the seven hills of Paris. Patiently working on maps and historical data to unveil these marvels and diving into the collective masterpiece that is being cocreated on the Internet add up to an experience similar to that of an archaeologist who patiently and amorously brings to light an age-old temple out of the subterranean realm.

Drawing only the network linking religious buildings (churches, cloisters, and abbeys), because most of them were anterior to the 1789 Revolution and the First Empire, I was dumbfounded to find that one prominent node of the churches' network was the Luxor Obelisk*— certainly extremely holy and sacred, albeit in the antique Egyptian civilization, where it was one of the two columns fronting Luxor's temple. Moreover, whole ensembles of buildings fit into vast structures based on sacred geometry. To give you an idea: a large golden rectangle, which has the Obelisk as a center, extends from Etoile Plaza to Châtelet Plaza. In addition, this golden rectangle is surrounded by a hexagon that shares the same center and is marked by important churches and avenues. Nested within both the golden rectangle and the hexagon, and having the same node, the Obelisk, is La Madeleine, a magnificent masterpiece of sacred geo-architecture. La Madeleine (a church devoted to Mary Magdalene) is embedded within a lily—or, more precisely, within the specific geometrical shape used to represent the central petal of the lily of France (a symbol of kingship) on blazons. Thus La Madeleine stands inside the sacred middle space of the golden rectangle, inside the mandorle (double ogival arc) drawn within this space, as if springing from another set of arcs originating at the Obelisk.

---

*The Obelisk, 3,300 years old, was given to the French King Charles X in 1829 by the viceroy and pasha of Egypt, Muhammad Ali, and was erected at the Concorde Plaza in 1836. Seventy-five feet high and weighing 230 tons, it was originally in the Temple of Amon and Mout in Thebes (Luxor in Egypt), built by Ramses II between the fourteenth and thirteenth centuries BCE.

Another exceptional geometrical and symbolic design is St. John the Baptist's pyramid. A large triangle is formed by three of the five churches dedicated to St. John the Baptist. The inner node of this triangle is the Obelisk. Both the western church and the triangle's center are on Paris's main east-west axis (called decumanus). The eastern side of the triangle goes through Saint-Sulpice Church (built above an ancient Isis temple), then passes in front of Carreau du Temple (part of the medieval headquarters of the Knights Templar's worldwide order), meanwhile another line in this structure runs into the prominent St. Denis Basilica. If we now connect St. Denis to the three St. John churches, the line creates the 2-D representation of a pyramidal shape. The symbolic richness of St. John's pyramid is astounding. It makes reference to Egypt and Isis (the Obelisk and Saint-Sulpice Church); the Knights Templar and their two patron saints, John the Baptist and St. Denis; and finally the Priory of Sion (Saint-Sulpice Church). The meaning revealed in this structure sheds new light on the emerging data suggesting that St. John the Baptist, highly revered by both the Templars and the Priory, was an adept of a Gnostic cult that originated in Egypt.[1]

The sacred network within Paris, while certainly inspiring, is not unique: high sites (that is, places of great and longtime spiritual energy) of different religions and ages are connected all over the planet. According to Philip Thomas, the grand east-west axis of Paris—which runs by the Luxor Obelisk at the Concorde Plaza and the Louvre's glass pyramids—when extended as a circular route around the planet, reaches Mount Sinai. Another circular route running mostly south of the Seine goes through Knossos in Crete, the Sphinx in Egypt, and Mecca, among other sacred sites.[2]

Decoding the sacred network and unveiling its history written in stone lead us to inevitable questions about its purpose: what is indicated by such a Great Work, which extends worldwide and spans more than eight millennia? What could be its planetary purpose? If temples and churches built at major crossings of sacred lines have a spiritualizing effect on people, what could be the all-encompassing effect of the planetary network? Was this grid intended to steer and accelerate the dawn of a planetary consciousness? This is where the two lines of research, collective consciousness and the sacred network, merge. Indeed, the formation of ever larger telhar fields—and their bewildering superimposition that sometimes happens at great distance—unveils the grand design to which we are individually called: the cocreation of a planetary consciousness. In this time of sparkling emergence and boundless opportunities for all questers, to know how to connect to the collective consciousness and function within it could mean more than a thrilling personal leap and the opening of an endless path of experience and discovery. It could well be the key to our future—to ensure that such a future will indeed exist and to ensure us of its quality. We are now living in a time of great tension for humankind as well as for the planet. We must deal with the imbalance of many ecological systems and the possibility that some of them may reach a threshold beyond which a collapse is triggered. Further, because all complex systems are interconnected, the collapse of a crucial system may have unforeseeable consequences on all coupled systems. With the sharp increase in environmental catastrophes, many people believe we are witnessing the precursor signs of the End Time and expect Armageddon to occur. It's true that the pace of ecological change is so rapid, while in contrast our political decisions and real actions are so timid, that our chances to reverse or merely lessen an ecological collapse are meager at best.

Yet there is a force that is never taken into account in the equation— and it has the power if not to reverse the process, then at least to curb its worst consequences. This force is collective consciousness. While it's evident that we are nearing the end of a time, there are many signs showing that a new cycle is in the making at a deep, underlying level, and this cycle will surprise us all when it comes to the forefront. We know that positive suggestion and visualization can trigger a healing process and prod the body to reorganize itself toward a healthy state. In the same way, we must view our planet as an intelligent organism. When our collective consciousness harmonizes and starts to send new signals—positive visualizations of cooperation—it will prod the biosphere to regain some balance.

The Great Work of our age is to learn how to create and connect ourselves to the planetary telhar field and, from there, to conceive and envision a workable future for Earth. And that's where the sacred network built in stone will be of immense help, because it has created the backbone on which the planetary telhar field can thrive. Indeed, an enormous part of this network, beyond the stones and buildings, dwells within the collective dimension of consciousness and compels us to weave connections among us all. The people who assembled and prayed together at ancient sacred sites were creating the first telhar fields. The interrelations—based on harmonic resonance—that are at play in telhar fields and expressed through the sacred network are an inspiration for launching our next evolutionary step as a humanity harmonized within itself and in harmony with our natural environment.

There are many indicators that collective consciousness will be the next leap in evolution on Earth—both opening new reaches of the mind and offering us the means to heal Earth. To become convinced that this leap is already happening, we need only to observe the emergences in terms of collective responsibility, ecological focus, heightened consciousness, and psi abilities (capacities such as precognition, clairvoyance, and telepathy). This leap should start a new cycle on Earth under the sign of collective harmonious spirituality among responsible individuals, each of us connected to our own higher Self. Yet there's no guarantee that we'll effectively succeed in completing this leap to another state of our collective being, because, standing in our way, are huge obstacles above and beyond the problems linked to the biosphere. Strangely, one of these is the nightmarish vision of the Apocalypse or Armageddon described in St. John's book of Revelation. From the perspective of SFT, the Apocalypse is a negative attractor in our collective psyche: it constellates our worst fears, defeatism, and self-culpability as much as it amplifies all warlike and lethal tensions. While endorsing this frenzied ensemble of broken pieces, any person or group may project onto our collective future whichever nightmare is plaguing him or it. Indeed, psychologist Carl Jung's in-depth analysis talks about a "shadow" within the psyche and reaches the same conclusion about the author of Revelations.[3] The dreadful vision of Armageddon has by now become a collective constellation, and therefore Jung's conclusion must be extended at the collective level. We are constantly projecting an atrocious vision of a "no future"—and because consciousness is energy, it is a powerful energy that is projected, so powerful as to be capable of weaving events and of bending probabilities toward this outcome. Moreover, to this lethal attractor are attached not only all similar prophecies, but also the no-less-nightmarish forecasts of science relative to the disruption of ecological systems—which are reinforced by daily news. As a result, the Armageddon semantic constellation has become a juggernaut.

Strangely, and to help tip the scale the other way, there are also glorious or at least nonterminal prophecies ("nonterminal" since prophecies can describe only major transformations). Theosophist Alice Bailey predicted that Earth will be a "sacred planet" when all people become harmonized in their spirit.[4] Several spiritual movements and/or secret societies hold the belief that a hierarchy of highly evolved beings and hidden masters is steering the spiritual evolution of the planet. One of their veiled yet persistent predictions is that the planetary hierarchy (conceived as one and the same at its top) will one day take the reins of politics all over the world—a comforting statement in the sense that there will still be a planet to govern! Yet let's hope it's not a *1984* scenario, but, instead, the user-friendly future of the creative Ur federation.* Let's also consider a heartening Sufi prediction about a future time in which will reign the "hidden imam"—that is, the imam hidden inside each person. In other words, each individual will be directly connected to his divine source, the Self (the higher Self of Jung, capitalized). I believe this time has come. As for predictions based on Hindu spiritual astronomy, which deals with cycles (or *yugas*) of twenty-five thousand years or more, the last cycle we went through was the Kali Yuga, a period of deep unrest and destruction. This cycle, however, is the shortest of all, and next comes a novel golden age.

---

*The Ur federation is an ideal society of self-responsible artist-philosophers, gifted with psi, whose whole social life—art, organization, politics, and especially science and technology—is geared toward the development of consciousness and its scientific understanding. They follow a "direct path" of knowledge—that is, a path of direct connection to the source, or cosmic consciousness—in which individuals strive for the blossoming of their mind potentials and have a mutual respect for their freedom. This Ur civilization is put into play in a science fiction novel: Hardy, *Diverging Views.*

Let us turn now to the Maya predictions. We are in the cycle of the Fifth Sun, started in 3114 BCE, the date at which the Mayan calendar began, which will end in 2012, on December 21. In his e-article "2012: End of the 5th Sun," Will Hart remarks that the Mayan calendar was tied to Venus transit—that is, the retrograde movement of the planet.[5] This transit is generally accompanied by a deep change in solar spots activity. Venus transit has marked events such as, for the 1518-to-1526 CE transit, the landing of Cortés in Yucatán. According to Hart, the transit of 2004 to 2012 (with a peak on June 6, 2012) ushers in the arrival of the new cycle, the Sixth Sun. Hart predicts a period of seismic activity and great disruption. On the 21st of December, 2012, an even greater cycle will be completed: the great zodiac precession cycle of twenty-six thousand years. This notwithstanding, instead of an end time, 2012 may turn out to be an "end cycle" before the new cycle starts.

Collective consciousness may prove to be a powerful anti- or post-Armageddon goal for our civilization to contemplate. To this idea there are eminent forerunners gifted with vision. Thus, for the sixteenth-century physician and alchemist Paracelsus, all living beings together with their physical universe form a greater whole: a unitary and evolutionary consciousness—in essence, God. This vision resembles the age-old Eastern concept of cosmic consciousness, called Brahman by the Hindus and Tao by the Taoists.* Yet the thinker who best developed this idea was the philosopher and anthropologist Pierre Teilhard de Chardin, who proposed that the next step for humanity was to make a leap in terms of collective consciousness.[6] Teilhard de Chardin calls the dimension of all biological entities the *biosphere* and the dimension of all consciousnesses in the living the *noosphere*. In Teilhard de Chardin's view, we are going to achieve a harmonized collective state of consciousness, although this will not be at the expense of our individuality—the hard-won achievement of the past cycle. We are to learn how to intertwine our minds and spirits and thus progress toward what he calls the Omega Point: the fully

---

*Brahman is a neutral term in Sanskrit, signifying cosmic consciousness, whereas the name Brahma (masculine) refers to one of the gods of the Hindu trinity: Brahma, Shiva, and Vishnu.

harmonized noosphere. Most of these predictions thus refer explicitly to an era of spiritual harmonization in which all individuals have direct access to the spirit dimension and collective or cosmic consciousness.

If we want humanity to have a future, we must build a positive attractor that can constellate our dreams and visions of a humanity harmonized with its planet. Only such a powerful spiritual attractor can counterbalance and defeat the apocalyptic attractor.

The future of humanity is in our hands—cocreated by each and every one of us. Collective consciousness steered by a vision could well be the only force able to take us beyond unfolding catastrophes toward a luminous future.

PART I

TELHAR FIELDS AND HARMONY FIELDS

In part 1, "Telhar Fields and Harmony Fields," we will explore states of deep harmony among people, during which they experience shared consciousness as well as telepathic contact. We will also explore the astonishing energy structures created by these shared states of consciousness, such as energy spheres with a precise boundary in space, a geodesic grid visible against the background of the sky, and a torus of circling energy created and shared between assembled individuals. These phenomena lead us to ponder the nature and properties of the energy of consciousness, that is, semantic energy, and to propose the existence of a deep dimension of reality in which consciousness and energy (matter) are one and the same. First, however, let me begin by recounting how I became aware of these telepathic-harmonic fields, or telhar fields, and how, through a special gift that allows me to see the energetic structures of consciousness, I was able to piece together over the years a global understanding of these fields and of their astounding dynamics. We will then explore the role of the field's node, the many ways to both create a telhar field and to sustain it, and the tangible benefits we may get from it.

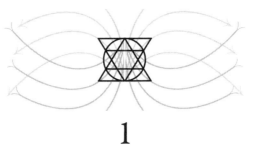

1

A QUESTER'S DIRECT PATH

Not long ago, I realized that there was a path of exploration I had pursued relentlessly over the years, gaining more and more expertise, and nevertheless I never sat at my desk to try to piece together all I had learned on this enigmatic subject. Of course, I had a number of reasons to think it was better to keep all this knowledge to myself. The weightiest one was that I had never encountered any mention of the type of phenomena I was dealing with—despite my reading of books ranging from ethnology, comparative religions, and transpersonal and depth psychology to esoterism, kabbala, alchemy, and tantrism. The second most important reason was that this path of knowledge depended heavily on some cryptic abilities that had surfaced in my life when I was nineteen, after I had started to meditate: a capacity to perceive, decipher, and interact with another dimension of reality—a dimension pertaining to consciousness and the spirit that I came to call the *semantic dimension*.

I was discovering a world in which each and every feeling or thought was in itself a meaningful energy that had its own influence on the world, however small. In its Greek root, *semantic* refers to meaning; this is why I called this dimension of reality the semantic dimension and the energy of consciousness the *semantic energy*.

Our consciousness, far from existing just as an intellectual abstraction, as if separated from the world, is instead continuously receiving and projecting a meaningful energy on its environment. I discerned that consciousness is in constant interaction with matter, imprinting objects and events and even modifying the way the world is organized; that all living beings (not only humans and animals, but also trees and plants) as well as inorganic systems (such as rocks and mountains) exist within this semantic dimension. They are endowed with a field of consciousness that I came to call a *semantic field*.

We don't usually realize how much diverse sciences, in the beginning, relied on perception and on machines enhancing vision and hearing (such as microscopes, microphones, and amplifiers). How could we ever have developed a science such as astronomy if we hadn't been able to observe first the regular movements of planets and stars? Sight, in fact, brings us a great deal of crucial information. It tells us where to look and which events are correlated and interacting. Observing a system allows us to come up with a prediction and a hypothesis that we can check through novel observations.

What I was seeing, in essence, was that the energy of thought and consciousness can take on many different forms, sometimes presenting spectacular dynamic structures. I was also seeing how these dynamic structures, created within and around groups of people, were precisely linked to their states of consciousness. A change of state or a thought affecting one or more people can disrupt the structure, and thus the collective field—and the inverse is also true: the creation of a structured collective field could modify the state of consciousness of the people participating in it.

The ability to connect with my inner Self and the semantic dimension had been activated when I began to read the foundational texts of Eastern religions, but the fact that I was an adolescent poet and writer and was often drawn into heightened states certainly had its influence too. When I was eighteen years old, I started teaching myself meditation with great ease, and about a year later, while vacationing in Tunisia during Easter week, I experienced my first transcendental state of consciousness. It was during this short vacation that, all of a sudden, I saw auras around people and had extraordinary mystical experiences.

One night, while I was sitting on a cliff overhanging the sea, a powerful energy lifted me up into an intense meditation. Suddenly, I had the vision of a sage meditating under a tree in a lotus position, his

golden-orange frock crossed over one shoulder. His head was a sphere
of radiant white light, hiding his face. Simultaneously, I felt and saw a
cylindrical ray about three inches wide, of an incandescent blue color,
reaching the center of my chest. It seemed to come from very far away,
where the sage was sitting. I was lifted into a transcendental state and
remained a long time in this beatific state, holding the vision. I had a
strong feeling that the sage had initiated the contact and was sending
me the ray.

As is often the case in deep meditative states, I saw all these details
of the ray while my eyes were closed. At the point where the ray had
touched my body, there appeared a round spot, about one and a half
inches wide, red and hot to the touch, which remained for a few days
afterward. More important, I realized I could reactivate the transcendental state by focusing my energy on that spot. While I hadn't the
slightest notion of psychic centers (or chakras) at the time, and without
being aware of it, my heart chakra had been awakened.

This life-turning experience triggered in me a permanent shift in
consciousness as well as the emergence of new mental capacities such as
the clear perception of the energy of consciousness.

In the years that followed, a process of progressive awakening of
the chakras—which Hindus and Tibetans call the awakening of the
kundalini energy—occurred within me and followed its natural course,
ascending and activating chakra after chakra along the vertebral column, up to the head chakra. However, I never felt the awakening of the
throat chakra, and the next chakra I became aware of was the forehead
chakra, or Ajna. A few months after the experience in Tunisia, I saw a
tiny spot of energy at the base of my nose and was drawn to meditate on
it. Upon focusing my energy on it, this point triggered an even deeper
state of consciousness: unknown to me, it acted as a preliminary activation of the forehead chakra.

I was twenty years old when the energy reached another threshold:
it naturally shifted to the middle of my forehead, the third eye. At that
time, I finally discovered a book describing the chakras and the awakening of the kundalini. I wasn't unhappy to have come to the conclusion,
all by myself, that it was a natural process, just like a child starting to

walk, and that I could therefore trust where it was taking me. I was especially content that the natural and progressive awakening I had lived was solid proof that this process was by no means an illusion or something born of suggestion.

It was a streak of serendipity when, a few months later, a traveler I met while on a short trip to the south of France told me about a community of monks that lived in a small village in Brittany, a northwestern region of France. What he said about their fantastic knowledge of meditation, esoterica, and astral journeys aroused in me a deep desire to visit the monks. He explained that they accepted visitors and gave me all the information to get there. I couldn't wait. On my return to Paris, I reported all this, vibrant with excitment, to my boyfriend, who was also my brother quester. Two or three days later, we drove to Brittany, and after a strenuous search, we finally found the village in which lived the dozen or so monks of this Orthodox Celtic order.

It was there that I experienced for the first time a field of collective consciousness. At the psychological level, a mysterious telepathic call to gather the monks, who were dispersed in the various rooms of the monastery and surrounding fields, was working perfectly well. More important, however, I could feel the minds of the monks constantly present in my own mind. This was very disturbing to me, because I had the impression that it robbed me of my intimacy with myself, something essential for a writer. To regain my inner state, I felt I had to go some distance from the monastery. While walking in the fields, I found a flat rock on which to sit, and from then on I spent hours there each day, reading, writing, and meditating. Altogether, this experience would have been nothing but shallow, anecdotal evidence of group telepathy were it not for two wholly unexplainable observations linked to space.

The first observation was my discovery of a precise spot on the path to the fields, beyond which, quite abruptly, I realized that I was alone with my thoughts again. It was so stupendous that I played with this "limit"—going within and beyond it—until I was utterly convinced that a single step brought me inside the consciousness field (sensing the others' minds crowding mine), while retracting that step brought me outside of it again. In the following days, the limit didn't change (I had made a kind of signpost on the vegetation), and the mental shift was just as drastic. It became evident that the persistent telepathic sharing somehow occurred within a precisely delimited space, and that within these limits, it was quite inescapable. At the time, I came to call it a telepathic field because, just like electromagnetic fields, it had a spatial component: the telepathic field was extended in space within a precise boundary. In contrast to the permanent inner whisper coming from within this field, when I would suddenly hear the telepathic call while reading or meditating on my faraway rock it was as if the calling came from outside of my mind, and it was no more disturbing than the sound of a loud voice.

A second unexplained observation in Brittany was a grayish grid that was neatly visible in the clear summer sky above the monastery. It was made of thin lines that intersected at near right angles and formed rectangles, imperceptibly curved, as if the geodesic grid was quite large. I had the impression that it was a dome covering the monastery and the small church nearby. The grid was a steady sight, day after day, and at the time it was rather unsettling to me, but I didn't make the connection between it and the telepathic field.

Apart from these two disturbing observations, the interactions and long evenings that we spent in discussions with the monks, especially the head monk, were extremely informative and quite exciting for both my friend and me. My stay was also very fecund in terms of transcendental states of meditation as well as spontaneous psi phenomena of great magnitude (such as telepathy, clairvoyance, and psychokinesis). It seems I was in a heightened state during the entire time I spent there. As for my friend, he must have had an even more transformative experience, because he found his vocation and decided to stay there. From my heightened state, I drew the strength to be happy for him, glad that he was now devoting his life fully to the quest, but on my way back to Paris alone, I was overwhelmed with sadness.

The next summer, no sooner did I receive my bachelor's degree than I left for a long-awaited journey to the East that was going to last about a year and a half. Right at the beginning of my journey, I awakened my head chakra and learned how to master astral journeys under the guidance and protection of a marvelous Sufi sage. A Sufi prayer, called Dikhr, led to a wonderful experience in terms of collective consciousness fields—a shared spiritual state and a harmonious attunement of souls reaching for a heightened state of consciousness.

On arriving in the Himalaya Mountains in northern India a few months later, I confronted again the reality of the grid in the sky as well as that of a telepathic field. In Manali, then a big village, there lived in perfect peace an ancestral Hindu population and newly emigrated Tibetans. I discovered the magnificent consciousness of the Tibetan people and had daily interactions with them. When I saw the exact same grid that I noted in Brittany while simultaneously feeling the continuous presence of a telepathic field, it dawned on me that the two are somehow interconnected. The Manali field, however, was so strong and its extent so great that it was spread over the whole village and its surroundings. In order to have some time to myself for writing or reading, I had to go far away, toward the rice fields, or else walk down to the river and then climb up the mountain on the other side.

One or two months later, on arriving in the sacred town of Nasik, near Bombay, I experienced an extremely harmonious and blissful telepathic field and confronted again the reality of its precise spatial boundary. Nasik is one of the four most sacred towns in India, and there the holiest of all gatherings, the Kumba Mela, happens every twelve years. While I walked for the first time toward the magnificent temples set along the river, I experienced an abrupt shift into a heightened state and found myself immersed in a field of collective consciousness. The Nasik field had an extraordinary quality. Suddenly, it seemed as if all the barriers surrounding individuals—and behind which the ego reigns—were brought down, and instead there was a flow of white light that was given and received by all. Each and every person was in a heightened state, each was connected to his Self. Each was in deep harmony with all the others and with the sacred city—its numerous temples, sacred baths on the river, and sacred trees. It was a communion of souls, each person recognizing and welcoming the innermost being of everyone else: the all-cognizant Self called *purusha* in Indian Vedanta philosophy. The whole town was bathed in white light, and it was a sharing and an attunement that implied our core being. This quality of harmonious exchange was so striking that I called it immediately a field of harmony. Telepathy was a natural consequence of this deep sharing in the absence of ego barriers, but harmonious attunement and sharing were paramount—for while telepathy is quite common in India, this kind of harmony field nowadays is quite rare and very special.

Though in Brittany I had recoiled from an invasion of my privacy, and though I had some difficulty adapting in Manali, in Nasik the harmony field triggered in me a blissful expansion of consciousness, a heightened state shared with others without the least embarrassment. In contrast with my two previous experiences, and since the pilgrims' house where I was staying was outside of the field's boundary, I would go to the river and spend the whole day bathed in this harmony field, meditating in temples and on the river's *ghats,* leaving it only at night. Very early on, I realized it was always at the same spot on the road leading to the center of town that I was abruptly swept into the harmony field. Just as in the Brittany field, the Nasik field had a very precise boundary in space. At this very spot, while climbing down toward the river each day, I experienced a shift to a higher state of consciousness and, on returning, I turned back suddenly to my individual self. What's more, I could also see very clearly the grayish grid on the blue sky.

This time around, I understood with absolute clarity that the harmonic-telepathic field had a particular energy structure, a sort of giant half-sphere that, in a still-enigmatic way, was embedded in Earth at this location. It had a precise boundary in space delimited by an energy grid, one that was all around it but that I could see only against the uniform color of the sky. Created by the high state of consciousness of the numerous sages, ascetics, and pilgrims who meditated day and night in the sacred town, the field was anchored to the countless temples, sacred baths, and altars. The harmony field had thus acquired stability both at a consciousness level and at an energy level. How wonderful for the several thousand people living in the core of town to remain continuously in this heightened state of shared consciousness! And what an even greater feat that this harmony field was shared by millions of people during the Kumba Mela, the great spiritual gathering that takes place in Nasik every twelve years.

What I learned during that time in India was to disengage from my ego while I kept my consciousness centered on my higher Self. This certainly was made easier by the fact that I was willingly without any money and had been since soon after my arrival, and thus I was now dependent on the magnanimity of people to offer me shelter for the night and sometimes to share their meal. In the holy towns of Nasik and Vrindavan (the birthplace of Krishna, the god of love), I could easily find a canvas bed in a pilgrims' house, and once in a while, a family or a group of pilgrims invited me to share their meal. I wasn't eating every day, but I was generally lucky enough to get one or two glasses of milk tea. Whenever I was on the road hitchhiking, interspersed with stays in particular places, I always spent the evenings and nights in temples with the wandering ascetics—the *saddhus*. On seeing the sun about to set, I would ask my driver of the moment to stop at the next village. There, I would walk toward the first saddhus' temple devoted to Shiva that I could spot in the vicinity—they were so numerous at that time that anywhere I looked I could see one, visible from afar by its red flag. Everywhere, the saddhus welcomed me as one of their own. Women saddhus are quite rare, but they do exist nevertheless. Time and again, I joined the circle of a few saddhus sitting around the sacred fire where they would cook their meager meal, generally just a few chapatis. After sharing the food, we sat in silent meditation until well into the night. Later on, each one moved to a corner of the room and lay down to sleep. What the saddhus taught me was how to direct and control my own kundalini energy, raise the energy to higher chakras, and maintain it there constantly in whatever action I might be performing, whether meditating or cooking food. They showed me how, at each moment, to be hypervigilant and aware of the energetic dimension of reality. The saddhus' path is a highly personal and lonely one. Each one strives to attain enlightenment, and their ethic is to respect the particular path of each person and his or her ways of behaving and specific beliefs. True saddhus do not show the least tendency to gather disciples or to teach other people. Each quester is a fully responsible person who takes care of his or her own quest. Some of them choose not to talk anymore, but even when not bound by a vow of silence, they will talk only rarely. What might be happening to a fellow saddhu is none of their business. Nevertheless, they group with other saddhus in temples, sometimes just for the night, and share whatever food they have, spending the night together around the sacred fire. They are kind and inclined to give, and the rare ones I met who were still talking did express some of their wisdom, recounting their travels to sacred places all over India. Thus the saddhus pursue a strictly personal path toward knowledge of the Self and the achievement of total liberation *(moksha)*.

My wish at the time was to become transparent, and I was striving to be "like air passing through air" (my particular expression at the time). I wanted to live solely in the dimension of the Self and to let go of everything else. At first, I focused my meditation on Krishna and the quality of spiritual love. This path led me to experience mystical states of fusion and unity. Then I centered my meditation on Amitabha, the Buddha of Infinite Radiance and Boundless Life. At first, I had had the feeling that Amitabha emanated and represented a similar quality of cosmic love as that of Krishna. Indeed, Amitabha is the Buddha of spiritual love; however, it wasn't this quality that I was trying to evoke while meditating on Amitabha. In my mind, the infinite radiance translated into infinite space, and while I was following my own path of progressive fusion and identification, I devised a "yoga of infinite space." The practice consisted of projecting my consciousness within a sphere of energy created from my head chakra (the thousand-petaled lotus), high up above my head, then extending this sphere in all directions to spread my consciousness field more and more, while keeping my soul energy in deep fusion and harmony with the world. Progressively, with each lengthy meditation, I kept expanding this sphere, becoming fused with the landscape around me, then with ever-larger portions of space.

During my stay in Goa, I spent hours each day in meditation, and soon I was meditating for the greatest part of the day. I often reached a state of fusion with the One, the Whole. I also experienced three grand visions of Buddha in Goa, and another one later in Dharamsala, to which I traveled, with a quester friend, to see the Dalai Lama. While practicing the yoga of infinite space, I progressively approached a state of fusion with Amitabha, which I achieved one month later.

Around Christmas, about twenty of us gathered for a party at somebody's house. Because the large rectangular room we were in was devoid of furniture (there were only candles, incense, and a few musical instruments for anybody to play), we all sat cross-legged on the floor, our backs leaning against the walls. After sharing food, some of us started to play music. That night, drawing on my experience of the yoga of infinite space, I discovered how to extend my consciousness to the whole group and generate a telhar field that included all of us in the room. We all remained in a profound silent state for the whole night, our consciousnesses harmonized and the music soft and attuned, like a vibrant spring of energy. While I was able to sustain the field for hours, most of the night in fact, it was still a very difficult task and quite remote from a flow state, a state in which our psychic and mental functioning is easy and effortless. To the contrary, I had to keep my consciousness expanded on the whole group, reaching out to each person present without a second of inattention. It felt as if I was weight lifting and that I had to hold the weight at arm's length for six or seven hours. Basically, the entire time, I remained in deep, hypervigilant meditation. When dawn approached, I felt I had reached my limit. I left the collective field intact and very delicately pulled my mind out of it, centering my energy back into my own being. At the moment when I was tiptoeing out, so to speak, I was astonished to see a friend enter the focal point—the node of the field—and take my place in sustaining it. Thus, the telhar field and the state of deep harmony lasted until the end of our gathering at dawn.

Because I had no previous knowledge of how to create or sustain a telhar field—I didn't even know it was possible—this first experience brought me a great deal of information. I immediately devised a few novel words in order to be able to think about this new dimension of reality. In India at the time we hardly ever spoke about our inner experiences—even less so when they concerned the edge of the unknown, the vast reaches of consciousness for which we didn't even have words or concepts. In fact, we hardly ever spoke at all. Most of us, following the saddhus in that respect, had lost any desire to talk, because we were so absorbed in the density of what we were experiencing together in the "here and now." So, I created new expressions such as "to create a harmony field," "to take the node of the field," or, in short, "to take the field."*

During the following week in Goa, there was another small party at a church that had just been founded by foreigners. We gathered outside the traditional house they were using temporarily, sitting on the sand. Some tea and various niceties to munch were passed around among us. We comprised a group of forty to fifty people, and we were loosely dispersed on the beach. At the time, I was continuously in a heightened state of consciousness, entering quite often into *Samadhi,* the level of trancendental states that starts with the experience of oneness. That night, I was again able to create a telhar field encompassing all the people present. Yet I didn't sustain it as long as at Christmastime, and nobody took the node role after me.

After my first travel to India, the active exploration of harmonic and telepathic fields became a background canvas to my life. Whether I myself was initiating the process or encountering situations that triggered my awareness of telhar fields, their reality became a major knowledge path for me. Nobody had ever taught me about these telhar fields. I had never (and still have not) encountered in an ancient or modern text any clear-cut mention of how they can be put into action or experienced in an energetic way. By way of contrast, there are theories referring to the general concept of consciousness fields and even scientific experiments geared at collecting statistical proof of their reality. The most striking is Roger Nelson's Global Consciousness Project (GCP) at Princeton University. The GCP uses a great many random number generators, called eggs, dispersed all over Earth. These measure the distribution of randomness at the sites holding eggs. Then statistical means are calculated among all the eggs, the results of which are sent through the Internet at precise intervals. Nelson and his close associates have been able to show that the eggs' behavior was strongly affected whenever there was a world-shaking event. Looking at the graphs of

---

*For many years, I had used the term *harmony fields* or *telepathic fields*. Yet on undertaking the comprehensive study that is this text, I understood that I needed a clearer term and chose that of *telhar fields* (TELepathic-HARmonic fields).

mean outputs, we can clearly see the steep rising of the curve and that it remains high for some time, for many of the dramatic world events that happened in the past years.[1]

Also of note, Larry Dossey expresses a practical understanding of collective fields through the concept of *prayer fields*. He evokes the strength of collective prayer and shows some of its applications.[2] I'm inclined to think that the telhar field on the sacred town of Nasik was generated tens of centuries ago by cosmic guides or masters and that it has been sustained by the spiritual energy of all the saddhus and sages who constantly meditate in this sacred place. Indeed, it must have been created so far back that for generations of questers the sacred semantic field, the field of harmony, was already there, anchored to the sacred hills, stones, trees, rivers, and temples. In view of their very special semantic imprint, perhaps this was the reason that such towns were called holy towns in the first place.

There is of course a legend concerning the four holy towns in India where the great gathering of all ascetics and spiritual gurus takes place: the Kumba Mela. This feast occurs every four years in turn in Nasik, Allahabad, Ujjain, and Hardwar. The legend describes the *kumb,* the holy vase that contains the *soma,* the elixir of immortality of the gods. The gods and the demons started a war to take possession of the kumb until, after twelve days of fighting, the god Vishnu intervened and stopped the battle. During the fighting, a drop of soma fell on each of the four places, thus rendering them sacred.

However, India has a lot more sacred towns and places. Benares, for one, is such a sacred place that on arriving near the Ganges River, a sensitive quester will experience a powerful shift into a heightened state of consciousness. In fact, Ganga (the river's name in Sanskrit) is a goddess: the river goddess existed in heaven, and when she descended to Earth, her power was so great that she could have destroyed Earth. Shiva had to receive her on his head, whereupon she flowed peacefully.

I sojourned in Benares a few times, and each time I was awestruck by the beauty and the powerful energy of this sacred place. Yet I didn't experience the other essential features of telhar fields, such as the energetic aspects (precise boundaries and grids in the sky). I also didn't note the feeling of deep harmony or telepathy with all the other people there or the recognition of kindred souls. To be more precise, this feeling of deep harmony did happen, but only with the many extraordinary sages and saddhus I met there. This wasn't comparable to a collective harmony field that took hold of the whole sacred part of town, as in Nasik. Of course, I don't expect each telhar field to have all the features present at Nasik. The Brittany field, for example, didn't show the harmony aspect, but only the telepathic element. As for the telhar fields created in a small group, such as the Christmas group in Goa or in jam sessions (we will discuss these at length further on), they generally present very clear psychological features (harmony and telepathic fields) and distinctive effects on the music being played. They rarely, however, allow for a perception of their energy structures (such as a large encompassing sphere or a torus of light). Another point to consider is that the perception of specific features does say something about what's there but doesn't say anything about what's lacking. In other words, the perceiver may not have always the same acuity in his or her gift of vision.

HARMONY FIELDS DURING MUSIC PLAYING

To create these first telhar fields, it was necessary for me to remain in hypervigilant concentration and as immobile as a marble statue, not taking part in the music that was being played. It's only later that I discovered we can create or be the node of a telhar field while improvising music (in what's called a jam session) and that trance dance was one of the easiest ways to enter this rewarding state. I have traveled a great deal in many different countries during my life, and there have been many occasions to meet local musicians and start a jam at a tea shop, under a tree, in a temple in India, or at the house of one of the musicians.

Hindus spontaneously express their devotion by *pujas:* sacred songs of devotion chanted to their gods, goddesses, and gurus. For example, for Shiva's annual feast, millions of people flock to sacred towns and sites dedicated to Shiva, such as Omkareshvar on the Narmada River. The Narmada became Shiva's river after he appeared on its bank in the form of a huge lingam (similar to a black and polished egg-shaped standing stone) in order to save the *devas* (gods) who had been defeated by the demons.

When they feel ready, saddhus undertake a grand pilgrimage, walking along the Narmada from the sea to its source and back to the sea that, altogether, takes nine months, nine weeks, and nine days to perform. This is about the time necessary to accomplish a grand spiritual transformation that will lead them to the state of liberation, or moksha. In India, the spot where two sacred rivers mingle their waters, the *sangam,* is highly sacred. There is such a sangam in Omkareshvar, at the western tip of the sacred island. Furthermore, this island is situated about midway on the pilgrimage path, which makes it a very special place for the saddhus. There are so many special dates and feasts for deities and gurus that in the years when the devotion was still high, it was a frequent experience to walk in a street at evening and find people performing a puja in a temple, under a tree, or right in the street.

In Benares, during Shiva's feast, apart from scheduled prayers and rituals in the major Shiva temples, at any time of day and night there are hundreds of small groups performing pujas while sitting on the many ghats and temple terraces overlooking the Ganges. Devotees improvise on their favorite songs for a great part of the night. The puja is always open to anybody who wants to join in. Not only will people smile and greet a foreigner who sits among them, but they will also offer a musical instrument. As the collective trance state deepens with time, the music gets better and better. Indians have a fantastic knowledge of how to get into a high spiritual state—a state of connection to the divine and their Self. This state is always one of active participation, totally remote from bored or passive listening. In India, prayer and devotion make a feast in which the soul enjoys a reconnection to its immortal source and a harmonization with nature. Hindu religion has always stressed how blissful is the harmonization between the ego personality (*jiva*) and the Self (*purusha*), which opens the state of oneness, or fusion, with the cosmic consciousness. The mantra expressing the essence of cosmic consciousness, as well as the path to achieve it, is SAT-CHIT-ANANDA, meaning, respectively, essence-conscience-bliss. Many great gurus have the word *ananda,* or "bliss," in their initiatic name, showing that their path of knowledge includes the state of blissful fusion, the state of unity. The master Yogananda had in his name the root *yog* (meaning "yoga," but also "link"), plus *ananda,* "bliss" or "blissful connection."

The free spirit is by nature blissful and harmonized with all spirits around it. This is a state of grace, and certainly the state that was depicted symbolically by our concept of paradise. All Eastern religions, however, point to the possibility of reopening and experiencing this fusion—for it's essentially a transcendental state of consciousness. More than that, it is the responsibility of all of us to strive for reaching this liberated and enlightened state. In Eastern philosophy, this is exactly what we came here to do while incarnating on Earth. When we get to the end of our spiritual path—because each and every human will eventually attain it—then we'll close a series of incarnations on Earth and move on to another dimension of the universe in order to pursue our learning and spiritual development.

A DIRECT PATH

The rising of the kundalini to the opening of the head chakra was the path laid before humanity in the precedent cycle of Pisces. Because we just entered the cycle of Aquarius, however, as well as a new grand age of Earth, our knowledge path will be different—as much in terms of goals as in the array of paths and techniques to strive for them.

Our present-day goal is to strive for a collective harmonization, and the most direct way is for each of us to reconnect with our Self. New mental capacities will emerge in the process, such as the capacity to see the semantic dimension and to act within it, as well as the ability to experience a wide variety of inner states, such as states of deep interconnection and fusion with the collective soul and collective unconscious, directly linked to experiencing telhar fields.

The Five Ways of This Direct Path

The first way is to experience and learn to master a wide gamut of heightened states of consciousness, such as intuitive states, meditation, immersion in other cultures or life situations, creative and artistic activities, trance states, playing music, trance dancing, and so forth. This path of heightened states of consciousness is a prolonging of traditional Eastern and shamanic paths—that is, searching for a connection with one's own Self, itself immersed in the collective and cosmic consciousness. Yet in this new cycle, this path will be experienced differently, and novel capacities will spring forth. This emergence of novel capacities and sensitivities will certainly be full of interesting surprises, because traditionally, the knowledge was received from a guru or master, while in contrast, heightened states are now achieved through a direct path of connection with our own Self and the cosmic source. It should be noted, though, that a traditional yet ever-so-secret knowledge about a direct path (sometimes also referred to as a direct way, short path, or voie sèche in alchemy) was hinted to in the hermetic and esoteric lore. More and more, people are attracted to the joyful creative exploration of consciousness through innovation, creativity, music, trance dance, and art.

The second way is to pursue the exploration of mind potentials. From this perspective, we have to be open to the possibility of anomalous experiences and psi phenomena, and we have to intend, while they are happening, to memorize them in detail in order to analyze them afterward and integrate them harmoniously in our own life. Anomalous and psi experiences open windows into another dimension of reality, and this new dimension of consciousness is the one we are going to harness in the present cycle until we can function within it in our daily life. After a period of spontaneous emergence and transformation, we should focus on making sense of this new dimension of consciousness and of reality as a whole. The focused intention has in itself the power to trigger the emergence of a new kind of mental integration so that we can keep systematically exploring unknown possibilities with enough confidence to steer the process in the safest and most beneficial fashion.

The third way is to trigger the integration of the Self to the mind-body-psyche system. In the past two millennia, the aim of all Western and Eastern initiatic traditions has been to integrate the ego with the Self—that is, our personality (psyche) and habitual state of consciousness with our soul or immanent Self. This path was understood as a liberation from duality in the East, where it is linked to the opening of the head chakra. In Vedanta philosophy, this realization is termed the integration of the jiva (the ego) with the purusha (the spirit); it corresponds to the mystical marriage in alchemy and the loss of the ego in Theosophy. The goal of our age is to move a step forward and also integrate both our body and our intellect within our supraconscious Self. Concerning the integration of the body, this evolution was prepared through ancient martial arts, sacred dances, and trance rituals. Through this process, our body consciousness becomes intuitive and can trigger clairvoyant information, while our psyche reaches a higher sensitivity. As for the integration of the intellect, it is best understood as left-brain and right-brain harmonization, the fourth way.

The fourth way is to pursue the progressive but relentless integration of right-brain and left-brain capacities. The path lying before us in this new cycle is clearly to bring into synergy our two brain hemispheres and to develop crossbreed abilities through the fecund blending of intuitive and logical thinking modes, the feminine and masculine facets of our psyche, and also receptive and proactive positioning. Most true innovators and discoverers have generally been endowed with an extra touch of intuition to steer their overdeveloped intellectual capacities. A good right-brain–left-brain integration will trigger the emergence of such astonishing mental talents that we can hardly imagine how our mind will evolve. This is the path that will lead to a deep knowledge of consciousness and the nature of reality, to the most profound transformation toward more empathic relationships, and to stupendous discoveries and innovations.

The fifth and final way is to explore rhythmic collective harmonization. This is the first totally novel path of this new epoch, opening a new horizon, and what we have been able to achieve until now is but a first step in that direction. Of course, large gatherings for concerts and festivals as well as trance dance are a royal way toward the knowledge and mastery of telhar fields. As opportunities for very large gatherings are multiplied, these become very fruitful ways to practice telhar fields. The exploration of mind potentials is a path that hasn't been open to the collective in the previous cycle because it's based on the kind of spontaneous emergences that can happen only in a period of transition and abrupt change. Nowadays, the emergence of new potentials is already a fact in the lives of all individuals on a spiritual quest. It is the sign of the time because we are cocreating a new age of Earth.

THE TRANSMISSION FROM ANCIENT CULTURES

In the mid-sixties, sensitive minds in the West were awakened by powerful earthshaking energies, heralded by the first musicians with a politico-spiritual message, such as the Beatles and Bob Dylan, and expressing a new world vision whose motto was *drop out,* meaning "get out of the consumer society and explore consciousness." This novel political perspective triggered the first massive opposition to war (the Vietnam War, in this instance), with dramatic rallies and sit-ins orchestrated by hippies in the United States, and after two years, it launched the volcanic May 1968 student revolution in Paris, which spread progressively all over the world, to the Far East and South America.

It seems that in the early seventies, those of us forming the first wave of travelers with a quest were at the turning point between two worlds. Most of us went to India with a conscious expectation—or, rather, certitude—that we would find there (and only there) a way toward the knowledge of the spirit. We were there at the right moment to witness a whole culture that had been focused on spiritual knowledge since the time, millennia ago, when there had been devised an array of paths and practices to achieve spiritual reintegration.

We learned with saddhus, the wandering ascetics who had renounced the world, with Tibetans, as well as with great gurus from the diverse religions found in India. We were able to witness what had been the collective realization of this civilization before it was swept into a whirlwind of transformation and abrupt transition to the computer age. On returning to the West, we surfed the wave of change that was awakening Westerners to the reality of consciousness, inspiring a thirst for self-knowledge and self-development.

An alchemical process was started worldwide by a double attraction: the West for the traditional knowledge of the East, and the East for the technical knowledge of the West. The exploration of millennia-old knowledge systems thereafter spread to all ancient cultures. At that time, the road toward India that ran through Iran and Afghanistan was packed with hundreds of hitchhikers, and it was also traveled bimonthly by buses. In contrast, during my seven months of solitary journeying through West and East Africa, past the last hippie stronghold near Agadir—that is, from the Sahara Desert to Nairobi, Kenya—I met only a single hippie.

Not only had an epoch of brutal, order-enforcing colonizers all over the planet given way to an era of humble and empathic questers, eager to learn the ancient wisdom from wise men and women, but also, with a magnificent clairvoyance, the possessors of the ancient sacred knowledge—shamans, saddhus, monks, medicine men—realized that they had to pass on their knowledge beyond their own youth to these strangers on a quest. They understood, through visions, dreams, signs, or prophetic knowledge, that an era would soon come to an end and a new spirit was on the rise, and that in order to transmit their secrets, they had to adapt or transgress many of their traditional rules.

African elders gave initiation to white people, such as anthropologists Robert Jaulin and Jacqueline Rouméguère.[3] The Mother of the Saints, Maria-José, in the Brazilian macumba cult, gave many secrets to Serge Bramly; and a Zulu shaman of South Africa (called a *sangoma*) told her apprentice-initiate Adrian Boshier, who wondered how he could receive initiation given that his ancestors were not from Africa, that her ancestors and his ancestors had talked together and were in agreement on this.[4]

In his famous books, Carlos Castaneda recounts how his Mexican master, the Yaqui sorcerer Don Juan, had to put up with a new kind of apprentice in Castaneda. Traditionally, everything he passed on was remembered by rote, but Castaneda insisted on writing down all that was done and said.[5]

I myself enjoyed many out-of-the-ordinary privileges while receiving ancient sacred knowledge. My Sufi master gave me the Darvichi initiation without demanding that I become a Muslim. The initiation of women must have been an extremely rare event, despite the fact that there had been in the past in Iran prominent Sufi masters who were women, such as the poetess Rabe'eh (tenth century CE), one of four people to have achieved the highest degree of enlightenment. More than that, my Sufi master allowed his two women disciples to stay and live next to him in his own *rhonerah* (ashram), traditionally exclusively reserved for men, and to ensure that there would be no difficulties with this arrangement from other disciples, he went as far as forbidding them to come to the rhonerah except on prayer day. Like my Sufi master, the head of the order in Brittany allowed me to sleep for a few days on several occasions in the men's monastery, even though the women resided just a few miles away. I also was cleared by an elder to participate in a Native American Bear Dance ritual north of San Francisco.

While hitchhiking through sub-Saharan Africa, my spirit guide (whom I recognized as my own Self) made me transgress many traditional ethnic rules, and yet they were all accepted ad hoc, and I never incurred the deadly punishment reserved for transgressors. Several instances of this occurred in the Dogon country, which I explored with my sister, who was then a physician at a hospital in northern Mali, her colleague from Burkina Faso, and his Peul wife. At our first camp, after ascending the Bandiagara Cliffs, my spirit guide woke me in the middle of the night and prodded me to walk through the wilderness, solely by the light of the moon, until I found the "initiates' wood" (*le bois des initiés*), where I spent some time meditating. Further inside the Dogon country we had been given shelter by the chief of the village, who offered us a sleeping place on his flat roof. The chief's house was on top of a mountain, on the side of a plaza at the center of which stood the elders' house (*la maison des Vieux*).

While the others were sound asleep, I woke, and my spirit enjoined me to rise and go sleep in the elders' house. For the Dogons, this is the most sacred place, where only the oldest and most accomplished male initiates can set foot. I was not only white, but also a woman who was only twenty-three at the time—a far cry from the requirements. Yet I trusted the injunction of my spirit and had no fear. From a distance we had been shown this elders' house. Generally, such houses look like crisscrossing rows of wooden pillars on which, at two-thirds their height, are sculpted two large breasts. The pillars are about a yard high, just high enough for people to sit inside, but they have to crawl to get underneath. On top of the pillars, the straws from the harvest are piled.

Yet the elders' house I was preparing to enter was unlike any I had seen and would ever see in Dogon country. It was a very large and flat megalith supported by a circle of smaller stones, thin and standing. In other words, it was a perfect example of a dolmen, a megalithic chamber as we see them in France and Great Britain, but without the covered passage that usually leads to the entrance. Here, the entrance was just a hole in the circle of stones, as if one of them had been removed.

There are numerous megaliths in Africa, namely in Republic of the Gambia, Senegal, and central Africa—circles of small, nearly square stones and huge standing stones. What is interesting is the similarity of symbols between the Dogon culture and the culture of the megaliths people. In fact, on the stone marking the entrance to many dolmens, such as those found in the Epte and Eure valleys in France, there is a carving called the goddess with a blazon (*la déesse à l'écusson*), which shows two small breasts and below them a row of collars that have the shape of a blazon. Here, in dolmens, we find the same symbolism of the two breasts in a similar megalithic construction as we saw in the elders' wooden houses in the Dogon country.

It must have been around one o'clock when I silently arose, took the loincloth I was using as a sheet, and, barefoot as usual, climbed down the two stories to the ground floor. A large, empty space, perfectly clean, surrounded the elders' house, and the plaza opened in front onto a rather steep cliff. The village houses were farther back, on the smooth slope of the mountain; among them, only the chief's house could be seen from the plaza. Leaving the house noiselessly, I peeked outside and couldn't see anybody in the whole plaza. This was comforting to me.

I crossed the space toward the giant chamber, crouched to pass through the small opening, and then laid my cloth on the ground and sat down on it. So far, so good. Despite the moon illuminating the plateau, it was quite dark inside, with just a spare ray passing the tiny door. I knew I couldn't be seen from the plaza, so I relaxed. Inside, the stones were raw, and the chamber was totally empty. I was very conscious of the sacredness of the place, and I intended to do just what had been suggested to me. Sitting in the center of the circle of stones, I opened my mind to the forces converging on that spot. After a short meditation, I lay down on my cloth to sleep.

My idea was to get up well before daybreak so that I could return to the roof before anybody was up, and I gave myself this suggestion.

I did wake up before the first light of dawn, although on leaving the chamber, I was baffled by something I hadn't anticipated at all: surrounding the chamber and sleeping on the ground were very old men. The elders had come to sleep here! There were about fifteen of them, and that reassured me, because they obviously couldn't have intended to sleep inside the chamber, where only six to eight men could sit and no more than three could lie down. Fortunately, all of them seemed sound asleep—not the slightest movement anywhere. Yet there were so many of them that there wasn't a single way for me to exit from where I was that didn't oblige me to stride over at least two of the prone bodies—which, considering they were elders, was even worse than what I had already done. Nevertheless, I couldn't risk staying there and being seen in broad daylight, so I chose the best path—the way that seemed to have the most space for my feet between the sleeping bodies—and without breathing and with extreme care, I started this perilous performance, careful to maintain my equilibrium and hoping that nobody would awaken. At last, I reached beyond the elders and started toward the chief's house.

Back on the roof, I lay down noiselessly, and I was finally able to release all that tension. I had arrived and nobody had woken up or seen me. I went back to sleep until the others got up for breakfast. Just after, a man arrived, and, despite the fact that my elder sister usually came ahead of me, he offered me a snake skin, while looking me in the eye. I transferred this gift to my sister, because I would be soon hitting the road to hitchhike.

It took me many years finally to understand the underlying truths of what had happened during this trip in the Dogon country—in fact, until I wrote a book on this nine-month trip. Now, however, I have no doubt that whatever I did in response to the call of my Self was orchestrated in the first place by the Dogon elders. Anybody who intruded on their secret grounds would have faced the gravest of penalties. This is why, I believe, contrary to their habits, they hadn't slept in their own huts and came instead to sleep on the plaza. Because the injunction of my Self had been to sleep in the elders' house, it seems an event was bound to happen in the dreamtime—part of the semantic dimension—probably a meeting of importance with the elders that I wouldn't have been able to integrate consciously at the time. African initiates, just like Australian ones, are able not only to see clearly the spirit dimension—what the Aborigines call the dreamtime—but also to function within it. From that perspective, the elders certainly knew more about what I was doing in their megalithic chamber than my conscious self.

When I first returned to Europe after traveling for a year and a half in the East, I couldn't readapt. With what looked like a flip-coin decision, I had started on this journey through Africa from Montségur, a sacred site of the Cathars, where I had sojourned for about two months in a small community. (We will talk again about Montségur.)

From Morocco to Kenya, I had numerous occasions to play drums with local musicians. Africa taught me how to harmonize rhythmically with the Earth, how to harmonize myself with others into a collective trance (playing or dancing) in which bodies and psyches are in sync—the whole group or village being like one collective mind-body synchronized with Earth. Jam sessions and music playing are the most fecund contexts for practicing telhar fields. They are the most informative, since musicians, being sensitive to music frequencies, are able to detect the influence of their mind-set and feelings on the music, whether they play alone or in a group. Thus, jam sessions provide the perfect learning ground to understand and sort out the subtle laws of harmony fields. Any bad thought or drive from any one of the musicians has the power to crash the harmony state. Techniques to put the telhar field on track again can be explored and tested on the spot: the effect on the collective music will be immediate.

In sub-Saharan Africa, I also became able to detect the subtle resonance of places, objects, trees, and so forth in the spirit dimension. I could intuit their semantic quality, their force and underlying connections, and their influence on the surroundings. I was thus able to experience the specific energies, natural resonances, and hidden correlations that have allowed shamans since very ancient times to recognize the healing virtue of a plant or to decipher the secret communications of animals and plants with the spirit world. I could also see whenever trees or places were inhabited by nature spirits. Often, I was thus able to heal myself and others, either through psychic energy or through using plants or techniques that spontaneously appeared as full-blown images in my mind.

From the port town of Mombasa, Kenya, I embarked on a boat toward India. I used the last of the money I was forced to ask my family to provide for this crossing by buying five kilos of oranges for the ten-day trip. On arriving in India without a penny, I immersed myself again into the Eastern spaces of consciousness, in pure immobile yogic states. I started another nine months of travel around India, hitchhiking my way in a large circle (just as I had done the first time), connecting Benares, Manali, Delhi, Mumbai, and Goa. What we hippies had experienced a year and a half earlier with a few dozen people, we were now able to achieve with a few hundred interconnected minds. Despite the number, we were still playing the music ourselves for great gatherings. We always held a jam session with whoever came with an instrument or the desire to play. Only for small parties in individual houses did we sometimes play prerecorded music.

EMERGENCE OF COLLECTIVE HARMONY STATES

By the mid-seventies, Holland, true to its history of tolerance, came out as a forerunner of freedom of expression and social change. Novel cultural behaviors weren't repressed and heavily sanctioned, as they were in France and even in the United States, where the heralds of the counterculture and the precursors of a novel world vision often lost their jobs and were sometimes jailed.

In that epoch, I had an extraordinary love relationship with a Dutchman who was adept at tantrism, and part of my mind was constantly attuned to Holland. There were so many people with heightened consciousness in that country that telhar fields were commonplace. They would be created in coffee shops or in an entire part of town or would be extended to the whole country.

As had happened in India, in most cases I became aware of the existence of a telhar field because I had participated in its creation in the first place. I would thus have a clear sensation of its extension. But once, while I was shopping, I was suddenly swept into a telhar field as I walked on the street. On that occasion, I experienced an even more drastic shift in consciousness than in Nasik. I consider this kind of experience—an abrupt shift followed by an immersion in a large telhar field—to be absolute, empirical proof of the reality of these fields. In fact, once a telhar field is created, it draws within its boundary all sensitive minds so that they attain a telepathic and attuned collective state. At this point, the Great Work consists of connecting telhar fields from place to place and country to country, thus extending the network of interconnected minds. On the days when the cosmic energy is at its peak—solstices, equinoxes, full moons—or when the collective consciousness on Earth is at its highest (Christmas, Easter, New Year's, May 1), it becomes possible to close the circle on itself, as a wave or an ouroboros that would encircle and rotate around the planet. While spending the night in a jam session or in meditation, I have been able to detect a specific window of time (different on each occasion, but about thirty to sixty minutes long) during which Earth as a whole receives a dense influx of cosmic energy.

As more and more people now connect themselves to the diverse telhar fields that occur all over the planet, new possibilities emerge in terms of consciousness. Heightened states, anomalous phenomena, contacts with other dimensions of consciousness, psi capacities—all are rendered easier to attain and to develop for an increasing number of people. The path of consciousness evolution is now open to all who desire to try it, and we can start to envision the field of possibilities that soon will be available to humanity as a whole. The objective is now to create telhar fields more frequently and to join in with as many countries as possible. Our Omega Point is to aim for a permanent, stable, planetary consciousness state. This purpose was definitely at very close range at the turn of the century; however, since the crashing of the field following the disastrous 9/11 events, we still haven't recovered our Y2K collective state.

CONCERTS

Great concerts have always been marvelous events in terms of collective consciousness fields. The most exceptional ones for me have been those held in cathedrals, such as that of Tangerine Dream in Reims Cathedral in France and Harmonic Choir in New York's Cathedral of St. John the Divine. These concerts were, of course, conceived to create a spiritual collective experience, an attunement with the sacred.

Reims Cathedral is special in that it is where most of the Carolingian and Capetian kings were traditionally crowned. I'd never seen a cathedral so packed with people; in fact, my soul sister and I arrived late, and we were hardly able to sneak in along an aisle to a pillar halfway through the nave. Once there, we found just enough space to remain standing. I climbed onto the rim encircling the pillar so that I could get above the sea of heads and manage to see the musicians installed in the choir. In the whole cathedral, there didn't seem to be a single square foot free of bodies crammed into it. It was clear that everybody was in altered consciousness, and I was immediately swept into a powerful heightened state.

When Tangerine Dream started the second part of the concert, the crowd was instantaneously enraptured. Within a few minutes of the playing of a powerful electrical organ, the walls and pillars and then the whole architecture of the cathedral began to tremble and oscillate on its foundation. Somewhat panicked, I started pondering whether sound alone could bring such a building to collapse, but I decided to trust the cathedral builders who had conceived the magnificent arches resting their weight on flying buttresses. The cathedral—the mandala of stones based on the golden proportion—was like a well-tuned instrument, a single, magnificent resonance chamber. All this was a high-speed thought. The oscillations climbed to a peak, and suddenly, the whole building took off, tearing off the last chains that anchored it to Earth. It took off and started to dart out into space, heading toward the grand, cosmic eye. The cathedral turned itself back into what it had been conceived as: a magnificent vessel of cosmic proportion and cosmic purpose.

The cathedral had been thought of as a sacred vessel whose nave was the body of the ship. The builders' intentions were reflected in the word *nave,* because the root *nav* in English refers to "ship" (as in navy and navigate) and *nef* in French means "ship." Indeed, the overall shape of the cathedral looks like an inverted boat with its deck on the ground, as if the vessel was floating through the sky. For the remainder of the concert, the cathedral-spaceship, together with its five-thousand-plus enraptured souls on board, soared through the immensity of a luminous, golden space. Together with the sacred vessel, we had fused into one giant spirit who, liberated from the weight of matter, had recovered the wholeness of its being and its boundless consciousness.

What giant open-air festivals hadn't been able to do, the subtle architecture of the cathedral-cosmic vessel did. It created out of a whole crowd a unique, harmonized consciousness, a telhar field. A cathedral is mostly spirit; only a small part of it is matter. It has been spiritualized by sacred geometry and the golden proportion as much as by the builders' intention. Moreover, most, if not all, cathedrals, as we will see, are situated on millennia-old sacred spaces and temples, at the crossing of Earth's cosmo-telluric lines that, following its curved surface, turn around the whole planet, passing from one sacred spot to another, from one culture to another. The sacred semantic field of the cathedral pervaded all our minds and linked them in a tight network, a harmonized consciousness field made of five thousand vibrant, interconnected cells.

SACRED GRIDS

During one of my stays with friends at Montségur in the Pyrenees, we discovered an elevated spot in the mountains nearby. It was a clearing on a high hill, and it still bore the signs of a very ancient sacred site and Druidic mound, or nemeton. After my friends left the spot, I went back to meditate alone in a very specific place, high on the slope, that I had seen clairvoyantly and that was marked with an extremely strong energy. While concentrating at that "seat of power," I saw in front of me rays of light that fanned out at a wide angle. Following them, one by one, I arrived at sacred places of ancient religions, starting on my left with

Brittany and southwest England (Stonehenge, the Glastonbury-Avalon of King Arthur) toward, on my far right, sites in India, and passing through many other sites.

I had thus rediscovered one of the ancient master spots within a high site that initiates all over the world use to communicate with one another. I think it dated from at least the time of the Druidic religion that spanned the two millennia before Christ.

A LIFE VISION DREAM

After two more travels to sub-Saharan Africa, a trip to the United States, two journeys to India and the Far East, and a master's degree in cultural anthropology, I started a new cycle of my life with the writing and publishing of my first book. In it, I described and analyzed many anomalous experiences I had during my traveling quester years. Toward the end of the writing, I had a dream that would change the orientation of my research. In this dream, I was shown a very ancient stone model of a law: a torus generated by two opposite rotations. I was told this law functioned at several levels of reality, and three masters came toward me and explained this cosmic law: Albert Einstein at the physical, energetic level; Carl Jung at the depth-psychological level; and a third master at the spiritual level.

Reflecting on this dream, I understood that if I wanted to live up to it and achieve the goal it unveiled (finding the deep links between the three levels of reality and being), what I was absolutely lacking was an understanding of hard science. A short time afterward, I had two other dreams that told me I was going to meet many scientists and become involved in science. The first dream had been a life vision, showing me a new path of development for the next life cycle. Indeed, a few months later, through a series of synchronicities, I became involved in writing a book that presented a new paradigm in science, and I started meeting and interviewing the most innovative and visionary thinkers in France—each exploring a different scientific domain—and then, on a smaller scale, in the United States.[6]

With this book, I launched a scientific cycle that, about two years later, took me to the United States to work at the Psychophysical Research Laboratories (PRL) at Princeton University, where I prepared for my Ph.D. A few years later, I became involved in new scientific fields such as chaos theory, systems theory, consciousness studies, and cognitive sciences, and ended up with publishing a book on my Semantic Fields Theory (SFT).[7]

COLLECTIVE HARMONY VERSUS ECOLOGICAL COLLAPSE

Over the years, my "infinite space" meditation became a yoga of harmony fields. Whether I was in solitary meditation, jamming with a group of friends, at a concert, or at a trance dance party, as soon as I reached a heightened state, I started connecting with the giant telhar field that turns around Earth—the very field to which was connected the seat of power at Montségur.

My understanding is that there has been, ever since a very remote past, a network that permits high initiates from different cultures to remain connected to one another and to exchange information on a regular basis. In a very ancient past, this network encircled the planet high up in the atmosphere, and it possessed such a subtle mental frequency that only great masters could harmonize themselves with it and be part of this archetypal telhar field. This arch-telhar field was what is referred to in the scriptures as the "communion of the saints," which expresses a soul dimension in which all the saints are constantly in deep interconnection.

According to Pierre Teilhard de Chardin, humanity as a whole is following a path of spiritualization that is leading progressively toward a magnificent harmonization of spirits that he calls the Omega Point. The dimension of consciousness—what I call the semantic dimension—he called the noosphere (*nous* in Greek means "spirit"). In the last two millennia, he said, humanity's path was for each person to pursue his or her own individual enlightenment. But Teilhard de Chardin predicted that soon would start a new cycle in which the goal would shift from individual to collective spirituality. Thus, the new goal will be to pursue the harmonization of all consciousnesses on Earth in order to cocreate the planetary collective consciousness. In order to launch this new goal, more and more individuals must achieve the previous cycle's goal, which was set by the latest great guides and grand initiates.

It is my understanding that the arch-telhar field has been progressively growing nearer to Earth's surface, with just a minor reduction in its frequency while it becomes accessible to a greater number of questers—that is, to individuals who consciously seek to reintegrate their Self (or soul) consciousness. In the new cycle, which is opening now and which aims to trigger a leap in collective consciousness and to cocreate a harmonized humanity, the arch-telhar field is so near to Earth that it's accessible to any sensitive person who is seeking his or her own improvement.

Nowadays, numerous small or medium-sized telhar fields are elaborated everywhere on the planet, and connections are already forming between them. Eventually, the arch-telhar field will merge with the novel telhar fields once the latter have reached not only a planetary level, but also a stable state. At that stage, they will become one huge web of interconnection.

As Theosophist Alice Bailey predicted, Earth will become a "sacred planet." In the vision of Teilhard de Chardin, humanity and the noosphere will be one step closer to the Omega Point—the harmonization of all consciousnesses on Earth. Furthermore, it is to be expected that, while humanity makes a leap toward a higher consciousness, the animal kingdom will make a parallel leap.

At present, we watch the last jolts of two opposite movements. On one side, there are the worldwide companies of production and exploitation that generate profits, the interests of which are generally against the survival of the planet. On the other side, there is an increasing imbalance of numerous natural systems as well as the slow elimination of crucial resources, such as numerous metals and crude oil.

A growing number of people are aware that we must collectively change our ways if we want Earth to survive and that this should be done diligently, for the sooner changes are made, the greater are the chances for us to stop or avoid the collapse of many ecological systems.

Indeed, the damage done to a complex natural system such as drinking water (lakes, aquifers) through a wide array of pollutants (pesticides, fertilizers, industrial warming, and so forth) isn't simply linear—that is, following a gradual increase mirroring the increase of polluting and disturbing forces. All complex systems are nonlinear, and as chaos theory shows clearly, these systems don't have a linear development. Rather, they evolve through thresholds. They show periods of relative stability and then undergo abrupt changes. There are thresholds and bifurcation points beyond which a complex system leaps abruptly into another global configuration: its attractor will change and, together with it, its dynamical behavior (its trajectory). Not only can we not predict the exact timing of the bifurcation point, but we also cannot predict the global evolution of the system, one of the possibilities being a catastrophe—the collapse of the whole system. When such a collapse happens in one system, it may cause the collapse of other systems that are coupled with it (all ecological systems are more or less interconnected).

THE MEGALITHIC-CHRISTIAN SACRED GRID

While I sensed and worked with harmony fields in specific spaces encircled by a boundary, the Montségur seat of power showed me the use of stable rays to communicate at very long distances all over Earth.

While I explored all this, I had a recurrent experience of seeing arcs of energy darting out of sacred buildings, either from the center of domes or from steeples. In my student years, I very often went off on jaunts, either hitchhiking or driving my old car, but always on a discovery spree. My destination was unknown; I followed my intuition. While encountering many an enchanting place, there were magical, stirring moments for writing or meditating. One day, while meditating in a small, very ancient church, it occurred to me to stand under the exact center of the dome. My intention was to use the chanting of the *OM* to deepen my meditation. The *OM,* or *AUM,* is the most revered mantra of Hinduism and Tibetan Buddhism, symbolizing the state of unity through the harmonization of the three levels of being (ego-body, the Self, cosmic consciousness). When chanted in meditation on long expirations, it creates a deep, vibrating sound capable of harmonizing the Self with the cosmic consciousness and the world.

I wanted to feel fully the field of forces created by the sacred architecture, and that's why I was using the harmonizing chant at the exact point at the center of the choir. My aim was to harmonize myself with the energy field of the building and, notably, with its core vibration. I had centered myself at the head chakra and decided to try the *OM* on different notes, going up and down the scale until I found which note would harmonize me with the church. Suddenly, on a specific note, I heard a powerful resonance that seemed to extend to the whole building. Simultaneously, my internal state of consciousness became focused on the entire church. It was as if I had created a telhar field with the church itself and we were now in deep harmony, my Self in a fusion state with the church's semantic field. I stayed on this note and kept on chanting the *OM* on very long expirations, taking only short breaths, deepening the resonance and the wholeness of the harmony field. I was humming very low, and nevertheless the harmonics seemed to resonate very loudly. The church was like a huge resonance chamber: its absolutely perfect architecture was such a holistic form that it let the vibration flow in its entire stone mandala, following the geometric design of the numerous crossings of arches and stone pillars.

At that point, I found myself suddenly passing through the dome with the long, thin, vertical ray that I had emanated from my head chakra and perceiving very clearly the curved rays of light arcing out of the dome in a star shape—a crossing of sacred lines at exact angles, forming a 3-D mandala. The rays were moving up as a bundle to a place a yard or so above the dome, at which point they started to separate into lines. Each became an arc that climbed while moving out from the dome, then slowly descended toward another anchor point a few hundred yards away, only to rebound again. Discovering this was so exciting to me that I began doing this meditation in many of the ancient churches I stumbled on while driving or hitchhiking. Whenever I sojourned in a region, I explored its churches. I soon realized that churches received and bounced back arcs of light, these arcs reaching, at their peak, higher than the tips of the church domes or steeples. These arcs connected churches to other sacred buildings, which in turn made the sacred line pass and bounce to another anchor point situated farther away. What they were creating, at a regional scale, was a real network of sacred energies, embedded into the lines of the geomagnetic field of Earth, but steering these energies and rendering them even more sacred and powerful. These sacred lines were then able to lift even more the consciousnesses of people when they were gathered to pray or contemplate. Since it was mostly sacred buildings (cathedrals, churches, abbeys, and so forth) that were involved, I came to use the terms *sacred network* and *sacred lines*.

The anchor points of the network are generally buildings whose architecture was conceived according to sacred geometry (such as the golden proportion). This includes the near totality of sacred buildings in France. As I soon discovered, however, the sacred network is much more extended than the strict interconnection of sacred sites and sacred constructions. The network in Provence is quite easy to follow because the churches are often situated at the top of hills, from where I could search for the anchor points on surrounding hills and plains. While exploring this network, I saw that small anchor points—spots that received and subsequently bounced only one sacred line—could be a simple chapel or a cross on a hilltop or an old tower that was sometimes half in ruins. At the most important crossings (of four, five, or six sacred lines—that is, eight, ten, or twelve arcs of light), there were erected magnificent cathedrals or abbeys. The towers of sacred buildings often show the number and direction of sacred lines by the number of sides and angles in their geometrical form (for example, octagonal or hexagonal towers).

In large towns such as Paris or Lyon, the network is incredibly dense, and many city buildings have been constructed using sacred geometry and architecture. In such cases, fountains are often used to mark a star of sacred lines. Many fountains have a precise number of statues placed around them at regular intervals. See, for example, the two fountains flanking the Obelisk at La Concorde that show the northeast-southwest axis marked by rue Royale and Pont de La Concorde. Other such fountains are Place du Châtelet, with sphinxes, and Place Daumesnils (Félix

Eboué), with eight lions in pairs. Lonely statues in Paris often mark the passing of lines. Moreover, many civil constructions are integrated in the sacred network, which seems literally to make use of any artwork produced by this astonishing city, whatever its antiquity and whatever its civil function. The most noteworthy examples are the magnificent sacred architecture of hospitals, especially military hospitals such as Invalides (built by Le Nôtre, architect of Versailles) and Val de Grâce. I was dumbfounded when, while mapping the sacred network in Paris, I encountered a ley line linking no less than five hospitals.*

Of course, all government buildings are integrated, whether constructed during the monarchy, the empire, or the democracy. During the French Revolution, numerous churches all over France were savagely destroyed, and statues in cathedrals were beheaded or smashed. The two Napoleons greatly impacted the sacred network. The socialist president François Mitterrand inspired and supervised the most innovative and beautiful cornerstones of the whole sacred network in modern times, from the exquisitely esoteric glass pyramids of the Louvre, conceived by the architect I. M. Pei, to the perfect embedding of the Mitterrand Library at a key point in the overall network. Great castles and towers from all epochs, and of course their chapels, *hôtels particuliers,* manors, museums, and other buildings with novel architectural designs—most of these are also oriented within the network.

While I was exploring this new dimension of reality, I encountered much empirical proof of the validity of what I saw and sensed. For example, in a church situated on a hilltop in Provence, I sensed two lines crisscrossing and took a mental note of the directions so that, when exiting the building, I could try to spot the anchor points in the vicinity. Once I looked out in the four directions, I indeed found each of them, situated on top of a nearby hill or on the plain, at about an equal distance.

Another time, I sensed an underground straight tunnel and noted

*The line starts at Porte-de-Saint-Mandé (east of Paris) and passes by the hospitals Trousseau, Pitié Salpétrière, and Broca, the care center La Rochefoucauld, hospital Saint-Joseph, then Notre-Dame du Rosaire Church, and finally ends at Porte de la Plaine, in the south. We'll see more on Paris's sacred architecture in part 2.

that it followed a side aisle of the church. When exiting the building, though, I couldn't find any trace of it. Taking the long wall as a signpost, I started climbing down the hill through bushes, keeping in line with its direction and searching for ventilation holes or a door. I was surprised to find an entrance much farther down the hill and quite far from the church. Either the passage was at a second or third level underground or it had consistently followed a downward slope. The entrance was totally hidden in thick bushes. It was a massive, rectangular, wooden door with a huge, ancient lock. Because the stone above the door was a Roman arch, it left a small space between it and the straight top of the door. After I managed to lever my head up to that height, I was able to see a straight passage with a curved stone roof, slightly lighted by pale beams of sunlight coming down at intervals from apertures in the passage's ceiling and so well hidden by bushes I hadn't seen any of them while walking around.

On occasion, while driving, I have been able to sense the presence of a high telluric spot sometimes a few miles away. Leaving the main road to search for it along tiny lanes and dirt roads, I would finally find it in the countryside. To find such spots, some people use a divining rod or a pendulum. I have never used any material tool for deciphering the domain of semantic energy linked to space. On the contrary, I have developed a whole array of mental tools, and I keep conceiving new ones and testing them. I'm constantly testing my capacities, giving myself psi tasks to perform that only a fool could imagine would succeed, with the endgame being clear-cut success or failure so that I can assess immediately my results. Here is an example:

On visiting Hong Kong for the first time, I met an English expat at the airport, and that night we met to have a drink. He gave me the name of a club where we hoped to meet later, but he said he didn't know the address and that I would have to ask my way. He was in a hurry to leave, and on my tiny map, he indicated roughly the general direction with such a large circle that following it was useless. After finding a hotel on the mainland, I took the ferry around sunset. I abruptly decided that, because there was ample time until our appointment, I would try to find the club through relying only on my intuition. I wanted to know if it was possible (for in my opinion the collective unconscious possesses near-total knowledge) to find a place in an unknown town simply by knowing its name. When the ferry reached land, I started off like a bloodhound. Twice I was tempted to forget this stupid game and ask my way; I hate walking, and I feared I would have to cross the whole town the other way around if I happened to be going in the wrong direction. Twice, however, an inner voice, whispering with humor, replied that if I was indeed heading in the right direction, it would be even more stupid to ruin my chances to know if such a feat was possible. So I kept walking in tiny alleys and backdoor streets, even ascending stairs, until I decided I had enough. Since I still couldn't see any neon sign bearing the name of the club, I decided to ask a man standing in front of a porch. The little voice didn't disagree this time, and I approached the man. He made a gesture with his arm: "It's just next door, there." I noted the street name, but oddly, when I looked for it on my map the next day, I realized my friend's large circle was way off base.

All of these feats, and much more, were empirical evidence. When getting information through sensing the subtle energies of a place—its sacred invisible architecture and its semantic print—the positive proofs we receive from time to time take on a great significance. They are like an Ariadne thread in exploring and developing new mental capacities, allowing us to assess objectively what is achievable, to remain in touch with material reality, and, even more important, to give us enough confidence to pursue our quest.

2
MUSIC AND HARMONIC RAPTURE

MAKING EARTH RESONATE

Sensing the subtle semantic and telluric energies of places is just one domain in which the quester may, through the emergence of a new sensitivity, explore a whole new level of reality. The first-person experiences in Montségur and Hong Kong recounted above are only a facet of what can befall the quester who is eager to follow a path of direct connection with his or her Self. Some of the most ancient ways to create a telhar field were certainly in the context of music playing, especially when a group of musicians is improvising, as was the custom in drumming rituals all over Earth.

Musicians in North Africa, notably Berbers and Tuaregs, when playing drums, generate a loud collective call through the amplification of many drums in harmony. To deepen the trance, a musician will project the sound toward another person and then receive the counterpoint rhythm into his own drum. So the beat goes back and forth, as if the sound was used to play ping pong. Surely this technique has a name in musical science, but that name won't tell us what exactly it does in terms of collective consciousness. At the musical level, the drum is hit with a tiny delay (like a counterpoint), and from this slight imbalance, the rhythm is forced to bounce and turn. At the consciousness level, with each back and forth, the energy exchanged is amplified, and the collective trance state is deepened. Furthermore, the shrieking of women at precise peak moments triggers a higher level of synergy and trance. It electrifies the whole group and stirs the musicians to attain a more deeply altered consciousness state.

This playing technique re-creates the connection with other tribes, however far away. Immersed within the collective consciousness of its people, the playing group reactivates its connection to the semantic dimension and enters into a profound communication with the land, the desert, and the stars. Similar techniques to make the sound bounce back and forth between players are found in deep sub-Sahel Africa. They also have a traditional way to use the sound of drums as a complex language. When I passed through Rwanda in the seventies, the drums were calling and answering each other from hill to hill. It is truly amazing to watch village feasts in deep Africa, to see the way the musicians and all the attending people dance and are able to engage their whole body in the rhythm. It's as if any single part of anyone's body belongs with the music and the dance. In joining them, we can learn how to put our mind and playing in rhythmical harmony with bodily rhythms—not only with the beating of the heart, but also with deeper rhythms that I would be at a loss to identify.

The most extraordinary gift, however, of savanna and jungle people is to put Earth in resonance. They are able to create a collective rhythmic wave that makes the ground, the telluric waves, and Earth vibrate in unison, and they generate it by both the drums and the pounding of their feet on the ground during the trance dance. Of course, Africans, like Brazilians, have a natural, ingrained knowledge of trance states.

The group can detect a peak in the trance state of a drummer or a dancer, and other members will do whatever they can to stir and support this person's trance. For example, if a dancing woman or a man enters a stronger trance and starts dancing extraordinarily well, all the other dancers will make a circle around this person, and with clapping, shrieking sounds, and rhythmical gestures, they will increase and sustain the trance. Likewise, often a woman will start dancing right in front of a drummer, thereby giving him a great deal of energy and positive feedback—so much so that the musician enters a higher trance. This kind of mutual enhancement of trance states between musicians and dancers is customary in Brazil among samba drummers and dancers.

During my first travel in Africa, hitchhiking from Montségur all the way to Mombasa, Kenya, I had multiple occasions to participate in rituals and jam sessions. I had learned to play drums in France and, later, on the road and in India. When I reached Africa, I added a new gamut of rhythms to my playing, from Moroccan and Berber desert drumming to deep African forest sounds. The Indian *tablas* and, even more, the African *balafons* allow for both rhythmic and melodic composition, a fascinating merging of chant and rhythm. In the jungle, I saw balafons that were two yards long and could be played simultaneously by four musicians, two on each side of the enormous wooden planks. I was continually trespassing into the men's world while playing with them, since in the feasts and collective rituals in the equatorial countries I visited, the musicians were exclusively men. Conversely, when, while hitchhiking through northern Mauritania, I was invited into a women's secret society comprising Tuaregs and sub-Saharan Africans (in a proportion that reflected the general population there), I was thrilled to join the women who played drums for hours during their gatherings.

This is also the case in southeastern Africa, where the shamans, mostly women, accompany themselves with a drum, just as the Native American women do during sweat lodges and other sacred rituals.[1] In India, jamming during pujas had taught me how to connect to a divinity or a cosmic source through a direct link to my higher Self and how to sustain for hours such a high state shared with a small group. I had thus learned how to focus the mind on an energy source while my hands were left free to improvise and weave musical patterns. When the mind is focused on a high source of semantic energy, the music being played expresses naturally the frequency, feeling, and soul quality of this source.

In the desert, the stars are so huge and present, forming the only landscape beyond sand dunes or a flat desert floor, that they are like buoyant witnesses of the music. In the equatorial jungle, the hundreds of different, interwoven rhythms—of all types of animals and plants—weave a tapestry so complex that it is impossible to decipher or memorize it. Jungle people such as the Ibos, however, express this complexity in their music as if they were able to hear millions of interwoven rhythms piercing through the obscurity of the night. In this way, Africa teaches us how to talk to Earth and take her as a partner in the collective trance.

In Africa, drummers call their brothers from very far away, and the sound wave makes a whole landscape vibrate—this landscape being extended to infinity when the drumming occurs in the desert. Not only does the landscape vibrate with the sound wave, but also the wave is created in such a way as to send it traveling along Earth's crust, undulating its way around the planet. (There is more on these vertical waves in chapter 6.)

EXPERIENCING A HARMONY STATE DURING JAMS

As a drummer and a lover of jam sessions, I have repeatedly experienced entire groups of musicians reaching at one point a very singular state in which our individual consciousnesses become intertwined in such a harmonious and attuned way that it seems we form one collective mind.

From that point onward, the group is able to play together on a new level of sensitivity and awareness, reaching such a tuned-in state that the improvisation of each musician falls perfectly in sync with the others' music, creating an extremely beautiful ensemble composition. At that moment, each musician becomes literally entranced by the beauty and the strength of the music that is being created. Whether he or she is leading the collective jam at that moment hardly matters. The music seems to originate from another source: a higher state of consciousness. Enraptured by the whole pattern of the music, one is in a state of hyperawareness that makes it possible to hear at once each musician playing and the playing of the whole group—as well as one's own part in the global tapestry being woven.

Yet musicians in this state are not trying or willing to play specific music. Rather, while their minds are focused on a higher source and on hearing the whole group pattern, their hands seem to play all by themselves. In fact, they themselves are absolutely amazed at what they are capable of creating.

The collective harmony state during music playing has very specific features that are easily recognizable to sensitive musicians. Before diving into the stupendous dynamics of cocreation, I must state that for musicians relying on improvisation, any shift in the collective state of consciousness—especially such a dramatic change as the whole group suddenly shifting from a disordered collective state to a highly harmonious one—is immediately felt in a very tangible way.

Awareness of the Shift in State

In the disordered state, the musicians feel they are not in sync or that some of them are out of tune, or else that the instruments are not well tuned. They will be unhappy or bored or even upset. On the contrary, in the harmony state, they feel not only that they are in perfect sync, but also that they are creating music of superior quality. Enthralled by the creative process and the music, they feel they are in a state of heightened consciousness. Due to their sheer sensitivity to music and their awareness of each note and beat, this recognition is instantaneous. Suddenly, all the diverse instruments fall into place, and each improvisation from one player embellishes and supports all the other parts. Suddenly, the sound one experiences becomes extraordinarily good!

Accrued Sense of Beauty

The accrued beauty of what's being played is of course the most striking feature of the state of harmony. By nature, musicians hate disharmony; it feels ugly and repulsive. Harmony among players is not only enjoyable, it is also a must of their profession, a sort of basic state without which they cannot be creative as a group.

This is why all good musicians are extremely sensitive to a higher level of harmony—a kind of hyperharmony. Their sense of beauty rises to a peak: the music's entrancing and beautiful! They are spellbound by what they are playing, and the public (if there is one) experiences the same shift into an ecstatic state. Everyone feels that the music is incredibly good, that they are all in it, part of the collective state, enraptured in a blissful synergy.

A Participatory Creative State

The accrued sense of beauty creates a stronger connection, a synergy among all the participants. Everybody enters the trance and begins to accompany the music in a very active and creative way: swinging in rhythm, clapping, dancing, turning any object into an instrument, or adding vocals. The mood is upbeat, spellbound, enraptured—entranced in any possible way but never passive. Even in the case of a public concert of classical music, which never leads to dancing, the listening becomes an active participation—a participatory trance, highly creative, alive, and holistic.

Higher Connectedness

When the sense of beauty and the synergy grow strong, the links among musicians are reinforced. Everyone develops a greater sensitivity to the presence of others, to whoever leads the improvisation at the moment. Then, as soon as the collective state of harmony is created, each person feels in sync, not only with the music being played, but also with the minds of all the others. The separate and diverse minds have given way to a collective mind, to a sense of belonging together. All are unified or strongly interconnected within one unique mind: a consciousness field.

Creative Flow

Of course, in a jam session, the musicians gathered together in the first place because they had the intention to play together. Thus their minds were already focused on getting in sync and reaching a collective state as well as on being creative. Each individual becomes a hypercreative part of the consciousness field that builds up and grows into a state of creative flow, allowing each person's mind to be incredibly more acute and aware of the harmonious interconnection.

The concept of *flow* was introduced by Mihaly Csikszentmihalyi as an "an almost automatic, effortless yet highly focused state of consciousness" that involves "an element of novelty or discovery."[2] For Steven Pritzker, the artists in a creative flow are quasi-unconscious of the work they are doing, such as painting while in a trance state.[3] I, however, will keep to Csikszentmihalyi's vision: in the harmony state, the hands may be playing as if all by themselves, but the mind is in a sort of *supraconscious* state, hyperaware and intent on expressing a source of energy so subtle that only an innovative process can achieve it.

In this creative flow, the psychic energy of musicians remains in constant reinvention of itself, which allows for imagining infinite variations of even the most well-known songs. It's akin to a state of grace, because the creation of novel music seems to come by and of itself, without the slightest effort and especially without any thinking or planning. Yet it's magnificent, perfect, and astonishingly beautiful. It is as if the flow of energy itself created the music in the heads and bodies of not only all the musicians, but also of all people in the participatory audience.

Holistic Visualizing

For each musician, the state of hyperawareness translates into the synchronous perception of all the parts being played—as if the music was a giant mandala in which the lead musician of the moment is at the center. The last musical sentence is translated into a complex graphic design in which each musician's music is like a petal. It's as if time collapses: the complex graphic represents the wave pattern of the entire last musical phrase. Each musician can visualize instantly the whole pattern of his or her part in the next musical phrase. In fact, the state of interconnectedness is such that there's a subtle precognition of what the lead musician envisions as his next lead pattern, and each comusician envisions his accompaniment of that future music.

This is why, in jam sessions, there are so many nano-instant shifts in the music or the beat or the tone that happen in several people at once. It's not that musicians hear a shift that is initiated by the lead musician and then proceed to follow it; rather, these shifts occur in several musicians at once and in perfect sync. My feeling, though, is that there's even more going on: a collective connection to the very source inspiring the lead musician, and this connection makes it possible to "hear" the variations and frequencies in the source at the very instant when the lead musician hears them himself.

Higher Speed of Thought

We must figure that while musicians play music, the thinking process is connected not to language in words, but rather to musical language, feelings, and the overall state of consciousness. In this kind of trance, the speed of thinking is thus much greater than the speed of playing—which means there can be nano-instant recognition of the lead musician's changing mood and inspiration.

My experience of these states has been that I shift to a much faster speed of mental processing. An entire twelve-beat rhythmical sentence may appear in my mind as a one-shot visualization that my hands then perform—even if this performance is wholly outside the range of their usual capacity in terms of both complexity and speed. While I visualize rhythm with tune shades and melody, my fingers spontaneously find the perfect spots to hit the drum in order to achieve these fine tunes—yet I'm totally ignorant of tunes on a drum skin. This definitely hints at the emergence, in this collective consciousness state, of a new sensitivity to sound—a sort of creative clairaudience.

HOW TO CREATE A COLLECTIVE HARMONY FIELD

Spherical 360-degree Listening

In my view, this accrued sensitivity to sound implies more sophisticated modes of listening, such as what I call *360-degree listening.*

A particular mode of listening requires that players be attentive to all that's happening at once in the whole group of musicians. It's quite evident that no musician who is part of an orchestra can function otherwise: simultaneously, he must be able to register the playing of other musicians and be focused on the lead person (the conductor or lead musician). Spherical listening, however, goes further in the sense that it is the very creation of a 360-degree circle of attention and receptivity that, in a mysterious way, leads to the creation of the collective consciousness field and the structure of energy that underlies it.

Let me explain my own ad hoc method for achieving such 360-degree listening. In order to hear every musician around myself at once, my mind first makes my two ear chakras (the energy centers in the internal ear) function synchronously. Biologists have observed experimentally that neurons situated at great distance in the brain can fire in a synchronous way. This phenomenon, called *synchronous firing* and still unexplained, has been understood as evidence of quantum interconnectedness, and several scientists, such as Roger Penrose, Stuart Hameroff, and Danah Zohar, have proposed and are researching these quantum interactions in the brain.[4] Such synchronous firing could explain the perfect harmonization between the assemblies of neurons in the two ears. Only when my two ear centers are in sync can I achieve spherical listening. More precisely, I sense I have created an energetic field of listening. I have actually *seen* the energy structure of the fields created by the ear chakras in several instances, and I have been able to observe how it works. I have many reasons to think this energy generated by consciousness is not of an electromagnetic nature. We will discuss this subject throughout this book, but let's keep in mind that while I use the term *semantic energy,* or the short term *syg-energy,* to refer to it, it is clearly linked to consciousness, and its nature is still unknown.*

Thus, an energy field (made of semantic, or syg-energy) is created around the whole head of a person that permits 360-degree listening to all the other musicians. I believe that all great conductors of orchestras, and to a lesser degree musicians playing in groups, create, unconsciously, such a field around their heads. When I have done so, and while listening intently to the other musicians, I start to harmonize myself with others' fields, which leads to the creation of the collective consciousness field.

Even if, however, the similarity with quantum synchronous firing could lead us to infer that these (personal and collective) harmony fields are quantum fields, such a possibility is far from guaranteed. As we will see, some of the properties of collective consciousness fields are at odds with the quantum behavior of particles as much as they are at odds with electromagnetic fields' behavior.

---

*I take the syllable *syg* from the Greek letter *S, sigma,* to stand for the word *semantic.*

Emergence of a Collective Telhar Field

Once we have created such an individual listening field, straining to hear what the others are playing leads to the creation of the collective field. This is a very natural process: it shows how we can pursue a learning procedure until we achieve a higher performance. As soon as one musician is able to take the whole group into his or her mind, the collective field is created. Thus, the main qualities of a collective field are:

- A state of collective harmony (that remains in flow and constant evolution)
- The experience of being one mind as a group, of being connected telepathically
- A field that stimulates a highly creative flow in each person.

I therefore proposed to call it (from its two main qualities) a telepathic-harmonic field, or telhar field. We can say that we are experiencing a telhar field while playing in a group when we suddenly feel that all of us musicians are forming one unique mind, a mental mandala in which no one is left out. An important point in viewing it as an energy field is that the people usually just listening (the audience) immediately become creative participants in the field.

The Node of Telhar Fields

As for the mandala analogy, the field is like a giant flower with petals. Each musician is a petal, and at the center is the lead musician of the moment. I'm talking here of the energy dimension, for the musicians may be in any spatial organization, and furthermore, the musician holding the field may change even though nobody changes places in the room (see chapter 1). While the telhar field is being created, the flower as a whole reaches a higher energy level, lifting all the people who compose it.

The telhar field has a very peculiar energy structure. At any moment, it has a creative center: the person (in this case, the musician) who actually inspires the group and keeps the harmony field together. I call this person the *node of the field*. It is a neutral term, for we must remember that the node assumes only an energetic function, and the person occupying this role may change several times during the session.

The node is thus the one who, at a precise moment, has the highest state of consciousness and is in sync with all the others. From this perspective, the node is not always the formal leader of the music band—notwithstanding the fact that a band is often organized around a person who is able to instill in others cohesion and empathy. When, during a performance, musicians play a solo, they are naturally swept into the node position for the duration of that solo, and they reach a higher creative gear while everybody listens. Even without breaking into a solo, one of the musicians may enter a peak state. Suddenly, listeners feel that this musician is incredibly good, and the whole group seems now to follow him—precisely because this musician has become the node and is, at the moment, the person with the highest and most creative energy of the group.

Once a musician has become the node, the whole mandala of the group is oriented and reorganized according to this person's sensibility, feeling, and specific consciousness. The other people, recognizing that the music played by the node has an extra strength and quality to it, even a trancelike dimension, will tune in, supporting his or her trance and period of high inspiration.

Of course, this is done mostly by feeling: the sheer joy of somebody playing extraordinarily well makes us turn our attention to that person and follow his or her lead. We thus give our energy to the node, and the node, in turn, pulls the whole group into a higher energy state.

A comparison that springs to mind is the way electrons reach an excited state and shift to a higher orbit in an atom. This analogy, however, could be misleading, for what occurs in a musical group is much more complex and should be understood on its own ground.

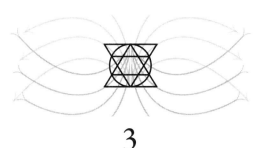

3

THE SECRET OF SHARED PRAYER

A situation in which telhar fields are often created is whenever people are assembled to pray or meditate as a group. All religions have a form of collective gathering, whether for prayer or sacred ritual. These gatherings have taken many forms, even in the Judeo-Christian heritage, that is, the Hebraic, Christian, and Muslim religions. Larry Dossey introduced the concept of *prayer fields* in reference to the great potency built up by people praying together. These fields, he says, can have a potent effect whenever people gather and harmonize their wishes.[1] The prayer field can generate positive changes, whether biological, physical, or even social, such as healing people and helping to ameliorate their relationships, work situations, or social environments. Based on my research, my understanding is that a group prayer will indeed have such potency whenever the participants have created a harmony field among themselves. To begin our understanding of this effect, let's take a tour of some praying rituals in the world.

GROUP PRAYER AMONG SUFIS

It was prayer day among the Sufis. The Iranian Sufi master Azra Darvichi had passed the traditional embroidered cape over his immaculate, long white dress. His ogival headdress, under which his long white hair totally disappeared, exhibited an intricate mandala made of tiny, multicolored crosses finely embroidered over a black material. The munificence of his age-old garment paled in comparison to the striking old face, the long white beard softening the otherwise too-intense look of his brown, keen eyes. His ashram (or rhonerah in Farsi) was a beautiful and peaceful garden with paths of fragrant white jasmine bushes around a sacred fountain that poured water in a small pool.

For now, Azra Darvichi was at the door greeting each newcomer, whether an initiated darvichi or a disciple. The traditional salute was a handshake in which the greeter and the guest kiss one another's upper thumb. The newcomer bows first, then the master gives his blessing. After this salute, the guests then headed toward the garden and the sacred fountain. They washed their hands and feet in a ritual way (I had done that much earlier), and then sat in the prayer room. Many a time, my Iranian friend Gazelle and I had sat in that room or in the comfortable garden chairs in front of its large double door for a peaceful and enlightening chat with Azra Darvichi. The master had taken us both into his inner circle, two women in their early twenties, for a special preparation prior to our initiation. I knew the sole decoration of the prayer room was Iranian carpets covering its whole floor. This room was in total contrast with the master's private meditation room, which was accessed by a terrace surrounded by flower trees and a flight of stone steps. That secret room, which only initiates (the darvichis) could penetrate, was richly adorned with ancient paintings and artwork—such as bronze travel bags looking like sailboats—that had belonged to ancient masters and darvichis, whose striking black-and-white photos could be seen on the wall.

We, the two women present today, wore white garments, and we sat cross-legged on the high terrace in front of the master's meditation room, mostly hidden from the prayer room by thick foliage. As women, we were not allowed to be in the same room as the men, but nevertheless, we were to participate in the Dikhr chanting and prayer. Despite appearances, women have had a great place in Iranian Sufism; among the four individuals having reached the highest spiritual state, one was a woman: the poetess Rabe'eh (or Rabee).

When all movement stopped in the garden and the men sat in the prayer room, there was a long moment of total silence while we entered a deep meditative state as a preparation. Suddenly, the chanting began in the prayer room. The Dikhr mantra of this school was simple: the name of God in two syllables, a breathing break, and then, on a powerful expiration, the sound Hû! *(pronounced as in "Hurrah!" but with the "H" more strongly aspired)*. The breathing that was performed while saying the mantra Hû! required abruptly and deeply forcing air from the lungs, which subsequently made the stomach muscles tense. At first, everybody started with their natural pitch of voice and followed the same breathing rhythm. Soon the choir grew in amplitude, its sound rounder and deeper as it reached a sort of harmonic resonance.

All the while, eyes closed and in a profound state, Gazelle and I were totally attuned to the group, if on a higher pitch of voice. I was deep in trance, and I could sense most of the men were in a very deep trance too. Soon, we had the impression that we were sitting among them; the thirty or so yards of distance seemingly disappeared through the depth of our harmony state. I was completely surprised when, after a lengthy deepening of our meditative state, one voice rose in an improvised stance high above the bass tone of the other men. He was still chanting the same mantra but much more rapidly, the pitch of his voice rising steeply, becoming more and more shrill. The impact it had on our group mind was tantamount: each person's state of consciousness reached a higher level. I had a strange, clairvoyant impression when this man started to get in a hypertrance state. I distinguished this particular voice (and person) in the faraway room with a well of light over his head—as if a ray that came from the cosmos was pouring light into his head and from his head into the whole group. His state stabilized at this higher, luminous level, his voice remaining high pitched. Some minutes later, abruptly, a second man entered into a hypertrance and also started chanting at a higher frequency, and I had the same image of a strong light pouring over him. Strangely, the second man getting into trance didn't displace the first one. The two high-pitched voices were distinct and at the same time in deep harmony, their joint effect on the group growing even stronger. Then, at one point, the first voice rejoined the rest of the group, and a third one suddenly irrupted into the hypertrance state.

The overall effect of this chanting was a strong collective harmony that created a large field of light. From time to time, a sudden flash of brighter energy erupted like a column of iridescent light, about two or three yards high. From two to four columns lighted at each moment, each one lasting about fifteen to twenty minutes.

As for the group, each new shift to a higher level of energy deepened our meditation and our connection to the divine source. At one point, I found myself in a fusion state, experiencing a very alive connection. I was not, however, aware of what my voice did, because I was mostly focused on the light.

The Main Traits of This Experience of the Sufi Dikhr

1. The specific mantra and breathing (with a strong expulsion of air) induces a deep meditation that reaches a trance state. While this breathing shows some analogy to hyperventilation techniques used to induce trance, this is not an explanation of what's happening during the meditation since such techniques can lead to a variety of trance states.

2. The impression is of a large field of light created by all participants at the beginning of the meditation (as a baseline consciousness state), from which erupt columns of iridescent light that correspond to the higher-level state of those entering a hypertrance. The overall sensation of a large field of light points to a telhar field.

3. The feeling of distance being annulled (between me and the far-away group of men): this trait points to the existence of a field, even if it has not been consciously registered as a field. (We will see this specific trait of telhar fields in other contexts.)

4. No telepathic events: in my view, the telepathic aspect only seems absent because, in group prayer, the shared state of consciousness is devoid of language and thoughts. Telepathy does exist, however, even if it is expressed not by an exchange of thoughts, but rather by a state of oneness, a shared consciousness.

5. Thus, through the harmonization of their rhythmic chanting, the participants form a harmonic choir and soon enter a harmony field.

6. After a two-hour Dikhr session, I feel nourished and replenished with a beautiful energy. Afterward, I remain in a higher state of consciousness, more alive and full of energy.

Telhar Fields during Sufi Prayer
- **Induction:** Harmonization of the rhythmic and synchronous breathing of participants
- **Inner experience:** Trance state, mystical fusion state (connecting oneself to a divine or sacred source)
- **Energetic aspects:** Large shared field of light plus a few columns of intense light emanated by Sufis in a hypertrance who are able to lift the remainder of the group
- **Nodes:** Several nodes—the Sufis in hypertrance, with columns of light above them. (We will see a similar feature in trance dance, discussed in chapter 5.)

A TELHAR FIELD DURING A MEDITATION IN MANALI

The experience that I'm going to relate now occurred in the foothills of the Himalayas, in Manali, which in the seventies was still a big village with half its population made up of Tibetan refugees. In the preceding months, I had practiced meditation several hours a day, but when I arrived in Manali, I started devoting less time to meditation and more time to practical learning under the guidance of a mostly silent teacher whose name was Karl. Karl was himself continuously in a state of meditative awareness, and that was what I was practicing and learning through him.

We were a few foreigners who lived in a wood house on the outskirts of Manali. The very simple village house was just a large room with a balcony and was totally bare apart from a stove on which we cooked our food. That night, four of us—Karl, me, and two friends who were also on a spiritual path—sat in a circle. We were sharing a deep state of meditative awareness with open eyes but in an inner silence, when, abruptly, this state spontaneously shifted to a higher level. We found ourselves to be one mind, and no more four individuals. This shift was so sudden and so strong that it was like a revelation of another level of reality. The abrupt transition was accompanied by a strange light structure that I had never witnessed before: I saw a large circle of white light that turned at incredible speed, forming a torus linking our head chakras together (the highest psychic center); this torus was a hand thick and about two yards wide. The torus of light appeared simultaneously with the impression of being in total telepathy with the others. I felt I was inside the minds of all of us at once. It was like a sudden explosion of light and an expansion of the inner state itself.

In utter astonishment, I realized that any single thing I saw within the room had an extraordinary, iridescent light. Everything glowed as if I viewed it through a soap bubble—everything had a peculiar shine. Moreover, the few objects dispersed throughout the room also had a sort of vibrating quality to them, similar to something viewed through a heat wave. As a result, the whole room, translucent and shining in a beautiful way, appeared totally transformed, especially with the glistening, circular torus in the middle. Yet the most striking feature was our shared inner state: the impression of being an individual entity no longer, but instead being fused with the others.

Then I grasped that the room appeared so because there was indeed a large sphere of energy (just like a soap bubble) that surrounded the four of us. This extended sphere (about four yards in diameter) seemed to be created by the torus of light that circled among our heads (and that was about two yards wide, at most). On focusing my gaze on the torus, I could see perfectly well that it was turning counterclockwise at an incredible speed and that it was, in fact, a luminous blur created by particles rotating at an enormous velocity.

I was awestruck and yet in bliss, and I sensed that those same feelings were shared by Karl, who sat opposite me, and the others as well. I didn't dare move. A thought passed between us that we were in a telepathic field: we were all in a unique mind space. When I understood how exceptional it was and how fragile seemed the bubble of light, I became afraid of breaking this stupendous state . . . and at the very moment I had this fear, one of my fingers jerked. I heard a high-pitched "cling," as if a crystal glass had cracked. The field abruptly broke down, and the torus disappeared. The room once again became a dull color. The feeling of oneness, the shared mind, was gone. I was back to my single self, in my separate place and in my individuality.

Reflecting on this experience later that day, I became convinced that there existed a second, clockwise movement of energy, which had not been visible because it was less pronounced and its energy was less strong. (We will see this double-rotation structure in more detail in "Torus and Counterclockwise Energy: Velocity," in chapter 6.) In my life, I have seen the torus structure a few times over the heads of individuals meditating alone, when they attained a very high state—a *samadhi,* or a transcendental state. It appeared as a small torus the size of an individual's head above the head chakra (the thousand-petaled lotus). Similarly, a few times, I have seen the iridescence of all nature and all the things around me when I was able to attain a landscape-sized telhar field—but in these cases, I couldn't see any torus. As for the spherical form, it seems to be a prominent, if not inherent, feature of telhar fields. In contrast, a telhar field blossoming from a shared samadhi state—creating a torus of light that links people and creating a sphere surrounding them—is a very rare and sacred experience to live.

In the Manali experience, the energy structure (the torus and enclosing bubble) added a new dimension to the inner experience of the shared state. Needless to say, it was an extremely clear and precise manifestation that lasted long enough for me to analyze it in detail. I concede that all participants may not have the specific ability I have to see the energy structures of fields, but they may, however, sense and know other features better than I. These are only individual variations in the way we sense energy fields.

In his book *The Celestine Prophecy,* James Redfield devotes an entire chapter to the ability to see energy fields around plants and trees. He then goes into a detailed account of how we may not only see these fields, but also learn to give energy to the plants. Redfield conveys that the learning can be quite easy. "It's the first time that's the most difficult; one has to learn how to modify one's own way of looking."[2]

Yet while we can sit in front of a plant until we have succeeded in seeing its energy field, telhar fields are much more elusive, and the way they work or emerge is still quite complex. Even when we feel and know that we are part of one, the precise seeing or sensing of their diverse features (extension, structure, quality, source, and nodes) is bound to change with each situation. Many factors are at play, both internal and environmental, for creating a field or for sensing it, and thus our interaction with them may be quite different from one instance to the next.

Meditation Telhar Field in Manali

- **Induction:** Deep state in silent collective meditation
- **Inner experience:** Inner sensation of energy turning between our heads and passing through our brains

   Impression of being one mind, of sharing a telepathic field, of feeling the others' minds inside our own

   No more sensation of a separate ego and emergence of a collective state of accordance
- **Energetic aspects:** Energetic structure forming between the four heads: torus of light moving counterclockwise at incredible speed

   Spherical bubble of light surrounding the participants completely

   Abrupt breaking down of the light torus and the sphere with a thought of fear; the breaking down is accompanied by a crystalline clinging sound
- **Nodes:** Due to the exceptional structure of the field, with the torus turning among our head chakras, it seems there is no prominent node; rather, the node role is shared equally among the four people who are in deep attunement.

THE CIRCLE-AND-NODE STRUCTURE

I'm now convinced there are different types of telhar fields. The perfect circling energy, in my opinion, is only one of the diverse structures they may take. In order for one to be created, there must be a particular number of people who can sit or play or dance in a circle. In fact, visualizing the energy circulating and rotating among a group of people sitting in a circle is the easiest way to create a telhar field. Once it is thus created, the energy seems to spin among participants at great speed. The Manali case, however, is one of the rare occasions in which I saw the rotation and the torus within a group with great clarity and precision.

In jam sessions, for example, I usually have only a fuzzy sensation of energy turning among people—a sensation both quasi-tactile and quasi-visual. (In chapter 6, we will see other cases implying the existence of a torus.)

Regarding the circling telhar field, however, let us note how many traditional dances—remnants of ancient times—use the circle as their basic structure. For instance, we can note the Celtic *fez noz,* the traditional, improvised feast still existing in Brittany. All the Bretons (descendants of the Celts) willing to dance form a huge circle. They hold hands and move their feet in rhythm and then turn in a circle for a few steps, back and forth, following an age-old pattern of movement. In many provinces of France, we find a similar pattern, *la ronde:* the round formed by people holding hands while dancing in a circle.

The Greek dance *sirtaki* is performed similarly. At one point, however, a specific dancer moves toward the middle of the circle for a peak improvisation. Everybody in the circle gives energy to him or her by focusing attention, but also by making encouraging sounds (more insistently beating the feet, whistling, high-pitched shrieks, and the like). Here, we can recognize another key feature of the telhar field: the presence of the node—the individual who enters a peak state and boosts the harmony field.

This feature is also found in African trance dance during village feasts—those that are based on improvisation and that stand outside ritual events. Suddenly, a dancer enters a trance, and everybody knows what's happening; everyone feels it. Immediately, everyone creates a circle around the dancer, encouraging him or her in any possible way: clapping in rhythm, shrieking loudly, and so forth. Meanwhile, the sensitive musicians, feeling (sometimes at a distance) the trance of a dancer, suddenly receive his or her energy, and they too enter a higher trance, playing louder and with a stronger beat. The whole village responds to the individual entering a hypertrance, because he or she is now like an antenna of cosmic energy, receiving it and giving it through the dance. All the people present not only receive it fully, but also help in sustaining and deepening the trance by giving back energy to the node.

A circular pattern of giving and receiving occurs between the node and the people, which enhances the energy of everybody. This exchange is accomplished in a spirit of joy, enthusiasm, appreciation, and excitement. When the dancer (generally worn out after a while) stops dancing, another enters the circle to take his or her place.

The Archetype of the Circle around the Node

Once the structure (the circle with a single node at the center) has been formed, it remains stable for a long time, sometimes for the remainder of the feast, with a new dancer replacing the center dancer as he or she becomes tired. Given its stability, it seems we have here an archetypal pattern of relations. The circle of people and the node at the center is an archetype, which is why we find it in so many traditions.

The archetype, according to depth psychologist Carl Jung, is a typical symbolic structure or image in the psyche.[3] It has its root in the collective unconscious and is highly charged with psychic energy. The hero, the mother, the fight with a dark principle—all are archetypes of the human psyche. This is why, explained Jung, we may find an identical symbol in the dreams of a Westerner and in an Australian Aborigine myth—with the myth generally unveiling the meaning of the dream. Jung explained that all humans are interconnected through the collective unconscious. Our minds have the same roots: the archetypes. The collective unconscious is thus a common reservoir of basic symbols charged with psychic energy. This is why, in our cultural and artistic creations, we often give new forms to ancient archetypes. We create new myths in art, novels, films, and so forth. For Stanley Krippner, evolution (cultural and personal) rests upon the creation of new myths.[4] A person who is able to analyze his old myths and willingly sets on creating more fulfilling narratives and symbols about his or her own future will very certainly achieve a better personal realization.

If telhar fields (collective fields of consciousness) are indeed an archetype, we should find the basic structure of this experience in much of the cultural or religious lore. And I must add that if indeed telhar fields exist, they have to be an archetype in the human psyche. The experience of seeing and sensing them may not be conscious; it may remain in the unconscious. But the structure of human relations—that is, of energetic interconnections—must exist in many instances in very diverse cultures. Jung proved the existence of archetypes by noting their presence and correlations in diverse cultures and religions. Of course, this was not the reason why his idea was so widely adopted. The real reason was that, on reading or on hearing about his ideas, people felt and knew they were true. His notions rang a bell. We realized symbols, and not only the ones in our dreams, drove and enhanced our whole psychic life. We understood that we were constantly judging situations and people according to basic matrices of thought and that these were precisely what Jung called archetypes.

In the same way, the existence of particular states of harmony or heightened consciousness in group settings is a fact of experience for many of us in a conscious way. Some of us have peeked at some of the very specific features, such as deeper interconnectedness, synchronicities, enhanced feelings of brotherhood or of belonging, telepathic occurrences, a shared sense of future unfolding of events, and so on.

The Ritual Circle

If we focus on the circle symbol in rituals and religions, an entire book would not suffice to assemble all its occurrences worldwide. We can note a few examples of a sacred circle of people. Many sacred rituals are based on the initiates forming a circle: the Aborigines of Australia, American Indians, and Africans (in animist rituals) all incorporate the circle. In the Dance of the Python among Masai warriors in Kenya, girls, for their puberty rite, form a large circle that represents a snake by pressing their naked bodies front to back, one after the other, while dancing. (See the films *Python Uncoils* by Jacqueline Roumeguère-Eberhardt and *Baraka* by Ron Fricke.)[5] In ancient rituals, the Druids form circles of initiates to symbolize "the three circles" of their religion. Druidism (or Bardism, the religion of the ancient Celts) views the universe as composed of three circles. *Keugant* (the void circle in Breton) is the circle of God, *gwenved* (the white world) is the circle of humanity, and *abred* is the abyss.

Native Americans have a "circle of initiates" in many rituals—for example, in the Sun Dance, the Bear Dance, and the Ghost Dance.[6]

Similarly, in the ritual of the calumet, the sacred pipe is passed among all the participants sitting in a circle around a sacred fire. This ritual gesture in the circle is believed to promote a spirit of brotherhood and sincerity and is specifically used for ratifying agreements among opposite groups—to seal them, so to speak, and commit them to memory. In the calumet rite, we very clearly see the telhar field archetype, both in the circle shape and in the harmonic bond created among people assembled. To use it to insure peace is even more revealing of the harmonic nature of the telhar field. The campfire at the center of the group is the symbolic node. Taca Ushte says, "The Indian symbol is the circle. The circle is the symbol of men and women assembled around a campfire, parents and friends meeting in peace while the calumet goes from hand to hand. The camp in which each tipi has its place is also a circle. The tipi is a circle in which people sit in a circle. All the families in a village are also circles in this circle, itself part of a larger circle made by the seven camp fires of the Sioux, which represent the Sioux Nation."[7]

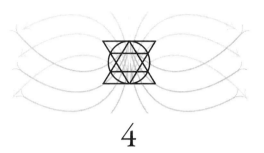

4

INHERITING SACRED PLACES

While visiting sacred places all over the world, we often feel much more alive, more energetic. Our minds seem to expand and give us the impression of being freer. We are filled with a sense of awe for the beauty of the site, whether Tiahuanacan in Mexico, Ellora in India, Chartres in France, or Angkor Wat in Cambodia. Walking on sacred stones replenishes our energy and thus we feel enthusiastic. At the same time, as we walk on sacred stones, we enter a kind of inner peace that makes us want to sit and reconnect with our deep Self. Stones, better than any other matter, retain memory. Temples are filled with a living memory of a people, of their specific connection to God and the spirit. This is why Native Americans consider stones sacred—*wakan* in the Lakota language.*

In the ancient territory of the Celts (mainly Great Britain, France, and Germany), an even more ancient people erected huge megaliths—vertical stones, or menhirs, and underground chambers, dolmens, tumuli, and cairns. The only thing we know about the megaliths people is that they erected these stones from 6000 BCE until the onset of the Celtic civilization. Then the Druids (priests of the Celts) used these powerful sites to perform their sacred ceremonies because they themselves didn't build temples prior to the Roman conquest. The Celts of France, the Gauls, led by Vercingetorix, were defeated at the battle of Alesia in 52 BCE, and the Druidic religion was forbidden under the

---

*For the Sioux (Lakota), *wakan* means "sacred, holy." *Wicasa wakan* are the shamans, the wise and holy men and women.

Roman emperor Tiberius (early in the first century CE). The only free Druidic society and priests that were left out of this huge civilization were in Great Britain and Ireland.

The megaliths people knew about telluric currents (ley lines and large cosmo-telluric lines) and that their crossing points had a great spiritual and uplifting energy and sometimes healing virtues. Thus, they erected standing stones at these points. Then the builders of Gallo-Roman temples and later of churches and cathedrals in France not only often chose the same sacred sites on which to erect temples or churches, but they also managed to keep these megaliths intact while they constructed on top of them. A magnificent network of old Celtic standing stones (which are still visible) is thus enmeshed within the more recent Catholic network of churches, abbeys, and cathedrals. No wonder that it is around a church built on a dolmen that I saw for the first time a telhar field in its spatial aspect—something rather incomprehensible for me at the time.

In this chapter, we'll explore in depth the telhar fields I experienced that showed a clear-cut spatial boundary, such as the ones in Brittany, in Nasik, and in Bièvres. I have already given a general view of some of these events in chapter 1, but we'll now dive deeper into the subject and analyze each occurrence in more detail.

GRID AND SPACE BOUNDARY AT A CHRISTIAN/DRUIDIC SITE

I and my boyfriend at the time were intuitively guided toward that monastery in Brittany where the community of monks had a very original spiritual way, at a crossing of Orthodox Christian and ancient Druidic traditions. The monks told us they were still cognizant of the ancient Druidic knowledge, as if this tradition had been passed on to them. The small church flanking the monastery, which is extremely beautiful, had been built on a megalith. As I noted in chapter 1, all the while I was there, I remained in a heightened state of consciousness. I had very strong meditations at the church, on my meditation rock, and also inside the monastery.

The community there was small and very poor. The monks subsisted by making and selling carpets and other crafts such as candles. Beyond devoting time to these tasks, each one of them also followed spiritual practices and helped run the place. They all seemed to be very busy during the day, one cutting wood, another tending the vegetable garden, another in deep meditation or reading in the prayer room, others carding and dying wool.

After dinner, we spent long evenings in the community room, where the monks, with somewhat of a Rabelaisian style of inner jokes, discussed their meditation practices and their spiritual quest. On arrival, they told us there were no rules governing their order, that everyone was a fully responsible person—so one of them explained to us the rule that was not a rule concerning meals: anyone who was hungry at any time could go to the kitchen and cook a meal for everybody. Because the rest of them were busy in the huge building or surrounding fields, the preparer, once the meal was ready, would call the others by using telepathy. It was an astonishing claim, and I was quite doubtful until the next day around noon, when I was sitting on my rock to meditate, I heard a very clear mental call for lunch! I suddenly felt hungry and came back to the monastery, where I was surprised to find the meal was just ready and everybody was already assembled there. It worked! I never missed a lunch, and I became respectful of such pragmatic ways to develop a new psi capacity by using our natural drives.

Through long evenings spent in discussions with all the monks assembled in the main room, I started to feel a great admiration for the knowledge and wisdom of the head monk. Yet two things disturbed me very much: the first, as I explained earlier, was a strange grid I saw in the clear sky of summer. It was composed of long, gray lines, thinly marked and crossing at near right angles so that they formed a sort of grid, with each elongated square being about one and a half times the diameter of the moon. It appeared as though a geodesic dome existed over the monastery and the adjoining church.

Not only was what I saw beyond my understanding, but also, having practiced meditation for barely a year and a half, I was still full of preconceived ideas, one of which was that gold, blue, and white were spiritual colors, but that gray certainly was not. If the grid had a gray color, then it was no doubt not very spiritual and might even be evil. The vision, which was limited to the sky, was quite stable; I saw it whenever I was outside the monastery or near the church, and I noted its presence on different days. It was not a happy sight, however, and I felt nearly fearful of it.

The second phenomenon that disturbed me was the impression that, while I was in the monastery or in the large field in front of the building, my thoughts could be read by everybody else and that there were other minds—the thoughts of the monks—crowding my own. Of course, this impression didn't surface in the evenings when we were all meeting and discussing in the main room, but in the daytime it was quite unbearable to be thus stripped of all intimacy with myself. Again, let me stress that, as a writer since my adolescence, I was disturbed to lose the profound and intimate attunement with my inner being that had become an angular stone grounding me. Therefore, very early on, to shun the odd disturbance, I ventured through the fields, intent on finding a spot that I could make my own for meditating, writing, reading, or daydreaming in peace. The perfect place was a huge flat rock overlooking a magnificent landscape, which became my meditation rock. It was such a relief and a great pleasure to realize that as soon as I was far from the monastery, I recovered the sense of being alone in my own mind, and I stayed there for hours each day.

The second time I went to the rock, on leaving the monastery and taking the small path toward the fields, I could sense inside me the shift from feeling my mind crowded with other minds to perfect intimacy. Suddenly, I had my mind just for myself. Indeed, this shift was so abrupt that I stopped walking, astonished, and I decided to retrace my steps slowly. A single step back, and there they were again: all the other minds! I went back and forth a few times, to test the shift and could hardly believe it! In this way, I discovered that the telepathic network had a very precise boundary in space, demarcated at this very spot on the path, something I was able to confirm day after day. Actively exploring the matter further, I came to the conclusion that all the minds at the monastery formed a telepathic field, presumably a sort of circle around the monastery and the church that was about 250 to 300 yards in diameter.

At the time, I made absolutely no connection between the grid in the sky and this telepathic field on the ground. I seemed not to realize clearly that I hadn't seen the grid anywhere but around the monastery. I didn't tell the monks about my experience; my inference was that they certainly knew about it, given that they used telepathy to call each other in the first place! I now have a larger perspective on these matters, and looking back, I'm not at all certain that they perceived the space boundary itself or the exact structure of the grid. Yet there's no way I can check back with them on this new inference of mine, for the monks I knew at that time have since dispersed. A second experience of mine, about a year later, clarified the connection between the telepathic field and the grid structure.

GRID AND SPACE BOUNDARY IN A SACRED TOWN IN INDIA

India has innumerable sacred places and holy shrines, which belong to a number of religions: Hinduism, Buddhism, Jainism, Sikhism, Islam, Mazdeism, and so forth. There are many holy towns there, but the most revered are the four sacred towns where the great gathering of all holy men, ascetics, and gurus is held: the Kumba Mela. This great gathering happens every four years in one of these four towns in turn, so that each of them holds it every twelve years. Nasik is in the southwest, not far from Ellora and the Ajanta caves.

When I reached Nasik a few months after I had stayed with the Sufis in Iran, I had one more year of meditation behind me since my time in Brittany, and I was both more mature and more knowledgeable than during my stay there. During this whole journey in the East, about a year and a half, I remained in a high state of consciousness, meditating a great deal, especially at all the sacred sites or in the temples I came upon on my way. (I must have arrived at the end of a golden age of freedom in India, for at the time there was no interdiction for anyone to enter and pray in temples.) Nasik is built within a circle of mountains crossed by the sacred river Godavari. In India, temples abound along the banks of rivers, especially when the rivers are sacred. In Nasik, many baths have been constructed using the flow of the river, and specific baths are designated for the saints and ascetics and then for each caste. The center of Nasik, where numerous temples stand along the river, is the most sacred part of town.

As soon as I had found a rope bed for the night in a pilgrim house on top of the hill, I went out to explore the sacred site. On that first day, while I climbed down the hill on a narrow street full of tiny shops and restaurants for pilgrims, I experienced a very abrupt shift in my state of consciousness. Suddenly, about midway down the slope, I felt I was swept into a higher state. My mind seemed to expand and tune in with all that surrounded me. My eyes widened, and I felt I was part of that town. Suddenly, all the people around me seemed to be in the exact same state: a state of heightened awareness and deep attunement to their own Self. All were extremely welcoming and benevolent, their minds wide open, as if conscious of their surroundings with a 360-degree awareness, a luminous energy field around their heads.

Abruptly, a realization struck me: I had entered a telepathic field, and it was extremely harmonious. With everyone I met, I exchanged glances of something more than just sympathy. It was as if we knew each other or recognized each other as belonging to the same spiritual quest, the same state of consciousness.

As I kept walking slowly toward the river, I had the impression that everything was bathed in a luminous energy. An identical state of consciousness—peaceful but at the same time extremely alive and aware—existed in all the people I saw, without exception. The feeling of interconnectedness and of being in harmony with others and the world around us was central—so much so that on this specific occasion, I came to call it a harmony field. When, at one point, I looked to the sky, I was stupefied to see the same grid I had seen in Brittany. As it had appeared earlier, it was gray. There was no doubt that it was linked to the field.

This heightened state and the feeling of mental interconnectedness lasted the entire time I spent walking along the river, visiting temples, meditating in some of them, and even having tea with some ascetics.

Then, when climbing back to the pilgrim house for the night, about halfway up the hill, I very abruptly shifted back to my usual state. People once again related as usual: expressing warm sympathy and greetings and exchanging pleasant comments, but there was no longer the silent participation of kindred spirits in a hyperaware state.

I remained in Nasik for a few days, and I spent most of my time within the sacred core of town. I went there each day for hours to meditate and stroll around the numerous exquisite temples. On getting there, each time, halfway down the hill—at the same place, in front of a small shop—the shift in my inner state occurred; and, on returning, I left the harmony field I had entered at the same spot on my way into town. There was no doubt in my mind that, once again, the telhar field had a very precise boundary in space. I understood then that it was this very field that appeared against the blue sky as a gray grid: thin, quasi-straight lines of a whitish, luminous gray. I fathomed that the grayish grid was the upper boundary of the field and supposed it was like a large dome over the center of town.

As far as I perceived it, the telhar field in Nasik was about a third of a mile wide and more elongated than spherical. If this field was indeed created by all the ascetics meditating constantly in hundreds of temples, then it would be spread along the river for about a mile and a half, its shape that of a wide tunnel or half tube, flat at ground level.

The question of what happens below ground, when a field is present above, remains unclear to me. Is the telhar field a sphere or tube extending below ground, or is it cut at ground level? I have no definite answer, but on the basis of other experiences, I'm inclined to believe it makes a whole sphere or tube. One day in Laos, I was lying down at the top of a hill, and I reached a state in which I experienced a very tangible sphere of energy around me accompanied by feelings of perfect harmony with Earth and interconnectedness with the landscape. I felt my body energy sinking into the ground, as if part of my body was beneath the level of the ground. The sphere of energy penetrated the soil and the stones as if there were no obstacles.

Another experience that revealed a consciousness field extending into the landscape and penetrating the ground was the spontaneous creation of an extended field while I drove on a highway in the far suburbs of Paris. (See chapter 6 for more on this.)

We can compare the main traits of the experiences in Brittany and Nasik. They have many features in common, the most important being the clear-cut boundary that I experienced while either entering or exiting the field—a tangible sensation of being in or out of a telhar field. The second common feature is the vision of the geometrical grid—certainly the upper boundary of the field. Third, in both cases, for the duration of my stay, I experienced a stable, heightened state of consciousness, shifting with great ease to transcendental states in meditation, as well as various psi phenomena. Fourth, in both cases I had a tangible feeling of a telepathic field, even if my experience of it differed widely in each incidence: in Brittany, I was bothered by the field, but in Nasik, I was totally open to it and felt it to be harmonic and blissful.

Telhar Field in Brittany

- **Induction:** Deep state and silent meditation during my stay in the monastery.
- **Global experience:** Sensation of a telepathic field; feeling burdened by the thoughts of others; the telhar field is felt as an intrusion and a loss of intimacy.

  I still don't know how to move within a telhar field, let alone how to connect dynamically with it. (I will learn a method of connection through creative jam sessions.)
- **Relationships:** These are somehow disturbing and invasive. Ambivalent relationship to the monks apart from the head monk, for whom I feel an extreme admiration.

  An empirical proof of telepathy is given by the fact that a telepathic call at an unspecified time works, and I and others hear it from a good distance.
- **Energetic aspects:** Discovery of a precise boundary—and just one step beyond it, I'm out of the telepathic field.

  Clear and stable perception of a geometrical grid in the sky, with thin gray lines that cross to form a geodesic structure of quasi-square parallelograms.

- **Inner experience:** Psychic energy is enormously increased.

   Permanent heightened state of consciousness during my whole stay.

   Several transcendental states in meditation (e.g., in the church courtyard).

   I experience several strong psi phenomena—psychokinesis and out-of-body experiences—both with positive reliable effects as empirical proofs. Also, I have some spiritual visions of the semantic dimension. These inner experiences, contrary to the intrusive field, are extraordinarily blissful and express a strong connection to my higher Self.
- **Inferences:** I don't make any connection between the gray grid and the telepathic field.

   I imagine the telepathic field to be spherical or to have a dome shape.
- **Nodes:** At the time of my monastery stay, I have no idea about nodes and their role in telhar fields; retrospectively, however, I see that the prominent person in the group and the one endowed with outstanding spiritual gifts is the head monk.

Telhar Field in Nasik

- **Induction:** Deep state and silent meditation for the length of my stay in Nasik.
- **Global experience:** Sensation of what I called a harmony field— participation in a deep interconnectedness among all people in a delimited space (e.g., the core of the sacred town), as well as a permanent flow state between the Self and the personality. Profound harmony with the surrounding world (temples, river, sacred trees, etc.).
- **Relationships:** Sensation of being in telepathic contact and in great harmony with all people, nature, and the surrounding temples; the state of harmony is fulfilling, peaceful, joyful, and open, one in which others are welcomed.

   Empirical sign of something special being shared among people, of a spiritual nature, through the extreme attentiveness and hyperawareness of all people in the sacred space.

- **Energetic aspects:** Clear and stable perception of a geometrical grid in the sky perfectly similar to the one in Brittany.

  Discovery of a precise boundary halfway down the hill to the core of the sacred town, beyond which the feeling of a telhar field appears suddenly.

- **Inner experience:** Heightened consciousness during my whole stay in the sacred town. Many transcendental states during long hours of meditation.

  Hyperawareness of connections in a spiritual dimension—with cosmic beings, human beings, temples, and sacred trees and objects.

- **Inferences:** I now infer that the grid is linked to the telepathic-harmonic field, and it doesn't seem strange or fearful anymore.

  I imagine, since there's a limit in space, that the grid in the sky follows a dome shape—and therefore that the harmony field must have a spherical shape, perhaps elongated along the banks of the river, with the rows of sacred temples. (This would mean it's about one and a half miles long and a third of a mile in width.)

- **Nodes:** I sense the field is created by all the yogis meditating all day long in the sacred town.

SEEING A TELHAR FIELD FROM A DISTANCE IN BIÈVRES

Later, I experienced more of the spatial features of a field, but in a totally different context. I will recount it here, for it points out the existence of some additional elements for us to consider.

The night had fallen already, but the springtime sky was extremely clear and dry, no clouds and no fog. I was driving back home from some appointment in Paris, and, as usual, I took a small road leading to Bièvres, a tiny town set in a valley in the midst of trees and fields. (I had taken this road for years and knew it inside out.) The road was lined with trees and front gardens and, once in a while, the facade of a house, but most houses were set farther back. I'd just passed a curve and was on a half-mile straightaway when I caught a glimpse, some two hundred yards ahead, of something very strange and abnormal. I adjusted my vision, hoping to understand it better. Above the asphalt was a large, hazy, circular area that appeared more whitish and luminous than the sky above and around it. It was nothing like a streetlight. Not only was it much more subtle and transparent, but it also must have been invisible to anyone but those who were sensitive to such things. Since I couldn't understand what it was, my first reflex was to reduce my speed drastically as I tried to observe it better.

What was striking was that the luminous, whitish haze made a perfect circle on the dark background of sky and trees—or, more precisely, it was a perfect slice of a round, as if the zenith had been more on the left and beyond the limit of the road. The side of the round that I saw touched ground at the level of the road on my right. It had no resemblance whatsoever to the much smaller glow of streetlights that appeared farther down. The haze, though whitish, was transparent, immaterial, and I had never seen anything like it. Though I was still driving very slowly, I was nevertheless approaching it. I kept looking at it and wondering what it was without being able to make up my mind. I was now about fifty yards from it, and I could see that on the left, at its level, there was a high wrought-iron fence, totally closed. Above the fence I could see the roof of a traditional stone house standing farther back. There was nobody on the road, and I couldn't hear any sound. I decided that the circle didn't seem dangerous, and I kept going.

As the haze grew nearer, I understood that it was a large sphere and that I had to pass through it slowly. As soon as I started crossing it, I experienced a sudden and abrupt shift into a very high state of consciousness. Without any transition, I entered a hyperawareness, and my mind felt incredibly expanded. Meanwhile, as I kept driving past the sphere, I saw that in front, the road had returned to its normal color. Simultaneously to the shift of my state of consciousness, I realized at once that the spherical haze had been what I called at the time a harmony field, and in it I felt I had switched into the deeply altered state of the people who had undoubtedly created the field in the first place. As I kept driving slowly toward home, a few miles ahead, I wondered how long this "contact high" (it felt especially real) would last. The expanded state I was experiencing was extremely vigilant, a heightened state with the altered vision and the frequency perfectly recognizable as an LSD state and altogether enjoyable. It was so unexpected and so fantastic that I took it with a dose of humor, and I was curious to see how it would evolve, how long it would last. It continued for about three-quarters of an hour.

I made a note to myself to go back there the next day to check if my interpretation was correct. At that time in France and Europe, only hippies—and we were all in our twenties—became involved in psychotropic experiences. Not only were we not numerous, but even among us, such LSD explorations were still quite rare, especially in that cozy valley. In about fifteen years of living there, the only local hippies I met were precisely the people of the house. Thus I concluded that either hippies (very recognizable by the way we were dressed) were living there and had dived into a psychotropic altered state, or else I was wrong.

The next day, under a beautiful spring sun, at around noon, I drove to the same spot. The wrought-iron fence was covered with iron plates; in order to get a glimpse of the house beyond, I had to climb on the cement wall that held the fence. Fortunately, along the perimeter there was a magnificent flowering tree, its branches bending to the sidewalk—which, in France, means that these branches belong to anybody and that anyone can pluck the flowers or fruits that hang into the street. With this pretext, I climbed the wall under the tree. When my head was over the fence, I caught sight of young people dressed like hippies; two of them were sitting on the lawn and a third one stood farther back. They saw me too, and we smiled at each other. I was gleeful that my inference was correct. After a few greetings, I asked them about the tree, and they told me that of course I could take a few flowers; they would get me pruning shears.

Features of the Bièvres Telhar field

Later, because I now knew for certain that the field had been created by people, I reflected on what it meant. I had already experienced the very specific vision and high consciousness state linked to LSD, and that's why I had been able to recognize it. In fact, whatever induces them, stable states of consciousness are one and the same—but LSD "tints" the vision and the thought frequency in a very unusual way. A few years back, twice I was able to ascertain the duration of a contact high with psychotropic chemicals (with only a glimpse at the probable source from afar), and both times my high was sustained for two hours. To be more precise, an LSD-induced high is for me the only state that is at the same time so deeply altered and so recognizable. During my nighttime drive, without an outside contact source, it would have been impossible to experience such a radical shift in state in a matter of a few seconds. (Biochemical induction takes thirty to forty minutes.)

As for the energy structure I noted on the road, it was evident, even if I saw only a circular limit detaching itself from the night sky, that the field above ground had been a half sphere. This was consistent with its zenith being somewhere over the house or the lawn. Its height was about three times the height of the fence—about seven yards in all. From the portion I saw, I believe that its diameter must have been about forty to fifty yards. Could it be possible that the sphere, because it was created by a loose group of people, was more wide than high, as if it were flattened at the top?

Another point: the spherical energy field was very clearly delimited, and its shape was unmoving for the dozen seconds it took me to drive up to it. This means (as in the other two cases in Brittany and Nasik) that the structure of telhar fields is quite stable.

Therefore, we have a new set of features to consider. The prominent specificity of the Bièvres telhar field is pointed to by the fact that I penetrated a telhar field coming from the outside and in a mundane state of consciousness. There were no cues in the environment that could have informed me about what to expect from this strange sphere (no other light and no sound and the house was hidden in the dark and behind the high fence). Yet the shift in my state was instantaneous. This is magnificent proof that (at least some) states of consciousness are linked to very specific energy structures and that interacting with these structures provides enough of a force to create major changes in consciousness. We see, in the instant, tremendous alteration of my state, that this energy field is itself a meaningful state—a semantic field instantiating consciousness as energy, which was created by the people living in the house. Linking this experience with the creation of an energy structure by the monks in Brittany and by four people in meditation in Manali, we can therefore reach this conclusion: a heightened and harmonized collective consciousness field can express an energy structure—a spherical telhar field (sometimes flattened or elongated). If one who is sensitive enters within its boundary, he or she can shift instantly to the heightened state.

The Telhar Field in Bièvres

- **Induction:** Normal waking state, alert and focused on driving.
- **Global experience:** Perceiving an anomalous sphere ahead on the road, a perfectly round haze against the background of the night sky. I don't know what to expect.
- **Relationships:** No interaction, I'm alone in my car.
- **Energetic aspects:** Clear and stable perception from a distance of a luminous, whitish haze that makes a perfect circle above the road. The perfect sphere shows that this telhar field has a precise boundary in space.

  The energetic structure of the sphere is neither broken nor modified by passing through an iron fence. Anyone can walk or drive through it without breaking it.

  It's impossible to know in this case if my physical and mental interconnection with the telhar field modifies the collective state of the people in the house.
- **Inner experience:** Instant shift of state of consciousness while driving through the sphere at low speed.
- **Inferences:** Recognizing the specific state of consciousness of LSD, I infer that those residing in the house by the road where I saw the sphere must have taken this psychotropic drug. I checked my inference the next day and gleaned a confirmation that the sphere was a LSD-induced collective semantic field.
- **Nodes:** I have no way of knowing if one or more people were able to take the node role and who the node was when I saw the sphere and went though it. My short encounter with three hippies the next day didn't give me a cue about the node(s).

PONDERING THE ENERGY STRUCTURE

By linking these three experiences (those in Brittany, Nasik, and Bièvres) to the spinning torus in the Himalayas, it now seems quite evident on empirical grounds that telhar fields are more than just a collective state of consciousness.

We must remember that most sciences have at first been based on observation—that is, on empirical knowledge. In astronomy, for example, firsthand observations were made with telescopes, and it's only on the basis of these observations that complex mathematics and physics were used to extract astronomical laws. Only afterward were predictions concocted through inferences based on these laws. In an ultimate phase, a law's accuracy—the predictions to which it gave birth—was checked against novel observations. For example, for a long time, our model of the solar system didn't fit the observed planetary orbits. Either the laws were not complete or the model was not correct. In fact, that's how we inferred the existence of new planets such as Pluto. As long as there exist slight anomalies in observed phenomena compared with the behavior predicted by a law, there's still something we haven't uncovered, and thus we have to make do with ad hoc corrections of the law's predictions.

Most of the new domains of science start with an empirical approach—either gleaned from the observation of new phenomena or by observation of anomalies in known phenomena. Very few sciences are created on the basis of pure mathematics or logic. Psychiatry started with the clinical study of hysteria using hypnosis, at the school of Charcot at Hospital Pitié-Salpêtrière in Paris, which Sigmund Freud attended.

Regarding telhar fields, I believe we are confronted with a totally new domain in cognitive sciences that exists at the crossing of transpersonal psychology, consciousness studies, and physics. If we are indeed talking about collective consciousness states that are linked to a perceptible energy structure, as I propose, then we face a major paradigm shift in the domain of psychology, with unknown repercussions in physics.

Telhar fields are based on a radically novel type of energy—syg (semantic) energy. This syg-energy is linked to consciousness and thought processes in a fundamental way. It also presents strange properties, behaviors, and energy structures that clearly distinguish it from electromagnetic (EM) fields and quantum fields. This type of reality, being both consciousness and matter-energy, has been envisioned by the psychologist Carl Jung as *psychoid* phenomena when it happens in the individual psyche; Jung also proposed that the underlying reality of the universe was a blend of matter and spirit, a unified universe referred to as *Unus Mundus*.

My aim, beyond postulating and predicting the existence of such an energy, is to gather the phenomenological data and to lay the groundwork for a theory exposing its functioning and its basic properties in terms of consciousness fields. My empirical conclusions up to now concern the properties of telhar fields, at the psychological level and at the energetic and physical level.

On the Psychological Level

- States of great interconnectedness within a group are linked to the creation of an energetic field—a telhar field—that has the qualities of heightened consciousness, harmony, spiritual bonding, and telepathic communication.
- All connected individuals share a common heightened state.
- An individual who enters such a field from the outside will be immediately swept into the collective state.
- This abrupt change happens at the spatial boundary of the field.
- In the case of groups focused on a creative or artistic task (such as music improvisation), telhar fields bring a higher speed of thought, precognition, holistic visualization, and greatly enhanced creative potentials.

On the Energetic and Physical Level

- A half-spherical structure is visible above ground (further on in this book there are more details on a sphere that extends underground), sometimes flattened at the top, sometimes elongated.
- Telhar fields can be small when they are created by a group of people or can be extended over a larger area. We have seen here

two spherical telhar fields with diameters of fifty yards (Bièvres) and five hundred yards (Brittany) and an elongated tubelike field that was about one and a half miles long (Nasik).

- Telhar fields don't seem to be broken or disturbed by buildings, rivers, or iron fences.
- Once formed, they have a very regular, stable shape. Telhar fields are not permanent, though, unless people constantly reinforce them in meditation or prayer.
- Viewed from the outside, telhar fields can appear to a sensitive as a luminous, whitish haze.
- Viewed from the inside, telhar fields show a luminous grid of grayish lines that appears against the sky as geodesic, slightly elongated squares about one and a half times the apparent width of the full moon.
- Their spatial boundary is very precise and instantiates the boundary of a consciousness state.

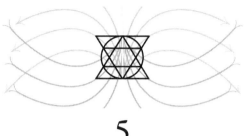

5

WEAVING THE COLLECTIVE CONSCIOUSNESS

We have now gathered enough phenomenological data on telhar fields to ask ourselves a crucial question: given we've concluded that telhar fields exist, how could they change something in our lives and in society at large? Let's start by considering how they impact our relationships.

INTERACTIONS AND NODES

In terms of our day-to-day lives, the most appealing example of the benefits of telhar fields is the jam session. In a jam session, all individuals participate actively in the creation of improvised music. Roles do not matter, whether the participants are skilled musicians, amateurs, or just listeners. The node of the field, the person around whom the field is structured, could be anybody anywhere in the room. I have seen a listener take the node by simply swinging his or her body in a most interesting, creative way.* I have seen people take the node by improvising a song, and others by trance dancing.

---

*I will use the term *node* to mean: (1) the person—or node of the field—who creates or masters the collective telhar field at any moment; (2) the control center of the telhar field. The node is generally a person, but it can also be a pair of speakers in a room, in which case the telhar field is created and sustained by the music being played and the consciousnesses of the musicians whose music is played; (3) a role, as in "to take the node," meaning to take the wheel, the control of the telhar field.

The node of a telhar field is the individual who has, at a given moment, the highest and most intense psychic energy, the one who is the most connected to his or her Self or to a source of energy (trees, lake, the place, a cosmic being or source, and so forth). This individual, then, could just as well meditate with eyes closed and body immobile— and still become the node of the field. Suddenly, the music being made is colored and informed by this person's energy for as long as he remains connected to the cosmic source and his or her Self. When the node's semantic energy starts dwindling (due to distractions, emotions, and the like) and he becomes less connected to his Self, the musicians immediately feel that the energy starts to flounder. At that point, they detach their minds from this node and remain hanging and oscillating until another person in heightened consciousness suddenly takes the lead.

Whenever we get connected to our Self, and that can be as simple a state as getting attuned to our inner being or to be in a deep listening mode, we can receive an enormous inflow from the planetary semantic field and become the node.

Indeed, our Self is a well of supraconscious energy that is able to connect itself to any other source in the cosmos. This is why, as soon as we connect ourselves to our inner Self, we receive instantly such a huge increment of psychic energy that it's as if we have become intensely alive, highly aware, and much more charismatic. For musicians who have trained themselves by listening to others and becoming attuned with them, the sudden intensification of the psychic energy of another person is a tangible sensation: the "vibes" emanating from the other person are not only stronger, but also more beautiful. Indeed, even if this subtle perception of inner connectedness is missed, they will "hear" how great and enthralling is the music of the node, and very naturally, they will harmonize their own playing with that person.

The Node's Trance

If the node role is taken on by a musician, this person starts playing a music that is generally way beyond his or her normal skill and sensitivity. The state of connected trance (when we are connected to our own Self) is a well of creative power. New ways of singing and playing and new rhythms come to the fore, and the creator feels a surge of sacred enthusiasm, an elevation of his or her spirit.

To become the node in a telhar field is a surprising peak experience. Our energy is enormously amplified not only at the beginning of the state (which in fact allows an individual to take the node role), but also as long as we remain the node. Most of the time, exiting the telhar field is due not to an inherent lack of energy, but rather to a disconnection from its source or distracting thoughts or emotions. As soon as we are in the telhar trance state, our being exists at a higher level of energy and awareness, and we do everything in a most superb way: when we are jamming or dancing, we are totally astonished by what our hands or bodies are able to perform. We are in an open space of creativity, and nothing of what we do has been programmed by rational will or by following a blueprint (such as a known song). In fact the opposite is true: the key to the node state is to be able to connect with our own Self and to put aside completely the ego and its way of thinking.

Inner connection to a higher energy puts the node (and all participants in the field) in an intuitive and spiritual cognitive mode. This mode is global, synthetic, and holistic; it involves thinking, intuiting, and feeling. It uses a much greater speed of thought to enable us to view in a flash the whole musical sequence that is created. The node nevertheless remains in such deep communication with his or her environment that he can sense any subtle change in the group. Consequently, the music being played by the node is a subtle weaving of his or her energetic source with the energy of all the other participants. Yet the quality of the node's own spiritual source remains the strongest influence.

Whatever the node creates (music, dance, etc.) is always much better than normal because the ego has let go of the reins of the personality. The person is now either strongly connected to Self or fused with it, and it is the person's own supraconscious Self who is now at the steering wheel, playing the music, dancing, and so forth. This specific trance of the node is literally a learning process for the individual. Indeed, we can learn so many things from our inner Self—new connections, new rhythms, new ways of mastering the collective field. I remember one day that, while my Self played an interesting and totally novel rhythm, I tried to memorize the rhythm and the hand movements. This is possible and will not destroy the trance, provided that we allow the expression of the Self to be totally free (without judgment) and that the part of the mind that observes (the vigilant) remains detached and in the background (so to speak). In fact, whatever we have been able to do at one time in a node state or trance state is now memorized in our body-mind-psyche (in a dynamic type of memory), and the know-how is part of our being. Even if we don't remember consciously or clearly the music we performed and wouldn't be able to play it again intentionally, our unconscious knows it, and one day, such music will suddenly spring up again, fully elaborated.

TELHAR FIELDS EVIDENCED BY
THEIR BREAKDOWN

The most pragmatic evidence of telhar fields can be found in why and how they break down. If we have participated in a jam session, a trance dance, or a collective meditation or prayer, then surely we have noted what could take us instantly out of heightened consciousness: namely, any thought or emotion that originates in the ego. And in this respect, the great interest of a jam session, in terms of learning about consciousness, is that as soon as we lose our heightened state, we can hear immediate and clear-cut effects on the music: it gets disharmonious, awful, or else just stops. In contrast, if we lose our focus during a meditation, no outside signals can make us aware of it and shake us up. In a jam session, a broken field makes the music so awful as to be unbearable.

Telhar Fields' Breakdown: The Why
Telhar fields tend to be disrupted by negative emotions or thoughts. Here are a few examples of disturbing thoughts.

- Being overly aware that what we are creating or doing is great. This is followed by a kind of showing off, thoughts of vanity. In short, we make the fatal slide from "It's great!" to "I'm great!"
- Any emotion linked to fear or self-culpability—especially the fear of the field breaking down.

- Any negative thought about anybody or anything around us—any bad thought in general.
- Any subconscious drive, such as a craving, a sexual impulse, anger, feeling hungry, and so forth.
- Any disruption that catches our attention: ambient noises, conversation, and so forth.

As we can judge by this list, telhar fields are very moralistic teachers! They set a high standard, and nothing less than a non-ego state will do. Due to such stringent conditions, what's happening generally during a jam session among friends is that a long time is devoted at first to the music, and during this early stage, high states that are able to induce telhar fields may be achieved. After this, everybody becomes hungry, and it's meal, joke, and discussion time. When the jamming starts again later, high states and telhar fields are more difficult to attain.

There are two other reasons why a telhar field may break down. The first additional reason is because the node is actively exploring this new level of reality, whether the telhar field or his own source and trance state, and is thus pushing it too far, beyond his own limits at that time. This is certainly a very praiseworthy way of crashing a field and one of the most instructive. Furthermore, the limits that are encountered by the crash must be explored, because this is how they will constantly be pushed back and how new possibilities and phenomena will appear. The second additional reason a telhar field may break down is that the node, in a perfect non-ego trance, creates music that is so original, so difficult to grasp, so fluid and changing that the remainder of the group is at a loss to follow or to accompany it. As soon as the group no longer supports the node, the node crashes and, usually, the telhar field crashes with him or her.

Learning to Walk by Falling: The How of the Breakdown of Telhar Fields

How a telhar field breaks down is also very informative. For example, I enter an inspired state and connect deeply or fuse with my Self. In that state, I start a rhythm. If everybody connects with it in a deeply harmonious way, a telhar field is created. I'm connected to a source (often my Self) and am completely focused on it. Once the telhar field is created, my impression is that I'm listening to the music that my hands are playing (rather than willing that I play something). At one point, I think it's really great, but I linger on that thought and give it too much room, and as a result, I'm no longer focused 100 percent on the source. Crash! Instantly, the harmony and interconnectedness among people is gone. Simultaneously, the music has no more power. Its extraordinary quality (whatever it was) is gone. Immediately, of course, I realize my mistake.

At this point, either someone will make the music rebound and will thus become the node, or else this piece of music comes to a stop because it's simply not interesting anymore. It's also possible to catch ourself quickly enough to rebound and reestablish the connection to our source—but we must practice to learn how to do this. Generally, the disconnecting thought or emotion is fatal to the node and therefore to the whole telhar field, and the crash is loud.

Yet it's the fate of everybody to crash the field, for it's our best learning procedure. An infant learns to walk by falling. The fall illustrates that she is walking instead of crawling! We must remember that it is a pure gift to be able to create a field in the first place! Slowly, we realize that, though there are a hundred ways to crash a field, there are also a hundred ways to put it back on track at the speed of thought. All the learning is henceforth devoted to pulling up the field when the node fails—whether the node is someone else or ourselves.

INTERACTING CREATIVELY

The traditional jam, such as in jazz, triggers a very creative mode of interaction among people that is quite uncommon in normal relationships. While practicing improvisation—beyond the bedrock ability of musicians to listen to and attune with each other—we have to give free rein to our own intuition and creativity. This creativity, however, must abide by the silent rules of the game: to keep an overall harmony and to stay in sync with all participants. In such a setting, the musicians naturally develop a great sensitivity for detecting the one who is the lead person during a given improvised piece. Very often, it's the one starting after a pause who defines the piece, and other people start playing in turn when they feel they have something to add to the tapestry being woven. At one point, a musician may suddenly play a solo and reach a higher trance state, and the beauty and original-ity of what he or she is playing commands other musicians to listen. They feel it's so good that they have to give him or her the full space, the lead in the music. This improvisation within the improvisation is often the very way a telhar field is created, and the solo musician, of course, immediately takes on the role of the node. There is no doubt that the traditional jam session had, intertwined in the group playing, real instances of telhar fields. This is why all improvising musicians have some knowledge of telhar fields, even if it's only on a subcon-scious level.

Interactions in the Traditional Jam Session

Here then are characteristics of the interactions among musicians in a usual jam session.

- Everyone listens intensely to all other players.
- Attuning to each other musically will generate a harmonization of the psychic energy of all players.
- The instant recognition of creations of great genius and beauty leads us to give the floor to the individual in a peak state.
- This musician (the soloist) enters an intense creative flow state.
- After letting the soloist takes the floor, everybody harmonizes with him and accompanies him.
- Everyone supports each other in turn.
- Everyone, at one point, gets the floor (i.e., the lead role).
- A long practice of jams endows a musician with a knack for rec-ognizing the increase or decrease of psychic energy, both at the individual and group levels.
- The musicians will become highly skilled at letting go of ten-sions and at sharing with others to such a depth that empathy is involved.

As we can see, the traditional jam session is a superb context in which to explore telhar fields. No wonder, then, that it's so easy for musicians to create them. The great difference between spontaneous groups and other music groups is that in a jam, everyone must remain in a flow state and a learning mode. It's the perfect way to explore new styles of interactions and to be creative.

Discovering and Learning through Telhar Fields

We saw the qualities and skills exacted by the traditional jam. The conscious practice of telhar fields, however, boosts these qualities and triggers the emergence of other talents.

The Greatest Gains of the Quester Who Experiences Telhar Fields

- Exploring creative states: how to trigger and sustain them
- Gaining practical learning about attuning to others and becoming harmonized with them
- Developing one's own originality
- Having respect for each other's states
- Supporting the qualities of others (creative brotherhood)
- Developing peer-to-peer relationships
- Having empathy and the capacity to interchange roles
- Learning how to enter a flow state.

With the experience of telhar fields, the sensitivity to any facet of music (tones, rhythms, feeling, etc.) is enormously increased compared with what we're able to access in a more usual state. What creates the harmony among people, both at the sound and at the psychological levels, is also an open path of learning and refining. Moreover, we can apprehend the numerous factors that can lead to the breakdown of a telhar field—some linked to our own inner state and others linked to the interactions within the group.

Ultimately, the crucial learning that takes place in telhar fields involves mastery of our own mind. Among the many talents we may develop are the concentration and unshakable focus that are necessary at the onset of the telhar field. In the long term, we will know how to connect to and fuse with our inner Self and how to create a link to a source of energy in the environment or in the cosmos.

As we can imagine, this path of learning is endless, but along the way, it brings its own extraordinary joys. A rewarding effect is a constant rejuvenation, for to keep discovering and exploring is the easiest way to remain full of energy, alive, and in great spirits.

Exploring telhar fields is also the most exciting way to build a stable connection to our Self, and this connection opens a direct path of spiritual awareness. The great inflow and exchange of energy that takes place during telhar fields enhances our capacities of intuition, of experiencing transcendental states, and of tuning in to our environment. It is a path of direct connection with the energy of the cosmos, a path of permanent exploration of who we really are. Moreover, it is a joyful and fulfilling learning.

In fact, practicing with telhar fields is definitely akin to having a guide in the exploration of another level of reality: the deep interconnection among all human beings and between us and our planet.

Toward Novel Human Relationships

Telhar fields are an experiment in balancing our own inner focus with the extended perception of a whole group. They are the perfectly balanced junction between inner and outer realities. The key is to make both the group and the environment part of our inner reality. In fact, the easiest way to create a telhar field is to connect with our Self and then to project our energy in a sphere that keeps expanding while we harmonize with our human and natural environment. It's a sort of yoga: the yoga of a double inward and outward meditation.

Beyond our social good sense is the possibility to experience our relationship to a group as a unified field in which each person becomes highly creative and thus original. We are used to thinking in terms of me versus others, or inner versus outer. Our common sense tells us that a collectivity will achieve only some sort of harmonization at the lowest common denominator: herd behavior. It seems unreal to achieve a state in which the deepest "I" is also a collective "I." Yet this is exactly what a telhar field does. It triggers the emergence of a totally novel way of relating to others, as if the whole group was now forming a new collective individuality—a metamind of exquisite richness, in constant exploration of itself.

One thing is sure: we all are in a dynamic of exploration in this matter. Despite the fact that we are now becoming conscious of the existence and workings of telhar fields, we are still a world away from understanding all the possibilities they may open for us in the long run. Yet we can be assured that the practice of harmonizing in a group and of finding inner and outer balance is a good path, and because its main effect is to increase the creative capacities of each person, we can also count on the fact that it is a path of living knowledge that can only heighten and replenish our energy. We can learn how to be supportive of each other's creative abilities, how to listen to the inner state of each participant. This is a relational mode based on listening and positive feedback in which competition is out of the game.

Telhar fields also teach us how to take the lead role while we remain in a listening, non-ego position. That alone may have immense repercussions on our ideas about leadership.

6
CONSCIOUSNESS AS ENERGY

Concerning our exploration of consciousness as energy, we cannot have a perfect grasp of the specific properties of semantic energy, or syg-energy, without observing it at the individual level, mainly because this energy is the same whether at work in an individual mind or in a group mind. Therefore, though individual fields and semantic fields of objects are not directly related to collective consciousness, they are extremely important for exploring further the purely energetic aspect of consciousness.

In this chapter, we'll look at the particular shapes assumed by personal energy fields—not so much the well-known auras, but rather energy structures linked to thinking or meditating. We'll also explore the energy glows around sacred objects created by the semantic projections of humans through faith, love, artistic feeling, and so forth. Indeed, when a person projects his feelings and thoughts onto a sacred object, his or her semantic field is imprinting directly the semantic field of the object. This is how the mind can influence objects as well as biological and inorganic matter—it will first modify the semantic field of the organism or object.

Finally, we will look at the many natural forms syg-energy shows and how these forms can be visualized, projected, and used by individuals. In fact, we are able, through specific visualizations, to create forms and fields in syg-energy (originating in our activated chakras) and then to use them for protection, as a medium for remote sensing and for charging objects, or as antennae for contacts. In this chapter, I will recount many of my experiences and visions, and then we will look at the general dynamics of syg-energy that can be synthesized or inferred from these cases.

PERSONAL ENERGY FIELDS

First, we must define what is meant by personal energy field, and then we must understand its link to consciousness.

Each person's semantic energy is different; it bears this individual's specific consciousness print (emotions, feelings, intellect, and spirituality). Any heightened state of consciousness (such as deep insight, spiritual connection, or creative inspiration) changes immediately our personal semantic energy: it enhances its strength, quality, and frequency and boosts its dynamics and flow. This uplift in our personal semantic field can affect objects around us (such as objects of worship or artwork) by raising the strength of their semantic field. I have proposed in Semantic Fields Theory (SFT) that the semantic dimension pervades the entire universe. It means that all matter has a semantic level of organization— from inorganic systems (mountains, crystals, lakes, all the way to atoms) to manufactured objects (vases, works of art, and the like). In short, objects and systems have a semantic field that reflects all the meanings with which they are associated as well as all their meaningful relations and links to other systems.

In humans, the semantic field is an extremely sophisticated, multilevel network that contains a multitude of subnetworks dedicated to various tasks and domains of life. Each one branches into the diverse levels of the mind-body-psyche system (that is, the entire personality), including the neuronal networks level.

Our semantic field is our consciousness—but in a dynamic and evolving sense. As the semantic field is a network that branches into numerous networks, all of them existing at various levels of the mind-body, our memory becomes a dynamic configuration (links and weights) in these networks. In a semantic field, the memory is dynamic. It isn't merely fixed data; on the contrary, it is the memory of the active connections and meaningful paths of feeling, thinking, acting, and relating. Of course, the most recent paths, as well as the most emotionally charged ones, are those that have the greatest weight in the network and thus are the ones that can be most easily reactivated. This is why traumas can bother us until, one day, we decide to confront them and start dismantling the semantic constellation. We do this by analyzing each connected element in the trauma constellation and branch it differently, connecting it to a novel outlook and positive values.

The consciousness energy pervading our Self (the greatest part of our semantic field) is semantic energy, or syg-energy. Syg-energy is not bound by space, time, or matter. Thus our Self is a part of our consciousness that transgresses the limitations of Newtonian space-time (the space-time of classical physics and the continuum we identify with in our daily life).

Because syg-energy isn't bound by time and space, the energy that is at one moment in the space-time coordinates of the body is not a person's entire semantic field. A part of that field—the supraconscious Self—can exist in any space-time coordinates. In physics terms, the Self is nonlocal. Yet, contrary to quantum physics, this isn't due to the fundamental indeterminism of the quantum field, and it isn't a function of probabilities. In contrast to quantum physics, the nonlocality of consciousness is steered by intention, will, desire, meaningful connections, synchronicities, and so forth—that is, by consciousness itself.

Our semantic field, however, is simultaneously connected to the multiple levels of our mind-body-psyche system (including neuronal networks), all the while using a unique connective process. The nonlocal part of our spirit, the Self, interacts with the brain via syg-energy and the semantic field. It thus creates the subtle energy field that expresses our long-term personality and history as well as our present personality (feelings, relations, sphere of interests, values, thoughts, and world vision). In short, it creates the psychic and spiritual auras—the more or less large sphere of syg light (the aura) that is perceptible by psychics and yogis and that some clairvoyant individuals can "read." We know that visible light consists of waves of photons. My hypothesis, however, is that the mostly invisible light of consciousness—that is, syg-energy—is linked not to photons, but rather to still unknown waves.

ENERGY GLOWS LINKED TO THINKING
OR MEDITATING

The human aura, according to the independent researches of O. Bagnall and J. Bigu,[1] is a composite field made of practically all the known energies that are able to diffuse through the skin. The natural physical aura is itself interlaced with an aura of semantic energy. This semantic aura is generated by the quality of consciousness of the person: his or her feelings, spirituality, goals, ethics, world vision, and so forth.

The energy of the aura is directly and deeply linked to consciousness. It doesn't belong to the electromagnetic (EM) spectrum (according to my thesis), but rather to the syg spectrum (non-EM). Large, luminous auras around people seem always to point to a high spiritual and ethical state of consciousness. Practitioners of left-hand, or black, magic are notably devoid of luminous auras. They present a contracted and darkened energy field that doesn't radiate around them but, on the contrary, acts like a sink. All living beings (animals, plants, cells) have semantic fields that are more or less developed.

Anyone, in a certain measure, can learn how to control his or her syg-energy field through meditation, yoga, martial arts, visualization, or an array of self-development techniques. The semantic aura of a person is thus organized, modified, and monitored by his or her Self. This is why a visualization can change the general shape of the aura to the point that the form visualized can be used as an antenna for connection, a bridge to keep contact, or a sphere for protection.

Torus of Light above the Head

My father, who was a caterer, was preparing himself for supervising a cocktail party, putting on his vest in front of a large mirror and checking his general appearance, when he saw a round halo of light above his head. It looked very much like a saint's halo—the round torus of light generally depicted above the heads of saints in paintings and drawings. He turned toward his faithful maître d'hôtel, who had become a friend, saying, "Come and look—do you see the light above my head in the mirror?" My father's friend came to the mirror, looked at my father's reflected image, and agreed that he too saw an aureole, clearly an extraordinary phenomenon.

My father was an atheist, and he joked a great deal when he recounted his story the next day at the family table. "A saint's halo! I'm no saint, so what could it be? But my friend could clearly see it too, a perfect, round halo of light that stayed above my head, even when I moved! Vraiment incroyable!"

My father's story is my only example of a torus of light that appeared on a person who was not in meditation or in a high state of consciousness. Given that my father attended only important cocktail parties and that he would complete most of the preparation himself, he necessarily had a few days of intense work before this event. Of course, we can't exclude the possibility that he had a potent archetypal dream the night before or that the stress of days of preparation for the party would have generated a heightened state, just as it does for a performance artist.

Yet I've seen this halo several times on individuals immersed in transcendental states of consciousness, and I occasionally saw the grand double aura of Buddhists on masters.

The torus of light above the head is linked to the deepest Samadhi states (transcendental states of meditation). It looks like a thick circle of white light that appears about two or three inches above the top of the head. It is as large as the skull and about two inches thick. (The reproductions on paintings are quite like the natural phenomenon.) Immersed myself in the transcendental void state, I was once able to have a clairvoyant image of the torus's structure. It is produced by particles that turn at a very high velocity, counterclockwise, around yet above the thousand-petaled lotus (the chakra at the top of the head). This chakra seems to act as the center of the dynamic structure and larger field that's generated all around the head, and the torus is only the inner circle of this.

I have inferred from another experience, namely a very clear initiatic dream, or life vision, that there are indeed other, larger, particles within the torus that turn clockwise, in a way opposite to the first ones. In my dream, one large, rectangular stone turned counterclockwise in an upright position while small, rectangular stones, also upright, turned clockwise. None of the rectangular stones ever hit each other—they behaved just like subatomic particles in the classical atom model (where each electron is in a different orbit). Let me recount this dream.

I enter a large, square paved yard surrounded by high stone walls. The heat is intense; the sun beats down on the place, and I have the impression that the courtyard stands amid an Eastern desert. At its center is a stone coping with an arc of metal, and I believe it's a stone well. A few people walk around, but when I approach the well, they exit the place via two doors in the walls. I realize the central structure isn't a well, because inside the round of stone is a flat surface, at the level of the ground, on which strange, rectangular stones stand erect. There are two great stones and about seven or nine tiny stones, all in an upright position. One of the two great stones is among the tiny stones that are arranged in virtual circles. The second great stone stands alone in the void in the middle space of the structure, but not at its exact center; it is displaced like the second center of an ellipse. This elliptical center is quite strange, because the entire system is encircled by the round stone wall, and the rotation movement of the small stones will be round. Looking at this system, I suddenly know it is an age-old model representing a cosmic law and that it has been built in stone by ancient sages to explain the functioning of the law. Even at rest, the configuration of stones, which is not geometrical, feels like an abstract design with an underlying, hidden meaning, just like a Zen stone garden. As I observe it, the stone system suddenly enters into motion.

The seven or nine tiny stones turn clockwise at a vertiginous speed, and one of the two great stones turns counterclockwise at a similar high velocity. They all remain in an upright position, and none of them ever collides with another. The great stone at the elliptical center remains immobile.

I know that this structure has to do with fundamental energetic dynamics, and I sense intuitively that the law the ancient sages have written in stone applies to all similar structures, from the microcosmic to the macrocosmic level of reality (from the atom to a solar system).

I then remark to myself that the great immobile stone is a center, or a factor, that has been functioning in the past but has no more reality nowadays. Judging that it's now utterly useless, I seize a hammer (a hammer appears in my hand at the instant I have this intention) and smash the stone, which disappears entirely. I'm abruptly overwhelmed by an intense remorse on remembering the sages who had erected this construction.

At that moment three grand masters arrive, walking: Albert Einstein, Carl Jung, and a third whose dignified face is familiar in the dream (but whose identity I couldn't remember on waking up). Einstein is walking ahead of the others, and on stopping near the well, immediately reassures me, telling me that I didn't make a mistake in breaking the stone. The three masters now stand at my front-right and around the well.

Then Einstein continues, explaining the dynamics of this strange field at the physical level. The main point I remembered after waking is that the energy of the system comes not from the apparent "center," but rather from the intense buildup generated by the two opposite rotations. Once Einstein has finished his explanations, Jung takes his turn and comments on this dynamic structure at the psychological and consciousness levels, in terms of the basic duality of the psyche and its fundamentally energetic and systemic organization. Finally, the third master explains the dynamic structure at the spiritual, esoteric level.

I went through the whole dream a second time during the night, and nevertheless, on awakening, I could remember precisely everything but the details of the explanations that were given to me.

As is often the case with archetypal dreams and grand life visions that set the stage for a new path of development, the information or the key to the dream is exactly what we have to pursue in life, or at least during a whole life cycle. Native Americans attribute an immense value to *grand visions,* called *wakanya wowanyanke,* which sometimes appear in dreams. They say that a grand vision shows a person his vocation or a great realization to accomplish and that it has the power to change an individual's destiny. Black Elk thought that the grand vision triggering a vocation contains all the elements of knowledge that the medicine men will use in their practice or in the major realization to which they will devote their life.[2] He underlines that the power of a grand vision is activated only when it is shared in part and put to the service of the community.

In fact, my dream of the temple of stones hints at the basic principle of the new paradigm in science: self-organization, which, by the sheer interaction of multiple forces in a complex, dynamical system, poses a continuous emergence of order and an increasing complexity. This principle also poses a force—creation and increasing complexity—complementary to the principle of entropy, or increasing disorder. Regarding the dream, however, self-organization also supersedes the arch-principle of hierarchy and of a sole organizing authority or center.

Torus and Counterclockwise Energy: Velocity

The dream explained a double-rotation movement that applied to the three levels of matter, mind, and spirit (soul). Concerning the torus of light above the head chakra (the psyche or soul level), though I haven't been able to see clearly the opposite, clockwise energy, I infer it is there, a part of the torus generated by the head chakra. However, my dream is not my only grounds for making such an inference; other considerations pointed to a double rotation in the syg-energy torus, but discussing them here would take us too far off the subject.

Apart from the dream, I have seen the counterclockwise energy on several other occasions, and my perception was clear enough for me to note that the energy's velocity could vary.

Just after my twenty-second birthday, in India, I went through an excruciating spiritual trial, during which I was plunged into a kind of darkness for about three weeks. This occurred after some of the highest states of consciousness I have experienced in my life (namely the void state, during which I saw the torus above my head). It was as if my aura had exploded and I was utterly naked, without any protective shield. I was plunged into the ocean of the collective unconscious, and the thoughts of all people passed through my head, which made me think I had gone mad and lost the way.*

---

*This immersion into the collective unconscious has been described by Jung in his autobiography. His trial seemed to have lasted quite a few years! See Carl Jung, *Memories, Dreams, Reflections* (New York: Vintage Books/Random House, 1965).

After a fortnight in pure hell, when my state improved, I was able to see the torus again, moving at a very low velocity, as if the energy had just started turning again. Over the next days, it took on more and more speed, and when it reached beyond a certain threshold of terminal velocity, I once again entered Samadhi. In the meantime, my entire aura was rebuilt, however differently, and I found myself centered at the head chakra and in absolute peace all of a sudden. Having escaped hell, the bliss was extreme.

Grand Auras

Many times, I have seen the grand auras around people when they are in high states of meditation. One day, I saw the person who was my master during my first journey in India immersed in a deep transcendental state, sitting in the lotus position on a rock overlooking the sea. I could see clearly the double aura represented on Tibetan paintings around Buddha. For Tibetans, there are innumerable Buddhas, because they mark the achievement of the spiritual path to which we are all destined. The Eastern religions state that each and every human being will one day achieve the state of illumination (nirvana, the Buddha state, moksha) and that we are incarnated on Earth precisely to pursue this aim. On reaching this state, the person becomes free from the wheel of reincarnation on Earth and will then shift to another dimension of reality. This is the meaning of the vow of the Boddhisattvas ("Buddha essence," in Sanskrit), the sages who, on reaching the gate of nirvana, decide to remain on Earth to help until everyone reaches illumination. Surrounding the head is the first aura, a sphere of about thirty inches in diameter with a light that is much more intense than that of the bodily aura. The second is a large sphere, about one and a half yards in diameter, that encompasses the whole body as it sits cross-legged. It is my belief that the head aura is a field generated by the high-energy torus of light.

Insight Lightning

Jungian psychology notes that our unconscious knows things that we are ignorant of in our daily lives. This knowledge is often expressed through age-old sayings and proverbs as well as through nonverbal symbols that are universally recognized. Verbal expressions such as "good or bad vibes," "to be in sync" with someone, and "her face lit up" all convey the luminous and energetic dimension of consciousness, and there are similar expressions found in many languages. Nonverbally, semantic energy is also conveyed through symbols, such as how comic strips often represent the notion of people having an idea of genius (the famous "Eureka!") as a lightbulb turned on above their heads, and this brings me to my story.

I stood in a room in full daylight while my boyfriend at the time stood about two yards away, behind my right shoulder, so that, from the corner of my eye, I could see his silhouette. Suddenly, I perceived a flash of light at the very place and height of his head. Astonished, I turned around to ask him what happened, when, with his back to me, he exclaimed, as if to himself, "Whoa! I just had a great insight!"

This remark instantly brought to mind the comic-strip lightbulb: maybe an entire neural network fired simultaneously in my boyfriend's head! In any case, his head aura was suddenly alighted.

Extended Sphere around a Person
Now let's look at some Hermetic phenomena that helped me to understand that gifted questers, through repeated meditation, can create a much larger field. Sometimes, this field can be so large that those sitting next to meditating questers can find themselves within it. These fields can also be anchored to a room or a house.

A friend with whom I often used to meditate had entered a deep meditative state in a room on the upper floor of a house where she used to practice meditation. On entering the room, I could see that she was in heightened consciousness—she was extremely peaceful, with an aura of light that was slightly pinkish surrounding her. I sat down and joined her in meditation. When I entered a deeper state, I saw that she had created a large sphere of energy (her pink vibratory signature on it left no doubt as to its origin).

The sphere was about ten yards in diameter and occupied most of the upper floor (with its two rooms and landing under the beamed roof). I realized I was within her sphere, totally surrounded and infused by her specific soul energy. I experienced a pleasant, peaceful state that was extremely harmonious. Yet as I entered heightened consciousness ever more deeply, I felt the urge to connect to my own source of spiritual energy, to my own Self. To be able to do this, I understood that I somehow had to make a hole in her perfect extended structure.

I explained the situation, and she agreed on my plan. After I made a tiny hole (about a third of an inch wide) at the tip of the sphere, I was able to draw from the cosmos a tiny ray that had my own vibratory quality. The connection to my own source, imperfect as it was, was still rewarding; but I suddenly remembered states of fusion in which I would be totally immersed in my own spiritual source. Again, then, I asked her if I could enlarge the hole I had created, and she told me to go ahead. Neither of us really knew the ins and outs of an enlarged sphere of energy, since it was the first time either of us was aware they could indeed be created. At the very moment I enlarged the tiny hole to about the size of a hand's breadth, the entire sphere suddenly exploded like a bubble, and I was instantaneously in pure bliss, feeling as if a stream of lively energy was pouring on me. An instant later, however, I heard a sound that evoked a kind of sliding, and I had the impression that something was wrong. I opened my eyes to check on my friend. She had fainted, and her body was slowly sliding toward the carpeted floor. She had received such a shock from the breaking of her sphere that I had to spend the next hours healing her—that is, recreating around her head a small sphere that had precisely the same vibratory quality as her semantic field and then maintaining it around her.

Threads of Light above the Head

It's not unusual for me to see rays of light emanating from the heads of people and shooting upward. I have the impression that some individuals don't have this link, but for those who do, how high the rays can shoot depends on the person's connection to the realm of the Self. Sometimes they reach such heights that I lose sight of them in space. They are not exactly straight rays, like lasers; they feel more elastic, more supple. My feeling is that these threads of light have to do with the way people are connected to some personal source of energy. Such rays resemble what some psychics have described in the context of out-of-body experiences (the shamanic or astral journeys): the astral cord maintaining the link between consciousness and the body. My impression is somewhat different: I see that some questers always have this link, whatever their state of consciousness. What follows is a specific phenomenon that could be linked to the subject.

One day, a quester friend with whom I had meditated often and shared many spiritual experiences told me that he was using a specific technique of visualization. The aim was to create a personal temple or secret refuge in the astral dimension and to charge it regularly, so that he had a private place, full of energy, to go to in order to recharge himself whenever his own spiritual energy was depleted. Using a visualization technique, this private place had to be created high in the atmosphere. Later that day, we sat to meditate. He was already meditating when I realized that I saw his ray of light, and I became absorbed in this vision. Suddenly, I saw a large bulb of energy, and at the same instant, I received such an enormous mass of energy that it poured into my mind and body like an electric shock. The blow was so strong that I was nearly knocked out. I realized my stupidity a bit too late. I was afraid that I had inadvertently discharged his secret refuge merely by getting into energetic contact with it, and I felt so ashamed that I couldn't say a word. He didn't leave his meditative state.

One thing that was certain for me was that his visualizations had indeed worked: in a short time, he had been able to accumulate a great deal of energy in his secret refuge. "Surely he will be able to recharge it as quickly," I thought with fervent hope.

HOW SEMANTIC ENERGY WORKS

All these occurrences reveal the way semantic energy works through specific structures and dynamics. Let's summarize the ones we have encountered.

Specific Auras Linked to Heightened Consciousness
In high meditative states, an aura of light can surround the head or the whole body of the yogi. In the highest states, the meditating individual

can achieve the double aura of the Buddhists—that is, a great luminous bulb around the head that blends into a larger aura enveloping the body. This spiritual aura is a field of semantic energy, the high energy of consciousness, and is distinct from the natural aura linked to the emotional and biological levels, which is itself a composite field.

Torus Structure of the Head Chakra

A torus of light above the head can appear in transcendental states when the head chakra is opened and activated. The torus is in fact one of the very specific energy structures that can be generated by the head chakra. It consists of a double rotation of semantic energy turning at great speed. Described thoroughly in Buddhism is a transcendental state of meditation called the void state. In this state, the meditator is devoid of thoughts, and he or she experiences pure consciousness "without content." While in this void state, I saw the torus structure above my head chakra. In fact, I believe the torus to be the energetic structure of the void state.

Inflow of Semantic Energy from Our Self

When we are connected to our Self (soul, solar angel), we can receive from it a sudden inflow of energy that can be correlated (at the psychological, conscious level) with having a great insight or entering a state of heightened consciousness. The inverse is also true: entering a heightened state will activate the deep connection between our ego consciousness and our Self and will permit the inflow of energy from our Self. In the semantic dimension, events always have a meaningful, consciousness aspect (insight, state) as well as an energetic aspect (dynamical structures, fields, etc.), because semantic energy exists at a deep level of reality where consciousness and matter-energy are one and the same: the semantic dimension is the dimension of consciousness-as-energy.

It's the energy of this dimension—having the characteristics of blending both consciousness and very subtle energy (and not abiding by the same laws as EM energy)—that I call syg-energy.

Forms Created in the Semantic Dimension

The repeated visualization or contemplation of a sacred object amounts to accumulating syg-energy in that object: it creates or reinforces its semantic field. Sensitive people can see and sense its energy (the aura around an object) as well as its meaning (its positive or negative influence, its history, etc.). A form can be created (out of nothing) by visualization in the semantic dimension and can be charged with semantic energy.

This is how specific types of visualization or meditation techniques enable a person to create a large sphere around himself or herself, which has many advantages: energy can be accumulated inside, it can protect the individual, and it can filter bad energies. Yet it doesn't have the strength and resilience of the natural aura. These "thoughtforms" (as they are called in esoterica) have a "real" energy with a specific form. Nevertheless, they do not belong to the EM and quantum spectrum: they are not perturbed or stopped by matter as are usual light rays or laser rays (even if some lasers can penetrate biological matter to a certain extent). They are created out of pure will and intention, and the semantic energy of another individual can affect them.

Spherical Shapes and Semantic Energy

We have encountered circles and spherical forms in many instances.

In terms of dynamical structures:

- The spherical telhar field (on the road in Bièvres)
- The torus of light that appeared among four people meditating and the sphere surrounding them
- The large sphere created by my friend in meditation
- Spherical auras and thoughtforms around a person
- A torus above the head chakra.

In terms of archetypal settings leading to the creation of telhar fields:

- The circle of people around a node (such as a dancer, a fire)
- The round harmonization for smoking the calumet.

ENERGY FIELDS AROUND (SACRED) OBJECTS

The sphere is thus one of the natural shapes assumed by semantic energy. Spherical glows, however, sometimes involve sacred objects, not just people. There are also notable energy forms other than the sphere, such as straight rays and arcs of light.

Many times, I have seen a clear, luminous aura, mostly around sacred objects used for rituals or around personal objects that are symbolic, sacred, or highly meaningful to an individual. Here are a few examples.

- At the monastery in Brittany, the head monk performed a Mass, and since the monastery was very poor, he used a very simple vase as a chalice. When he lifted the chalice above his head while offering the sacred words of consecration, I saw the vase glowing with a light that extended a few inches around it.
- Even in my ordinary state of consciousness, I can see the auras of sacred objects in temples or around objects that hold great meaning for people. In India, not only are there a great number of beautiful and rich temples, but also there are small altars everywhere in the streets. These small altars generally consist of one or two statues of divinities in stone or papier-mâché set into a small cubic temple with a dome or else of a sacred Shiva lingam (an oval standing stone) under a sacred tree. Sometimes, these altars are simply a formless mound of papier-mâché with eyes painted on it. In front of all the altars hangs a bell, which people ring when they begin their devotions. Many times I have seen the eyes of these sacred statues light up or their aura becoming more intense when people started to pray.
- On one occasion, a well-known young Hindu guru, venerated as a reincarnation of Krishna, was going to give a speech to an immense audience gathered in a large square in Delhi. A platform had been erected, and it was decorated with two statues of papier-mâché standing approximately the height of a man. One statue represented Krishna, the god of love, and the other depicted Ganesh, the god of wisdom. Having climbed on the platform,

with his mother following him, the guru came to the foreground in front of the microphone, and he stood there a short while. At the exact moment he started his speech, the two statues were lit up by a very subtle and intangible light that surrounded them like an aura. This light was no trick, because it must have been invisible to most people, especially in broad daylight. The statues remained aglow until the end of his speech.

• When I want to recharge my own sacred objects and replenish their energy, I perform a laying on of hands on them, and in effect, I see their aura increase. Generally speaking, the objects we wear are naturally charged with our semantic energy. For example, the jewels of a person in good health will have a pleasant, vigorous aura, while those of a sick person will exude an aura that appears somber and as if tarnished.

• On two separate occasions, I have seen the auras around jewels I was wearing disappear suddenly, as if they had been turned off like a lamp, at the moment a person would touch them. (This is the exact opposite of the auras of sacred objects that suddenly become more intense when people pray in front of them or to them if they are representations of divine beings.) I didn't feel any particular antipathy or aggression toward these people touching my objects. Nor did I feel any aggression from them toward me. They were merely curious, as were many other people who touched them without any consequences. These people, however, apart from being curious, seemed more or less skeptical about such objects. It was as if they had an unconscious sensitivity to the objects' semantic imprinting, but a negative one: an unconscious refusal of them. It's also possible they had an energy totally antithetic to my own. One of these objects was a silver pendant I had worn for a long time. A parent of my boyfriend at the time, a patent skeptic, grabbed it one day on my chain out of curiosity to have a better look at it. The intense aura of the object disappeared instantly. The other jewel was a velvet African belt decorated with shells, and its aura, too, disappeared instantly on being touched. In the case of the silver pendant, I was so annoyed by what had happened that I tried to recharge it through a laying on of hands and reciting mantras, but nothing worked—and that was very strange, because I used to charge objects quickly this way. I asked a renowned psychic friend to help me recharge it. The object began to glow weakly, but it was nothing compared to the bright aura of months and months of gradual imprinting.

- On one of my returns to France from India, I bought a tiny bronze statue of Krishna as a child, an antiquity that had a broken leg but a splendid blue aura. I bought it because I had never seen such a beautiful aura on an antique piece. I purchased it just prior to my departure, and as I intended to give it to my father, I kept it wrapped until I saw my parents. (So there was no imprinting or laying on of hands from me.) As we often do in France, I pulled out my gift at the end of the meal, at dessert time. My father was an amateur collector of antiquities, and very pleased, he began to turn around the statue in order to observe it better, all the while praising its craftsmanship. Midway through his observation (but not at the first touch, as in the two previous cases), the aura abruptly disappeared, and I "plunged my nose in my plate," so confused and sad was I.

I could go on with more stories of auras around objects, but without adding any information. Let us review what we have gathered thus far.

Auras Linked to Matter: Generalities

- Objects are naturally charged with the semantic energy of those who wear them or look at them with admiration, love, and a great deal of feeling—as we do, for example, with objects that remind us of somebody we have loved.
- A laying on of hands has the capacity to imprint or charge objects more quickly. Prayers, religious rituals, and mantras can transmit the semantic energy of people to the sacred objects.
- If a person's semantic energy bears a quality that is vastly different from our own or has a quality that is incompatible with our own, this energy can annul or diminish the imprint we have given our own objects.

Traditional religious rituals are meant to build up the semantic energy of participants, and while they do so, they also build an aura on all objects used ritually. However, a specific faith or school of thought is a collective semantic field with a specific quality, frequency, and so forth. Consequently, the influence of the collective field on the energy field of devotees (and ritual objects) will bear the specific qualities of that faith—that is, its meaning, inherent values, as well as its spiritual and psychic imprint.

RAYS AND ARCS OF LIGHT

In order to understand what's going to follow, let me explain a psychological process that can be achieved by questers who work on their sleep and dream states. There are many traditional ways to control the sleep state. For example, the Tibetan yogis have developed techniques to become connected to the "clear light of the Self" during sleep, and Australian Aborigines have a great mastery of the dreamtime. There are also modern techniques to become lucid during our dreams—that is, to be able to trigger our own awakening from within the dream or normal sleep state.[3]

Command for Waking Up Originating in the Unconscious Self

Since I have experienced this process quite often, let me recount the most striking episodes I have seen.

Lucid dream: I had a dream that featured a fire starting in my basement. Then, while still in the dream state (it became a lucid dream at that moment), I reflected on the dream I just had and decided I'd better wake up and go downstairs to check the basement. I started walking down the basement staircase of my previous house when I realized I was still dreaming. It's not that I realized it was the wrong staircase, but rather, I noted that the walls at my sides were not passing me by at the correct speed according to my body movements. Again, I told myself that I absolutely had to wake up and go down to the basement, that with such a dream of a fire in the basement, something was bound to be wrong down there. So I made an incredible effort, and finally I was able to wake up. I went directly to the basement and found that my iron was still turned on at a high temperature and that it was resting on the ironing table. I had thus succeeded in driving into my brain-body the command to wake up and in fulfilling my unconscious aim, which was to suppress the danger I had seen clairvoyantly. The exceptional feat, in this instance, was not the lucid dream per se, or even the clairvoyant information; it was the fact that the command to wake up and perform an action had originated in my unconscious mind, within the dream state. This lucid dream shows clearly that it is indeed possible, within the dream state, to think, reflect, and decide with our unconscious mind.

Immaterial presence: Another time, when awakening, I opened my eyes just a tiny bit. They were already turned toward the immaterial shape of a young wise man who sat very peacefully, crosslegged, by my bedside. When he realized I had woken up, he swiftly rose. I sat up quickly, and looking at him while he was turning his body to get up, I asked him telepathically to stay and explained that I could stand such a vision of the other dimension. Yet he crossed the room and passed right through the door, making both the wooden floor and the wooden door creak.

In this case, as in the case of lucid dreaming, the command to wake up and look at the immaterial presence had originated in my unconscious Self during sleep. This is consistent with the fact that I had hardly opened my eyes, so that the wise man wouldn't realize I had woken up. I felt immediately that I knew him as a friend and that we had been in discussion for a while before I opened my eyes.

Rays Establishing Connections

On several occasions, I perceived nonphysical rays that seemed either to create a connection between me and a sacred object (or other semantic source) or to express an existing connection. It generally happened when waking up in the morning that I would see rays of light dashing from one of my higher chakras toward a specific location in or out of the room. The rays were very thin, perfectly straight, and nondiffusing (just like lasers, the beam didn't get larger with distance). Though they were all nondiffusing rays, they did vary in their width, color, and the chakra to which they connected. Here are a two examples:

- **Connection to a sacred source:** One day I saw a ray of white light, about two-tenths of an inch wide, that connected me to an Indian painting hanging on the wall—a painting representing the goddess Kali, the archetype of the Great Mother goddess and the vanquisher of the devil. Kali has several forms and names, according to the qualities and forces she can activate. As the spouse of Shiva, the Creator, yogi, and ascetic, she is Parvati; as the protector of villages and families, she is represented as Durga. The representation I had, painted on paper by village women from Rajastan (who normally paint the outside walls of their houses), was Kali the vanquisher, dancing in trance after her victory over the body of the slain devil.

- **Rays toward the stars:** On two occasions close in time to one another, I woke in the middle of the night to perceive a thin, whitish ray that started from my head and shot straight through the opened window toward the starry sky (although it may have been the other way around—it may have come toward me from the stars). My mattress was set on the wooden floor covered with carpets and next to a low window.

Each time, on awakening, I opened my eyes slowly without moving my head or body so that my gaze was already directed toward the vanishing point of the ray, and I saw it right away. This points to the fact that the command for waking up had been initiated from my unconscious Self. Indeed, when I opened my eyes without moving my head, my gaze was already turned in the precise direction of the ray. The first time it happened, I was dumbfounded, but still I had the good sense not to move my head until I was able to note the form of the ray and its direction. Since the luminous, laser-like ray was passing less than one inch below the upper part of the window frame, I took a mental note of its distance from the right top corner, using as markers scratches in the wood frame. The only problem was that when I rose to draw a mark on the wood, I forgot to note the exact position of my head and the time of the event. It must have been around 4:00 a.m., for I used to go to sleep very late.

Then I tried to determine which stars were in the direction of the ray, roughly south-southwest (the ray was at about a 50-degree angle from a second-floor height), but I wasn't knowledgeable enough about stars to get anywhere. I made a sketch, but didn't have a map of the stars to use when I observed the sky the following nights.

Two or three weeks later, I woke up again in the middle of the night (around the same time), and a similar ray sprang forth toward the stars, passing at about the same spot just under the window frame. This time, I took note of the position of my head, but I forgot to write down the exact time. I devised a strategy for the next time this would happen, and I was ready, but unfortunately there never was a next time. Eventually, I forgot about these events, and I lost the drawing as well as the dates.

Rays Triggering the Awakening of the Kundalini

What follows was the first grand spiritual experience of my life, at the beginning of my nineteenth year. When it occurred, I had been meditating for about a year, easily entering deep states and remaining effortlessly in meditation for a half hour or hour at a time.

While vacationing in Tunisia, I was one evening with my friend's sister at a traditional café high on a cliff in Sidi Bou Said. We were sitting cross-legged on mats for a long chat accompanied by mint tea, when I felt a call to meditate outside, and I told my companion that I was going out for a while to get some air. I found a fantastic small terrace overlooking the sea—the perfect spot for meditating. I sat down cross-legged and entered inner silence. Soon, I felt my mind was lifted, and I knew that such a sensation preceded a shift to a higher state of consciousness. That time, however, the sensation was so strong that I had the impression, for twenty or thirty seconds, that I was in an elevator sliding up at a hypervelocity. When I reached a new level of consciousness, my state became peaceful and stable, and I felt my mind expand. Eyes closed, I suddenly saw two things at once, and this vision remained stable the entire time I kept on meditating—about thirty minutes. A straight ray of an intense, magnetic blue, beautiful and vivid, reached my chest, exactly at its middle. It extended out as far I could see; it was nondiffusing and about three inches wide. Simultaneously, I had the magnificent vision of a wise man meditating in a lotus position under a large tree. He was slim, like an archetypal Asian ascetic, and dressed in a long golden-orange garment that covered only one shoulder. Above his shoulders, where should have been his head, only a large sphere of light of an intense luminosity was to be seen, totally hiding his face. I was enraptured, and the vision brought me into pure bliss.

While pondering this experience much later, both the quality of the exchange we had and the presence of the beam linking us left me no doubt that the sage was a real person. Since the coast of Tunisia is facing the east, and he had appeared very far on the horizon at the other end of the ray, I came to think he was living in the Orient (the East). I became convinced that one day, when I realized my great dream of traveling to the Orient, I would meet him physically. The energy I received that night was such that it opened a new level in my meditations. In the following days, I realized that I could return to this transcendental state if I centered my energy on the very spot the ray had touched (and where it left a reddish circle, an inch and a half wide and hot to the touch for a few days). I was puzzled by this mixing of consciousness states and spots on my body. I had read some of the classic books of Eastern religions, but I had not yet encountered any mention of the chakras or of the kundalini. I had taught myself meditation with a beginners' book of hatha yoga, which contained only a half dozen basic postures. Given that I was a poet and already knew how to immerse myself into inner states of poetic contemplation, I quickly reached deep states in meditation just by using the most classical posture.

Unknown to me, my heart chakra had been opened and activated that night. The process would follow its course during the next year without my conscious knowledge of it. It was only after I had opened my forehead chakra and meditated on a round, blue, intense light at the middle of my forehead, which was visible with my eyes closed, that I finally ran into a book describing the rise of the kundalini energy from chakra to chakra into the thousand-petaled lotus at the top of the head.

A Hex Ray

After my first grand journey to the East and a year and a half of immersion in another dimension of consciousness, I found myself unable to get back into materialistic Western culture. I hardly spent two months or so in a house in the woods near Paris before departing to live in Montségur. After about four and a half months in France altogether, I left France on a hunch and started toward an archetypal "South." This led me to North Africa and then across the Sahara to Nouakchott. After I had crossed the desert, I decided I wouldn't turn back and would instead return to India by way of sub-Saharan Africa. That was how I hitchhiked from the south of France all the way to Kenya—without money and barefoot, with a blanket on one shoulder!

In Cameroon one evening, a very nice man had given me a lift down the final stretch of road toward the big town of Yaoundé. I immediately felt secure and at ease with him, and when he offered me to stay in his house for the night, explaining that his wife and kids were gone for a few days and there was a void room I could use, I accepted gladly. That evening, very pleased, I set up in the room, and we shared some dinner and talked. The next morning, he offered that I myself cook the food for lunch. I was thrilled while cooking fried potatoes à la Provençal because I hadn't eaten French food for six or seven months. The lunch ready, I called my host. While I glanced at the appetizing food set on the table, I suddenly didn't want to eat—something rather strange since I was feeling okay at that moment. A bit confused, I stayed at the table to talk with my host; yet a few moments later, I felt very nauseous and, excusing myself, went to my room.

There, I saw a ray darting toward me through the open window, straight and thin like a pen. Not knowing what it was, I tried to sense it with my forehead chakra. Abruptly, I began to experience a very high fever; I shook all over and sweated as if I had a fit of malaria. Having seen the ray, I had no doubt that the fever was caused by it, and I remembered that two evenings earlier, I had rubbed the wrong way the pride of a male taxi driver: returning to Douala with his taxi empty, he had taken me for free as long as he was without customers. Fair enough. On arriving in town, however, he had stopped, and leaving me in the taxi, he went to an open-air stall nearby, where he started to drink heavily. After ten or fifteen minutes, I thought I'd better leave the car and find a place to sleep. I located a Protestant church in which the pastor, occupied with directing a chorale, kindly offered me shelter for the night. When I left a half hour later to find something to eat, I fell on the driver again, who, drunk and upset, was searching for me in the streets. He refused to believe I had found shelter at the Protestant center, and he decided to follow me there. I got rid of him only by staying within the open church, where the pastor was chanting with his pupils. That all occurred on the evening before I met my host on the way to Yaoundé.

Immediately, I blocked the wicked ray with a visualization that created an energetic closure on the whole room. It worked well; the ray no longer came through the window. I soon realized, however, that this didn't stop the fever that was already in me. I then tried to use a healing stone, but that didn't work. Perplexed, I called my Sufi master for help and heard in answer a faint voice telling me to open the door. I was afraid to do this: wouldn't the ray hit me again? Also, conscious that the fever was starting to muddle my thoughts, I didn't dare trust the voice I heard. The fever increased very quickly. I was at a loss as to what to do next when, very naturally, my host opened the door to check on how I was doing and saw me trembling with fever—a symptom that any person living in Africa can read on the spot. Immediately, I felt some relief, and I knew a healing process was on its way, with extrordinary speed. (I later came to the conclusion that if my visualization was blocking the malevolent syg-energy, it was also impeding my master's healing syg-energy from reaching me.) My host insisted on taking me to the hospital, but I was back to normal about ten minutes later, well before we reached the hospital. At no time in my life, either before or after this episode, have I suffered a fit of malaria.

The distance between the towns of Douala and Yaoundé is about 150 miles, and the dirt road at that time was one of the worst I ever saw.

This could only mean that the taxi driver must have sent this energy ray from that far. Yet, even if this syg-energy was very negative and had such an ill effect on me, it doesn't necessarily mean that the upset driver projected it willingly as a hex, with a magical word or ritual. Though I doubt it in this case, it could have also been the expression of anger in an individual who possessed strong mind power.

Luminous Arcs

Semantic energy can also take the form of smoothly curved arcs. Examples of this are the rays that emanate from the architectural centers of churches and other sacred monuments. In France, I have observed that these curved rays climb progressively to about seven or eight yards above the height of the roof (depending on the importance of the church) and then begin curving down, forming arcs that link the church to other sacred buildings. I can both see these arcs from outside of the building and *feel* them and follow their path, eyes closed, from within the church. They exist on most sacred buildings in France, and they generate the Christian-Druidic network connecting cathedrals, churches, abbeys, and megaliths. (To this grid are also connected lay monuments based on sacred architecture and the golden proportion, such as museums, castles, arcs de triomphe, etc.)

The grid of churches thus branches into the old megalithic-Druidic grid that has connected dolmens, menhirs, and the sacred mounts (*tertres*) of the Celtic (Druidic) religion. Both grids follow the natural lines of the geomagnetic field, and this is why they are interlaced and form one single grid. (We will explore this grid in detail further on.)

An Amazing Diversity of Forms

We have seen that semantic energy can take quite a few forms—but these tend to fall into general types. Each type of form (sphere, ray, and so forth) has its unique properties, and thus the way they can be reinforced, steered, or used requires particular knowledge and techniques. Moreover, the still mysterious semantic energy seems to be interlaced with the EM spectrum, such as the geomagnetic field of Earth or the natural physical human aura. Here are the main types of forms.

- Spherical or ovoid auras around people and organisms. The natural physical aura (a composite field of EM frequencies) is itself interlaced with an aura of semantic energy (syg energy, non-EM), derived from the activity and quality of consciousness. All living beings, from animals to cells, have semantic fields, more or less developed.
- Spherical auras around objects, made of the projection of semantic energy on revered or loved objects.
- Straight, nondiffusing rays emanated by people and used for long-distance semantic connections. (Because they're also used in negative magic, they're not always good or ethical.)
- Arcs of energy of the sacred network that enrich and modulate the lines of the geomagnetic field—that is, EM waves interlaced with syg-energy waves. These arcs are activated through sacred architecture, and they raise the consciousnesses of people.

SENSING THE SEMANTIC ENERGY INSIDE

This chapter wouldn't be complete if it left the impression that semantic energy is something that we can perceive only from the outside. In fact, inner sensations are much more common. Most individuals who have had some practice in self-development techniques or in martial arts have, to some degree, experienced psychic or semantic energy. Even the novel workshops on emotional and relational intelligence often underline how psychic energy can be best exchanged and shared between people.

Empathy is the capacity to feel another person as if from inside and understand his or her viewpoint. The latter description, however, shows only the psychological level. At an energetic level, empathy is the capacity to harmonize one's own psychic-semantic energy with that of another. It's as if some people have a knack for creating a telhar field capable of including another person and their psyche is so flexible and open that they could do that with many individuals.

Bodies Can Talk

Surely, we have an unconscious knowledge of semantic energy since we have words to express it that are often quite similar in several languages.

We feel a place gives us energy (*nous donne de l'énergie*), that meeting a very optimistic person will pump us up (*nous regonfle*), or on the contrary, that a person may suck energy out of us (*nous pompe*). We judge that people have good or bad *vibes,* and so forth.

The fact that these novel expressions exist in diverse languages shows they are part of the zeitgeist (the spirit of the time). It means that we are now able to sense how our energy and our state of consciousness are modified while the changes are occurring. In other words, we are becoming more and more sensitive to semantic energy and capable of perceiving how it affects us beyond what occurs at the mundane level. For example, the individual who "puts us down" could, in fact, be quite nice, and the fact that we "feel down" after a chat may have nothing to do with what has been said. The feeling is deeper. It's an energetic sensation: the recognition of how this person affects our energy field.

The Sensation of Being Centered

Another energetic sensation that's now part of social knowledge is the awareness of being centered. In French, we say, "After that great workshop, I feel centered" (*"Après ce super atelier, je me sens bien centré"*); or "This exercise recenters me" (*"Cet exercice me recentre"*). These terms were first used in self-development books.

The verb *concentrate* reflects a purely intellectual level: to be focused on a mental task. In contrast, *to be centered* expresses an energetic level. To feel centered is also different from feeling articulate or wide awake. It's a sensation based on the fact that our energy is strong and grounded, which generally means that it is gathered in one of the psychic centers (the chakras). In many performance arts—especially singing and acting—it is essential for the artist to be centered. All singers learn very early on how to ground their voice in the belly by belly breathing. Similarly, one of the key lessons of martial arts is how to breathe through the belly and how to center one's own energy in the *hara* (the chakra situated about one inch below the navel). The hara not only allows for maximum strength and physical balance (thus protecting our individual field), but also stimulates psycho-motor coordination. This is why this chakra is essential in all martial arts. To be centered in general enhances our mental capacities, and this is why there are many techniques in yoga, t'ai chi, qigong, and so forth that aim at gathering or centering our energy in one specific chakra.

Sensing How and Where Our Energy Is Centered

However, there's still another array of inner sensations concerning semantic energy: that is how to sense from the inside in what qualitative state is our personal semantic energy. We can learn quite easily how to center our energy in a chakra by using visualization techniques. Of course, some chakras—such as the hara and the heart chakra—are much easier to feel than others, because their energy is much stronger. If we keep practicing, we'll soon be able to sense the energy of several chakras, and we'll develop a keen inner sensation of where our energy is gathered at any moment.

The energy of the main chakras can be extended in many different ways to create fields that have particular shapes and properties. This happens spontaneously (and unconsciously) during meditation practice, but once mastered, it can be done willingly.

One example of this is the large sphere my friend created with her heart chakra. This loving and harmonious field (resulting from her continuous meditations) gave her the capacity not only to protect herself and to accumulate energy without dispersing it, but also to harmonize herself with great empathy with people around her.

Here is another example of a large personal semantic field that spontaneously expanded on the environment.

I was driving on the highway (on a stretch of road I'm accustomed to) and listening to music for about a half hour. The landscape consisted mainly of fields and spots of trees, green and refreshing. I was looking at it, how beautiful it was, when I realized I was in an astonishing state of consciousness—something I was not used to experiencing. I felt that my mind was enlarged to the landscape around me and deeply attuned to the whole environment. I shifted my car to the right lane and began driving in a slow, stable way; the highway was mostly empty. Then I opened my mind to understand the state I was in, and by doing so, my mind became hypervigilant and very sharp. I was able to simultaneously be immersed in this expanded state of consciousness, to drive, to sense cars around me, and to observe and reflect on my state.

I realized what was strange and novel about my state: it was my bodily sensations, rather than my mind, that were expanded onto the landscape. As I often do, I started using the soothing bass sound of my engine to deepen my trance. My bodily sensations were extraordinarily extended and more immaterial. I got the clear sensation that with my bodily energy field I was sweeping through the fields and trees, but even more so (and this was very strange to me) through the earth deep in the ground. As I passed smoothly through grass, bushes, and trees, I was feeling an array of diverse, subtle sensations, as if my skin had been stroked by feathers or light flowers. From the part of me that swept through the ground, I ascertained the sensation of something more rough and weighty, yet still enjoyable. With my enlarged body, I swept as far as one hundred yards on both sides of the car. I felt perfectly centered in this extended field, in control and at ease. I had never experienced this type of sensation—of having my bodily energy field extended spherically on the environment.

At that time, I knew only large and extremely large energy fields of a pure consciousness quality because experiencing these had been one of my favorite meditation techniques. This time on the road, however, was akin to touching the surrounding landscape with my body and sliding through it.

I grew curious about how this extended field emerged and which chakra was responsible for it. I knew it had to come from a lower chakra, for I was so accustomed to the higher chakras' fields and activation that I would have recognized them. While I was still in the trance, then, sweeping through the landscape and cautious to sustain the state, I tried to feel from where this extended sphere originated in my energetic body—to no avail, however. I could sense the entire sphere around and below me, about two hundred yards in diameter, yet I couldn't feel its center.

Then I tried another strategy: I gathered all my energy into the hara. The energy was totally different, much more masculine, strong and warriorlike. Then I tried to center myself on the higher chakras, one by one. I recognized these fields, for I'm used to creating them. Of course, they had nothing to do with this particular state, since with each new field I thus created, the quality of the energy was totally different from that of the novel field. Finally, I tried to focus all my energy on a chakra I knew hardly anything about because I had never "felt" it before: the navel. And that was it! It had the very specific frequency and quality of the field. I was feeling the field again, extended on the landscape. The energy was very subtle and smooth, harmonious, soft, and penetrating.

In fact, as I write this, reliving my state to express it as finely as I can, the particular energy of the navel field that day reminds me of two hexagrams of the I Ching describing a soft influence. The first one, The Wind (number 57), shows that a progressive and gentle persuasion, such as a yielding and yet enduring breeze, can in fact exert a powerful and lasting influence. The second, The Influence (number 31), expresses that openness to others and a state of receptivity to them make others connected to us so that they can later be influenced. The same is true of complex natural systems. This experience thus showed me that, interestingly, one of our chakras can be in full activation without us sensing more than some of its effects. It's thus possible for us to create a field of grand proportions without being aware of its energetic source. And while we are considering how much our unconscious can do without us being aware of it, let me point out that, in the "exploding sphere" case, my friend hadn't the slightest idea that she had created a large, stable field during her meditations, let alone that it could affect other people around her.

Before we get back to our main topic, let me note the features of this extended field of the navel chakra, because even if it is a personal field and not a collective one, it presents unusual and important traits.

Features of the Extended Field of the Navel Chakra

- The structure of the field is spherical, and in my experience, it plunges into the ground.
- It is possible to experiment with our own semantic field and chakras while remaining in a heightened state of consciousness and, thereafter, to dive again fully into the heightened state.

- The feat in my experience was to be able to move with the extended navel field through the landscape at the low, smooth, speed of driving, while keeping the field structure perfectly intact, for about forty to sixty minutes. In fact, I could have prolonged that state easily, because it was only when arriving near Paris and entering heavy traffic that I had to detach my attention from my inner state in order to focus fully on the road.

For those who think I took daredevil risks in driving: from the start, there was a hypervigilant component to my expanded state. I was literally sensing the approach of each one of the rare vehicles that passed me on the two left lanes because the field also extended behind me. Not only that, but I also felt I had an out-of-the-ordinary control of myself, of my car, and of my state. I was in a hyperlucid state, with a higher speed of thought and quicker reflexes.

HUMAN ENERGY FIELDS

To conclude this chapter on experiencing energy fields linked to meaning and consciousness, let me summarize what we have discussed:

- Human beings have a semantic field (the semantic aura) that surrounds them and that can be enormously expanded in heightened and altered states of consciousness. The biological aura is a much smaller composite field generated by the diffusion of many different energies of the EM spectrum.[4] The semantic field blends into it but can be much larger.
- Syg-energy (and therefore the semantic field) is consciousness-energy: it is at the same time energy and consciousness, matter-like and mindlike. It is a whole spectrum of energy different from the EM spectrum and thus showing different properties, for it is linked to the working of consciousness. So whenever we talk about an aura (of a person or an object) being lit up, let's remember we are not talking about photons or physical light—proof being that these rays are not stopped by matter.

- The human semantic field is organized (bioenergetically speaking) around the psychic centers, or chakras, and their consciousness-energy (called kundalini energy or *shakti* in India, *chi* in China, and *ki* in Japan). The energy radiating from activated chakras creates the semantic aura. This is why the human semantic field is imprinted by the specific qualities and frequencies linked to the activated chakras.

- Through the practice of meditation and self-development techniques (such as visualization, martial arts, healing practices, etc.), we can increase our ability to sense our own inner energy. Furthermore, we can learn how to elevate intentionally its quality and frequency and thus enter heightened consciousness. We can also learn how to harmonize better with our environment—to the point of experiencing a harmony field within this environment. Of course, we can also learn how to generate telhar fields with other people.

- Consciousness is able to modify its own organization (its semantic field) at any given moment. In fact, an act of will or an intention has the power to change not only our inner state of consciousness, but also the energetic configuration of our semantic field. For example, an experienced person who enters deep meditation can intentionally shift the energetic center of his semantic field from where it is usually focused and move it upward to a higher chakra. This can be done easily by using visualization. Visualization techniques are very potent and permit us to achieve a great variety of states of consciousness and objectives—such as to expand willingly our own semantic field, to achieve a state of oneness with our environment, or to connect to a distant space (clairvoyance) or time (precognition). Also, experienced questers can visualize and create particular forms of syg-energy. These forms can be projected around ourselves (such as spheres used for screening energies and protection) or can be anchored to a place (such as rays for stable connections to specific sources of energy). Of course, willingly changing our state of consciousness will modify our energy field; inversely, changing our energy field will have an influence on our state. Besides practice and intention, many factors have an influence on our states of consciousness—such as human environment, natural environment, activity, as well as biological and emotional health. For example, the psychological and chemical factors that are able to induce altered states of consciousness have been well studied in transpersonal psychology.[5]

- Shifts to a higher state of consciousness can occur spontaneously whenever we are deeply connected to our Self (soul, solar angel), our guides, or kindred spirits. Also, such states might be initiated by a connection with powerful semantic sources, such as sacred places, whether in our proximate environment or at a distance.

PART 2

THE SACRED NETWORK

In the first part of this book, we have seen that telhar fields—states of deep harmony among people—show very specific structures made of syg-enegy, such as tori and spheres. In this second part, we will now turn to the network of cosmo-telluric lines linking all sacred sites worldwide as well as specifically oriented monuments within a city. The Montségur seat of power exemplifies how deeply interconnected are these two themes: the sages of the past created a fan of syg-energy rays linking various Indo-European sacred sites, but they had to be in a high state of consciousness to open this communication channel. In the same way, the Zuni Indian elders of a village who wanted to communicate telepathically with elders from faraway villages would get into a deep inner state in their underground chambers, or *kivas*. We will discover that sacred sites and monuments, all the way to megaliths from 6000 BCE, have been erected at the crossing points of cosmo-telluric lines and in accordance with sacred geometry, with the long-term aim of spurring a higher consciousness in humanity. We are now at the beginning of a new cycle of Earth during which we will decode the lattice of the sacred network and reach its aim: the collective harmonization of our minds.

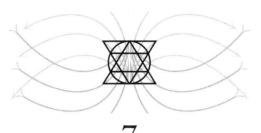

7

CATHEDRAL BUILDERS
AND MEGALITHS

France has a dense network of Catholic churches, cathedrals, and abbeys going back as far as the eighth or ninth centuries or even earlier, to the sixth century for some old walls or remnants integrated in more recent constructions. Yet the placing of these edifices, which were regularly destroyed by fire and rebuilt anew using a different architectural style, didn't occur at random. At the beginning of the twelfth century, the Gothic style rose as striking and innovative features (like the ogival crossing) were introduced into otherwise Roman-style buildings in Ile de France (Poissy, completed in 1120; Saint Denis, completed in 1144) and in England (Durham, completed in 1140). These innovations seemed to have launched a building spree that spread at incredible speed. A factor that greatly helped this building craze was that the construction of churches was no longer undertaken by the monks, but instead was given to civil guilds. Between 1050 and 1350, eighty cathedrals, five hundred large churches, and tens of thousands of minor churches were constructed in France.[1] The building rules, however, were secrets that were jealously kept by the builders' guilds. Though we have several examples of a transition from the Roman to the Gothic style, mainly around Paris, and the first ogival crossings appeared in Poissy and Morienval in 1118, some researchers remain perplexed as to how such a novel architectural design appeared so suddenly. They hint at an influence and novel ideas brought back from the Holy Land via the First Crusade, started in 1095.

PERMANENT SACRED SPOTS

Both the orientation of religious buildings and their precise location are noteworthy. We know that churches are generally oriented toward the east, their choir pointing to the exact degree where the sun rises on the day of the feast of their patron saint. Take, for example, Chartres Cathedral, dedicated to two patron saints, the Virgin Mary and St. John the Baptist, whose feast falls on June 24, the summer solstice. The cathedral is oriented along the solstice axis, with its choir facing 47 degrees northeast, where the sun rises on the summer solstice. Its nave (where the two towers flank each side of the great rose window) points toward the place where the sun sets on December 24, the winter solstice.

If the orientation follows a known rule, the exact spot where churches are constructed remains more mysterious. The experts on sacred architecture and occult history give very sparse—but nevertheless insistent—information as to ancient altars or temples that exist underneath a number of religious buildings.

Thus, the Nautes Pillar, discovered under the choir of the cathedral of Notre-Dame de Paris, was a gift of the Parisian Nautes (the guild of sailors) to Emperor Tiberius, who reigned at the turn of the first century CE. It was dedicated to Jupiter and featured six Gallo-Celtic gods and goddesses as well as six Roman gods and goddesses. It was surmounted by a statue of Jupiter and carved with images of Mercury as well as the Celtic god Cernunnos (or Kernunnos), among others. The latter, with stag horns, is the god of abundance and the lover of the Mother Goddess. He was identified as Mercury (the Greek god Hermes) by the Romans. The main feast of the Celts, Beltain (or Beltane), on May 1, celebrated the sacred union of the stag god and the goddess Ceridwen. It was a feast of fecundity that marked the ascending of the light, and in which a Druid was chosen to impersonate the god and a priestess the goddess.

Ruins of Gallo-Roman or Egyptian temples exist under several Christian churches. We have seen, for example, that the cathedral of Notre-Dame de Paris is erected above the ancient foundations of a temple to the Roman goddess Diana, and that Saint-Sulpice Church is built above a temple to Isis.

Jean Markale gives us other examples in France, underlining that a complete list would be much too long to draw. "The Christian sanctuary Mont-Saint-Michel stands at the location of an old Mithra temple, itself situated where a Gaul sanctuary dedicated to the shining god Bélénos was."[2]

Gwen Le Scouëzec offers another piece of information about Mont-Saint-Michel, one of the most sacred sites of France, situated at the boundary between Brittany and Normandy. He states, "There were megaliths at the tip of Mont-Saint-Michel."[3] Its ancient name was the Tomb Mount, but it was also referred to as the Two-tomb Mount. As for the tiny island close to it, now called Tombelen, it was called Tomba Beleni—that is, the Tomb of Belen, the Celtic god of light, Bélénos. The other tomb would be that of Gargan, who, according to Le Scouëzec, was a pre-Celtic, megalithic god of light—the one who was replaced by the cult of St. Michael on the very same sacred sites. There are very ancient sculptures, predating the St. Michael cult, that depict a warrior riding or overcoming a dragon without slaying it.

Regarding St. Michael's Chapel on the hilltop of Mont-Dol in Brittany, Le Scouëzec also mentions: "The Mont-Dol bore a pagan temple the remnants of which are still clearly visible beneath the Saint-Michel chapel."[4]

Let's pursue this topic further with Markale:

> At [the megalithic site of] Carnac (Morbihan), the church devoted to Saint Korneli replaces a sanctuary to the horned Gaul god Kernunnos; [the cathedral of] Notre-Dame de Paris is situated above an ancient pagan temple dedicated to a mother divinity. At Langon (Ile-et-Vilaine), the actual Sainte Agathe chapel is the very building constructed during the Roman empire to worship Venus (the magnificent Gallo-Roman fresco showing a naked Venus coming out of the waters being a living proof of this cult), and was afterward a sanctuary dedicated to a mysterious 'Saint' Véner or Vénérand. As for [the cathedral of] Notre-Dame de Chartres, the local clerical tra-

dition itself claims that at this precise spot the Druids were worshipping a *Virgo Paritura* [madonna, or virgin,* with her newborn].[5]

Philippe Court-Payen mentions that the southwest tower of the cathedral in Le Mans had been erected on a menhir of green granite, which is still visible. The plaza in front of it was previously called Place Saint-Michel.[6] Paul Devereux, the greatest specialist on leys, mentions in his book *The New Ley Hunter's Guide,* "In June, 601, Pope Gregory wrote to Abbot Mellitus as he prepared to leave for England: 'I have come to the conclusion that the temples of the idols in England should not on any account be destroyed. Augustine must smash the idols, but the temples themselves should be sprinkled with holy water and altars set up in them in which relics are to be enclosed. . . . I hope the people (seeing their temples are not destroyed) will leave their idolatry and yet continue to frequent the places as formerly, so coming to know and revere the true God.'"[7] And finally, in *The Old Straight Track,* Alfred Watkins quotes from Johnson's *Byways in British Archaeology:* "It is on record that Patrick, Bishop of the Hebrides, desired Orlygus to build a church wherever he found the upright stones or menhirs."[8]

The Catholic authorities therefore provided instructions to build churches on the exact spots where ancient temples and megaliths stood, and, in practicality, to cover them. The most important point was that they should not be destroyed, and the order of the pope specifies this three times. In fact, the mandatory nature of these instructions so bypasses the rationales invoked that, when reading them, we cannot exclude an ulterior spiritual (if not occult) motive.

Jean Bayard, in *La tradition cachée des cathédrales* (translated as *The Secret Tradition of Cathedrals*), speaks of a standing stone just outside of Saint-Julien Cathedral in Le Mans adorned with carvings that represent undulations. He cites two churches built above Roman baths: Notre-Dame de Reims Cathedral and Saint-Etienne Church in Beauvais—which means that water is flowing underground in the crypts of these churches.[9]

---

*Let us remember that the ancient meaning of the word *virgin* (*virgo* in Latin) was "a sacred and powerful woman."

Bayard goes on to explain that churches and cathedrals must be built on a mount and that this mount should have a spring (or well). "In general churches possess a well; interestingly, nearby such alive water often sits a Black Virgin."[10] The enigmatic Black Madonna statues (called *Vierges Noires* in French), depicting a definite black complexion, were extremely revered and are found in many churches and cathedrals in France. Still a mystery, they have nevertheless been associated with ancient cults to the Mother Goddess, a fact rendered more plausible because they often guard the sacred healing water. The mount is a clear reminiscence of the Druidic open-air cults, which were always in clearings or on sacred mounds (knolls), especially if there were standing stones on these mounds. Thus, in Great Britain, some cairns (megalithic mounds with an underground tomb or chamber) have standing stones above the mounds. Further, the spring was an essential sacred presence in ancient Egyptian and Greco-Roman cults as well as in Druidic cults. Bayard adds very enigmatic and occult information when he says that of course, wells have pragmatic functions, however "these are just the consequences of a sacred principle, for where water can be harnessed, there the temple can settle."[11]

These sacred spots were chosen and consecrated millennia earlier, given the existence of megaliths under several churches, such as Les Sept Saints in Brittany and especially under Chartres Cathedral. We will see how deeply the network of Catholic churches is interwoven with the ancient sacred grid of standing stones as well as with Druidic cult places. We know that the megaliths people preceded the Celts at least by four millennia. At the sacred site of Carnac in France there are megaliths that date as far back as 6000 BCE. The megaliths, which, strangely, are found nearly everywhere on Earth, were so sacred to the Druids that they used to perform their holy rituals in front of them during Celtic times (starting in 2000 BCE). Indeed, Chartres Cathedral may still have surprises awaiting us: according to trustworthy notary reports, underneath it there exists a megalithic astronomical temple. Early in the fifteenth century, the architect Jon Guygnard was called after a tremor to check on the foundations of the cathedral.[12] He reported finding an arc of twelve menhirs that formed an ancient megalithic solar calendar. The menhirs were placed along an elliptical arc, and the sides of the stones facing the centers of the ellipse were carved with runes and geo-metrical structures. Astronomers would use this type of stone structure to calculate various astronomical events. Usually, these megalithic astro-nomical temples were surrounded by a circular enclosure. The author of the 1982 article recounting the event was himself able to access the crypt in 1957, using an ancient tunnel, and he corroborates the archi-tect's earlier description. The tunnel was walled up immediately after.

There is some uncertainty about the exact location of this sanctuary. One possibility is at a third level of depth, below St. Lubin's Crypt (on the second level) and St. Fulbert's Crypt (the first underground level, which, in the past, was at ground level). Some authors hint at the existence of a grotto that, according to Markale, would be at this third underground level. Another possibility, more credible, because these temples were gener-ally at ground level, would be that the arc of menhirs is surrounded by the very strange horseshoe shape of the gigantic St. Fulbert's Crypt. The aisles of the crypt are indeed astonishingly narrow compared with the width of the cathedral, but they run the whole length of the building, following the outside walls. Markale remarks that in the old times the people com-ing to pray had to climb to the cathedral from the crypt. Nowadays, we still have quite an unusual flight of steps to climb on both sides, even if the declivity is somewhat masked by the magnificent porches.

One of the builders' secrets was thus to construct a church at the exact same spot where ancient cults had set their temples. As says Bayard in a rather terse formula: "The sanctuary is edified at the exact location of an ancient temple."[13] He goes on to explain that this made the task of laying the foundations and building the church much more ardu-ous. The motive must therefore have been beyond any material consid-eration. It was very likely linked to the sacredness of the site and its specific and rare qualities in terms of cosmo-telluric energies and their effect on consciousness.

The use, through the ages, of the exact same place to erect and rebuild temples that belong to different religions is by no means specific to France or even Europe. The extraordinary spiritual site of Pilar in India has seen many cultures and religions since it was the ancient city of Govapuri, then Sindabur—built on a hillock at the bottom of which was the port of Gopakapattana. The site, situated a dozen miles south-east of Panaji, Goa's capital, points to an early settlement of Kharvas fishermen circa 4000 BCE, then of Brahmins and Kshatriyas.*

Interestingly, Christian crosses with four equal branches that have been dated to the seventh century were found around Pilar. They bear inscriptions in Pahlavi, the language of the Persian Sassanid dynasty that took over the trade with India after the fall of the Roman Empire in 476 CE. In Pilar's Archaeological Museum, there are many remarkable statues and bas-reliefs—one of which depicts a magnificent, long-haired Mary Magdalene surrounded by highly sacred emblems and an angel bringing her presents. The name Maria Magdalena is carved on the stone above it. (We will see this stunning stone carving and analyze it in detail later in this chapter.) The book compiled by the museum's director states, "Interestingly Christianity had already taken roots in India when Thomas is believed to have come to India in AD 52 but it was believed that Christians were isolated to Kerala and Mylapore."†

---

*At the time, Goa was part of the Mauryan empire (circa 300 BCE), the port of Gopaka-pattana was thriving and made use of a large surface of lands reclaimed from the sea through a network of bunds, or *khazans,* the ruins of which are still visible in the sea. Roman coins and fragments of terracotta testify to a trade with Rome that ran at least from 30 BCE to 337 CE, the end of the reign of Emperor Constantine. After this, Govapuri was ruled by the early Kadambas of Karnataka, from the fourth to the mid-sixth century CE, followed by the Chalukyas of Badami until the mid-seventh century. The Shilaharas ruled Goa from 765 to 1020 CE and made Govapuri their capital. The Shilaharas were feudatories of the Rashtrakutas emperors, who reigned on the region surrounding the Ellora Caves near Mumbai. This is why the magnificent statue of the god of wisdom, Ganesh (the god with an elephant head), found at Pilar resembles the Dvibhuja Ganesha statue unearthed near the Ellora Caves.

†The Goa Kadambas then ruled part of Goa from 960 CE and had, for a capital, Chandrapura, near Godavari on the south. They captured Govapuri around 1020 CE and made it their capital in 1053. A magnificent statue of a lion—their royal emblem—was found in Pilar. The Kadambas, who ruled Govapuri till 1354, installed a very tolerant, cosmopolitan culture with a Hindu king of Jain descent and a Muslim prime minister, and Buddhist monks also enjoyed many privileges. The area seems to have been a major knowledge center with a university. Medical tools, a road, and irrigation works attest to a highly sophisticated civilization. The Muslims, in 1313, ransacked Govapuri, then Chandrapura, and finally they installed their government in the first town, now called Sindabur. The Muslims ruled over Goa until the arrival of the Portuguese in 1510, but bizarrely, they destroyed Govapuri before the end of the fifteenth century.

In 1610, Spanish Franciscans built the Church of Our Lady of Pilar, dedicated to the Virgin Mary because she appeared standing on a pillar (or *pilar* in Spanish) to hearten the dispirited apostle James in Spain in Saragossa. In the nineteenth century, Carmelites, and later on, St. Francis Xavier's missionaries, resided at the Pilar monastery. It is now a seminary comprising several educational centers.

As with so many high sites—places of great spiritual energy through time—the seminary building at the top of the hill opens on all sides, revealing breathtaking views, and at its center there is an interesting pillar as well as a several-centuries-old tree.

MEGALITHIC ALIGNMENTS AND LEY LINES

Another enigma concerns the persistent and omnipresent alignments of sacred spots and the precise structures they form between them. Alignments of stones—together with stone circles—were already one of the building principles of the megaliths people. Rows of standing stones, sometimes in parallel, are very common, especially in Carnac. Alignments (called ley lines or leys) were first spotted by an English businessman, Alfred Watkins, in 1921. While looking at a map, he saw that from one hilltop to the next, in a perfectly straight line, there were placed standing stones, various megalithic constructions, or ancient sites and buildings as well as old tracks, aligned so that they could be seen from afar. In his 1925 book *The Old Straight Track,* Watkins coined the term *ley lines* and thought they were prehistoric trading routes. He spent the rest of his life doing enormous amounts of fieldwork with a group of ley hunters assembled around him. Next, Dion Fortune, a renowned occultist, wrote in a novel that the leys were lines of power between standing stones. Thereafter, leys were linked to the field lines of the geomagnetic field of Earth. In the sixties, some UFO researchers linked leys to trajectories found in UFO sightings.[14]

Leys in Great Britain

Leys found in England, Scotland, and Ireland show an extreme diversity of megalithic artwork. To give an example of their richness, Ian

Taylor has completed an interesting study of leys and standing stones in the North York Moors in Yorkshire, and his article and photos have been posted on the website started by Devereux. He found eight leys and six standing stones covering an area of about twenty miles by twelve miles. The standing stones, as usual in megalithic leys, were set with their flat sides pointing to the direction of the ley they were on. Some of them showed a carved hole high up, a frequent feature in megaliths of Great Britain that experts believe was used for astronomical observation. In an earlier study, Taylor explored other parts of Yorkshire, but he is now working on this sacred site and has posted his preliminary results.

Impressive in Taylor's discovery is the number of markers on each ley: "Ley No. 5: 2 standing stones (one holed), 8 cairns, 1 mark stone, 2 springs. Passing by the hamlet of Beck Hole. Length: 13.75 miles. Ley No. 3: 1 tumulus, 2 standing stones, 2 cairns, 1 mark stone, 3 springs, 2 fords, and 2 churches. Passing by Danby and Kildale villages. Length: 19.5 miles."[15]

A point of interest to us is that beyond the cairns, tumuli, and prehistoric earthworks that mark the leys, more recent monuments—such as Roman sites, castles, and churches—are also perfectly aligned. Thus, along the eight leys Taylor describes, there are no less than four churches or chapels, two castle sites, two Roman sites, eighteen springs, fourteen cairns, five tumuli, and six fords. Ley 8 also crosses the well-known hill called Roseberry Topping, remarkable for its very unusual, large conical shape. This shows that the preliminary sacred network designed by the megaliths people was not only protected and revered, but also was made more complex by later cultures—just as is the case with Paris's sacred network.

What is also noteworthy in Taylor's mapping is the discovery that the crossings of ley lines show nearly geometric or at least regular structures. Some basic geometrical shapes resemble those I came across while mapping the sacred lines of Paris and of the region of Touraine-Centre in France. The difference is that whereas I generally hit upon extremely precise regular structures, Taylor's North York Moors leys are only nearly regular. For example, Taylor's ley 5 and especially ley 6 cross at near right angles to ley 4. Also, a quasi-regular shape is formed by the intersection of four lines (eight vectors) that somewhat delineate the outer lines of a imperfect Maltese cross (see figure 9.2, Maltese cross). By contrast, on Plaza Denfert-Rochereau there is a perfect intersection of four sacred lines—an embedded double cross formed by eight (4 x 2) vectors all interspaced by 22.5-degree angles. This quite-extended plaza is set upon an underground complex that was holy to the early Christians around the fourth century CE.

Taylor gives the rough date of post-2100 BCE for his group of leys, based on astronomical observations that could have been performed using the standing stones and especially their observation holes. Taylor specifies that these groups of leys are limited only to a county or tiny region and that other counties will have their own network of leys without connection to these. This is not of course the opinion of all researchers. In fact, a Michigan ley hunter arrived at the exact opposite conclusion. Doug Masselink has found that prehistoric sites were very precisely aligned across the state.[16] When he plotted their exact location with the use of a global positioning satellite (GPS) receiver, he noted that several Native American earthworks (circles and mounds) he found were situated on the exact same latitude or longitude as two or three other sites—sites that are sometimes as distant as the other end of the state. And that definitely points to alignments across vast regions, as we will see them in France, for example, with cathedrals reproducing the shape of constellations. Masselink plans to pursue his fieldwork into the state of Ohio, the center of the ancient Hopewell/Adena culture. Michigan's Native Americans still perform sacred rituals on these sites and revere their sacredness.

Continuous Expansion of Alignments and Megalithic Sites

We have clear-cut evidence that megalithic sites have been continuously expanded in various ages, which signifies that they have been used in different periods. Stonehenge, for example, shows three circular rows of stones, each one made of a different type of stone and built in a different period. The same is true for Carnac in Brittany and many other megalithic sites.

Carnac has the most striking megalithic alignments existing in France. The larger one is a slightly curved band of several lines of menhirs that runs northeast-southwest for 3.7 miles. It includes a covered alley (dolmen) and ends to the southwest, next to a circle of standing stones, a cromlech. On the summer solstice, the rising sun illuminates the whole alignment to the cromlech.

At Carnac, alignments are mostly longitudinal, some of them perfectly east-west and others northeast-southwest or the exact perpendicular, northwest-southeast. North-south alignments are extremely rare. At the site of Kermario, well known for its alignments, three menhirs are much more ancient than these alignments and are perpendicular to them. According to the specialist of megaliths, Jean Markale, these three standing stones are the sole remnants of a rare north-south alignment.[17] For Markale and several other specialists, the most ancient megaliths known up to now are dolmens with a covered passage that have been estimated to reach back as far as 5000 to 6000 BCE. They include a dolmen (a great stone table that tops a chamber), and this dolmen is accessed by a covered passage on which the entrance stones often show a sculpted goddess (a collar and two breasts). Some of the most beautiful examples of such dolmens are in the Eure and Epte valleys as well as in Brittany.

We thus have clear proof that in England as well as in Brittany, cairns and dolmens stand near other types of prehistoric works and megaliths of different antiquity. This means the sacredness of megaliths was continuously revered through the ages—which we can ascertain right away because we know that the Druids made sacred use of what were already millennia-old megalithic sacred sites and stones. In doing this, they no doubt kept alive the knowledge of sacred stones and alignments and their astonishing properties in terms of consciousness and health.

The Mont-Saint-Michel Sacred Line in Brittany

An extremely interesting Druidic-Christian alignment has been discovered in Brittany by Gwen Le Scouëzec, great Druid and eminent expert in Druidism, megaliths, and secret Brittany (See figure 7.1).[18]

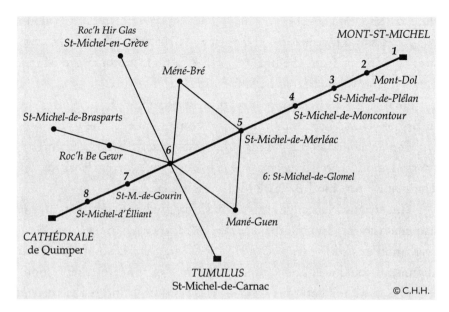

Figure 7.1. The St-Michel line in Brittany by Dr. Gwen Le Scouëzec. Reproduced through the courtesy of Gwen Le Scouëzec and Le Corps à Vivre Association. Digital artwork by Chris H. Hardy.

The straight line crosses Brittany from east to west and connects no less than eight sites dedicated to St. Michael, all of them on hilltops open to all directions, sometimes with breathtaking views, apart for one that stands a little below the summit. The line starts in the northeast, at the well-known sacred site Mont-Saint-Michel, with its magnificent abbey standing on a steep hill surrounded by the sea at high tide. The eighth site is St-Michel-d'Elliant. The line, however, does not end there: farther to the west, it passes through Quimper Cathedral. The line thus traverses about 130 miles. Eastward, it is aligned with the rising sun on May 1 (the Celtic feast of Beltane), and to the west, with the setting sun on November 1 (the Celtic feast of Samhain, at the end of summer).

Investigating the whole region, Le Scouëzec found additional alignments linked to the archangel. A near-perfect perpendicular line links St-Michel-en-Grève to the gigantic St-Michel tumulus (or cairn) in Carnac, with this line crossing the long St-Michel line slightly east of the sixth site (St-Michel-de Glomel). Then a perfect diamond or rhombus appears, linking the fifth and sixth St-Michel sites (the node) to two sites equidistant from the line: Méné-Bré (a high summit) and Mané-Guen, or the White Sacred Mountain in Breton.

Finally, the second most important site dedicated to St. Michael in Brittany—St-Michel-de-Brasparts—is on an oblique line to the center (St-Michel-de-Glomel). This line passes exactly by another highly charged mount near Huelgoat: Roc'h Be Gewr, or the Rock of the Tomb of Gheor, another name for the giant Gargan.

This magnificent alignment is thus expressed by a similarity in the names of the sites, most of them related to St. Michael. In my sense, however, another striking feature of this St-Michel line, beyond the spatial alignment, could well be the time alignment—or time superimposition.

The most ancient time layer of the St-Michel line is that of the megaliths. We have two megalithic sites on the line: first a very ancient tumulus in Carnac (a region abounding in megaliths), and second the megaliths that were standing on the hilltop of Mont-Saint-Michel. The medium time layer involves pagan and Celtic cults that existed before the Christian religion took over: there are still traces of a Mithraic cult (bull worship) at Mont-Saint-Michel, and the rock at St-Michel-en-Grève (Roc'h Hir Glas) was a well-known pagan site, and according to a local legend, a magical treasure is hidden there. Moreover, explains Le Scouëzec, two places were Celtic high sites: both St-Michel-de-Montcontour and Roc'h Be Gewr are surrounded by sacred sites (the latter has sacred sites disposed in a circle around it).

The third time layer is that of the Christian St. Michael. There are two major St. Michael shrines: the magnificent abbey of Mont-Saint-Michel and St-Michel-de-Brasparts. In addition, there is the cathedral of Quimper and a church in the village of St-Michel-de-Plélan. Finally, there are three chapels: one at the tip of Mont-Dol, ruins of a second one on the mount of St-Michel-de-Merléac, and a third one standing at midhill at St-Michel-de-Glomel, where, moreover, a cross was standing on top of the hill. Altogether, for the Christian layer: three high sites, four churches or chapels, and one cross.

Following up with Le Scouëzec's discovery, Court-Payen lengthened the St-Michel line toward Normandy and found two additional St-Michel sites and a menhir.[19] Both authors have discovered that the name Mont-Saint-Michel was given to mounts previously called Mont-Mercure or Mont-Hermes—sites dedicated to the Roman god Mercury or Hermes in Greek mythology—and before that these sites were called Mont-Belen, dedicated to the god Belen, the god of light at the age of the megaliths people.

Court-Payen traced a complex network of lines over the whole of Europe, connecting sites linked not only to St. Michael, but also to the light (*luz* in Latin; its derivations include Lux, Lucie, Lucia, etc.). An interesting one is the line connecting Mont-Saint-Michel in France to Saint-Michael's Mount in England, at the extreme tip of Cornwall (near Penzance). This line, to the south, runs through several eminent spiritual sites, such as Vierzon's cathedral, Bourges' cathedral, Sept-Fons Abbey, St-Michel-de-Maurienne, and Castel Saint-Ange in Rome.

Urban Alignments

If alignments can go back as far as four or five thousand years, they have also shown an impressive resilience up to the present day. The implementation of this principle of energy lines has extended to urban architecture, right up to the most recent architectural complexes. Paris offers a good example of this alignment principle with La Défense, the business quarter near Paris, or the famous glass pyramids of the Louvre.

It is immediately evident for any lover of architecture that Paris is built along a main east-west axis whose perspective is breathtaking: it passes through the Louvre, the Arc de Triomphe of Carrousel, the Concorde Obelisk, the Arc de Triomphe of L'Etoile, and the Grande Arche of La Défense. Because this axis 1 is the preeminent alignment in present-day Paris, I use the ancient Roman name *decumanus* and call it West Decumanus, or axis 1. (See West Decumanus—starting at A and ending at B—in plate 1: Main axes and leys in Paris.)*

---

*Note that in plate 1 all the axes and leys are marked at each end with A and B, wherein A is showing where the line starts and B is where it ends. For a detailed description of major axes and leys, see appendix 1.

Soon after Julius Caesar vanquished Vercingetorix in 52 BCE and thus conquered Gaul, the Romans installed themselves on the left bank of Paris—the Latin Quarter, south of the Seine river—while the city of the Parisii was mainly on the core island on the Seine (the actual Ile de la Cité). The Parisii were an ancient Gallic people whose domain was separated at Rambouillet from the Carnutes Gauls established in Chartres, Orléans, Blois, and the center of France.

Under the Roman Empire, the city became Lutecia Parisii, or Ile de Lutèce. The Romans brought into the newly named Lutecia (from the latin *lucis,* "light") their principles of urban architecture—that is, two major perpendicular axes: *decumanus maximus* and *cardo maximus* (nowadays called *decumanus* and *cardo*). The ancient Roman cardo is slightly east of Châtelet Plaza and cardo; it's perpendicular to the East Decumanus at St-Jacques Tower (see node S in figure 9.4, page 219). Long before the Roman conquest, however, the actual Châtelet Plaza was already marking the first-ever wooden bridge built on the Seine at l'Ile de la Cité, thus making it a core node of the ancient city, as is exemplified by the magnificent ten-pointed star centered on that very node. Under Napoleon I and Napoleon III, with the design of new avenues and quarters, a new node was created at the Obelisk, on Concorde Plaza. Like Châtelet Plaza, the Obelisk is situated on the West Decumanus, and so is the Arc de Triomphe of L'Etoile. This is why I called the axis perpendicular to the West Decumanus at Concorde the Obelisk Cardo, and the one at Etoile Plaza the Etoile Cardo (see these cardos in plate 1).

Yet the research on prehistoric leys shows that the Romans often placed their roads over previous Celtic thoroughfares. It is attested that Iron Age Britons used chariots and that, consequently, suitable roads for cartwheel traffic existed prior to the Roman conquest and the Roman creation of new roads. Indeed, traces of ancient paved roads have been found underneath Roman ways.[20] Furthermore, Roman ways in many instances follow the prehistoric leys that connect, in straight lines, megalithic standing stones. It is very probable, then, that the city of the Parisii, which had a busy port and a powerful community of sailors (the Nautes), already had Celtic roads and axes on which the Romans built their large paved avenues.

What is astonishing is that in the two-millennium span of time that we can historically assess—from the early Gallic and Roman city of the first century CE (with its huge Nautes Pillar erected at the very site of the actual cathedral) to late-twentieth-century democratic Paris (with astounding buildings such as the Louvre's glass pyramids)—all the governing leaders, whether Gallic chiefs, Roman emperors, kings of France, emperors, or presidents, have respected the fundamental sacred network of Paris and France, its sacred geometry and orientation. Indeed, respect of this network involves much more than straight alignment, which could be attributed to pragmatism and a simple predilection for order on the part of these leaders. The crucial point is that fundamental principles of sacred geometry are involved in this network: the symbolism of forms and the golden proportion, the reality of which has a clear demonstration in stone on the facades of cathedrals. There is more, however: the design of the constellation Virgo is expressed through the locations of eight cathedrals in and around Paris whose names all start with the words Notre Dame—the Virgin.

The evidence we can gather from alignments and architectural axes, as well as from the choice of locations to insure precise global patterns, makes it rather clear that the sacred network has been the Great Work of organized groups of professionals who have had a plan and a purpose. We know that one of them, the Compagnons, had a huge impact on the building of Gothic cathedrals.

THE CATHEDRAL BUILDERS

It was early in the fourteenth century that the Compagnons guild was created. From then on, they took over the task of building cathedrals and churches. A veil of mystery, however, lingers on earlier times. We can recall that as early as the fourth century both Chartres and Paris had built the primary version of their cathedral.

Astonishingly, in the early twelfth century, just at the start of the Gothic age, the church handed to secular entrepreneurs the building of cathedrals and churches. This is surprising because so many orders of monks were building their own monasteries that one of them could easily have been assigned the building of all Catholic churches and cathedrals. The Cistercian order, for example, boosted by Bernard de Clairvaux, built numerous new monasteries in their own traditional-ist style, which was seemingly impervious to the Gothic architectural revolution that was taking place. The Cistercians even opposed the so-called luxury deployed by the Cluny order, which was supportive of the new Gothic style. As we will see, however, the personality of Bernard de Clairvaux—head of the Cistercian order and author of austere theologi-cal treatises, but also writer of an eulogy of the Templar order and of their Rule, and who exercised immense political clout in the major royal courts—seems complex and multilayered enough to make us ponder its apparent contradictions.

In the Middle Ages, the monks at the monasteries produced whatever they needed, copying tons of manuscripts, using calligraphy and illumi-nations. In this way, they internalized whole libraries of books—not only Christian texts, but also Greek and medieval philosophy and science—thus carrying the knowledge of the time. Two Cistercian abbeys—the abbey of Cîteaux and the abbey of Clairvaux (founded in 1115 by Bernard, hereafter referred to as de Clairvaux, who was promoted to be its first abbot)—were devoted to translating Hebrew and Muslim texts brought back from the Crusades by the Knights Templar. The École de Chartres was the predominant center for scholastic philosophy until the founding of Paris University in 1215. The ecole flourished under the influence of Bishop Fulbert (around 1000 CE), who after the burning of the Carolingian cathedral, supervised the construction of the crypt (the Fulbert Crypt, which still exists) and the Roman-style cathedral (mostly destroyed). Yet after peaking under the exceptional leadership of Bishop Jean de Salisbury (the ancient secretary of Bishop Thomas Becket in Canterbury), the École de Chartres was already in decline at the time of the cathedral's great burning in 1194, which triggered the construction of the Gothic cathedral that is practically unchanged today.

Let us look in more depth at the Compagnons order. It seemed to be a secular guild, but in fact it was organized as a secret society that had its own secret knowledge of the building arts—the *secrets du métier,* the craftsmen's professional secrets. The order of the Compagnons comprised the entire spectrum of the diverse crafts (or *corps de métiers*) that were necessary to build a sacred edifice: stone carvers, wood carvers, masons, and so forth. At the top of this hierarchical structure were of course the architects, who planned the ensemble of the buildings: their location, positioning, and global architecture.

Though the Compagnons were divided into many crafts (painted glass, formation of arches, creation of rose windows, carving, geometrical design, etc.), all members were versed in symbolism, the golden proportion, and holy texts. The apprentices were sent all over France to learn with masters, one after the other, so that they acquired firsthand knowledge of the many crafts necessary to building a church. At the end of their apprenticeship, they chose which craft they were going to pursue as a profession and, subsequently, had to accomplish a masterpiece in order to attain the degree of Compagnon. Some of these masterpieces can be seen in the museums of cathedrals—in Chartres, for example. In his masterpiece, the Compagnon had to show his mastery of the specific craft he had chosen and of sacred geometry based on the golden proportion. He also had to master symbolism in all its facets—symbolism of numbers, geometry, allegoric figures, myth, and more—and had to evidence in his work his knowledge of holy scriptures. During his *tour de France,* he would visit many sacred sites and temples of knowledge, where he was able to contemplate the works of masters of the past, whether in reality or through reproductions—for example, the works of Greek and Egyptian architecture. All of these facts can be gathered through the many books on the Compagnons and cathedral builders.

According to some sources, the order of Compagnons was created by Jacques de Molay, grand master of the Templars, when he sensed the Knights' order was in great danger. In fact, a whole month passed between September 14, 1307, when King Philippe the Fair decided to arrest the Knights, and the arrests conducted all over France by the king's armies on October 13, 1307 (during which time, de Molay was arrested). Another seven years passed before the burning of de Molay and three other high dignitaries of the Templar order in Paris in 1314, following the dissolution of the Templar order by Pope Clement V in 1312.

We also know, however, that several new secret societies were created between 1312 and 1316, and that numerous Templars joined them. We must remember that the Templars were arrested and persecuted only in France. In other countries, they were either unmolested or were recognized as innocent through trials. Yet, because the Templar order was abolished worldwide, all Knights, whatever their nationality, either affiliated with other already existing orders or created new ones.

We can clearly decipher that artwork adorning the cathedrals made reference to much more than the strict Catholic orthodoxy (above and beyond the fact that this orthodoxy had been evolving through the centuries). We find, for example, allusions to diverse initiatic knowledge systems, such as Greek sacred geometry (the Pythagorean school), alchemy, and so forth. This distance from strict orthodoxy is one more sign that cathedrals and churches were built by a secret society that had a certain independence and a perspective on sacred knowledge that reached further back in space and time than the Catholic framework. As for the handing down of this tradition, we might note, as an example, a secret society such as the Freemasons, whose name and evident knowledge of sacred architecture and symbolism suggest a connection to the builders of cathedrals. The Freemasons might have been the corporation of architects and philosophers who oversaw the lesser corporations of diverse crafts necessary for building. (The Compagnons still exist as an order, and it trains apprentices in diverse crafts, following the tradition.) Freemasonry has several branches and exists all over the planet; furthermore, its members are allowed to belong to more than one secret society. A persistant rumor hints at the existence of a very mysterious group whose specific mission is to keep open the interconnection, not only among various Freemasonry lodges and branches, but also with other secret societies. All this would then happen above and beyond the continuous petty or nasty wars waged among secret societies or lodges to control the levers of power. Can this mysterious group's mission imply more than just communication, and extend to supervising? Theosophy and the esoteric lore state the existence of a higher-order organization—called the Hierarchy—leading the spiritual development on Earth, and therefore all initiatic societies, and whose *Unknown Masters* would be immortals. But are they? As far as the sacred network is concerned, and just on the basis of the objective, geoarchitectural proofs we can observe, we can be certain that for centuries at least one group has been in control of a global plan—at the very least for all matters linked to the planning of cities and the architecture of major buildings, even civil ones. And that means quite a large and powerful organization or leader who acted and directed major architectural planning without the far-reaching aim being known to civil society: a "grey eminence."

With respect to the French sacred network, who are the most likely candidates for the grey eminences responsible for the sacred architecture? We can refer to Napoleon I, who was instrumental in enriching Paris with masterpieces of sacred architecture, such as the Arc de Triomphe of Carrousel and the planning of the Arc de Triomphe of L'Etoile, both precisely located on the major axis of Paris and incorporating clear initiatic symbolism. He pompously supported a resurgence of the Templar order, initiated by Bernard-Raymond Fabré-Palaprat. Fabré-Palaprat's claim of a direct affiliation with the apparently defunct order is far from accepted by all experts, but we know, however, that Napoleon gave him a powerful hand in organizing a grand ceremony to memorialize de Molay in a church in Paris on March 28, 1808, the anniversary of de Molay's burning. Another likely candidate in the twelfth century is the complex and rather strange figure of St. Bernard: he defined and wrote the Templars' rule while fustigating the luxury of Gothic style, and yet he is supposedly the unknown architect of Chartres cathedral.

WORLDWIDE CONNECTIONS
AMONG SACRED SITES

Many large towns in France have been built around similar decumanus and cardo axes, which may have been constructed on previous Celtic ways. These axes do not seem to end at the limits of towns, however; rather, they follow energy lines that connect them to other major towns or that link sacred buildings between them at great distance, such as the sacred lines between cathedrals that delineate the Virgo constellation.

The knowledge about axes passing through main sacred sites, or of geometrical structures linking them, was only hinted at in older books on megaliths, Druidic sites, and sacred geography—for example, on Jean Phaure's maps.[21] Now, however, there is a trend to decipher the arcane interconnection between grand cosmo-telluric sites that have been revered as sacred by most religions and faiths.

Several authors are now researching great circles or circle routes that turn around Earth and pass major high sites of diverse cultures. They use GPS receivers and sophisticated mathematical tools to calculate the coordinates of monuments and the circles around the globe (which must have Earth's core as center). Their precise mappings suggest that holy sites all over the world are energetically interconnected. Jim Alison made a remarkable discovery in finding a great circle that connects many ancient high sites: it runs exactly through major magnificent sacred sites such as Giza, Easter Island, Nazca, Ollantaytambo (near Cuzco), Paratoari, and Tassili n'Ajjer.[22] Aligned within one-tenth of one degree with this line are Petra, Perseopolis, Khajuraho, Pyay, Sukothai, and Anatom Island; aligned within one-quarter of one degree are the Peruvian sacred sites of Cuzco and Machu Picchu, the Indus Valley sites of Mohenjo Daro and Ganweriwala, and the Oracle at Siwa in Egypt. Angkor temples are one degree from the circle, apart from the pure jewel temple of Preah Vihear, which stands at one-quarter of a degree.*

Yet how could such an interconnection have been in existence since ancient times, when sacred sites belong to widely different cultures and time frames? There are two possible explanations: the first, which we have already discovered, is that architectural planning was undertaken by a secret society and according to sacred geometry. This would explain sophisticated regional designs such as the Templar geo-architecture of Bornholm or the cathedrals that form the design of constellations in northern France. In no way, however, can it explain the very ancient sites or the sites held most sacred by each particular religion. The second explanation, able to account for worldwide energetic connections,

---

*The information on Jim Alison's website is exhaustive and includes marvelous photos: http://home.hiwaay.net/~jalison (accessed June 16, 2010).

is that most ancient traditions made use of the lines of the geomagnetic field of Earth and of ancient leys built during the Neolithic, Bronze, and Iron Ages. The crossings of major field lines could have been used for building temples, given that the energy at these crossings is very strong and has an uplifting and spiritualizing influence on human consciousness. Remember that megalithic sites, held sacred through the ages, have been used for rituals and have been continuously expanded in a time frame that covers millennia.

It could be that wise men of the ancient civilizations everywhere on Earth (whether shamans, priests, monks, seers, or ascetics) had the gift of sensing or seeing these energy lines. They must have been able to detect and mark the places of power that the Mexican Yaqui sorcerer Don Juan talks of in Carlos Castaneda's books. They must have marked minor crossings of ley lines with simple altars, sacred trees, standing stones, or small temples. At the crucial crossings of major cosmo-telluric lines, they built gigantic temples and sacred sites, such as Stonehenge and Carnac, Angkor Wat, Teotihuacán, Borobudur, Ellora, the Cairo pyramids, and, more recently, cathedrals, great abbeys, and castles.

We have proof of that knowledge in Chinese geomancy, or Feng Shui: by using this age-old science, Feng Shui masters can perceive, know, and map precisely the *paths of the dragon* (or *lung mei*). This science states that lung mei crisscross each other and turn around Earth. It is said that ancient monuments have been erected at the sites where several of them converge. In 1947, in the province of Shensi, near the ancient Chinese capital of Sian (Xian), a pilot spotted about a hundred pyramids of various sizes. Most of them seem to be about three thousand years old, yet some could reach back to 6000 BCE. Satellite photos show magnificent, huge pyramids, and according to witnesses, some are aligned. Should this be confirmed, the site could be considered a point of convergence of *lung mei*. Japan has a similar body of knowledge, and its own experts that are called in for any architectural project.

We find such a convergence of multiple leys in other sacred sites around the world. In the state of New Mexico, there exist absolutely straight lines that converge on (or radiate around) Chaco Canyon, the most sacred site of the Anasazi, who were the ancestors of the Hopi and Zuni Indians. We have several examples of straight, prehistoric leys that show a converging (or radiating) structure in local networks. Moreover, we can note converging (or radiating) rays around the two central energetic nodes of Paris, the Obelisk and Châtelet Plaza, rays that create the marvelous star structures of Paris's sacred network (see the regular spikes forming (out of center G) the hexagon in plate 4 and the double pentagram in plate 6).

Let us ponder the hypothesis that sages, Druids, and shamans of ancient civilizations were indeed able to see and understand the laws of cosmo-telluric flows and energies as well as their influence on human consciousness. We can consider that they used this knowledge for building sacred sites or temples on the crossings, which were charged with a highly beneficial energy—places in which telluric energies (Earth) and cosmic energies (spirit) meet harmoniously. If we consider that this abstract knowledge can be transmitted even when the gifts of seeing and sensing are receding, then the initiates receiving such transmitted knowledge would protect the sacred sites they already knew of and would keep constructing on and around them. As we have seen, this has precisely been the case throughout time: the exact places where sacred altars are situated don't change over time, even when new faiths replace ancient ones. And that, retrospectively, gives weight to our hypothesis.

This gift of sensing positive telluric spots has been attributed to the Templars. Lynn Picknett and Clive Prince cite two researchers who investigated the Templar sites in the Pyrénées mountains. They state that the two researchers found documents showing that the Templars possessed a deep knowledge of Earth and were very careful about the locales on which they constructed. In one case, they had to buy land in order to build a hospital, and they chose a soil that had curative properties.[23]

We also know, from the magnificent network of round churches built by the Templars on Bornholm Island that they precisely chose the locales of these churches in order to form global sacred structures. Henry Lincoln and Erling Haagensen have sorted out a pentagram that points toward the famous Rennes le Château in the south of France (where a Templar and Priory of Sion treasure is said to be hidden) and is also connected to Jerusalem.[24] Moreover, they have unveiled another set of structures that includes a Star of David. Haagensen studied Osterlars, which has only two opposing tiny windows on its third floor, and the axis that links them passes through a hole in the central pillar. He discovered that on the winter solstice, one window is illuminated by the first ray of the rising sun, and the sunrays follow the axis.[25] With Bornholm, we thus have confirmation of a Templar geo-architecture that used groups of oriented monuments to form global symbolic structures and that was also oriented according to astronomical events.

TWO HUGE TELLURIC CURRENTS

Being naturally sensitive to cosmo-telluric lines, I am able both to feel the energy and see the lines crossing space. On two occasions I felt and saw extra-large cosmo-telluric lines: the first in the south of France, in the vicinity of Cannes, and the second on the campus of Rutgers University in New Jersey. Both were about the same size: huge tubes of energy of about 1.20 yards in diameter. The one at Cannes was slightly above ground, its base about eight inches above the pavement. Where I saw it, in a suburban area, it came from the direction of a cement courtyard and crossed a small street perpendicularly. The one at Rutgers ran through a large expanse of lawn, and at the spot where I saw it, it touched ground. I was attending a scientific conference and knew my friends and colleagues would be skeptical if they were to receive an unsubstantiated piece of information. At the same time, I thought that such a phenomenal cosmo-telluric line offered a unique occasion for them; it was so large that some of them should be able to sense it, even if unconsciously. I decided that I had to conceive of a test that would satisfy their minds bent on science. After some pondering, I told them there existed a huge telluric current out there, and if some people were interested in a blind test, they should come with me. I then took them, one by one, some thirty yards away, placed them right in the middle of the flow, and instructed them to lie on the grass and move their body in all directions until they felt which axis was most comfortable. I figured that the body would naturally sense this energy and feel comfortable only in one direction, the axis of the flow, and, contrarily, would feel great discomfort when lying sideways across the cosmo-telluric line—which I knew could disturb sleep, even with a normal-sized line that was about one-fourth the size of this one. With such a huge line, I was quite certain they would be able to consciously "hear" their own bodily sensations if they tried to align themselves with it. Indeed, all of them did finally set their bodies in the direction of the flow. Of the five or six scientists, no one missed it.

The architecture of the university building used for our evening gatherings was at odds with the cosmo-telluric line (something that would never happen in France): the building was set across the line but did not face it. A house set sideways in this way can generate health problems for its residents beyond the disturbing of sleep—especially with such a strong current. When I discovered the line earlier that day, I sat in the middle of the flow (facing its source) and concentrated on it. I felt it reached, a few hundreds miles to the north, into an ancient Native American sacred spot. The name I heard was Cherokee Lake. When, later, I was able to check it on a map showing the whole of America, I didn't expect this ancient Indian name would appear there, but I was happy to see that the Cherokees lived in that region.

Undulating Telluric Lines

The portion of the Cannes line that I saw was slightly oscillating, while the Rutgers line was more stable, but was also nearest to the ground at that spot. I believe the change in height is due to the fact that these geomagnetic lines (which of course have a wavelength) are undulating vertically. At one point, a wave is at ground level, and then the wave ascends to describe an elongated arc. At the other end of this arc, it touches the ground again and then follows another arc, plunging into the ground and then rising back to ground level. Thus the undulation goes upward (a half wavelength) then downward under the surface (a half wavelength), on and on. (See figure 7.2.)

In neither of these two occasions did I have the idea of following the actual path of the cosmo-telluric line on the ground. If it was impos-

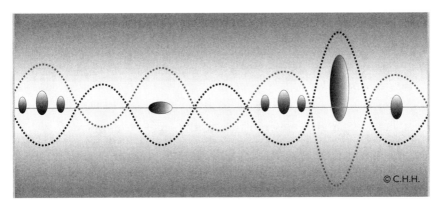

Figure 7.2. Vertical cosmo-telluric lines undulating aboveground and belowground. Digital artwork by Chris H. Hardy.

sible in France (due to the presence of houses all around), it would have been easy on the large, grassy campus. In following it, I would have had a chance to check on its vertical undulation and get a better idea of its height from the ground at the apex of the arc and its wavelength.

We have, however, information that supports this idea in Chinese Feng Shui since the path of the dragon is said to be undulating. Attracted by the crest of mountains, it turns around Earth. This is the yang telluric energy. In contrast, the feminine, or yin, telluric energy moves in straight lines. The harmonious meeting of these two energies is said to happen on mounds or knolls sitting in valleys. Of course, it's impossible not to think about the sacredness and power the Druids ascribed to mounds.

THE INTERLACING OF DIFFERENT TYPES OF ENERGY

To understand how initiates of all cultures made use of our planetary geomagnetic field, we must imagine more than a crisscrossing of the field lines on the surface of Earth. Two interlaced electromagnetic grids have been discovered and tested by specialists. The Hartmann Grid (H Grid) is a crisscrossing of geomagnetic field lines at very regular intervals, oriented north-south and east-west. According to some authors, it forms squares of about one and a half yards, but others say it describes rectangular shapes of about six and a half feet in the north-south axis by eight feet in the east-west axis. The Curry Grid (C Grid), said to be "geoelectrical" and oriented north-west and south-east, runs diagonally to the Hartmann Grid. Its square sides are said to be about six yards at the equator and three to four yards in northern countries.* These two grids, however, bear no resemblance to the sacred network we speak of here. In fact, the H and C Grids are as regular as checkerboards (the Curry is superimposed diagonally on the Hartmann), and most of their crossings are of two lines (four rays), with an absolute maximum of four lines (eight rays). Furthermore, their lines are flat on the surface of Earth. In total contrast, the sacred network shows crossings of eight, ten, or more cosmo-telluric lines. As a result of these complex crossings, the sacred network resembles a neuronal network that links together complex 3-D pyramids, stars, and rose windows—a far cry from a regular checkerboard. Furthermore, both the H and C Grids are fine and small; the distance between field lines is much too small to fit the energy flow that connects sacred monuments. Therefore, it's likely that H and C Grids have little to do with the sacred lines.

The telluric grid that has been used to define the locales of sacred buildings consists of large telluric lines showing undulating flows and a tubelike shape of a diameter that varies from 1 foot to 1.20 yards. Furthermore, these lines undulate vertically—going belowground and then surging aboveground—and keep turning around the planet. In regions that are still wild and free, the desert for example, I estimate that their half wavelength (an arc or arcade) is about six hundred or seven hundred yards. The peak of the arcs rises about six to seven yards aboveground, and the wave then plunges about the same depth belowground. In their wild state (unfixed by stones or buildings), the field lines that compose the grid constantly oscillate with local variations of the geomagnetic field due to a host of factors such as pressure and magnetic storms, but also astronomical events such as sunspot activity. An abrupt change could make the line move a few yards horizontally from

---

*I merely report the information I've found in books, for I never saw or experienced these Hartmann and Curry Grids, and unfortunately, each specialist seems to offer a different measurement.

its normal course, and the line later would return to its normal mean path of flow.

To my knowledge, it's at important points of junction of the field lines that sacred sites have always been consecrated, whether by revering the place as a "sacred forest" (as in tropical and equatorial Africa) or by erecting standing stones or temples. In Europe, it's at the lines' crossings that standing stones were erected by the megaliths people (from 6000–5000 BCE to 2000 BCE, during the Neolithic Age and into the Bronze Age). It's also at these crossings that Druids had their sacred gathering places above mounds or in clearings (*nemetons*) in Celtic times (2000 BCE to about 50 BCE in France). In addition, at these same spots, the Greeks and Romans constructed temples, and, later, the Christians built churches or, in the south and east of Europe, the Muslims erected mosques.

Four Effects of Erecting Stones at the Crossing Points of Leys

Erecting stones or temples at crossing points enhances the natural energy of the place and, together with specific rituals and prayers, heightens the consciousness of people. In fact, it has four definite effects on the natural wild grid itself.

1. The first is to fix or anchor the line on the specific spot. Because telluric lines are magnetic energy lines, they are naturally subjected to minor variations and oscillations while running on the surface of Earth and around the globe. Erecting a standing stone at a crossing point drives the magnetic flow into this needle that punctures Earth, just as an acupuncture needle drives the chi energy into a specific spot on the body. In fact, it is worth noting that in the Chinese language, the same word meaning "well" is used both for acupuncture points and for strong telluric spots, "the wells of the Earth."

When a church or a temple is built on a crossing point, the incoming field lines—arriving as ascending or descending arcs of energy—are attracted by the highest point of these buildings (the steeple or the top of a dome), and they move toward that point, following the field lines of the architecture, upward or downward. The smaller the attraction point on the architecture, the more precisely the sacred line is anchored to that building.

2. The second effect (directly derived from the fact that energy lines follow a building's architecture) is that the lines will rise above the high point of the building in arcs that arrive at or spring from a megalith or temple—and that's high indeed, when we talk about the Eiffel Tower or the Tower of Pisa!

As a result of Effect 1 and Effect 2, the undulating lines make a U-shape in dense, urban networks with many tall buildings.

3. In addition to these telluric lines, there exist cosmic rays that hit Earth and can be attracted or fixed through any antenna-shaped monument, whether a standing stone, steeple, or tower. Cosmic energy is also naturally attracted by tall trees and mountain peaks, which is why very old and large trees are revered in many cultures, such as those in India and Japan, and by the Indians in the Americas. Mountains peaks are also deemed sacred in many cultures, and this is why they are often places of choice for setting temples and the rituals of cults.
4. Finally, these energy lines are imprinted and strengthened by the semantic energy generated by people who pray there and by the shamans and artists who conceived and constructed these buildings. With the passing of time, some telluric lines and of course their crossings become highly charged with semantic energy and spirituality.

All these forces together create the specific sacredness of a sacred site in a given place and culture. This is why we call the web that connects sacred buildings the sacred network. There is definitely an interlacing of three types of energy: the planetary geomagnetic field (EM spectrum) is charged with cosmic energy and, moreover, is imprinted with the semantic energy generated by the consciousnesses of people—

which, I propose, belongs to a different energy spectrum, the syg-energy spectrum.

As we have seen, telluric lines in the sacred network are vertical waves undulating aboveground and belowground. Only the biggest waves—scalar waves of huge proportions, such as those I witnessed in Cannes and New Jersey—keep turning around the planet. Because their undulation is vertical, they appear as nearly straight lines on regional maps—the curve of Earth showing only on a larger scale. As for smaller field lines (with shorter wavelengths), they assume a U shape when they are running across monuments in dense cities. In deserted lands, however, their undulations are much smoother, and they run low on Earth's surface unless a standing stone or a building makes them spring up. It is possible that the properties of these two types of lines—huge, planetary scalar waves and smaller field lines—differ, as Feng Shui states clearly. The Chinese experts distinguish two types of telluric waves. The first one, as we have seen, the path of the dragon, is male and yang and moves in undulations; the other, yin, proceeds in straight lines. The dragon lines are said always to pass along the peaks of hills and mountains, and the yin lines follow the valleys.

The leys investigated at prehistoric sites (such as the ones found by Ian Taylor and described earlier) fit the description of long, undulating, crisscrossing waves, whereas they do not match the description of H or C Grid lines. In effect, their various types of crossings include multiple rays radiating like spokes of a wheel from a single central node, and this specific feature is nowhere to be found in H and C Grids. As for the fields of menhirs found in Carnac, they comprise several parallel lines and may run for about one and a half mile, and the distance between stones is generally about 2.5 yards. Markale has found out that these alignments show a slight curving, forming a crescent shape, at two places in the vast site of Carnac: in Kermario, for example, there are ten rows and more than 900 stones (most of them were lying down and have been picked up), covering 1,250 yards in length and 100 yards in width. The direction is grossly east-west, with a crescent shape set from north-northeast to south-southwest. In the second case, Kerlescan (on the eastern side of the site of Carnac), there are thirteen lines covering 963 yards in length and 152 yards in width and totaling 240 stones; their curvature goes from north-northeast to west-southwest with a concavity at the northwest. Markale notes that though the space between the two sites is actually covered by pine trees, traces of alignments are still visible and are marked by smaller stones. Speaking of the Kermario alignment (in which one menhir shows carvings of serpents) and its extension, he remarks, "This suite of alignments goes *over* a more ancient knoll, that of Manio, crowned by a menhir presenting also at its base serpent-shape signs. . . . Yet according to scientific studies, the knoll—and the menhir—of Manio are two thousand years older than the alignments."[26] The oldest dolmens in Carnac, such as the one sitting near the famous Tumulus Saint-Michel (a cairn) are dated around 4000 BCE, early Neolithic. This great Saint-Michel cairn of 125 yards, which, as we saw, is part of the Saint-Michel line discovered by Le Scouëzec, is a man-made mound with about ten chambers underneath built at different epochs, two of which are evident necropolises.

If this type of curving is corroborated by GPS, does it suggest that large cosmo-telluric lines, undulating vertically, also present some (even if slight) horizontal undulation, in accordance with Chinese Feng Shui? Perhaps the omnipresent design of snakes on megaliths and in so many ancient cultures represents the snakelike winding of cosmo-telluric lines.

Markale, despite his sensitivity for the sacred and for invisible realms—realms whose access doors, according to Breton legends, are only open on specific dates and at these ancient sacred sites—concludes: "The fact of deliberately going over a sacred knoll to pursue the alignments supposes, on the part of the builders of alignments, a kind of rejection, if not a disdain, toward older sanctuaries."[27] In my opinion, for the megaliths people to set new standing stones in more ancient alignments is just the opposite of a rejection: it rather exemplifies how the worldview and knowledge about cosmo-telluric forces and other dimensions of reality was perpetrated through the millennia. It also shows that this knowledge must have been central to the multi-millennia megalithic civilization in order to inspire the erection of megaliths along the same principles, and that people belonging to different millennia and devoted to this sacred task shared a perfect concordance of goals. The sacred constructions at different epochs were intentionally centered on the same sacred nodes, following and harnessing the very same lines of force in the cosmo-telluric network.

Vertical Undulations, A Spots, and G Spots

If we imagine telluric lines as vertical undulations, their effect on consciousness is easy to discern. But first, let's call the undulation a *high arc* whenever a cosmo-telluric line surges from the ground and makes an arc above ground; and let's call it a *deep arc* whenever a cosmo-telluric line plunges into the ground and makes an arc below the ground. The energy of a high arc is uplifting, connecting with cosmic forces, while the energy of a deep arc is grounding, harmonizing with Earth. Any crossing of two or more telluric lines, if such crossings occur at the peak of arcs or at their dip, will have a powerful effect and will be highly beneficial for the mind as well as for the body.

We thus have two main types of crossings of telluric lines. (See plate 2: A Spot and G Spot at crossings of cosmo-telluric lines.)

1. The crossing happens aboveground (at the peak of the curves of two high arcs), and it creates an *ascending energy,* which we can call an A Spot.
2. The crossing happens belowground (at the dip of the curves of two deep arcs), and it creates a *grounding energy,* which we can call a G Spot.

Now, if you look at the global shape created by the lines meeting aboveground at an A Spot, does it remind you of something you might have seen at a magnificent megalithic site? It did for one of my friends who used to live not too far from this site. She exclaimed, "It's just like Silbury Hill! It's such a strange shape—nobody has any explanation for it!" Silbury Hill is less high than our A Spot model (see plate 2), but the shape of the hill is strikingly similar, with its spectacular and rare flattened top—which also appears on Mayan and Aztec pyramids. Further, if, keeping in mind that this is a man-made mount, you scrutinize diverse photos of Silbury Hill, you will detect that, at its base, there are several near-straight sides. I believe that the trajectory of the sides, if extended, would show the direction of several lines crisscrossing at the hill, resembling the four crossing lines (eight vectors) at Aigue-Vive abbey. (The lines at Aigue-Vive abbey are marked by an octagonal steeple.) This Silbury-type A-Spot shape is exactly what occurs whenever crisscrossing leys have a long, five-hundred–yard half-length, as I believe is generally the case in the countryside. In dense towns, the cosmo-telluric lines are higher, U-shaped, and shortened, due to the effect of high monuments.

BACK TO MEGALITHS

At the major crossings of lines, the ancient people from the Neolithic Age generally erected megaliths. In France, we don't have as many types of remnants from prehistoric times as there are in Great Britain. Earthworks, designs on the ground, and moats—if there were any—practically don't exist in France anymore. Now, as far as megaliths are concerned (in the strict etymological sense of *huge stone*), there are two predominant and well-defined types, each one with variants.

Menhirs

The first type of megalith, called a *menhir,* is an erected stone—a huge block two to six yards high, a gross parallelogram with round angles, or an egg-shaped block. In France, there are some menhirs of exceptional height. The menhir of Kerloas, or Kervéatous (Plouarzel, Finistère), sitting high up on the 410-foot-high Léon Plateau and dominating the sea and all surroundings, was the tallest menhir still upright in the eighteenth century. It measures 31.17 feet, which is less high than it had been because its top was broken by lightning, and researchers estimate that earlier it was more than 32.8 feet. The Champ-Dolent menhir (Dol, Ille-et-Vilaine) also measures 31.17 feet. As for fallen menhirs, the longest one is in Locmariaquer, a central megalithic site (near Carnac) that, during Celtic times and until 56 BCE, was the main harbor of the Gaul Venètes, whose fleet was defeated by Caesar's fleet. This *Grand Menhir* (as it's known in French), also called *Pierre de la Fée* (Fairy's Stone), has a diameter of 16.4 feet and weighs 347 tons. It reached a peak of 68.88 feet before it was toppled long after the Roman conquest. Now broken, it lies in four pieces. Another fallen menhir in Kergadiou (Plourin district) measures 34.44 feet and sits near an upright menhir that is 28.86 feet high.

Some menhirs have carvings. The Manio menhir has serpents and undulating lines, and the Kermaquer menhir (Landes of Lanvaux, Morbihan) depicts crooks that look like a bishop's bent staff. That of Saint-Denec (Finistère), lying down, depicts axes. Both axes and crooks are carved on the menhir of Saint-Samson sur Rance (Côtes du Nord).

Menhirs can appear solitary, in rows (one or several parallel rows), or in circles (and in this case, we call them cromlechs). Many circles of menhirs show they were used as astronomical temples beyond being sites of sacred gatherings. Of course, the magnificent, complex ensemble of Stonehenge is the most strikingly beautiful and significant open-air temple that remains on Earth from the megalithic period. Its majestic lintels, supported by elegant menhirs (the trilithos), are absolutely unique. It radiates a powerful energy. On the morning of the summer solstice, the first ray of the sun touches what has come to be called the Altar Stone, the node of the site and of the three circles of stones (which, in effect, are ellipses). Moreover, this first ray falls exactly on the path heading to the temple.

Africa has many megalithic sites. An interesting site in Cambia shows a complex global structure comprising several circles of megaliths. The megalithic site in Nabta (near Alexandria, Egypt) has been studied by Professor Kim Malville of Colorado University. It features six alignments and a total of twenty-four megaliths. Each alignment radiates outward from the node of the structure. Professor Malville found that these lines pointed to the rising positions of three bright and visible stars during a period from 4800 BCE to 3700 BCE: Sirius, Dubhe (Ursa Major's brightest star), and a star in Orion's belt.*

Dolmens

The second type of megalith, the dolmen, is a huge, flat, round natural stone called a *table,* made of one block that is two to four yards in

---

*This study was made by students of the South African Astronomical Observatory in Cape Town, in collaboration with the National Research Institute of Astronomy and Geophysics in Helwan, Egypt. Nabta is about sixty miles northwest of Abu-Simbel, in the Sahara Desert.

diameter and looks like a round table or altar. It rests on smaller standing stones that fit to it tightly, and with them the table forms a round chamber whose access is a long passage made of small standing stones topped with flat rectangles. We call these "covered passages" (*allées couvertes*). Some covered passages are so low that it is necessary to crawl to access the chamber. Along the Epte and Eure valleys sit interesting dolmens with covered passages showing the megalithic Mother Goddess carved at the entrance. As mentioned earlier, she is called Goddess with a Blazon (Déesse à l'Écusson) because the carving depicts rows of collars in the shape of a blazon, surmounted by two tiny breasts. The Goddess with a Blazon has a discreet but meaningful presence at many megalithic sites. The representation is as insistent as it is sparse: indeed, time has erased most of the carvings, and one has to look for them.

The usual ancient interpretation was that the chambers were used for death rituals, but archeologists and researchers in the past have generally shown a down-to-earth approach, reflecting the materialistic paradigm of their time. Confronted with strange temples or caverns from the Neolithic Age or a time even more distant, they saw only two usages: hunt magic or death rituals. Yet even in the great cairns or tumuli that have several chambers, only one or two of the chambers were used as tombs or necropolises (the ones where skeletons and bones were found). In contrast, bones haven't been found in most dolmens or in all chambers of complex cairns.

Menhirs vs. Dolmens

So what was the basic difference between erected stones (menhirs) and underground chambers (dolmens)?

One explanation could be that the upright menhir marked the ascending, uplifting spots, and dolmens marked the grounding spots. This interpretation is derived from the forms of the structures and their energetic aspects. The dolmen chamber is round, flat, and partly underground, which implies the symbolism of caves and reconnection with Earth (Mother Goddess) and with the forces of nature. Furthermore, the dolmen was at one time covered with a mount of small stones (a tumulus or cairn) and would appear only from the outside as a mount (a *tertre*).

This interpretation is corroborated by the omnipresent Mother Goddess sculpted at the entrance of the passage.

Menhirs, in contrast, are huge, monolithic blocks that stand erect, and their form symbolizes an antenna, a needle planted in the ground to establish the connection between Earth and the cosmos—just as all sacred buildings pointing upward do, such as steeples, towers, Shiva lingams, or stupas. Menhirs can stand alone or they can be arranged in circles (or cromlechs, such as Stonehenge) or in alignments (Carnac). One thing is certain: the megaliths people placed megaliths at major power spots that, as we have seen, were again and again the sites chosen for religious rituals and the building of temples over a few millennia. We can thus infer that their seers and priests (at the very least) were endowed with the capacity to detect cosmo-telluric lines and the very strong energy emitted at their crossings. In that perspective, menhirs, then, mark A Spots, and the alignment connected to them (if any) shows the course of the cosmo-telluric lines. In contrast, dolmens mark G Spots, and their alignment also points to the direction of the lines.

The two types of energy were no doubt used for their specific effects. The first, ascending energy enhances connections along the Earth-sky axis and was used for rituals geared at uplifting consciousness. Circles of menhirs (cromlechs)—for example, those at Chartres and Stonehenge—marked the most powerful A Spots and were used for collective rituals and major gatherings. This Earth-sky axis goes two ways wherever an antenna-shaped monument has been erected. The grounding telluric lines create an Earth-to-sky flow, while simultaneously the antenna attracts cosmic energy toward Earth. To take a posture reinforcing such a vertical Earth-cosmos axis is a basic practice in yoga and qi gong; by practicing it, we can connect with our higher Self and cosmic consciousness. In the rituals of the Native Americans, the shaman bows first to the four cardinal directions and then to the sky and Earth.

The second, grounding energy favors reconnection with Earth in the cardinal directions (reflecting a basic technique in many rituals and martial arts) and in as many directions as the number of lines crossing there. Thus the flow of energy (toward Earth's center) allows the influx of cosmo-telluric energy to nourish and replenish the body and its vital energy (beyond charging the sacred site, of course). It prods the body to connect to forces of nature (underground water, earth, grottos). Both these influxes—cosmo-telluric energies and forces of nature—have a healing and vitalizing effect. Moreover, if an antenna-shaped monument is erected above a chamber, the inflow of cosmic energy hitting the antenna will flow vertically toward Earth, thereby nourishing it. Such is the case with a menhir that stands on a cairn or with a cathedral and its crypt.

In light of what we've discovered, healing temples would have a greater potency when situated on such grounding spots and in caves; and in fact, this is exactly the case with the healing caves (or asclepieion) used in Asclepios* healing rituals. The most important features of such sleep temples, beyond provoking dreams, were the *cave* and a *spring* that held healing properties. Patients were to drink the sacred water and then sleep in the cave underneath the temple in order to receive a dream. The priests would interpret the dream the next morning and propose a cure. This healing tradition comprising a cave, a sacred spring, and interpreting dreams also existed in Egypt and indeed originated there. Healing rituals based on sleep and dreams exist also in several other shamanic cultures, such as the Senoi tribe in Borneo and Native Americans.[28]

Since Celtic times, a similar healing ritual existed at the very locale of the actual Chartres cathedral. The site was, I believe, the most powerful and prominent Druidic site in the whole of Gaul, and, with its circle of twelve huge menhirs standing on the sacred hill as well as its magical source, it was a place for spiritual gatherings and healing. Healing rituals around a miraculous well existed at this Druidic sacred site even before the first cathedral was built there during the fourth century CE, a building that was destroyed by the Vikings in 858 CE. (Indeed, mod-

---

*In the Hermetic tradition, Asclepios is the disciple of the Egyptian god Thoth, whose Greek name is Hermes. Asclepios was the Greek god of medicine, and in the third century BCE, his cult and his sleep-healing rituals became widespread in Greece. We should keep in mind that there was always a very alive connection between Greece and Egypt, especially during the reign of the Ptolemy in Alexandria. Also, some of the most preeminent Greek thinkers and philosophers, such as Plato, Pythagoras, and Apollonius of Tyana, had been initiated in Egypt.

ern radiesthesists detect an underground rivulet spreading in several branches under the actual choir—which is not rare in cathedrals.) These healing rituals were testified to at the time of the Carolingian cathedral (858 CE to 1020 CE), the ground floor of which was at the level of the actual St. Fulbert's Crypt, and its own crypt (smaller than that of St. Fulbert), called St. Lubin's Crypt, was underneath (actually, now the second level of depth). Along with the well or spring (*le puits des Saints Forts,* which was said to have miraculous healing power), a Black Virgin (*Notre-Dame-du-Pilier,* actually at ground level now), a relic (the veil of Mary), and a statue of the Virgin (the ancient statue of *Notre-Dame de Sous-Terre*) attracted many pilgrims. According to Markale, this well, the site of pre-Christian cults, was situated outside the Carolingian cathedral. Since the building of the larger Gothic cathedral (consecrated in 1260), however, it now stands within the St. Fulbert's Crypt, which itself forms a horseshoe that encircles the Carolingian construction on its outer perimeter. Ailing people used to live and sleep in the crypt, praying and drinking the holy water until they were healed. Some specialists hint at the existence of a grotto beneath St. Lubin's Crypt.

Yet we have seen that beneath Chartres Cathedral is a megalithic solar calendar of twelve menhirs that form an arc. There are thus two complementary energy nodes in Chartres. The underground crypts and cave mark the grounding G Spot. In Celtic times, the ascending A Spot was marked by the astronomical temple with an arc of twelve megaliths (which then sat on the hill of Chartres), and since Christian times it is marked by the cathedral and its steeple, which has been set higher with each reconstruction.

Interestingly, the same is true for the magnificent Asclepios temple on the island of Paros, which stands on a mountaintop and opens to all directions: this location shows that the aboveground temple (just as Chartres Cathedral) is a crossing of cosmo-telluric lines on an A Spot. (While meditating in this spot, I indeed felt strong connections to several other sacred sites on Earth.) Furthermore, as with all Asclepios temples, it had a cave (underground telluric currents) and a spring (vital energy ascending from underground), which together generate health and vitality.

It thus seems that both the Asclepios temple in Paros and Chartres

Cathedral could be complex sites with an interlacing of both ascending and grounding flows, rendering them the most extraordinary type of sacred spots and so holy that it would explain why the sacred hill of Chartres was chosen by the Druids for their most sacred annual gatherings.

Let us ponder the astonishing energetic properties of a sacred site that does include both an A Spot (temple, dome, steeple) and a G Spot (cave, source, underground river, and thus a well). The ascending energy of the spring (expressed so nicely in the phrase "to spring forth") originates below the ground; in contrast, the energy of the dome or steeple, and the resulting crisscrossing of cosmo-telluric lines, originates from a higher place.

There are, then, three basic types of sacred spots (see plate 2).

1. A Spots: the crossing of cosmo-telluric lines at ascending energy spots (aboveground), marked with menhirs and steeples
2. G Spots: the crossing of cosmo-telluric lines (underground) at grounding energy spots, marked with dolmens, caves, and crypts
3. AG Spots: complex double sites, with both an ascending flow and a grounding flow.

Crossing of Two Cosmo-telluric Lines (Four Vectors)

Now, let's see more complex graphic representations of the cosmo-telluric lines: see plate 2 to get a global understanding of the energy flow, and then follow the text with figure 7.3 (on page 174) to undertand the specific energy structures.

In figure 7.3, we have two sacred lines (thus four vectors) linking four cardinal points far away in the landscape and crossing aboveground at the A Spot. If you were to look at the crossing from above, you would see a perfect cross: two perpendicular straight lines. The figure shows the perspective as if you were at ground level, in front of a small hill inside which is a cave and above which is a menhir. Let's first look at the A Spot: one line ascending from the ground level (to meet the other one), which keeps climbing and then plunges back to the ground. This can be represented by a vertical triangle with its apex pointing up. (This is only a schematic and makes an abstraction of the curving of the line.)

But if you now visualize the two ascending lines running perpendicularly to each other to meet at the A Spot, then the two perpendicular triangles form a schematic pyramid shape that is somewhat flattened. The real shape, smoothly curved, as we have learned, resembles Silbury Hill (see plate 2)—a shape that has remained a mystery to researchers.

The schema is inverted for grounding energies and G Spots: one line plunges to meet the other underground and then moves upward again—represented by a schematic triangle with its apex pointing down. If we imagine two lines (four vectors) descending and crossing each other perpendicularly underground, the four vectors meeting at the G Spot would make the schematic shape of an inverted pyramid, its apex pointing down.

In those extremely special spots where two ascending lines cross high up in an A Spot and two more descending lines cross each other underground at a G Spot, the schematic result is an upward-pointing pyramid that is base-to-base with an inverted pyramid underground—an octahedron.

Sri Yantra 3-D Mandala

If, however, the two bases are slightly displaced—if the upward-pointing pyramid has slid down and the downward-pointing one has moved upward, we obtain a very sacred Sri Yantra 3-D mandala: an upright pyramid embedded in an inverted pyramid, or a 3-D Star of David (see figure 7.3 on page 174).

What could provoke the sliding of the two bases? A spring or well, as an ascending flow coming from deep underground, would set the base of the uplifting energy (upward-pointing pyramid) lower than the ground. Add to this menhirs on top of the mound, and the ascending flow would be raised higher than the natural up-and-down undulations. A cave or grotto aboveground—like dolmens situated high on natural hills or in chambers under man-made tumuli mounds—would put the base of the downward-pointing pyramid higher. Thus, the base of the upward-pointing pyramid would have slid down, and the base of the downward-pointing pyramid would have moved upward. Once again, Chartres has a prehistoric well with curative powers and an underground grotto—all

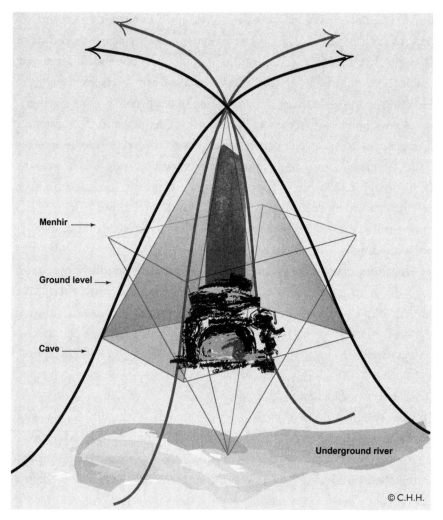

*Figure 7.3. The crossing of two sacred lines to form a 3-D Sri Yantra
Digital artwork by Chris H. Hardy*

situated on the hill of Chartres, on top of which, in megalithic times, was a magnificent arc of twelve menhirs.

These complex sacred spots where a 3-D Sri Yantra is perfectly assembled, the double-energy spots with both an ascending flow and a grounding flow, were no doubt held as highly sacred, for, through them, individuals could achieve a perfect balance between elevation of soul and harmonization with Earth.

Crossing of Four Cosmo-telluric Lines

We merely have to double the structures at each level to visualize four cosmo-telluric lines (eight vectors) crossing each other.

Four ascending lines mark an ascending pyramid in which is embedded another pyramid in such a way that, looking from above, their interlaced bases create an eight-pointed star: a double pyramid. Further, four downward lines (that is, eight vectors of energy meeting underground) mark an eight-pointed star: a double inverted pyramid.

WORLDWIDE SACRED NETWORK

In France, Montségur is one of the most interesting high sites—places of great spiritual energy that have been the sites of sacred rituals and spiritual gatherings through the centuries. Together with Chartres, Mont-Saint-Michel, and the entire city of Paris (to cite only a few), Montségur is a sacred place.

The best or maybe only way to understand such a place is to travel slowly toward it and remain there for some time until you enter a heightened consciousness and inner receptivity. Sit in meditation, reach a state of inner silence, and connect yourself to the energy of the site. You will feel a force uplifting your spirit toward a higher state of consciousness, and perhaps, from that state, you'll be able to sense the network of energy connecting Montségur to other sacred sites in France and beyond—to other sacred sites on our planet.

The Montségur "Seat of Power"

In Montségur, one of the main sites of the Cathar religion, I discovered the existence of a very ancient and immaterial grid that connects some of the most sacred places on Earth and has been used by high initiates of different cultures to communicate amongst themselves. Montségur sits in the Pyrénées mountains in the southeast of France, not far from Rennes-le-Château. It was near there that the following events took place.

My friend Edouard lived in Montségur village, just at the foot of the Cathar castle, and one day, he wanted to take me and two other friends for a stroll to a nearby mountain—not the steep peak on which sits the castle, but to a spot near enough to belong to the energetic node of Montségur. Edouard drove to a high hill, and we left the car and went on a long walk, crossing canyons and hills, and slowly climbing.

Edouard thought this mountain had a very special and high energy. He sensed it, but had not found any particular energy spot. We reached the top of a high hill when our group stopped, puzzled by a long, high wall of massive stone that was standing alone in the otherwise bare field. Its shape was striking: it consisted of two long stretches of a monolith that were well aligned and that climbed the hill, leaving a large, square hole that looked like a door in between them. The structure appeared natural, but the smooth top and the alignment were so astonishing that I wondered if the huge stones were carved. Everybody was silent in thought while observing the place. We walked toward the door or gate and crossed it. At the other side of the opening, there was a large rectangular field.

On the inside wall there was a carving of a face with an enormous third eye: a circle perfectly centered in the large forehead. This carving was either stylized or time had eroded part of it. Some features were absent, but we could recognize clearly the eyes and the forehead chakra, the skull, a cheek, and the chin. Again, it was impossible for me to decide if this carving was natural or not, but it was certainly highly charged: it was as if the face was alive and looking at us with a clairvoyant force.

One length of the rectangular field was partly delineated by the wall and the other by small trees. The field climbed the hill on its length, save for its lowest portion, which was flat and formed a quasi-rectangular platform. On this platform we could see, well delineated on the ground by what seemed like years of use, a circle in which seven or eight people could have sat cross-legged.

All together—and without talking save for a few exclamations—we went to sit in that spot, forming a circle as if it was evident to us that it was the place to do so. Once seated, we looked at each other with round eyes, refraining from talking, as if we were expecting something to happen. Then we each entered a silent, receptive state. I could feel the presence of ancient sages meeting there around a fire. We stayed at that spot for a long while, in a meditative state. I *felt extraordinarily at home in this place, and a surge of well-being and peace came over me. I could feel the magic of the place. After a time, we all stood up and began walking separately around the site. I ventured into the woods, and I remarked that, because of worms, all the trees were devoid of their bark. Yet in the wood, the worms had carved galleries that formed some of the strangest designs I had ever seen. They were so intricate and undulating that they looked like some sort of calligraphy.*

While seated in the circle, I had remarked on the upper third of the grand rectangle—a small place that had no vegetation and had a neat, flat, round spot at its center and overlooked, it seemed, the large circle below, where we were sitting. I was both seeing the luminous syg-energy of this spot and feeling its power. Given its energy, the small place seemed to me like a special seat for only one initiate, the leader of the group. Because my friends were leaving the site and I wouldn't be able to find my way alone back to the car, I thought I'd better catch up with them. On passing through the gate, I saw they were a bit higher up, heading for the hilltop. My intention was to join them, but as soon as I had taken a few steps outside the site, I stopped, gripped by a strong urge to return alone and to sit at the single person's spot. The pull was so compelling that I retraced my steps without even signaling to my friends, my mind totally absorbed by this call. Thoughtfully, I bowed to the site upon entering, patting the stone of the gate (my expression of a salute), and then climbed straight to the seat.

Sitting in meditation, I emptied my mind and entered a receptive state, expecting to pick up some images or impressions. I could feel how charged this spot was, and how some very special people had sat there—certainly the heads of this little community. Yet nothing more precise happened, and after a while, I decided to climb down and find my friends. When exiting and saying good-bye to the site, I caught a glance of my group, nearly turning around the hill and disappearing from my sight—but as soon as I had moved out a few steps, again I was possessed with the strong pull to return and sit at the place of power, and again, oblivious of all else, I climbed back to the high spot.

I sat, opened my mind, let myself become limpid and without thoughts, and waited. Nothing happened. Three times I went through the entire process of exiting the site, feeling the urge, reentering, and going to sit at the seat of power. The third time, as soon as I had closed my eyes and blanked my mind, a clear image began forming in my mind's eye. I saw thin rays of energy darting from the precise spot where I was, at the level of my forehead, and spreading out like the sticks of a paper fan. The rays were white and about one-fifth of an inch wide, and they appeared to shoot straight from me, the whole array fanning out in front of me from my left to my right and covering about a 110-degree angle.

What was astounding was that these rays were perfectly stable, as if they existed there permanently and that opening my vision had merely permitted me to perceive them. I was seeing, eyes closed, another dimension of reality—a higher level of energy.

I intuitively read the lines as energetic connections to other places of Earth, and I started to attune my mind to the ray farthest to the left. Following it (as if sliding on it), I reached Brittany. In this way, following the rays one by one brought me to several great sacred sites in the Northern Hemisphere. The last one on my right was the connection to India (Ellora and Nasik). Among the rays was a connection to Glastonbury and also Stonehenge (the oldest part of which is dated to about 4000 BCE).

I understood that I had penetrated a very ancient grid used by initiates of the diverse cultures of Earth to communicate with one another.

As we have seen, the grid of Catholic churches is deeply interwoven with the ancient grids of megaliths, themselves used by the Druids for their rituals during Celtic times. Glastonbury, before being the site of a prominent Christian abbey, was the mythical site of Avalon Island, a central place in the saga of King Arthur and the Knights of the Round Table at the end of the fifth century. The legend of the Holy Grail—a symbolic tale veiling a deeper truth—expresses a strong semantic link to both Montségur and Glastonbury when it recounts that Joseph of Arimathea brought to the Occident the holy cup used by Christ at the Last Supper and in which he, Joseph, received Christ's blood before burying him. Legend tells that he made a stop at Montségur before proceeding on to Glastonbury. What's more, according to legend, recovering this Holy Grail became the most important quest of the Knights of the Round Table. At this point, of course, we must follow the trail uncovered by Michael Baigent, Richard Leigh, and Henry Lincoln and later developed and fictionalized by Dan Brown in *The Da Vinci Code*.[29] In the ancient etymology, the Holy Grail (*Saint Graal* in French) was spelled *Sangreal* or *Sangraal*—that is, Sang Real, or Royal Blood. The Sangreal in fact referred to the bloodline of Jesus, who was married to Mary Magdalene—the woman who was highly revered in the Gnostic gospels, especially the Gospel of Philip, which hints at the fact that she received a secret teaching from Jesus. According to Picknett and Prince, she was the first and foremost disciple of Jesus and, like him, was of royal lineage.

For evidence of this, we can look at the magnificent stone bas-relief of Mary Magdalene found at the Pilar high site. (See figure 7.4.)

Figure 7.4. Above: The Magdalene of Pilar. Below: Detail of cup and skull. Photography: Chris H. Hardy.

An entire story unfolds in the stone representation. The most crucial message is conveyed by the cup (the Graal containing the Royal Blood) and the fact that this cup is adorned with a cover resembling the headdress of a pope. It sits next to the skull (the dead or absent father, Christ) and leads to a rod blossoming with three flowers (suggesting three children). I had never heard about the three children of Mary Magdalene, but this is what I read in the stone. In all appearences, the Magdalene is shown praying and repenting for her sins (she is not eating, and the rod also looks like a whip); her seclusion and ascetism are so severe that angels come to bring her food. The hidden symbolism, however, has not escaped the monks of Pilar, because they see in this rod the representation of the Shiva lingam (the most sacred symbol of the god Shiva). The symbolism of repentance now appears very shallow compared with these underlying meanings. We can also note that the name of the would-be Portuguese sculptor has been carved clumsily on top of numerous skillful ancient inscriptions, as if to mask them.

Distant Communication between Initiates

Let's reflect on the meaning of the existence of a grid between sacred sites.

It seems the initiates of old had found a stupendous mode of communication that covered great distances and relied not only on telepathy, but also on a stable network of energy lines. (Of course, since Earth is round, the rays that appeared to be shooting straight in front of me were in fact curved over great distances.) The stable, curved rays that linked sacred sites no doubt kept the connection-channel open at all times and facilitated enormously any telepathic exchange. Two aspects are worth noting regarding the specific fan of energy lines that I rediscovered in Montségur.

The first is that the seat of power was not at the top of the hill, which limited the possible connections to the open space in front and on the sides of the hill. Moreover, the fan I was able to explore was even smaller, covering an angle of about 105 to 115 degrees.

Now, the lines of the sacred network (on which churches, Celtic sacred sites, and megalithic standing stones are situated) generally run through the very tops of hills and mountains (whenever the landscape permits it). Thus menhirs and temples (whatever religion they belong to) are visible from afar and are well placed geometrically within the landscape. The crossing of cosmo-telluric lines at the top of a mountain or hill is always open in all directions, forming a dense geometric structure around the site. The castle of Montségur, now fallen into ruin, was a sacred site for the Cathars (also called Albigensians, because one of their main towns was Albi). It is a perfect example of a building that stands at a crossing of cosmo-telluric lines: it sits at the very top of the mountain and is open in all cardinal directions.

Montségur Castle, sadly, is also where, in March 1244, three hundred Cathar "heretics" were burned—the last atrocious act in the infamous Albigensian crusade, which started the Inquisition and was soon to be followed by the persecution of the Templars.

Under the command of the abbot of Cîteaux, an army of northern knights devastated and destroyed the highly refined culture of the Languedoc region (the whole south of present-day France), where philosophy, the arts, courtly love, and the Holy Grail quest flourished. According to several researchers, the Templars didn't participate in the crusade and more often than not gave shelter to the Cathars.

It is also worth noting that the seat of power is not very far, as the crow flies, from Montségur Castle. Of course, nothing certifies that the seat of power had been used by Cathars or even that it was created by them, but the proximity suggests a link. The energy rays that I saw imply that the seat is much more ancient than the Cathar religion. Then it could be the other way around, with the Cathars choosing to settle in Montségur because of the existence of a powerful cosmo-telluric site. The Pyrénées abound in such powerful spots: these mountains are where the Templars built the majority of their castles and preceptories *(commanderies).*

The fact that this seat of power was not at a main crossing of cosmo-telluric lines, that its angle of open space was limited by the hill at its back and its sides (while mountain peaks with a 360-degree perspective abound in this region of the Pyrénées) point to a grid that was artificially created for a specific purpose: to sustain communication with other northern Indo-European high initiates. Moreover, the type of ray used at the site doesn't resemble one of the sacred network. The energy lines extending out of crucial nodes in churches or religious buildings are arcs of whitish light and are rather thick. In contrast, the lines converging on that precise seat were sharply delineated straight rays, thinner than a pencil, fanning out at about the height of a sitting body. There is a quality of light in the sacred lines above churches, an alive and vibrant luminosity that was lacking in the Montségur rays. The latter were more like tiny laser waves piercing space (just as did some of the connecting rays we saw in chapter 4).

Of course, there could be other seats of power around Montségur, which would cover other fans of sacred sites: to the west toward the Americas and the Pacific, and to the south toward the Middle East, Egypt, North Africa, sub-Saharan Africa, and all the Muslim countries. (Remember the lines are curved over such a distance and that one needs to use a globe to visualize them.) What if there were three fans, each of a 120-degree angle?

If the link to other Indo-European sacred sites was the purpose of the Montségur seat of power, then it would imply that each of the high places that were connected had its own seat of power in the vicinity of the main temple (or node). And just with the fan I found, we are talking about more than a site for each ray, since each line crosses a few sacred places while following the curvature of Earth.

The Montségur-to-Nasik line, for example, connects (among other sites situated along the curved ray) Rome, Mount Athos (and Thessalonica, in northern Greece), then Ispahan (a sacred site in ancient Persia, which is now Iran), before reaching Ellora and Nasik (two very close sites in the proximity of Mumbai, and after exiting India around Madras, it jumps toward Australia.

The fanning lines between Brittany and India, in fact, cover all the Nordic and Eastern countries. The line that links Montségur to the holiest mountain in Tibet—the Kailash, abode of the gods—also goes through Angkor, the magnificent jewel of the Khmer civilization, before reaching the sacred Mount Arnhem in Australia and then New Zealand.

Furthermore, great sites are often the meeting places of several religions. For example, three religions—Hinduism, Buddhism, and Jainism—have their temples side by side in the magnificent mountain cirque of Ellora, and all consider it an extremely holy site. This may be the reason why the seat of power in Montségur is not situated within the sacred building of a specific faith, such as the stronghold of the Cathars. The southwest of France, once called the *pays d'Oc* (with its own language called *langue d'Oc*), is where the Visigoths (a Teutonic people that came from central Europe) had settled. The Cathars claimed them as their spiritual ancestors.

It is evident that if high initiates, belonging to widely diverse cultures and religions, felt the need to keep a channel of communication capable of crossing the centuries and millennia open between them, then the sacred spot where it was anchored should preferably remain on neutral ground, above any specific faith. In addition, if only to sustain and protect this channel through such a long span of time, it would be better if the place weren't easily accessed or marked by any obvious sign, such as the temple of a specific religion.

It's difficult to assess how long such a grid between initiates has existed, but if sites from the ancient Celtic, Nordic, Persian, Roman, Greek, Tibetan, Hindu, Khmer, Chinese, Japanese, and other Oriental religions were connected, then such a grid could have been in existence for centuries—and simply been expanded as new religions and novel sacred sites and temples came into existence. Another possibility is that a network of initiates, at any point in time, decided not only to communicate among themselves, but also to keep the energy of ancient sacred sites in activation because such places were situated on the same geomagnetic grid they used for communication.

Some may think there is another possibility: that the Montségur grid was created and used by initiates of a specific doctrine who would have traveled and started small communities all over the Indo-European area.

These initiates would have discovered a way to communicate telepathically at long distances. In this kind of practice, we have the example of the Hopi and Zuni Indians in the state of New Mexico, who had rituals of contact held in underground chambers. Their common ancestors, the Anasazi, after seven centuries or more of a nomadic life, started constructing villages around AD 700, such as the ones we can visit in the Chaco Canyon complex. In the astounding village of Pueblo Bonito, an extremely sacred place, there are many deep underground chambers called *kivas*. Apart from grand ceremonies, the initiates used the kiva to enter heightened states of consciousness and then to communicate not only with the spirits, but also telepathically with other tribes, from kiva to kiva.[30] Nevertheless, it is doubtful that a widely dispersed group that adhered to a single faith could explain the Montségur grid, which, on the contrary, definitely points to a grid of communication across diverse religions.

Though I discovered the Montségur seat of power in my twenties, it's still unique in my life in several respects: the fan shape of the energy structure; the neat, permanent rays that exist in a higher dimension (called by some the etheric level of Earth); and the enigmatic nature of these rays.

In contrast, I've reenacted several times the specific way of keying to the memory of a place, even if I have performed it each time with total spontaneity. Countless times, I've meditated at the sacred core of temples, pyramids, churches, or sacred mountains and was able to sense their connections to other sacred sites—in Western Europe, ancient Greece, Crete, Egypt, the Middle East, North Africa, India, Southeast Asia, Mexico, and the United States. Though I have spent a great part of my life traveling and visiting many sacred places from all religions, my experience with complex regional networks—the sacred grids linking churches—is much more comprehensive and precise within France. The fact is that many of my spontaneous experiences occurred in France, and in France I was able to conduct a systematic observation of several regions. Nevertheless, it's evident to me that this type of network exists in most countries, and—this is my central thesis—a sacred network among all sacred sites of Earth exists and is permanently activated at the global planetary level. That the megaliths people, who erected the network, existed at the very least eight millennia ago gives weight to the hypothesis Colin Wilson proposed in *From Atlantis to the Sphinx* that, in a very distant past, a highly developed and spiritual civilization had lived on Earth.[31]

8

UNVEILING THE CHRISTIAN-DRUIDIC GRID

The *OM,* the mantra of harmony, is chanted throughout India for meditation. It consists of centering on the hara (the abdominal chakra) and breathing with the belly, then uttering the *OM* sound in long expirations with a low, deep-throat voice. After a normal intake of breath, we start another long *OM* on exhaling. The sound *OM* is derived from the three Sanskrit letters *AUM,* which together form the most sacred mantra of both Hinduism and Tibetan Buddhism. The mantra *AUM* (or *OM*) signifies the integration of the three levels of the individual (body, psyche-mind, divine spirit), which express the three levels of the cosmos (matter, sentience, cosmic consciousness). The mantra is in itself a path toward reaching inner harmony and attunement with our immortal soul, the Self.

HARMONIC RESONANCE OF CHURCHES
AND ARCS OF LIGHT

I was sixteen or seventeen when I started a hitchhiking spree, alone or with friends—I couldn't imagine anything more enjoyable than being carefree à l'aventure for a few days, beginning a journey on a whim with whatever small amount of money I had at a particular moment. At eighteen, when I woke up to the consciousness of my Self and started meditating, I experienced a new sensitivity to subtle energies. I started visiting the many churches I found along roadways, meditating and sensing their energy fields. My greatest pleasure was to dive into a musical meditation whenever I found a harmonium in a conveniently deserted church. However, I would always go into a deep meditation to sense the energy fields as well as the crypts and underground passages. This is how (as I have recounted it in chapter 1 of part 1) I once sensed that there was an underground, straight tunnel under the church in Provence, as well as its exact direction, and was able to find its access door, which was quite far from the chuch and totally hidden by thick bushes. Feeling the syg-energy of an underground passage is the same type of sensitivity that allows one to "sense" and "see" the arcs of the sacred lines: it's a sensitivity to semantic energy, or syg-energy, that can be learned. And indeed, this sensitivity slowly increased in me until a few years later, when I happened to make a great discovery.

One day, I was drawn to meditate at the geometric node of the choir within a small, ancient church. I stood there, uttering the sound OM while exhaling slowly, when I had the idea to climb up the scale progressively. I experienced a strong shift of state and found myself in heightened consciousness. I gathered all my energy at my head chakra (the thousand-petaled lotus) and created a vertical ray along my kundalini channel, ascending in an Earth-sky flow toward the center of the dome of the structure.

At one point, on a specific tone, my voice became suddenly naturally amplified and got in resonance with the whole building. The effect was something like the harmonics chanted by a harmonic choir, with a Gothic "surround" effect. The whole edifice, due to its perfect architecture, had entered in resonance in its totality as if it were a whole and unflawed resonance chamber.*

My mind shifted to an expanded state, and I felt that I harmonized with the whole church. I had the impression of being one with the exquisite stone architecture. As I kept humming the OM on the same note, thus deepening the strength of the harmonics, my consciousness, following the ray linking me to the center of the dome, suddenly went through the roof and followed the vertical

---

*A harmonic choir follows a chanting technique that generates harmonics on higher scales. The chanting group called Harmonic Choir has rediscovered this ancient chanting style and made it popular by performing in well-known cathedrals and abbeys, such as the Cathedral of St. John the Divine in New York and the abbeys in southern France.

Earth-sky ray shooting upward. After sliding along this ray with my consciousness for a few dozen yards, I suddenly saw beautiful lines of energy arcing out of the church; I saw them so clearly that I could perceive their number and the direction of each flow. I was dumbfounded and at the same time in awe, and I understood that I was seeing field lines bouncing in and out of that spot on top of the dome, which no doubt linked the church to other sacred buildings or sites of high cosmo-telluric energy. I had never heard or read anything about rays emanating from churches; I had only read about the existence of ley lines.

After that first experience, as I kept traveling and meditating in churches and sacred sites I met on my way, I systematically included in my meditations the sensing of worldwide sacred lines as well as the detection of crypts and highly charged spots. My practice amounted to a yoga of harmonic resonance *with temples and sacred sites. Using it, I learned a great deal about these arcs of energy linking sacred sites. Whenever I would be visiting a region or a country, I would detect part of the network that we call the sacred network—the network connecting sacred structures and the oriented edifices between them all over France and the world.*

As we have seen, cosmo-telluric lines have a natural tendency to oscillate, but buildings standing at their crossings (and conceived according to sacred geometry and with a spiritual intention) anchor the current and fix it to a precise spot. I know now that the architecture of a church—in order to receive and rebound the sacred lines and to act as a resonating chamber for the syg-energy—must be designed according to principles of sacred geometry and, in order to function, must also remain intact and complete. (Just imagine a hole in a drum skin: what kind of sound would you get?) Additionally, if there are repairs to be done, they must be carried out with the utmost respect for the ancient architecture. Intention—one of the strongest semantic energies of consciousness—is crucial. Both the intention presiding at the construction and the specific architecture of the building add particular qualities to the natural cosmo-telluric energy. A sacred building may vibrate in total resonance no matter its architectural style; it simply must be pure and balanced in its proportions. Its walls and arches must also be perfect and whole to allow the sound waves to pass through them in a fluid way, unobstructed and unswerving. For example, layers of different materials stop the flow, unless they are metals and knowingly assembled. It's as if the building itself has to be in a flow state.* It has to be pure enough to do what it was conceived for: to be an antenna that receives cosmic energy and redistributes this energy through the sacred networks of Earth, while simultaneously orienting and fixing the telluric currents.

Different architectures, however, introduce subtly different heightened states of consciousness. There is no doubt that circular or half-circular shapes (domes and Roman arches) instill a state of inner silence and attunement. The Gothic arch—the ogival rib, or *ogive*—induces an upward thrust, an uplifting of consciousness. Gothic arches also evoke a quality of spiritual love that is well expressed by the symbolism of the heart of Christ and, of course, by the feminine path of love exemplified by the Virgin Mary, or *Notre Dame*. This path of spiritual love also exists in India, where it is called *bhakti yoga,* the yoga of devotion. It consists of awakening the kundalini through the heart chakra by being in an extended state of consciousness triggered by a spiritual love for all humankind, Earth creatures, and the planet.

TELLURIC ENERGY, COSMIC ENERGY

In churches and temples, there are two types of energy: the first one is the telluric energy (energy of Earth) we have talked about. The second is the energy of the cosmos released into the sacred buildings through the channeling of cosmic rays linked to the stars.

Telluric and Semantic Energy

Suppose we have a crossing of two ascending cosmo-telluric lines—that is, two currents of energy arriving on an A Spot (aboveground). Beyond the crossing, each current will move away following its own particu-

---

*The flow state is generally restricted to individual consciousness. It means a dynamical state of mental fluidity and inner harmonization, without blockage or hindrance to the flow of consciousness. As a result, intuition and creativity are enhanced.

lar direction of flow. If, however, a church or temple has been built at this precise A Spot, the structure increases the strength of the energy at the crossing point and imprints it with the quality of consciousness of the people who pray or meditate there—with their semantic energy. Furthermore, part of the flow of energy will be deviated from the main current and will ascend vertically from the center of the dome of the structure or along its steeple or spire.

The sacred building directs the telluric energy in its ascending flux along the field lines of the architecture, and while doing this, it anchors it to the stone, wood, or metal. The temple will thus be charged and imprinted with energy. The building has a second effect on the telluric flow: the current is heightened and lifted upward, just like a fountain channels water flow. Imagine the simplest fountain: a water pipe in the ground brings the water into a vertical tube that is neatly cut at its top. The water surges upward, and on arriving with force at the open end of the tube, it squirts out in all directions in graceful arcs. The water falls back on the ground, making a wide circle—and the more pressure, the wider the circle.

Similarly, in churches and temples, most of the telluric energy that springs from the ground is drawn upward, following the walls, columns, and arches, all the way to the dome or steeple if the building is perfect. Just like the fountain, all the telluric energy then gathers and keeps rising vertically at the exact center of the choir or beyond the tip of the steeple, thus creating a vertical ray that shoots upward and divides itself into the exact same number of currents that it had on arriving at the crossing. (See plate 3: flows of sacred lines around an obelisk and cave.) These currents then start bending downward, forming the lines of the sacred network.

Cosmic Energy

The second major inflow of energy received by a temple is the one that comes from the cosmos. The spire is a natural antenna, and it attracts some of the most mysterious energy from the stars. Indeed, it's quite common to see a long, vertical ray above steeples or domes; this ray is created partly by cosmic inflows and partly by telluric currents that have been channeled upward by the architecture. Thus, currents of energy arrive from the cosmos and descend following the steeple, spire, or towers or along the dome or the arches. They follow the architecture until they plunge into the ground, where the energy charges crypts and the Earth beneath the building and is eventually channeled along the underground telluric arcs and currents.

Indeed, many sacred buildings are located or oriented according to astronomical measurements. Some cathedrals and temples are even linked to specific constellations or stars. We can look in more detail at the eight Gothic cathedrals that reproduce the Virgo constellation. We owe this discovery (or disclosure) to Jean Phaure, the renowned specialist of the secret architecture of France, who includes it in his book *Introduction à la géographie sacrée de Paris Barque d'Isis.*[1] The cathedrals were built at about the same time in the north and northeast of Paris, and they include Notre-Dame de Paris. Because they were all devoted to Mary, all of their names begin with Notre Dame—the Virgin—which gives them a symbolic link to the constellation of Virgo. The eight were the cathedrals of Notre-Dame de Paris (star έ of Virgo), Beauvais, Amiens, Noyon, Senlis, Laon, L'Epine, and Reims (star β of Virgo). Phaure, however, shows on his illustration much more than only the Virgo constellation. He draws the projection of several constellations onto the north of France. Chartres, for example, is the projection of Arcturus. This is quite baffling, and there is certainly more to understand about this association.

Anchor Points

The overall effect of locating a sacred building on telluric lines is to amplify these lines while charging them with a spiritual quality. After crossing at the vertical energetic center of a sacred building, the lines of energy—whatever their numbers and the direction of their flow—part again in as many currents and follow their natural undulation paths. These arcs reach higher in space (or lower in the ground) than they would without the edifice. In the ascending flow, past the crossing point, the arcs either move up for a while or start to bend downward. Whatever the case, they bounce toward their next natural anchor point on Earth. Note that if lines cross at the top or trough of the waves, it creates a Roman arc (that is, nearly a half circle, as in plate 2) but if the crossing occurs at midheight, especially on a wave that is pulled higher by a building, it creates an ogival arc (as in figure 7.3, page 174).

In some regions of France, at each point where the arcs are anchored—arriving and departing—there's a sacred anchor point. Some of these anchor points are simply crosses on top of hills or tiny chapels, but they exist to anchor and spiritualize the network.

When I chanted the *OM* in France, for example in the hilly countryside of Provence, after I sensed how many lines crossed within a church, I went outside, and, since these churches were often on hilltops, I looked in the precise directions in which I had sensed the arcs. I was astonished to perceive the anchor points in each direction on faraway hilltops: here a small church, there a chapel, a cross, or even a beautiful castle.

Once in a while, I could sense an anomaly. I might feel very precisely three arcs, but I knew there must be a fourth, because the arcs must keep flowing, like rivers. I inferred, in such instances, that the fourth arc had been broken by the destruction or partial damage of whatever edifice acted as an anchor point for it. A bad restoration can damage the integrity of a building, especially when the rebuilding has altered the structure's overall proportions or when different materials have been used for the repair, thus blocking the natural flow in the stone arches. Fortunately, and due to the handing down of traditional knowledge and craftsmanship, bad restoration has, until now, been quite rare in France. It is much more common to have churches or chapels disappear because they were destroyed by wars or the Revolution. In France, it is quite rare to see churches left in ruins or disrepair.

The meaning or *raison d'être* of many configurations of sacred sites that anthropologists have found so mysterious becomes crystal clear when we decipher such places with the sacred grid in mind—if we see, for instance, a central, star-shaped node and small anchor points all around it. For example, an interesting feature of Pueblo Bonito is the system of lines radiating in all directions around the village and leading to small shrines. Yet a great part of the knowledge pertaining to this energetic dimension has been lost through the millennia. There are so many energetic laws embedded in a temple that only so much has been secured and transmitted within the traditional knowledge. This is why it is extremely risky to pursue all at once a massive restoration of a single building, with teams working simultaneously in different spots of the structure. (As an aside, it's sad that the funding policy for repairing monuments often tends to create this type of situation.) If we consider the semantic field alone (that is, the quality and meaning of spiritual energy and not the telluric energy itself), several teams are extremely aggressive and dangerous for the semantic memory contained in the field. In effect, each team of workers generates a novel imprinting loaded with the values, interests, and worries of their present situation. The greater the number of workers, the less they will be inclined to create a deep empathy with the church and a link between their own Self and the spiritual field of the church. A link of that sort would have the power to maintain harmony between all their gestures and the semantic imprinting. A few people working alone are more likely to establish such a connection and remain in meditation within it, thus producing a perfect restoration.

EMPIRICAL SIGNATURES OF THE GRID

Let's now ponder a question regarding the purely energetic aspect of the grid: if a church's first function is to enhance and anchor already existing cosmo-telluric lines, why is an arc broken if the anchor building is damaged? Shouldn't the natural current be flowing freely even if it is loose and oscillating? The answer is yes, the current of that precise arc is flowing freely, but on the ground and not through the church where I'm meditating, and therefore, from my perspective, it's broken. In fact, the building of so many churches has added a novel, complex network to the natural and ancient grid: the very network between sacred buildings I call the sacred network. This network connecting sacred buildings (or stones) is not only anchored to the natural telluric grid but is also perfectly enmeshed into it, forming a seamless and balanced mandala. The natural geomagnetic grid, however, has already become something entirely different, novel, and sacred, with the creation of the first megalithic network.

Through the centuries and with each new civilization, this natural grid has been keenly expanded, magnified, revered, and embellished—with Druidic sacred sites, Gallo-Roman temples, and finally Christian churches and cathedrals. Monuments that are not overtly religious but which have nevertheless been built according to sacred geometry are also fitted tightly into the sacred network. These include the libraries in Paris; the royal palaces (such as Versailles); castles; *hôtels particuliers;* public buildings; fountains; bridges; oriented avenues and crossings; and, of course, the temples of secret societies and minor faiths.

Thus, my discovery of arcs of light arriving and rebounding on churches, along with my systematic exploration of their connections, made me aware that most (if not all) churches in France are interconnected. Furthermore, I understood that they form a gigantic interlacing network of sacred buildings that pertains to different ages and faiths and that sustains itself through time. At this point, I made another stupendous discovery, and in a very strange way.

Over the years, I had explored five regions of France and had been able to see that in these regions the network of churches and castles was still very much alive and strong, providing a web of spiritualized energy that constantly uplifted the spirits of the inhabitants. At one point, I decided to buy a writing house in the countryside—a cozy retreat away from the stressed capital that I could use exclusively for writing and meditating. Once I purchased it, I started exploring Touraine and the Centre regions, using maps to check the many places I found while driving intuitively, guided by my sense of energy flows.

One day, looking at my map of the region, I had the idea of taking a ruler and, if I saw three churches in a straight line, drawing this line. My map was great because it included not only churches, but also castles and even megaliths and ruins. So I included all these in the drawing of lines, since, as in the case of the royal castle of Amboise, they are often crucial cosmo-telluric places. That's when I noticed the lines I drew passed by megaliths and other ruins that were also marked on this map. Soon, I had covered part of my map with a dense network of crisscrossing lines—and that's when I observed a most improbable structure.

There it was, neatly formed by the lines, a crossing of four field lines on an abbey. The mandala couldn't have been more perfect in terms of symmetry: a star with eight lines fanning out at perfectly regular intervals. In additon, the name of the abbey was evocative: Aigue-Vive, which is a derivation of the Latin aqua viva, *"alive water," thus suggesting that the place might have a spiritual energy and possibly a miraculous spring.*

The next day, I went on a stalking spree in my car. I turned around again and again in the place designated on my map, but there was a dense forest and not a single signpost. It was quite strange indeed for such a high telluric spot! Finally I saw a dirt road—or rather a bridle path—penetrating the forest, and I took it. After a while, I reached a large clearing, and there it was: a magnificent abbey, partly in ruins and in the process of being repaired, with just a couple of opulent houses around it, guarding it like watchdogs.

As I walked around it, seduced by its beauty, I stopped, spellbound, when I noticed that its tower had an octagonal structure. This was surely no coincidence. Here was a high spot (or site of great spritual energy) well hidden in the forest, and its meaning was encrypted in the stone, readable by initiates and seers!

This junction of eight rays at precise angles (that formed a perfect octagon, or an eight-pointed star in a circle) was material evidence of the grid that linked the churches I had explored intuitively during my whole life thus far. I was happy to see such proof.

Another fact I discovered was that Druidic sacred sites were enmeshed with the Christian network to form a unique grid. I had known that some cathedrals and churches (such as Chartres and the small church in Brittany) were built on megalithic sites, but after seeing all the field lines on my map, it became downright evident. The megaliths had been placed on specific telluric spots (or nodes in a network), and the network of churches had been superimposed on these megaliths, and they had been preserved in the process. Both churches and megaliths were anchored on the network of cosmo-telluric lines and nodes. Building in this way had not only kept the Druidic network alive, but it had also considerably expanded it and made it more complex, if only by the sheer number of the network's buildings after the churches were completed.

Moreover, all of the oldest castles had their own private church or chapel, and some of these are jewels of the secret and sacred knowledge. Amboise Castle is a magnificent example: within the ogival arch around the tympanum of the entrance gate, where there are usually bas-reliefs of Christ, the Virgin Mary, or saints, there is instead a carving of a stag. In addition, at this church, stag horns have been built into the steeple at midheight, extending outward in all four directions.

Cernunnos (also spelled Kernunnos) was a prominent Celtic god represented by a human face and stag horns and was revered in Gaul and Great Britain. The stag—the emblem of Cernunnos—was thus a sacred animal for the Druids. To find a stag sculpted on the tympanum in the royal chapel at Amboise is especially significant when we know that among the kings who inhabited Amboise castle was François I, who invited Leonardo da Vinci to Amboise and gave him a beautiful manor to live in quietly nearby until his death. The story goes that François I so much enjoyed discussing with da Vinci that a subterranean passage (maybe built by da Vinci himself, given that he was such an expert in these types of construction) permitted the great genius to visit the king *sans cérémonie*.

In 1771, a pillar, called the Nautes Pillar, was discovered under the choir of Notre-Dame de Paris. It was erected by the Nautes, dedicated to the god Jupiter, and offered to Emperor Tiberius at the very beginning of the first century CE. As we have seen, the Nautes were a Gallic sailor people who lived in the city of the Parisii since around the third century BCE. On this square, stone pillar with four levels in decreasing size were sculpted several Roman gods and goddesses (among them Jupiter, Mercury, Juno, and Mars), as well as several Gallo-Celtic gods and goddesses. Among the latter was the god Cernunnos.

On the Gundestrüp Cauldron (from Denmark), another antique piece on which Cernunnos is represented, the stag horns clearly form the letter *V* above the god's head—a sign that, for any Hindu, would indicate a spiritually accomplished master who had a fully awakened head chakra. Moreover, Cernunnos has a very lean human body and face; he sits cross-legged and perfectly centered, with one heel pointing to the kundalini channel—a yoga posture that makes him look like a Hindu god. To top it all, he is beardless and holds in his left hand a snake, the attribute of Shiva. His right hand brandishes a *torque*—that is, a torus with a thin aperture, emblem of the Great Goddess. Cernunnos is one of the two lovers of the goddess Ceridwen, sharing her favors with Taranis, the god with a wheel.

Interestingly, in India the sacred consciousness energy is called *shakti* (feminine), but Shakti is also a goddess, and the awakening of the kundalini energy is sometimes referred to as awakening the inner shakti.

When the psychic energy reaches the thousand-petaled lotus at the top of the head, shakti enters in sacred union with *shakta* (masculine), and the two poles of the human psyche (masculine and feminine, yang and yin) are finally harmonized. Let's also remark that the word *chakra* means "wheel" in Sanskrit and that each psychic center is represented by a lotus with a specific number of petals (that are arranged geometrically, as in a wheel or a mandala). As we have seen, the awakening or uplifting of the head chakra puts the psychic energy into motion in a torus movement.

Cernunnos is the lover of the Great Mother Goddess, and on the Celtic feast of Beltain (May 1), a man of royal descent or a great Druid, bearing a headdress of stag horns and empowered by the god Cernunnos, had a sacred union (hierogamy) with a woman who incarnated the Great Goddess and wore a crown of flowers. It is said that many descendants of the Pendragon royal line—the family of which King Arthur is the paragon—had been conceived during this sacred ceremony. Cernunnos is sometimes represented with two or three heads, and interestingly, the Hindu god Brahma sometimes is represented with four heads, facing the four directions (the one at the back would not be seen on a carving). Cernunnos, after the Roman conquest, became Herne and was identified with Apollo and Hermes or Mercury. In later legends, he was conflated with a giant hunter, and in Christian times he became St. Korneli, patron of the megalithic sacred site of Carnac.

9

THE SACRED NETWORK OF PARIS

The Obelisk Node

THE SACRED ARCHITECTURE OF PARIS

It is quite evident to the keen observer that all the architecture of Paris, whether religious constructions, royal palaces, or public buildings, all the way to fountains, plazas, and bridges, is built according to axes and perspectives of deep symbolic meaning.

In *The Da Vinci Code,* Dan Brown narrates some of the secrets pertaining to the astonishing planning of Paris: for two centuries, the world's Zero Meridian, positioned since 1884 in Greenwich, Great Britain, ran through the core of Paris—specifically, through the Paris Observatory. This observatory was built in 1672 especially for the purpose of establishing the meridian's reference system just after a French scientist had calculated the exact measure of a degree from the circumference of the world. Louis XIV approved its construction in 1666. The ancient Zero Meridian (called Méridien de Paris) is still marked in the observatory with a copper line that runs along the floor of the Casino Room. (See the vertical blue line marked MD 0 in plate 1, roughly in the center of the map.)

The Paris Meridian—or, more precisely, the Observatory Meridian— should not be conflated with other meridians within Paris. A *meridian,* or perfect north-south axis, can of course be calculated from any point or significant monument in a city. In the same way, a *parallel,* or perfect east-west axis parallel to the Equator, can be drawn at any point. The meridian marked with a copper line in Saint-Sulpice Church is thus a particular meridian: that of Saint-Sulpice. It runs through Paris just about parallel (save for the curvature of Earth, which is imperceptible on such a small scale) to the ancient Zero Meridian to the west. A line of bronze medallions—a recent work of art—marks the ancient Zero Meridian all across Paris. Called the Aragon Line, each of its original 135 medallions is stamped with the name Aragon as well as an indication of north and south. (The medallions, however, keep disappearing, and the meridian hunters often find only holes left in the pavement where they once were.) To the north, the Observatory Meridian runs through the small eastern pyramid at the Louvre—one of the three that flank the great upright pyramid—and the Saint-Sulpice meridian runs near the inverted pyramid. All in all (and to make the matter a little more complicated for meridian and pyramid hunters), there are six pyramids in I. M. Pei's great work at the Louvre: one great inverted pyramid on the Carrousel Plaza, one great upright pyramid (at the center of the Louvre's courtyard), three small upright pyramids around the great one, and one tiny upright pyramid directly beneath the inverted one, its tip touching the tip of the inverted one.

Several architectural ensembles, such as Etoile Plaza, the Champs-Elysées, Concorde Plaza, and the elongated garden of Tuileries, are geometrically configured so that the main east-west axis of the city passes right on their center line. This axis, called the West Decumanus (see plate 1 for this and all the descriptions that follow) runs precisely through the centers of the Grande Arche at La Défense, the Arc de Triomphe of L'Etoile, the Concorde Obelisk, and the Arc de Triomphe of Carrousel. If we take as a reference point a parallel virtually drawn at the Obelisk, the West Decumanus runs at an angle of 26 degrees to this parallel and points east-southeast.

The Seine River between Pont de la Concorde and Pont Royal—called Cours Royal de la Seine, meaning Royal Flow of the Seine, and running from Concorde all along the Tuileries—is perfectly straight and parallel to the West Decumanus. The West Decumanus follows the central geometrical line of the large architectural ensemble formed by the Tuileries Garden (the garden's castle, Tuileries Castle, was destroyed) and the large western side of the Louvre; at this level the museum building is perfectly aligned with the West Decumanus on its length. Then the eastern part of the Louvre building is oriented at another angle in order to follow the Seine, which flows slightly more to the north, so that at the eastern end of the Louvre (on rue du Louvre) the West Decumanus axis reaches practically the southeast corner of Cour Carrée and runs along the southern wall of Saint-Germain-L'Auxerrois Church.

The Louvre shifts from the axis of the West Decumanus and the Tuileries at the level of Arc du Carrousel, where ley 12 meets the West Decumanus and the East Decumanus (see plate 1). It then configures a different axis, the East Decumanus, which follows the median line of the horseshoe building of the Louvre and runs through the exact centers of the two great glass pyramids. The great pyramid aboveground stands in the middle of the main plaza and serves as the main entrance to the museum; the square base of the inverted pyramid can be seen at the exact center of the circle formed by Place du Carrousel: it plunges underground, and at floor level, its pointed tip meets the tip of a tiny third pyramid that points upward (which can be seen at the level of the underground gallery).

The East Decumanus then reaches the central porch of Cour Carrée on rue du Louvre, at the exact center of the pediment adorned with the magnificent bas-relief called *La Gloire distribuant des Couronnes* (sculpted by Pierre Cartellier). Both the decumanus and the western porch of the Louvre face the dome of the Cloister Saint-Germain-L'Auxerrois. Then the decumanus runs through major city monuments such as Saint-Jacques Tower and the Bastille. It was during the presidency of François Mitterrand that the Grande Arche at La Défense and the glass pyramids of the Louvre were designed. Mitterrand, a Freemason, is said to have had a crucial role in the conception and launching of these two sacred geometry masterpieces, as well as the design of a few others, yet the extent to which he influenced their planning is unknown. That these recent constructions are perfectly positioned along the East and

West Decumani is a clear example of the relentless care given to the secret architecture of France.

Beyond the decumani, other important axes in towns that existed in the Roman Empire are those drawn at right angles to the decumani, and, as we've learned, are called *cardos*. Given that Paris started to develop within and around Ile de la Cité, it's clear that the East Decumanus was the original one. In 360 CE, two massive wooden towers called the Châtelets guarded two ends of the first wooden bridge on the Seine on the eastern side of the island. Similarly, the traditional Cardo of Paris is at a right angle to the East Decumanus, the two axes crossing on the northeast of Châtelet Plaza in front of Saint-Jacques Tower. The traditional cardo on the Rive Gauche side follows rue Saint-Jacques, goes through Ile de la Cité, and then runs along rue Saint-Martin.

Thus, Châtelet Plaza is one of the main nodes of the sacred geo-architecture of Paris. On its northeast corner stands the magnificent Saint-Jacques Tower, which is crowned by the four evangelists characterized by their symbolic representations (Mark the lion, John the eagle, Luke the ox, and Matthew the angel). The square tower was added in the sixteenth century to the twelfth-century church St-Jacques-de-la-Boucherie, but it alone survived the destruction of the church during the French Revolution. This very mysterious building, in the midst of the Alchemist Quarter of Paris, is associated with Nicolas Flamel and his spouse Pernelle, the paragon of an alchemist couple dedicated to the Great Work, who had a shop on the northern side of the tower.

As we've seen, before the Roman conquest in 52 BCE, Paris had been, for about three centuries, the already vibrant Gallic city of the Parisii, practically enclosed within Ile de la Cité. This city was considered sacred and endowed with supernatural powers. "If we believe Grégoire de Tours, there were marvelous traditions concerning this city: She was sacred, fire had no hold on her, and snakes couldn't live there," wrote Théophile Lavallée.[1]

At the site of the cathedral of Notre-Dame de Paris, there very probably stood some megaliths, followed by a Druidic open-air temple. Ruins of a Gallo-Roman temple dedicated to the goddess Diana, as well as the famous Pilier des Nautes dedicated to Jupiter, were found underneath the cathedral. Finally, the direct ancestor of the Catholic cathedral was erected in the fourth century. Jean Phaure has calculated the orientation of several French cathedrals.[2] In Notre-Dame de Paris, the whole length of the nave, from the facade and main porch facing west to the center of the cross, is oriented at a 26-degree angle. Thus the median axis of the nave is parallel to the West Decumanus, because the cathedral is more to the south. Then, from the center of the cross through the area of the sanctuary—that is, the choir—the cathedral is oriented along an angle of 23 degrees, 30 minutes.

With a different configuration, Chartres Cathedral, according to Phaure, is oriented at 47 degrees along a solstice axis. Its choir, oriented toward the northeast, faces the rising sun at the summer solstice (on the feast of St. John the Baptist, June 24), and its facade, oriented toward the southwest, faces the sunset at the winter solstice at Christmas.

A METRO MAP DISCOVERY

If a grid connecting churches and megaliths using cosmo-telluric lines existed in some regions, it was likely the whole of France was organized in a similar way. That's the conclusion I had reached after exploring five different regions of France: Brittany, Normandy, Ile de France, Provence, and Centre-Touraine. All of them showed a very alive network. Luminous auras girded churches, rays and arches darted over steeples—and only occasionally were these rays absent (that is, the link was broken). Though I kept in mind that this giant network could be damaged or totally destroyed in other parts of the country, I was now sure that it still existed in some places and had been there in the past.

In Paris, my hometown, I had explored the grid over the years, but less systematically. I knew what most Parisians had remarked, that is, the town was built following numerous axes on which architectural construction was precisely set—the Défense-to-Louvre axis being the most remarkable one. Let me remark, though, that even such experts as Phaure hadn't detected the change of direction and slight angle shift of the decumani to be aligned with Cour Carrée; for all Parisians, there's only one decumanus, and it runs through the centers of the two Louvre pyramids all the way to Etoile and La Défense (which is false since it's the East Decumanus that runs through their exact centers; see plate 1).

Apart from the key buildings we have mentioned, these axes incorporated all kinds of architectural works that were perfectly placed in the global geometry—from sacred monuments, fountains, museums, plazas, and bridges to sculptures and even military buildings (École Militaire) and hospitals (Invalides, Val-de-Grâce), and of course the most famous of all: the Eiffel Tower.

While pondering this one day, I grew curious to see how the main axes of Paris were ordered within the entire city. Because, at the time, I was in Brazil on a long journey, I used what I had: a common Metro map that every Parisian acquired. I began delineating the well-known axis passing through La Défense, the Etoile, the Concorde, and the Louvre. Then I followed more or less the same formula I had used for drawing the cosmo-telluric lines in Touraine and the Centre Region, but using Metro stations (Metros) instead, for they are reliable markers of important monuments and nodes in the city. I expected to find these Metro lines running parallel to main ley lines, though slightly displaced because the station entrances are often at the sides of avenues. I expected that I would still be able to sort out precise structures, and then, later, correct the slight displacement using a detailed city map. Yet, as I was soon to discover on detailed maps, icons for Metros are often drawn at the precise centers of plazas—and this is how, in fact, many icons sit exactly on the sacred lines, or city axes, that connect churches and monuments. Thus, they were much better markers of city structures than I expected.

After a good deal of intuitive tracing of lines between Metros (my rule of thumb was to have no less than three stations aligned in order to draw a line), large geometrical structures began to appear. What I ended up with was beyond anything I could have expected in terms of structure and complexity. I was dumbfounded by what it revealed about architectural planning. Basic rules of sacred geometry were obviously respected and applied through the centuries, despite all the changes in architectural styles and technologies, as well as in politics and governance.

My drawing of axes and lines was far from perfect and lacked precision on such a small scale, but it was precise enough to give me an inkling of the complexity of the grid. First, the inverted pyramid stuck out as a major node in a structure that took form around a central cross: the West Decumanus and the cardo (or perpendicular) drawn at the inverted pyramid.* (See plate 1.) Yet it's clear that the grid in Paris involves something vastly larger than just two main perpendicular axes.

The most astonishing global geometrical structure I found is a very large Sri Yantra, or Star of David—that is, two inverted triangles superimposed, one on the other. As we've learned, the Sri Yantra, or venerable mandala (or geometrical figure), is a very ancient symbol in India that was often drawn on temples. It represents the perfect harmonization of the body and psyche with the soul, or Atman. It is also used to represent the heart chakra, generally described as a wheel turning (the word *chakra* in Sanskrit) and depicted as a lotus flower with six petals (see figure 9.1 on page 204).

The center of this Sri Yantra was the inverted pyramid of the Louvre. This structure has four main nodes, one of which is Bibliothèque Mitterrand, a huge library conceived during Mitterrand's presidency. Four main axes (eight rays, or a double cross) of this Sri Yantra meet at the inverted pyramid. I later discovered that Paris possesses several such main nodes, around which certain global geometric structures can be drawn. One such node can be, at the same time, the geometrical center (the main node) of a couple of structures and a secondary node for another structure that reorganizes the cosmo-telluric lines and the monuments. This is the case, for example, with the Obelisk—on one hand, it is the main node of three concentric geometric structures: a golden rectangle, a hexagon, and a Sri Yantra. On the other hand, it serves as a secondary node in the St. John the Baptist pyramidal structure.

This inverted-pyramid Sri Yantra remains the largest sacred structure I have found thus far in Paris, for it spills into suburban areas.

---

*At the level of the inverted pyramid, the two decumani just begin to separate from the Arc du Carrousel, and they both run eastward through the inverted pyramid, which, from the sky, appears as a glass square: the East Decumanus passes through its center, and the West Decumanus passes at its south corner.

Figure 9.1. The heart chakra as a Sri Yantra, depicted on a Nepalese thangka.
Photography: Chris H. Hardy

The first lines I drew also gave me an idea of some of the basic principles used in geo-architecture. The geometric structure illustrated, for example, the role of the Seine River within the global geometry. First, there were precise junction points between the Seine and Musée de Sèvres and the river and Pont de Levallois. Second, the Seine's natural direction of flow was used in several places (such as at Musée de Sèvres, Les Côteaux, and between Basilique de Saint-Denis and Puteaux, via La Défense). In this respect, we must remember that a river's flow generates a current of ions that runs in the atmosphere above it.

This Metro map also showed a near-perfect eight-ray star on Denfert Rochereau, just as it appeared on my subsequent work with leys (see plate 1, bottom center, the red cross perfectly imbedded within the blue cross). At this plaza stands the main entrance to the catacombs, the old caves where the first Christians of the fourth century gathered and prayed in secret and where some of them lived in hiding. Later, the network of tunnels and caves was expanded for various mining projects and was used as an ossuary at the end of the eighteenth century. I beamed when I found that this double cardinal cross (formed by four leys) is precise on larger maps, with eight spokes at 22.5 degrees. (See plate 1.) One of the spokes (belonging to the blue cross) is no less than the Trocadéro-to-Eiffel Tower axis (axis 4 on the map*). Its perpendicular at Denfert Rochereau Plaza is ley 14, which goes through one of the most beautiful Parisian plazas, Place des Vosges. As for the two other lines (the red cross), the first is the exact meridian at the Denfert node (ley 8, passing by Saint-Roch church), and the second is the Denfert parallel, running through the geometrical center of Bibliothèque Mitterrand (ley 16). What's interesting to note here is that a near-perfect eight-pointed star (double cross) appeared on a very small-scale map that included only Metros, and this same star was also found to be perfectly exact on large, detailed maps.

---

*The leys and axes are numbered from 1 to 17 in a clockwise manner starting at the northwest with the West Decumanus. All ley numbers are placed near the outside frame of the map and are followed either by letter "A" showing where the ley begins or "B," where it ends, that is, in their portion crossing Paris.

Moreover, I had found an oddity in the eight-pointed Metro-map structure: the doubling, at a small but perfectly similar angle, of all four main axes meeting at the inverted pyramid. This in itself is absolutely remarkable, and though I couldn't understand it at first, I was hoping it would reveal something of interest on larger maps. Then I discovered the slight angling of the Louvre's eastern part, Cour Carrée, to accommodate the change of direction of the Seine River toward the north. I then deduced how and why the decumanus changed its angle (and then called it the East Decumanus). The bewildering feature of my Metro-map structure suddenly was explained: the city planners used the two decumani and their two cardos, thus creating a doubling of the main perpendicular axes at a small angle, as if the cardinal cross had slightly turned on itself. I was dumbfounded: we had, on the inverted pyramid node, a slight turning of a wheel-mandala-chakra, creating the eight spokes forming a St. John's cross,* even if the angles forming the splayed-arms ends are somewhat thinner than usual (this cross has four pairs of spokes). If we assume the West Decumanus to be the most charged with syg-energy in our epoch (with the city expanding toward the Etoile and the new business quarter at La Défense), then the wheel is turning clockwise. The stupendous conclusion is that the inverted-pyramid Sri Yantra has at its heart a Maltese cross, also called *John the Baptist's cross* (see figure 9.2). It reveals that St. John the Baptist has a very deep and extended presence in the sacred network of Paris. The inverted-pyramid Sri Yantra's whole structure, beyond its dedication to St. John the Baptist, contains at major points several monuments—such as the inverted pyramid, Mitterrand Library, and La Défense Grande Arche—that were inspired by Mitterrand and conceived during his presidency. The inverted-pyramid Sri Yantra is a recent Great Work indeed!

---

*St. John's cross, also called John the Baptist's cross, has arms that are splayed at the ends. This cross has many shapes (straight or concave arms, forked ends) and many names (Maltese cross, pattée cross), one of which is John the Baptist's cross. It was the cross of the Knights Hospitaller in the Holy Land, the order of knights that was in competition with the Templars, but to which many Templars rallied after their order was outlawed. (See the end of this chapter.)

*Figure 9.2. The Maltese cross or St. John cross,
also called St. John the Baptist's cross.*

The Metro map's Sri Yantra structure, despite its unavoidable lack of precision due to the small size of the map, was enough for me to infer a more global and complex sacred geometry. At the time of my Paris discoveries, I was in South America, where I lacked good tools and good maps. However, as it sometimes happens with creativity, I believe I had the intuition to look for global patterns precisely because I was far away and didn't have detailed maps. As the saying goes, "Necessity is the mother of invention."

MAJOR AXES IN PARIS

Major axes as I define them are striking alignments of urban constructions—avenues, palaces, churches, or bridges—that run through the length and breadth of the city and even beyond, depicting an energy line that connects sacred or oriented monuments. The French-speaking Freemasons use the past-tense term *orienté* (oriented) to refer to a building that is facing a specific direction and, more generally, to refer to a building conceived and located precisely according to sacred geometry. It is derived from *orient* (east) and points to the tradition of constructing cathedrals with their choirs facing the east.

When I returned to France, I was able to work on large and detailed maps. I started drawing all the straight lines that connected a minimum of three monuments, starting with the major axes that appeared so clearly on all the maps. I ended up with three large Michelin maps covered with lines, and on each of them a different geometric structure appeared, centered on two specific nodes. The first structure I found was the upper part of the Obelisk Hexagon. This geometric design was indeed so present in the leys and so clearly marked in the city that it showed on all my maps, even when I pursued the examination of other nodes and structures. You can see it in thin brown-gray lines underneath the shiny blue color filling the sides of St. John the Baptist's pyramid (see plate 8). First, find the West Decumanus (thick brown line) starting from the northeast and linking the Obelisk to J2. Then turn the map upside down so that the Obelisk points downward and the north arrow faces up. If you follow the spokes fanning out from the Obelisk, you will see the three isoceles triangles (in faint brown) forming the half-hexagon set on the West Decumanus.

Because they are based on alignments, these axes are a perfect fit with Alfred Watkins's description of a ley line as an alignment of prehistoric and megalithic artwork interspersed with hilltops, springs, and old tracks. The only difference is that urban leys and axes such as these make use of monuments and urban artwork instead of prehistoric and megalithic artwork, and of avenues instead of dirt paths or Celtic roads.

Major axes are only prominent leys; they are the first sacred lines that I drew in a maze of lesser leys that eventually revealed overall geometric structures. There are many leys in Paris, and in plate 1, I have tried to highlight some that were not part of the striking great geometrical structures that we will explore here.*

The whole geo-architecture of the city is organized around the major axes, and, as we will see, we can draw many large geometric structures, such as golden rectangles, hexagons, and pentagons. They are like basic coordinates in a city that has many centers, or nodes, in a network of architectural ensembles. What becomes crystal clear when we start studying the connections between axes and monuments is that a whole constellation of diversified buildings may have been conceived as forming a single geometric structure. We know this was the case with the Concorde: La Madeleine was conceived to close geometrically the newly built Plaza Louis XV (the actual Concorde), as was the Bourbon palace facing it from the other side of the Seine River (the actual Assemblée Nationale). Later, Napoleon I had the whole facade of the palace rebuilt

---

*For a complete description of these lesser leys, see appendix 1.

in a Greco-Roman style, with a row of columns, similar to La Madeleine. A more recent example, though less easily decoded in terms of its inner coherence, is the group of glass pyramids at the Louvre: according to principles of Hermetic science, a giant upright pyramid, such as the Egyptian pyramids at Giza, calls for, or more precisely creates, an exact inverted form beneath it—that is, an inverted pyramid. An upward-pointing pyramid placed base to base with an inverted pyramid directly beneath it form a huge octahedron—the same shape, incidentally, that is created by a double crossing of lines at an A Spot and G Spot.

This is why I coined the term *geo-architecture,* referring to global structures that comprise several elements extending over a large part of town. In other words, a geo-architecture is an architecture that uses as elements many diversified buildings spread over a broad area in space. A good example of a geo-architectural complex is Teotihuacán, in Mexico, with its magnificent sun and moon pyramids overlooking myriad lesser constructions. Not only are there many such geo-architectural master-pieces in Paris, but also, as we will see, they are superimposed on or enmeshed with one another.

In Paris, many monuments, as well as the main avenues linking them, were drawn under Napoleon I and then by Haussmann under Napoleon III. The 3,300-year-old Obelisk was, as we have learned, originally one of the two columns in front of the temple of Luxor in the ancient city of Thebes in Egypt and was given by Muhammad Ali, viceroy of Egypt, to King Charles X in 1829. It was erected in 1836 at the center of La Concorde Plaza on the main axis of Paris, the West Decumanus.

The West Decumanus (Axis 1), Etoile-to-Concorde-to-Louvre

As we have discovered, the West Decumanus is the prominent align-ment that crosses Paris from west to east (precisely west-northwest to east-southeast) and makes an angle of 26 degrees with a parallel drawn at the Obelisk. Look at plate 1 in the insert: first find La Défense in the top left corner, and then follow the West Decumanus from A (where it begins on our map) to B (where it ends). Altogether, it runs through no less than 13 monuments plus 2 churches and passes exactly through

9 of their porches (a porch is the main portal of a church or a monument, and is always set on the facade of such monuments). In fact, the West Decumanus reaches far out of the city, and it is along its axis (and specifically around the Grande Arche that stands on it) that the western business quarter of La Défense was conceived during Mitterrand's presidency. We will start from the west, and you can see in parenthesis where exactly the line passes on the monument. The lines runs through: (1) La Défense's Grande Arche and (2) Esplanade, (3) Neuilly Bridge (Pont de Neuilly), (4) the Arc de Triomphe at L'Etoile Plaza, (5) the Obelisk at Concorde Plaza, (6) the Tuileries, (7) the Arc de Triomphe of Carrousel, (8) the Louvre Museum, (9) the inverted pyramid (southern part) and (10) the Louvre's pyramid (southern part), (11) the fountain at Châtelet Plaza (the line runs through its center), (12) the Flamboyant Gothic jewel of Hôtel de Sens, and finally (13) Quinze-Vingts Hospital (southern part).

The two churches are the magnificent St-Germain-l'Auxerrois, facing the eastern side of the Louvre (the axis runs along its south wall) and St-Antoine-des-Quinze-Vingts (its southern aisle). Of course, axis 1 is the path we follow when we walk down from l'Etoile Plaza toward Concorde Plaza, because it follows the median of avenue des Champs-Elysées, and we are still on this path when we stroll along the median of the garden of Tuileries to the Arc de Triomphe of Carrousel, facing the inverted pyramid. We can also note that this alignment is perfectly parallel to the Seine River from Pont Neuf to Pont d'Arcole. In addition, axis 1 continues its course far beyond Paris and even France. According to Philip Thomas, the great circle route of La Défense-to-Obelisk runs through Mount Sinai (along a route that is 116 degrees south-southeast). A second circle route, which Thomas calls the Royal Axis, runs through the Grande Arche and Palais du Luxembourg (120 degrees south-southeast), then goes through the Giza pyramids in Egypt to Mecca.[3] Given that Napoleon I took scientists with him all through his Egyptian campaign and there launched modern archaeology and the restoration of monuments, and given that Napoleon III erected the Obelisk at La Concorde Plaza (among other such *oriented* monuments), it seems that both emperors must have known a great deal about Egypt, sacred lines, and the planetary grid. In fact, the modern sacred network of Paris owes much to these two emperors, as we will find out.

The careful planning, along centuries and based on sacred geometry, of geo-architectural structures encompassing ensembles of monuments and avenues has been a magnificent opus major that can be deciphered!

The Etoile Cardo (Axis 5), Etoile-to-Trocadéro

We can see, for example, the remarkable Etoile Cardo that passes though Etoile Plaza and the Trocadéro monument. Look at plate 1 in the insert: first follow the West Decumanus from the west until you find Etoile, where you see the Arc de Triomphe representation. The Etoile Cardo is the perpendicular drawn at the center of the plaza (and the exact center of the Arc de Triomphe). This ley is very well marked: it runs along the median of two avenues—Kléber and Wagram—and is perfectly perpendicular to the West Decumanus Etoile-to-Concorde (the median of Champs-Elysées). Both axes appear in geometrical structures of vast proportion, such as the Obelisk's golden rectangle. The Etoile Cardo—starting in the north near Porte de Clichy and ending at Quai d'Issy—runs through 4 monuments: the Arc de Triomphe (central line running its length), Maison de la Radio (tangent on the east), Pont Mirabeau (midpoint), and Pont de Garigliano (eastern end). In doing so, it passes 3 geometrical points. It also goes through 8 plazas and no less than 5 Metros. Because the ley is drawn on the median of the lengthy avenues, the five Metros on its route show my point about the alignment of Metro icons with axes and leys.

The city (enclosed within the *périphérique,* or circular highway around the city) fits in a rectangle of about 7.5 miles by 6 miles, and as we have learned, an axis can run through Paris and progress toward other towns in France or other countries, linking sacred sites along the way. Let's have a quick view at the remaining major axes, described as if we traverse them from their western or northern tip (called A) toward the east and south (called B). (Keep referring yourself to plate 1. For more details on these major axes, see the appendices.)

The East Decumanus (Axis 2), the Louvre's Pyramids-to-Bastille

The East Decumanus runs through twelve monuments and, while doing so, through the exact center or front porch of 8 of them. These monuments are (1) the Arc de Triomphe of Carrousel (the line runs through its center); (2) the Louvre's inverted pyramid (the line passes through its exact center) on Carrousel Plaza; (3) the Louvre's pyramid (the line runs through its exact center); (4) the Louvre palace and (5) the fountain of its Cour Carrée; (6) the eastern porch of the Louvre with *La Gloire* bas-relief (through its center); (7) St-Jacques Tower (through the south facade); (8) Hôtel de Ville (Paris's town hall, the line runs through the north wall); (9) the Bastille's column topped with Génie de la Liberté (Liberty's Genius) at the center of the plaza. To the west, the axis meets (10) Petit Palais (through the front porch); (11) Grand Palais (through the northeast corner of the cross); and (12) Musée National des Arts. It also crosses through 3 churches: the tower of the cloister of St-Germain-l'Auxerrois, St-Germain-l'Auxerrois Church (through north of the choir), and St-Paul-St-Louis Church.

Imagine that we are turning clockwise around the Obelisk. On the **western side**, we see the Arc de Triomphe of L'Etoile towering over the view of the Champs Elysées—that is, we see the West Decumanus (axis 1), which goes all the way to the Grande Arche of La Défense. If we keep turning clockwise around the Obelisk, we reach its **northern side**, and, looking beyond the fountain, we are now facing the Obelisk Cardo with the great view of La Madeleine and its row of columns that stands between the two hotels, resembling two towers at the end of rue Royale. This is the northern side of Obelisk Cardo, which runs perpendicular to the West Decumanus.

The Obelisk Cardo (Axis 3), Obelisk-to-Madeleine

We will discover that the breathtaking alignment of the Obelisk Cardo acts as a major sacred line in all the structures organized around the Obelisk node. The Obelisk Cardo is the spine of the most exquisite geo-architectural structure in Paris: the stupendous Madeleine mandorle, with its lily petal enclosing the Madeleine Temple like a jewel.

If we keep walking around the Obelisk (following our imaginary tour in figure 1) to its **eastern side**, we now have our back to the Champs-Elysées and face the immense garden of the Tuileries, the eastern side of the West Decumanus, that is, perfectly prolonging the Champs-Elysées alignment. If we were to take a walk through the Tuileries, following the median of the garden, we would reach the Arc du Carrousel; then, follow the median of the horseshoe Louvre building to its Cour Carrée, slightly slanted toward the north. The East Decumanus begins at the Arc du Carrousel, and it is this line that follows the median of Cour Carrée.

If we take a few more steps, we stand on the **southern side** of the obelisk and, beyond the second fountain, we view the Obelisk Cardo (axis 3) toward the south. We face the magnificent view of La Concorde Bridge, beyond which stands an ancient palace of the Bourbon royals (now the Assemblée Nationale). Axis 3 runs nearly parallel to the eastern wall of the palace and reaches the east side of the south front porch.

Eiffel Tower-to-École Militaire (Axis 4)

And finally our final major axis, axis 4, is the one we see when we stand at dead center underneath the Eiffel Tower and look toward the Seine and the Trocadéro. (The exact center beneath the tower is marked on the ground by a tiny concrete round.) If, looking at plate 1, you spot the Eiffel Tower icon (center left), then Axis 4—Eiffel Tower-to-École Militaire—is the line darting northeast toward Trocadéro and La Défense, where it meets the West Decumanus at the Esplanade. It runs in the exact center of Trocadéro Plaza, Palais de Chaillot (also called Trocadéro Palace), and the Pont d'Iéna. After passing the tip of the Eiffel Tower (remember, this sacred line is heightened all the way to the top of the tower and beyond), the energy line runs through the elliptical and diamond-shaped garden mandala that is Champ de Mars. It then runs along the median of École Militaire and into three plazas that are major nodes in Paris: Plaza de Fontenoy, Plaza de Breteuil, and Plaza Denfert-Rochereau (which makes a perfect double cross).

GOLDEN RECTANGLE ON THE OBELISK NODE

The Golden Rectangle and Sacred Geometry

The golden rectangle is one of the geometrical figures based on the golden proportion, a mathematical proportion held sacred since Egyptian times and that was part of the sacred geometry developed by Pythagoras. The length of a golden rectangle divided by its width results in the golden proportion, called phi: 1.618. Inaccurate but easy-to-remember proportions that approximate phi are 5/3 and 21/13. The golden proportion has been widely used in architecture, especially for building cathedrals, churches, and city monuments. It has many interesting properties and is also found in many natural shapes and phenomena. It can be used to create golden rectangles, golden triangles, and golden spirals. In these structures, the relationship of two sides equals 1.618 (the number phi). (See figure 9.3, opposite.)

Imagine a golden rectangle (AEFD, top left in figure 9.3) of 5 inches by 3 inches (an approximate golden proportion), so that its length is horizontal. Imagine now that you take its width (AD, 3 inches) as the side of a square that you draw on the left inside the rectangle (the square is ABCD). Now you have a square on the left inside the rectangle, with the same width (3 inches), that reaches past the midpoint of the rectangle's length: it is called the **internal western square** (on the left). Now look at the top right of figure 9.3 and do the same with the small side on the right (EF) to draw the **internal eastern square** (EFGH, on the right). You end up with two squares that are overlapping (the width of the area of overlap, HB, is one inch). This is what you see now: two smaller rectangles on each side standing on end (AHGD on the left and BEFC on the right) and a **middle space** (HBCG) that is enclosed by them. Now, each of these smaller rectangles standing on its end is also a golden rectangle showing the golden proportion. If you take one of them (BEFC) and take out the square, you end up with yet another smaller golden rectangle (IFCJ), shown in the lower half of figure 9.3.

This step can be repeated indefinitely. If you keep going, you will draw the path of a perfect spiral called the golden spiral, as shown in the lower half of figure 9.3.

A Golden Rectangle and its Sacred Middle Part

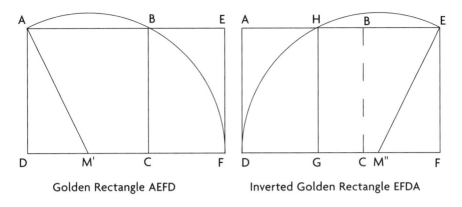

Golden Rectangle AEFD

Inverted Golden Rectangle EFDA

1. Draw a square (3 x 3) ABCD
2. Put your compass needle at point M' (halfway along DC) and draw the circle passing by apexes A and B. You get point F on the prolonged basis of the rectangle.
3. Draw the perpendicular EF to the basis: AEFD is a golden rectangle.
4. Do the same on the opposite side, drawing the square EFGH, then the circle of radius M"E. EFDA is a golden rectangle.

    AEFD (or EFDA) is a golden rectangle: its length AE divided by its width EF equals 1.618 (phi).

    HBCG is the sacred middle part.

    BEFC, the rectangle (on end) added to the square, is itself a golden rectangle.

Embedded Golden Rectangles and Golden Spiral

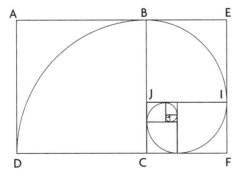

1. In each golden rectangle (on end), extract the square.
2. Draw an arc having as a radius the side of the square and you will get a golden spiral.

Figure 9.3. Golden rectangle, golden spiral, and the golden proportion

Following the Pythagorean tradition, the cathedral builders consider the middle space of a golden rectangle sacred (HBCG, the rectangle left over in the middle when you take off the left and right rectangles standing on end). (See also OQUW in figure 9.4 on page 219.) We will see how, in the geo-architecture of Paris, the builders have adorned this space with even greater symbols of sacredness.

Before we move on, however, it is important to briefly introduce another aspect of the golden proportion, that of the Fibonacci series. The mathematician Fibonacci discovered a numerical sequence that has an intriguing property: any number divided by the previous one results in a number approaching the golden proportion: phi.* We have seen already how phi was used to create golden rectangles and spirals; further in the discussion, we will discover how phi is applied to architectural structures within the sacred network.

The Obelisk Golden Rectangle

The first structure of the sacred network we are going to explore is a large golden rectangle that has the Obelisk at its center. It is so large that it extends to three quarters of the city, from the Etoile all the way to Sainte-Chapelle on the Cité Island. Take a look at plate 4: Obelisk golden rectangle plus hexagon. From the obelisk at the center, follow the horizontal line (the decumanus) toward the left to the Arc de Triomphe icon. Perpendicular, if you remember, is Etoile Cardo, or axis 4, going down (following avenue Kléber) to the elliptical shape of Trocadéro, precisely to the exact center of the Trocadéro plaza. (The map has been

---

*Here is how to calculate the Fibonacci sequence: 1 + 1 = 2; 2 + 1 = 3; 3 + 2 = 5, and so forth. The beginning of the sequence is thus 1, 2, 3, 5, 8, 13, 21, 34, 55, 89, 144, 233, 377, 610, 987 . . . As the sequence progresses toward large numbers, the proportion between two sequential numbers keeps approaching the golden proportion, or phi (1.618, also referred to by the Greek letter ϕ). One way to show this is to divide a number in the sequence by the previous number in the sequence. Thus, 8/5 = 1.6000, 13/8 = 1.6250, and 21/13 = 1.6153. Beginning at 55/34 = 1.6176, we are very near to the value of phi. At the proportion 233/144 = 1.618055, we are exact at four digits beyond the decimal point (that is, exactly 1.6180). Continuing to divide according to the rules of Fibonacci results in 6,765/4,181 = 1.6180339; that is, the more we go in the sequence, the more the numbers approach the phi value.

rotated to better show the structure; see the north arrow at the top left corner.) I started thinking about the perfect crosses at right angles set at the very center of (1) the Obelisk, (2) the Arc de Triomphe building, and (3) the Trocadéro Plaza.

This configuration, being in itself spectacular, prompted me to measure the segment from the Arc de Triomphe to Trocadéro Plaza and the segment from Arc de Triomphe to the Obelisk. I erupted in joy—there it was!—the golden proportion. I had stumbled on the exact length and the exact width of a golden rectangle! Then it was easy to find the whole structure, because the distance between the Obelisk and the Arc de Triomphe was exactly identical to that between the Obelisk and Châtelet Plaza. That made the Châtelet Cardo (the cardo of the ancient Celtic node of Paris) the eastern side of the golden rectangle. Furthermore, the perpendicular to Etoile Cardo at the precise center of Trocadéro Plaza (thus parallel to the decumanus) was running exactly through the splendid dome of the Invalides, which is the dome of a church called Eglise du Dôme. The Invalides's huge complex was built under King Louis XIV. It was started by the architect Bruant and was added on to by Mansart, the architect of Versailles, who built the dome. Strangely, the Invalides not only possesses a second church called St-Louis, but also the choirs of the two churches face each other and, of course, are aligned. Ley 15 (see plate 1), which connects Sainte-Chapelle to St-Gervais-St-Protais Church and which is a perfect east-west parallel drawn at the latitude of Sainte-Chapelle, crosses exactly between the two choirs, though at a slight angle to the perpendicular axis of the building.

The planning and building of the main markers on the golden rectangle (excluding Châtelet, which was a Celtic node)—namely Arc de Triomphe, the Concorde plaza, La Madeleine, and the large avenues along the rectangle's sides—were carried out by both Napoleon I and Napoleon III (we will see that the nephew followed up on Napoleon I's esoteric plans, even magnifying them, despite the fact that the monarchy was reestablished from 1814 to the 1848 revolution). But in case you could still doubt that the golden rectangle was intentional and not just a nice geometric grid, the builders didn't use two random segment lengths: they used exactly two lengths derived from the Fibonacci sequence, 13 and 21, thus ensuring that they embedded the golden proportion and that they would make a golden rectangle. In effect, on the precise map of Paris that I used,* the length of the small side of the rectangle (the segment Trocadéro Plaza-to-Brésil Plaza) is 26.5 centimeters—that's 2,650 meters, or 2,900 yards. This number (26.5) is roughly 13 doubled, and 13 is a number in the Fibonacci sequence. As for the length of the rectangle, the distance between the Arc de Triomphe and Châtelet is 42.25 centimeters—that's 4,225 meters. Forty-two is 21 doubled, and 21 is the number directly following 13 in the Fibonacci sequence.† In this respect, the numbers are so revealing of sacred geometry and of intent that any cartographer with a ruler can infer (just as I did) that each segment showing a Fibonacci number must be part of a golden structure.

The precise building of monuments and streets to form geo-architectural structures is rendered evident by the perfect alignments of axes that are central to the golden rectangle. Look at figure 9.4, and you will see that the West Decumanus is the median in the length (YS) of the golden rectangle, while the Obelisk Cardo (on which La Madeleine stands) is its median in the width (PV), and the Obelisk stands at its exact center. In addition, the Etoile Cardo (axis 5) is its small left side (NX), while the Châtelet Cardo is its small right side. And finally, even minor lines such as the sides of the sacred middle part (OQUW) and the diagonals are very well marked. It is also evidenced

---

*I drew all the leys and searched for structure at first on the Michelin map of Paris no. 58, which incorporates a 1/10,000 scale—that is, 1 centimeter = 100 meters, and 10 centimeters = 1 kilometer. (The translation on the map is that 3.937 inches = 0.6214 mile). I later redrew my findings on the Michelin map Paris-Tourisme, no. 52, so that readers of this text could see the main monuments of Paris. On this map, 1 centimeter = 200 meters (0.3937 inch = 218.8 yards). I calculated that my margin of error (for example between the actual center of a plaza and the ley passing) is only a 33-yard error in 2,900 yards—that is, 1/90. The possibility of drawing the perfect centers of diagonals, at the Obelisk and Arc de Triomphe, allowed me to back-calculate the measure of the width of the golden rectangle: 4225/1.618 = 2611.25 meters.

†Let's remember though that the small difference with a perfect 13 or 21 may be due to my own imprecision and margin of error. I'm calculating on maps with a ruler, while the architects had much better tools to draw the avenues and monuments; let's also remember the scale of these golden rectangles: the long side of this particular one is 4.225 kilometers.

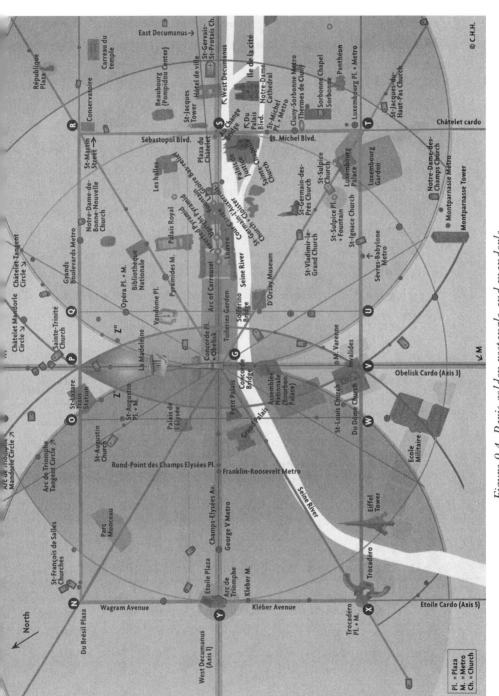

Figure 9.4. Paris golden rectangle and mandorle

North

© C.H.H.

East Decumanus→

West Decumanus

Châtelet cardo

Obelisk Cardo (Axis 3)

Etoile Cardo (Axis 5)

West Decumanus (Axis 1)

Seine River

Seine River

Ile de la cité

République Plaza
Conservatoire
Carreau du temple
Beaubourg (Pompidou Center)
Hôtel de ville
St-Jacques Tower
St-Gervais-St-Protais Ch.
Notre-Dame Cathedral
Du Change Bridge
Du Palais Blvd.
St-Michel Pl.+ Metro
Cluny-Sorbonne Metro
Thermes de Cluny
Sorbonne
Sorbonny Chapel
Panthéon
Luxembourg Pl. + Metro
St-Jacques-du-Haut-Pas Church

Sébastopol Blvd.
St-Martin Street→
St. Michel Blvd.
Plaza du Châtelet
Palais de Justice
Sainte-Chapelle Church

Notre-Dame-de-Bonne-Nouvelle Church
Les halles
St-Germain-des-Prés Church
St-Sulpice Church
St-Germain-de-Grand Church
St-Vladimir-le-Grand Church
St-Ignace Church
Luxembourg Palace
Luxembourg Garden
Notre-Dame-des-Champs Church
Montparnasse Metro
Montparnasse Tower

Grands Boulevards Metro
Opéra Pl. + M.
Bibliothèque Nationale
Vendôme Pl.
Pyramides M.
Palais Royal
Louvre
Upright Pyramid
Inverted Pyramid
Carousel Arc
Arc of Carrousel
Tuileries Garden

Châtelet Tangent Circle
Châtelet Mandorle Circle
Sainte-Trinité Church
La Madeleine
Concorde Pl. + Obelisk
Concorde Bridge
Solférino Bridge
Soléférino Garden
D'Orsay Museum
M. Varenne
Servès-Babylone Metro

St-Lazare Train Station
St-Augustin Pl. + M.
St-Augustin Church
Palais de l'Elysée
Petit Palais
Assemblée Nationale (Bourbon Palace)
Du Dôme Church
St-Louis Church
Invalides
Ecole Militaire

Arc de Triomphe Mandorle Circle
Arc de Triomphe Tangent Circle
Parc Monceau
Rond-Point des Champs Elysées Pl.
Grand Palais
Franklin-Roosevelt Metro

St-François de Salles Churches
Du Brésil Plaza
Etoile Plaza
Champs-Elysées Av.
George V Metro
Arc de Triomphe
Kléber M.
Eiffel Tower
Trocadéro

Wagram Avenue
Kléber Avenue
Trocadéro Pl. + M.

Pl. = Plaza
M. = Metro
Ch. = Church

by the perfect embedding of larger geometrical structures around the golden rectangle, such as the hexagon. My attitude became one of respect for whatever the sacred lines were showing: they revealed such an amazing world of significant and symbolic stories!

The Basic Structure of the Golden Rectangle

- **Following the outside of the golden rectangle.*** Refer to figure 9.4 on page 219: Starting at Trocadéro Plaza, we turn clockwise around the golden rectangle. From the Trocadéro (point X), the **side XN** follows axis 5 (Etoile Cardo) along the large **avenues Kléber and Wagram**, passing through the **Arc de Triomphe** (Y) at its midpoint, and then reaches apex N at Place du Brésil. The **NR side** of the golden rectangle passes through Gare St-Lazare (train station), Mogador Theater, Grévin Museum, Metro Grands Boulevards, and **Notre-Dame-de-Bonne-Nouvelle** Church, and ends at rue St-Martin (apex R). On the **RT side**, the golden rectangle follows the Châtelet Cardo, that is, rue St-Martin along the **Conservatoire**, then, farther down, Sébastopol Blvd. to **Plaza du Châtelet** (point S). It then crosses the Seine on **Pont au Change** and follows **Du Palais Blvd.**, parallelling the facade of **Palais de Justice** (where sits Sainte-Chapelle). The golden rectangle then runs through **St-Michel Plaza** and its Metro station, and from there follows **St-Michel Blvd.**, running through Metro Cluny-Sorbonne, very near to **Thermes de Cluny**. It ends at Luxembourg Garden. After apex T, the **side TX** of the rectangle (ley 17) meets **St-Ignace** Church, Metro Sèvres-Babylone, the church **Eglise du Dôme** within **Les Invalides**, then reaches **Palais de Chaillot** (the palace of Trocadéro), and returns to Trocadéro Plaza (point X).
- The **YS median of the golden rectangle** is the West Decumanus (axis 1)—the grand axis Etoile-to-Obelisk-to-Châtelet. From **Arc de Triomphe** (Y), the line runs through **Etoile Plaza, Champs-Elysées Av.** (Metro George V, Metro Franklin-Roosevelt); **Pl.**

---

*To make it easier to follow the discussion of the maps in part 2, the names of all important monuments are shown in bold.

Rond-Point des Champs Elysées; Pl. Clémenceau (Metro
Champs Elysées-Clémenceau); Pl. Concorde, Obelisk (point G);
central line of Tuileries; Arc de Triomphe of Carrousel; the
Louvre palace, the Inverted Pyramid; and Louvre's Pyramid;
it crosses the southern part of Cour Carrée; follows the southern
wall of St-Germain-l'Auxerrois Church; runs through Metro
and Pl. Pont-Neuf, then parallel to the Seine from Pont-Neuf to
Pont d'Arcole; and finally crosses Pl. du Châtelet and its fountain with sphinxes (point S).

- The PV median of the golden rectangle is axis 3, the Obelisk
Cardo. It follows rue Tronchet, then runs through La Madeleine,
rue Royale, Metro Concorde, Concorde Plaza with its two fountains and the Obelisk, Concorde Bridge, Assemblée Nationale,
and Invalides (point V, where it meets ley 17, the XT basis of our
golden rectangle).

- The internal left square of the golden rectangle (NQUX) is
delineated by the QU line on the right side of the middle space.
This line, which separates the square from the added space QRTU
to form the golden rectangle, is itself very interesting, for it passes
through (from point Q), the very center of L'Opéra Plaza, then
Vendôme Plaza on its southeastern side, and crosses the Seine on
the Passerelle Solférino to reach Musée d'Orsay and the Metro
Solférino, then to point U.

- The internal right square of the golden rectangle (ORTW) is
delineated by the OW line on the left side of the middle space.
(Keep following figure 9.4 on page 219.) This OW line is very well
marked since, after meeting Plaza St-Augustin and its Metro,
it travels along the wall of Palais de l'Elysée (the Presidential
Palace), moves up the dome of Petit Palais, where there is a view
of the garden of Grand Palais bordering the Seine, doesn't take
any bridge to cross the river, and wants to jump toward the Metro
École Militaire, but meets the base of our golden rectangle before
reaching it.

Diagonals of the Obelisk Golden Rectangle

The diagonals of any golden rectangle are crucial features in the unfolding of sacred geometry because an endless series of embedded golden rectangles can be drawn along them. Let's explore the diagonals of our Obelisk golden rectangle. Keep looking at figure 9.4 on page 219.

- **The XR diagonal** seems to love to skirt the outer reaches of great palaces: it touches the north tip of **Palais de Chaillot**, then the south tip of **Palais de Tokyo** (facing the Seine). It approaches Pont de l'Alma only to have a quick glance at the Seine before following the lawns of both **Grand and Petit Palais** and crossing the Concorde Plaza toward the Obelisk (point G). It passes the south corner of **Jeu de Paume** museum, then the Metro Pyramides, before reaching apex R of the rectangle at **Conservatoire** des Arts et Métiers.
- **The NT diagonal** starts at Plaza du Brésil (N), runs through **Palais de l'Elysée**, the **Obelisk**, and the **Orangerie Museum**, and crosses the Seine at the southern tip of the small bridge Solférino. It then passes through Musée d'Orsay, **St-Vladimir-le-Grand Church**, the choir of **St-Sulpice Church** (a major node), and **Palais du Luxembourg**, and then reaches apex T of the golden rectangle. If it is extended past this point, it runs north of **St-Jacques-du-Haut-Pas Church** and Plaza d'Italie.

Embedding of Golden Rectangles

The golden proportion seems to have an astounding capacity for reproducing itself. It's as if it touches something so deep in the fundamental reality of life that it is a constant pulse. We have seen that with respect to numbers in the Fibonacci sequence, but it is also the same in terms of objects. Indeed, the spiral shape seen in many types of sea shells is perfectly expressed by the Fibonacci sequence as well as by an endless embedding of smaller and smaller golden rectangles (from the large end of the spiral).

We have seen already that, when a square is drawn using the short side of any golden rectangle, you end up with a space that is itself a golden rectangle standing on end. And that if the same operation is done using this resulting rectangle, you get its embedded golden rectangle, and so on infinitely until the increasingly small rectangles ultimately resolve in a point. This is how we drew a perfect spiral in figure 9.3.

Now, here is another astonishing case of the self-reproduction of golden rectangles. Imagine you extend the diagonals of your golden rectangle; then you place the needle of a compass on the center of the rectangle and trace a circle of any radius around it. If you draw the four lines between all four points of intersection of the circle and the extended diagonals, you will end up with a larger, embedded golden rectangle. Your radius can be of any length. In short, if on two proximate diagonals you have two churches equidistant from the center of the golden rectangle, they mark the side of a larger, embedded golden rectangle. This is what happens for two churches situated on the eastern side of Paris: **Notre-Dame-de-Lourdes**, farther east along the XR diagonal, and **St-Hippolyte**, farther to the southeast along the NT diagonal. The distance from these churches to the Obelisk is 5.22 miles.

THE CIRCLE AROUND THE OBELISK
GOLDEN RECTANGLE

If there are still any doubts of the geo-architectural validity of the Obelisk golden rectangle, then the following exercise should dispel them. We can draw a circle through the four tips of this rectangle: this circle runs through 4 major churches, including **Notre-Dame de Paris**, 2 chapels, 4 plazas, 8 crossings, 5 Metros, and 1 train station. It also espouses (as a tangent or an arc) no less than six streets or monuments. (It is represented by a double blue line in plate 4, and the golden rectangle is traced in a thick blue line.) We can turn clockwise from the southwest apex (see apex X in figure 9.4 on page 219) of the golden rectangle, at Trocadéro Plaza, to note the prominent features of this circle: it passes through **Ste-Thérèse Chapel**, **St-François-de-Sales Church** (the southern one), Metro La Fourche, Montmartre Cemetery, Theater Abbesses, the plaza in front of **St-Jean-de-Montmartre Church**, Metros Abbesses and Strasbourg-St-Denis, **Conservatoire** des Arts et Métiers, and then it makes a perfect arc on the western facade of **Hôtel de Ville**. The circle crosses the nave of **Notre-Dame de Paris** (the arc of the circle is nearly perpendicular to the nave), then the **Sorbonne Chapel** (the choir and the western tip). It then passes through the plaza and Metro Luxembourg, **Luxembourg Garden**, the **church Notre-Dame-des-Champs** (boulevard Montparnasse), the plaza and Metro **Montparnasse-Bienvenue**, and runs in front of Tour Montparnasse (be careful to distinguish the 3-D view of the tower from the line; the line passes through the plaza in front of the tower and not on the tower itself), and, finally, through Metro La Motte Piquet-Grenelle.

HEXAGON CENTERED ON THE OBELISK NODE

When I traced the leys within Paris on a large map, one of the first geometric structures that I noted from the maze of lines was the top half

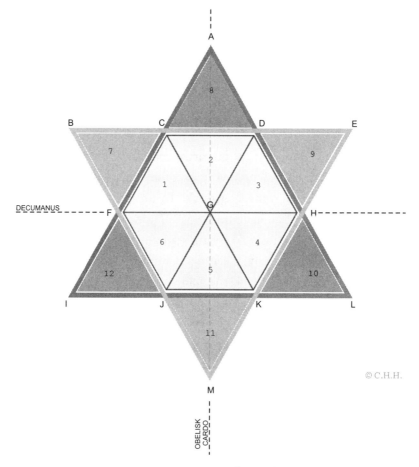

Figure 9.5. Sri Yantra (Star of David)

of a large hexagon centered on the Obelisk. Its median was the West Decumanus. The structure appeared as five imbricated equilateral triangles (see plate 8: St. John the Baptist's pyramid)—the three triangles of the upper half of the hexagon (triangles 1, 2, and 3 in figure 9.5), plus one on each side (triangles 7 and 9). These two additional equilateral triangles (7 and 9) could be incorporated into contiguous hexagons in a large hexagonal grid, as shown in figure 9.6. All triangles that form a hexagonal grid are equilateral (that is, they have equal sides and three angles of 60 degrees each), and the grid can be organized in three different patterns of imbricated hexagons, the most common being the hexagonal tile floor shown on the upper left of figure 9.5.

I was to discover later that the equilateral triangles 7 and 9 formed a larger triangle pointing downward (see figure 9.5). This larger triangle was composed of an upper row of five triangles (7, 1, 2, 3, 9), a second

Figure 9.6. A hexagon grid

row of three triangles (6, 5, 4), and a bottom row with just one triangle (11). This larger equilateral triangle pointing downward and made up of nine smaller equilateral triangles was, of course, part of the large Sri Yantra structure. Calculating all this on a new map, I found another large triangle pointing upward. I ended up with a Sri Yantra (Star of David) that extended across three-quarters of Paris, and the central node (G) of this was on the Obelisk. I found the upper part of the Obelisk hexagon well before the discovery of the golden rectangle. However, since both the hexagon and the golden rectangle had the same central node on the Obelisk, I decided to superimpose one on the other on the same small map—and astonishingly, the sides of the hexagon (FCDHKJ, in thick red in plate 4) just slightly cut the apexes (N, R, T, and X) of the golden rectangle (drawn in a thick blue line) as well as the circle drawn on the rectangle (the thick double blue-violet line).

Keep looking at plate 4: Obelisk golden rectangle plus hexagon. In total, the Obelisk hexagon runs through 10 churches, including **Notre-Dame de Paris** (the choir), **La Madeleine** (the choir), and 2 fifteenth-century Flamboyant Gothic churches: **Cloître des Billettes** and **St-Gervais-St-Protais** (node H). It also crosses 10 plazas (including Opéra, Concorde, and St-Augustin), 10 monuments (including the seventeenth-century Porte de Saint-Denis), and 10 Metros.

The Upper Half of the Obelisk Hexagon

In plate 4, we can see very clearly that the sacred lines forming the hexagon are marked by major churches and monuments. The hexagon apexes are F, C, D, H, K, and J, and the central node is G. The upper line linking the five triangles (line BCDE) runs through 4 churches, 3 major plazas and Metros, a town hall (generally of classical style), and a seventeenth-century hospital.

The three-triangle structure I first discovered was clearly marked by major churches. On the eastern side, **St-Vincent-de-Paul Church** marks the D node, nicely fitting within the angle formed by the two hexagon sides CD and DH. Similarly, at the eastern node H of the hexagon, **St-Gervais-St-Protais Church** is nested between sides HD and HG (the West Decumanus).

- **The side DH** (on the right) is thus clearly drawn: starting at **St-Vincent-de-Paul Church (D)**, it moves on to the ancient **Porte de Saint-Denis** (seventeenth century) and its plaza, a survivor gate of the ancient Charles V surrounding wall, the **Cloître des Billettes** (Flamboyant Gothic, fifteenth century), and finally, **St-Gervais-St-Protais Church** (H, Flamboyant Gothic, fifteenth century, save for its facade).

- **The diagonal GD** goes through the Metro and **Opéra Plaza**, then Metro Cadet, and ends at **St-Vincent-de-Paul Church**. If we lengthen it eastward, it crosses the northern station (**Gare du Nord**) at its geometrical center, then Metro and Plaza Crimée, and ends at Cité des Sciences, where it runs inside the building, parallel to its length.

- **The top side of the hexagon, CD**, runs through the crossing St-Ouen–Clichy and Metro La Fourche, Abbesses Plaza and church Notre-Dame-de-l'Assomption, and 2 theaters, then on to **St-Jean de Montmartre Church**.

- **The side FC** (on the left) is marked by Plaza General Patton (marking the node F on the decumanus), **St-Ferdinand-Ste-Thérèse Church**, and the two churches of **St-François-de-Sales** (the old and the new), meeting at their choirs but sideways, with the ley running in between.

- **Diagonal GC** (a few degrees from being a meridian) is an interesting ley since it runs through two important churches: first it follows the northeast side of St-Augustin Plaza, around the magnificent **St-Augustin Church**, and then runs into **Ste-Marie-des-Batignolles Church**.

- **GA, the hexagon's central vertical axis**, is the Obelisk Cardo, the breathtaking alignment from Concorde Plaza, following **rue Royale** to the splendid Greco-Egyptian temple of **La Madeleine Church** (and running through its median and choir). Higher up, this GA axis runs through **St-Louis-d'Antin Church**, the German Evangelist church, Metro Lamarck-Caulaincourt, and then it heads straight toward Porte de Clignancourt (the exact center of the plaza).

All these markers make the upper half of the hexagon so apparent that I drew it in color, but at this stage of my discovery, the lower half of the hexagon still remained obscured.

The Lower Half of the Obelisk Hexagon

When I started redrawing precisely the northern half of the hexagon on yet another large map, I became even more persuaded that it was well grounded within the city's sacred architecture. Pursuing my search, the lower half of the structure suddenly appeared with absolute clarity. Of course, such a prominent axis as La Madeleine-to-Obelisk (the AGM line in plate 4) demands to be extended all through the city: the segment GM was indeed quite well marked. To follow the line discussed in more detail below, continue to refer to plate 4: Obelisk golden rectangle plus hexagon.

- The **GM section**, beyond **Assemblée Nationale**, runs through Metro Varenne, then crosses the Invalides axis on **Vauban Plaza**, in front of the building (and passes at the geometrical center of this hemicycle), and meets a side of the golden rectangle just above. Extended, it passes through Villa de Saxe Chapel, Metro Ségur, **Unesco** (at its geometrical center), **St-Seraphin de Sarov Church** and Paris-Plaine Theater, to end at Porte de la Plaine.
- From node F, if we move counterclockwise, **the hexagon side FJ** crosses transversally the elliptical building of **Palais de Chaillot** (apex X in figure 9.4) on the palace's east wing, and then crosses the Trocadéro-to-Eiffel Tower axis 4 (which we saw in plate 1) on a line that joins the tips of the Trocadéro's wings. Then it goes through Metro Bir Hakeim, and when extended, meets with Porte de la Plaine at its exact center.
- **The southern side of the hexagon (JK)** follows two boulevards (on their southern edge): **boulevard de Grenelle and boulevard Garibaldi**. Then the side meets four Metro stations (Dupleix, Motte-Piquet Grenelle, Cambronne, and Sèvres Lecourbe). This axis is also clearly marked because it passes exactly at the center of the plaza between the Montparnasse Tower and the

Montparnasse train station. (Extended, this axis is parallel to the northern side of both **Montparnasse Cemetery** and the garden around the observatory, then passes slightly below the center of Place d'Italie.)

- **Hexagon side KH** starts with node K on Bobino Theater and Metro Edgar Quinet, runs transversally to Luxembourg Garden, crosses the Sorbonne University on the **dome of the Sorbonne Chapel**, passes through the **choir of Notre-Dame de Paris**, and then reaches node H on the West Decumanus. Extended, it runs through the large Crossing Lenoir-Voltaire (at its center), then passes slightly above Metro Ménilmontant and **Notre-Dame-de-la Croix Church** (node E du Sri Yantra in plate 5), and then reaches Porte des Lilas (slightly north of its Metro and center).

- **Diagonal GJ** doesn't seem to have significant features apart from pointing to Porte de St-Cloud (southeast). **Diagonal GK** meets the golden rectangle circle at Metro Montparnasse and the node K at Bobino Theater. Extended to the south, it marks **Mairie du 14ème** (at the northewest corner), then the southwestern wall of **St-Pierre-de-Montrouge Church**, after which it runs through Metro Alésia. The church is thus perfectly nested between GK and the continuation of the eastern side of the golden rectangle.

GRAND SRI YANTRA AROUND THE OBELISK

Saint-Antoine-de-Padoue Church sits inside the apex node M of the Sri Yantra (see plate 5: Obelisk Sri Yantra). Similarly, the large circular **Plaza d'Italie** nearly fits inside the apex L. The apex E sits about 22 yards to the north of **Notre-Dame-de-la Croix Church**. Axis DE, however, touches this church's choir just after this apex. We will see in detail only the two bases because we have already seen the other lines previously (when I described each side of the hexagon, I also gave the main markers for the lines extended in both directions).

- **The upper line BCDE** is marked by 4 churches, 3 major crossings, and an ancient hospital. It runs through the small plaza situated on the south of Cimetière des Batignoles, then through **Sainte-Reine Church**, Metro La Fourche, and **St-Jean-de-Montmartre Church** (near Metro Abbesses). It then passes just above **St-Vincent-de-Paul Church**, which marks the D apex of the hexagon. After this, it passes through **St-Louis Hospital** (seventeenth century), the Plaza and Metro Belleville, and touches the choir of **Notre-Dame-de-la-Croix Church**, just after node E. Extended, it meets the Metro and Plaza Gambetta and **Mairie du 20ème** and ends at Porte de Bagnolet Stadium.

- **The lower line IJKL** starts above and beyond Porte de Passy, then meets Crossing Raynouard-Lamballe. It then combines with JK, the southern side of the hexagon: It follows two boulevards, **boulevard de Grenelle and boulevard Garibaldi** (on their southern edge), then meets 4 Metros (Dupleix, Motte-Piquet-Grenelle, Cambronne, and Sèvres Lecourbe). It passes through the exact midpoint between Montparnasse Tower and Montparnasse station. The axis then runs parallel to the northern side of both **Montparnasse Cemetery** and the garden around the observatory, and it finally reaches slightly below the center of **Place d'Italie**.

OBELISK MANDORLE
An Homage to the Magdalene

After hearing that I was working on the sacred network, a Freemason I met at a cocktail party who was well versed in symbolism and sacred geometry (I suppose it's a tautology) confided to me that the closure of any work on a geometric structure was always to draw a circle around it. If I hadn't already had a bent for arcs, curves, and undulations, as well as a natural tendency not to feel satisfied (or just balanced) unless a map showed curves to compensate for too many straight lines, the advice would have been priceless. I did remember, however, that such closure doesn't consist of just any curve: it must specifically be the one encircling the mandala. This, of course, doesn't rule out embedded circles and arcs and the most sacred of inner crossings of arcs: the mandorle.

The Arch-Mandorle

Architects use the mandorle to draw ogival arcs, for in fact a mandorle is composed of two ogival arcs that meet at their base on the horizontal line (a figure that fits in a diamond). The arch-mandorle (from the greek root *arch,* meaning "first," "primary," "archetype," or "model")— the model of all mandorles—is drawn from two circles having the same radius and embedded in such a way that each circle runs through the center of the other one. This gives the sacred proportion of the ogival arc used in Gothic churches, which is why this arch-mandorle is the one sculpted on the tympana of cathedrals and churches to nest the sculptures of Christ or Mary in glory. In Chartres Cathedral, the magnificent tympanum on the western porch features, within the mandorle, the Four Living Creatures from the book of Revelation surrounding Christ in glory.

The Obelisk Golden Rectangle Mandorle

In general, however, the term *mandorle* is used for any two symmetrical arcs that form ogival ribs of varied proportions (more or less high, more or less curved, etc.). Thus, the two arcs drawn inside the sacred space in the middle of a golden rectangle form a mandorle: this mandorle is the heart of a golden rectangle.

Let's see the mandorle inside our golden rectangle (see figure 9.4). The sacred middle space of the rectangle, if you remember, is OQUW, the central smaller rectangle standing on end that corresponds to the overlapping section of the left and right squares. In the middle of this sacred space stands the vertical median (PV) of the whole rectangle: the Obelisk Cardo, which is the grand axis La Madeleine-to-Obelisk. And perperdicular to the Obelisk Cardo is the horizontal median of the golden rectangle: YS, which is the West Decumanus.

Keep looking at figure 9.4, and find the middle space OQUW. Now, imagine drawing the golden rectangle mandorle. Put the point of your imaginary compass on the midpoint of the right short side, point S on Châtelet Plaza, setting the compass to fall on the midpoint of the top long side (point P), and then draw the arc to the midpoint of the other long side (point V). Try to follow the circle on the map, and imagine you continue to draw the entire circle. Then repeat the operation with the compass point on the midpoint of the left small side, Y, keeping the same aperture so that it falls on the same two midpoints of the long sides (P and V). You thus have drawn the two pink circles that form and delineate the mandorle space, itself colored in light pink.

Thus, by using as a radius half the length of the rectangle's diagonal and using as a center the two midpoints of the short sides, the golden rectangle's mandorle is created. The resulting two outer circles intersect to form the mandorle. Let's call the circle (on the left side of the map)—drawn with the Arc de Triomphe as a center—the Arc de Triomphe mandorle circle. The opposite circle on the right of the map is the Châtelet mandorle circle.

See figure 9.4 to follow the detailed descriptions below:

- The **Arc de Triomphe mandorle circle** draws an arc that delineates the proportions of the École Militaire monument (at the bottom left of the drawing): first, it links the northeast corner of **École Militaire** to its southwest corner, and then it runs through the small side of the inner courtyard (on its right side). All together, this arc shows the width and length of the rectangle on which the École Militaire is built. Further north, the circle crosses the southeast corner of the **Invalides** building (around point V).

- As for the **Châtelet mandorle circle**, it goes through the nave of **Sainte-Trinité Church** (just above point P), and marks the southeast corner of Petit Palais (on the left of G), then runs through the center of the **Montparnasse Tower** (bottom right of figure 9.4) and, farther, into the geometrical center of the **Observatory Garden** (see plate 5). A tangent to the arc is quasi-parallel to the back of Gare de Lyon and passes in front of **Ste-Marguerite Church** (rue de Charonne), then above Gare de l'Est, geometrically oriented toward the building, and then it reinforces the nesting of **St-Vincent-de-Paul Church** on the D node.

Two Circles That Are Tangent to the Obelisk Cardo

Let us now draw another set of two identical circles that seem to fit perfectly a golden rectangle, ones with a radius half the length of the Obelisk golden rectangle. They are drawn from the centers of the short sides (S and Y, the same centers we used for the mandorle), and their identical radii extend from these points to the center of the golden rectangle, G, the Obelisk. We end up with two circles that are tangent to each other on the Obelisk node. (See, in plate 4, the circles outlined in a double pink line, one soft pink and one bright pink.) These two tangent circles are thus concentric to the first two and slightly smaller.

The first, the Arc de Triomphe tangent circle, uses as a radius the segment YG from the Arc de Triomphe (Y, its center) to the Obelisk (see figure 9.4 on page 219). The second, or Châtelet tangent circle, uses as a radius (of identical length) the segment SG, Châtelet plaza (S, its center) to the Obelisk. It runs through several Metros and plazas, namely the one at the back of **L'Opéra**, and it passes in front of the choir of **St-Ambroise Church** and **St-Antoine-des-Quinze-Vingts Church**.

THE MAGDALENE'S ROYAL LILY

The drawing of these two tangent circles creates a stupendous geometric structure: inside the northern part of the mandorle, the two double-line inner circles create a fountain shape springing out of the Obelisk that perfectly embeds La Madeleine, a church dedicated to Mary Magdalene. The geo-architecture is adjusted so that the arcs precisely mark the width of La Madeleine on its front facade, ravishingly encasing this sacred Greco-Roman–style temple.* Below point P, these two inner arcs are cut (at points Z' and Z" in figure 9.4) by the two outer circles that form the top of the mandorle (in the shape of ogival ribs), creating a stunningly beautiful structure, as extraordinary in its geometrical conception as it is in the message it delivers though its geo-architectural symbolism.

---

*This doesn't show on our maps, because I had to enlarge the icon of La Madeleine for it to be properly visible.

Let's look more closely at figure 9.4 to see the shape delineated by the four arcs, GZ', GZ'' and PZ', PZ'', a kind of curved diamond shape created by convex arcs at the top and concave arcs at the bottom, with La Madeleine at the source of the springing concave arcs. Astonishingly, it corresponds to how one can geometrically draw the lily of blazons, symbolic of kingship in France. More precisely, it is the exact shape and proportion of the central petal in the blazon representation of the Lily of France—a large, central petal flanked by two small, differently shaped petals. Now the symbolism of this whole structure is even more amazing! Let's first have a look at the recorded history of the La Madeleine monument.

A previous building on a Diocese land was a synagogue until the expulsion of the Jews in 1182, after which it was consecrated as a church to Mary Magdalene. After the Plaza Louis XV was constructed, the old building was demolished and a large monument was conceived, oriented geometrically to the axis of the plaza. In 1777, the architect Couture drew the plans of a Greco-Roman temple and started building the portico. He finished it, but his work on the monument came to a halt with the 1789 Revolution. A few years later, a new architect, Vignon, assumed the task, changing the remaining plans. Yet nobody knew how to use the building, since churches were no longer in the zeitgeist. In 1806, Napoleon I contemplated making it a "Temple to the glory of the Great Army," but the Arc de Triomphe ultimately grabbed the title. Finally, it became a church again in 1842.

The geo-architectural complex of the Obelisk-to-La Madeleine, however, speaks otherwise. It reveals such an exquisite embedding of meaning, a whole semantic constellation in stone, that we can suspect the said "hesitation" about its final dedication—especially from such a geo-architectural initiate as Napoleon I—to be nothing but a smokescreen. It is beyond doubt that an overall grand design in architectural symbolism had all along presided over its construction. The final rectangular building of La Madeleine is surrounded by fifty-two huge Corinthian columns, making it look more like a temple than a church. To balance La Madeleine, the Palais Bourbon (which refers to the Bourbon royal line) was constructed on the other side of the Seine in the same style, though it is not perfectly aligned with the Obelisk Cardo (the reason escapes me).

As we have uncovered, La Madeleine is nested in a thrice-sacred space. Thrice sacred because it's within a golden rectangle, within the sacred middle space of this rectangle, and within the mandorle inside the sacred space. Remember that the great initiator of Egypt, the divinized Thoth (Hermes) was called Thrice Great.

To top it all, La Madeleine is nested inside a lily petal within the mandorle. The very center of all these embedded structures (Sri Yantra, hexagon, golden rectangle, mandorle) and the root from which the lily petal stems is the Obelisk from the Luxor temple in Egypt. In front of La Madeleine starts rue Royale, which penetrates into the Concorde Plaza through the space between two magnificent hôtels, looking more like two towers.

The Luxor temple's Obelisk is flanked by two beautiful fountains (their axis perpendicular to the two towers). Overall, the Concorde Plaza is in the shape of a rectangle with cut corners, thus forming an elongated octagon. The four short sides of this octagon are adorned, at their corners, with two statues each representing French towns: in all, there are eight statues of crowned women bearing scepters. In the southeast corner, in front of the Orangerie Museum, is the sculpture of Marseille, the harbor through which Mary Magdalene arrived by boat when fleeing the Holy Land. Interestingly, the crown of the queen representing Marseille looks like a medieval fortified castle and thus has the flavor of ancient Tarot cards.

To add to this royal symbolism, let's remember that in the seventeenth century Concorde Plaza was a royal plaza dedicated to Louis XV. The Obelisk was erected at the very place where the statue of Louis XV had stood.

Thus, Magdalene's temple, inserted in a lily as in a casket, surrounded by symbols of a royal line going back to Egypt and linked to France's royalty, faces the Obelisk through the space between the two towers. The two towers—a very important symbol in Freemasonry—refer to the two columns that flanked Solomon's Temple. Called, respectively, Jachin and Boaz, these two columns symbolize that those on a spiritual path must harness all complementary forces and harmonize duality. In fact, King Solomon and the Queen of Sheba, always side by side, are a persistent sight on cathedrals' porches. They stand on the right side of the front porch of Chartres, beneath the mandorle featuring Christ in glory surrounded by the Four Living Creatures from the book of Revelation.

La Madeleine is also embedded into another structure—a five-pointed star centered on the Obelisk. Imagine drawing a circle centered on the Obelisk (G) and using as a radius the distance GY (Obelisk to Arc de Triomphe): by doing so you will obtain the thin, orange circle seen in plate 5, Obelisk Sri Yantra. Inside this circle, draw a pentagon facing point A. The horizontal line marking the two upper apexes of the inner pentagon follows exactly the northern limit of the square plaza surrounding La Madeleine. Thus again, in this new structure based on the number 5 (the pentagram), La Madeleine is at a place of honor.

The whole geo-architecture of the mandorle, with the Obelisk at its center and La Madeleine at the place of honor on rue Royale, hints at underlying links between the Magdalene, royalty, and a French royal line. It illuminates the connection between Mary Magdalene and both Egypt and Isis as the Great Goddess; it hints at the Magdalene being of royal Egyptian lineage and the priestress of an Egyptian initiation cult. It reveals the Magdalene fleeing to France, and specifically to Marseille. Could this evoke the wondrous story of two initiates who had come from Egypt—Jesus and John (the future St. John the Baptist)—to settle in the Holy Land? The very clear symbols depict the Magdalene linked to a French royal line—being married to Christ and their lineage merging with the Frankish royalty and becoming the royal Merovingian bloodline. And then we have also the strange name of La Concorde, the root of which refers to the heart and the word meaning "harmony" ("hearts together") and a pact of peace. A harmony between Mary Magdalene and Isis, between the priestress and her initiatic lineage?

The royal lineage of the Sicambrian Franks (installed in the north of France but originally from Germany) underwent a key transmutation with the birth of Mérovée (or Merovech), who started the Merovingian dynasty. Mérovée was the grandfather of Clovis, who became the first king of the Franks in 509 CE and was the first to be crowned by the pope. The queen mother of Mérovée is said to have been already pregnant from her husband when, during a bath in the sea, she was impregnated a second time by an extraordinary Neptunian creature. Mérovée, thus born of two fathers, possessed extraordinary supernormal capacities, such as the gifts of healing, telepathy, clairvoyance, and magical powers related to longevity. The Merovingian royals in general, according to Michael Baigent, Richard Leigh, and Henry Lincoln, were initiates in arcane sciences and powerful practitioners—and for this reason they were called *sorcerer kings* or *thaumaturge kings*.[4] In fact, the memory of the arrival of the Magdalene in the Rhône delta, not far from the harbor of Marseille, accompanied by two other women whose names were also Mary, lingers in stone. At the small town called Les Saintes Maries de la Mer (The Holy Marys of the Sea), a most holy pilgrimage recalls their arrival in France. The story goes that the Magdalene then settled in a Jewish community in the south of France. Robert Maestracci, who mapped the secret geography of the Provence region, describes their arrival at Les Saintes Maries de la Mer and then follows Mary Magdalene toward Aix, then Marseille, and finally to La Sainte-Baume, east of Aix.[5] According to the French tradition, the Magdalene spent the rest of her life in this large grotto, which is quite high on a cliff topped by a towering rock called Saint-Pilon. Strangely, since Maestracci is not aware of the Goan Pilar and the Rishi grotto, where the magnificent bas-relief of the Magdalene was found, he nonetheless equates *pilon* in French to a rock *pilier* (with English translation *pillar* and Portuguese translation *pilar*). So in the two sacred sites of Pilar in Goa and La Sainte-Baume in Provence where the Magdalene has been present or honored, there are sacred stone peaks—a natural antenna of Earth.

Thus, geo-architecture is far more than an expression of sacred geometry and the golden proportion pointing to harmony and beauty within nature. It also reveals an entire story to those who can decode its energetic connections and read its symbolic language in stone.

HEXAGONS WITHIN HEXAGONS

Of course, symmetrical arcs that form mandorle shapes within a particular geometrical structure are found not only in relation to circles and golden rectangles. In fact, there is also a wealth of different mandorle shapes incorporated within a grid of hexagons, which can be drawn by moving the point of the compass without ever changing its aperture set on the radius of the hexagon. The method for drawing all the magnificent rose windows of cathedrals is to start with a perfect star (whatever the number of points), and then to draw circles from all the apexes and from all the crossing points—ad infinitum. The structure becomes increasingly more complex, an embedding of stars within stars, which, however, always retains the same numerical basis. For example, a six-pointed star (derived from the hexagon) leads to embedded six-pointed stars and hexagons with the constant doubling of the number rising with complexity: 6, 12, 24, and so forth. (See figure 9.6, A hexagon grid, on page 225.) This is true whatever the number of points in the initial star. A pentagon thus leads to rose windows of infinite complexity, and larger embedded five-pointed stars and pentagons lead to embedded ten-pointed stars and decagons—just like the two embedded ten-pointed stars around Châtelet. In the geometric structures in plate 5, the Obelisk hexagon is already so large that the first larger embedded 6-pointed star (the Sri Yantra structure) exceeds the edges of Paris (delineated by the surrounding highway, or *périphérique,* drawn in a grey line that follows the outer frame of the map). In drawing it, however, I didn't feel comfortable with the fact that it was leaving out the east side of Paris, so I decided to look at it from far away. Pinning the map to a wall to ponder it, I made a discovery: a second imbricated hexagon could be drawn to the east. I immediately checked to see if I could find geo-architectural markers showing that some buildings had been conceived on this geometrical canvas—and indeed I found quite interesting ones. The next node falls on Crossing Reuilly-Picpus (E), and the southern side passes through the Mitterrand Library, and the northern side passes through the perfect center of Nation Plaza and two churches, **Bon-Pasteur** and **Notre-Dame-de-la-Croix** (the eastern node E of the Sri Yantra).

We can also note the most important circle linked to the Obelisk hexagon: the one encircling it.

Circle Drawn on the Apexes of the Obelisk Hexagon

The circle drawn on the apexes of the Obelisk hexagon (see this in brown in plate 4) runs through several interesting churches. After crossing apex C and then the Obelisk Cardo (moving clockwise) it meets **St-Pierre-de-Montmartre Church**, which is quite remarkable. More leys converge on this small church than on the imposing basilica flanking it. The reason being that St-Pierre-de-Montmartre, originally Gothic in style, is much more ancient than the Montmartre Basilica (Basilique du Sacré-Coeur), dating from late-nineteenth century. The circle also meets **St-Jean-Baptiste-de-la-Salle Church** (after apex K), the node (J1) of St. John's pyramid and also a marker on ley 13.

The most fascinating feature of this circle, however, is that it runs through two churches strongly connected to the Knights Templar. After apex D is **Notre-Dame-des-Blancs-Manteaux**, and then both the circle and the western apex H of the hexagon are marked by **St-Gervais-St-Protais Church**, one of the few Parisian edifices in Flamboyant Gothic style (fifteenth century, just like St-Jacques Tower), save for its seventeenth-century facade. (See the details of this circle in appendix 2.) The name of the first church—Blancs-Manteaux (White Mantles)—is a reference to the Templar's clothing. The name of the second church resonates with another church, set in Gisors, that has this same double name. Apart from sharing their name, both St-Gervais-St-Protais Churches also have an ancient elm nearby. The Parisian church marked the border of the vast property of the Templars in Paris—the mother house of the entire worldwide order—which reached to the Carreau du Temple (west of boulevard du Temple, a marker in several structures), set nearer to where had been the location of their medieval fortified castle.

As for Gisors, it was under l'Orme de Gisors (a quite mythical elm) that took place, in 1188, a grand gathering whose guests of honor included Guillaume de Tyr (archbishop of Tyr), Henri II Plantagenet, (king of England and duke of Normandy), Philippe II (king of France and future Philippe Auguste), and a mysterious Jean de Gisors (an influential and charismatic Templar). At this gathering, de Tyr was in the process of rallying support for the Third Crusade, but the most significant event was a bitter feud that erupted between the two kings and culminated with the enraged Frenchmen cutting down the extremely old elm. It is as far as the diverse reports agree on this eventful day; the real motives of the quarrel, however, remain unclear.

In one version of the story, the feud was a skirmish in a permanent battle between the two kings for the possession of Gisors, whose strategic importance at the border of the two realms seems to pale when compared with its mysterious power and spiritual meaning. It is known that the two kings had numerous meetings at Gisors. The cutting down of the elm signified the end of their alliance.

Another version refers to the hidden tenants of Gisors, the Priory of Sion, the new name adopted by the ancient Order of Zion. This "Ordre de Sion" or "Ordre Notre-Dame de Sion" was founded by Godfroi de Bouillon (who ruled as the first king of Jerusalem but had refused the title) in 1090, that is, nine years before Jerusalem was conquered. The order resided on Mount Sion just outside of Jerusalem, in an abbey called Notre-Dame du Mont de Sion, which de Bouillon built over the ruins of a fourth-century Byzantine basilica. King Louis VII returned from the Second Crusade with ninety-five knights of the order (at this time, they were still called Knights of the Order of Notre-Dame de Sion). Many charters (notably from the town of Orléans) state that in 1152, King Louis VII gave to the Ordre de Sion a large priory at St-Samson and a small one called Petit Prieuré du Mont-Sion—both situated near Orléans. After the fall of Jerusalem in 1187, the order was forced to go back to France. It seems the order changed its name to the Priory of Sion at this time, in line with the priory they had been given.

The Priory is the secret society said to have launched the Templar Order and to have been its concealed head; this assersion is based on the fact that the grand masters of the two organizations were the same person, at least until that famous date in 1188. The cutting of the eight-hundred-year-old tree would have marked the decision of the Priory of

Sion to break with the Templars, who had already become a very powerful international order.

THE TRANSMISSION OF SACRED GEOMETRY

I have practiced the yoga of harmonic resonance and decoded the sacred network in many ancient ruins and temples all over the world. These experiences have shown me that grids similar to the one existing in France and Paris exist in other countries. Dan Brown's *Angels and Demons* unveils part of the grid that links sacred buildings in Rome, and *The Da Vinci Code* hints at a larger grid encompassing France and Great Britain.

The existence of a vibrant sacred network over a town or a region influences the very life of its inhabitants, not solely because space is centered and oriented, but also for the reason that a living and spiritual energy keeps flowing along the cosmo-telluric lines. The fact that such giant webs of standing stones and temples have been preserved and enlarged up to the present day reveals a global plan that spans centuries and, if not always directed from the highest levels of government leaders, is at least endorsed by them. If we take into consideration the interconnection of sacred sites across different countries and cultures, forming a web at the planetary level, then we have to infer the existence of stable means of communication allowing for intensive contacts among high initiates of various faiths and secret societies all over the world.

The question then becomes: Is the sacred network of cosmo-telluric sites of Earth linked to an active organization of interrelated initiates? Is there an arch-network connecting various secret societies, an arch-network that has remained in the shadows and yet has been highly efficient through at least two millennia?

One way to investigate such a question is to tackle an enigma that has long puzzled researchers and art historians: Which secret group had both the knowledge and the immense means necessary to build at the same time (in the novel Gothic style) so many cathedrals during the twelfth and thirteenth centuries?

In his book on Chartres Cathedral, Sonja Klug attributes such a role to the Templars.[6] Given that they invented exchange transaction between countries (through authenticated letters) and were the bankers of the world, we know that the Templars had the means. But what about the builders' knowledge? Of course, the Templars themselves built their numerous churches and *commanderies,* lavish with their own symbolism. But what about the emergence of a totally novel architectural style, the Gothic, the exact same year as the creation of the order, that is, 1118?

To understand the larger picture of the sacred network, spanning over two millennia, let's make a quick detour by Chartres (all roads lead to Chartres, it seems!), following Klug's analysis.

According to Klug, Chartres Cathedral was erected on a Druidic site comprising not only several menhirs (we saw more detailed information about them), but also a large dolmen (table), under which was a chamber. This dolmen would now be in the crypt, above (or rather under?) the statue *Notre-Dame-de-Sous-Terre.*

This statue, erected in 1857, was modeled on an extremely revered previous statue of the same name that was destroyed during the 1789 French Revolution and set at the same place. As we saw, the Fulbert Crypt was crowded by sick people who lived there until they were healed—just as in a hospital. We know that the Celtic site and the curative virtue of the well water and ancient spring had attracted crowds since the Druidic times. Did the mysterious statue also draw crowds— or were the crowds due to its specific location at a very ancient sacred node in what once had been a temple complex?

The Carolingian- and Roman-style edifices suffered six major fires through the centuries. After the last very severe fire in 1194, the cathedral was rebuilt in a Gothic style in only twenty-six years! This Gothic cathedral is the exact same one that we can visit today, for it never suffered any more fires or damage of vast proportions apart from the heartbreaking knocking down of many hands and heads of statues during the French Revolution. The case of Chartres is not unique: many of the greatest Gothic cathedrals have been built and consecrated in three or four decades—leaving only minor work and decoration to be completed in another decade or so.

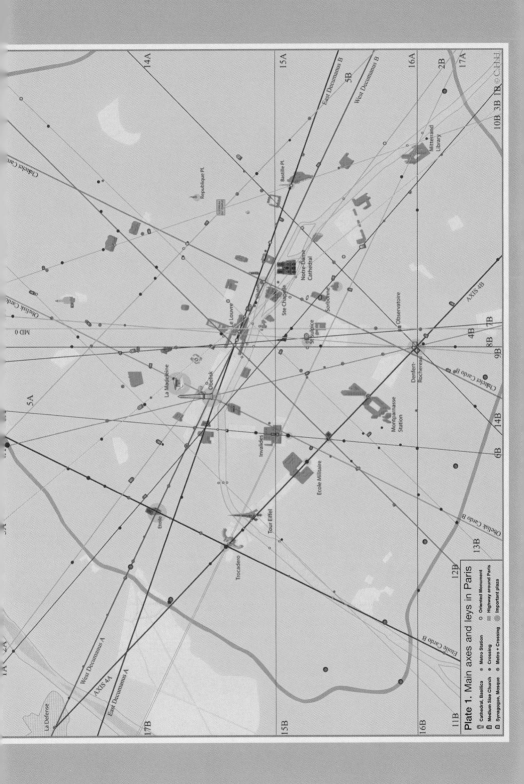

Plate 1. Main axes and leys in Paris

- Cathedral, Basilica
- Medium Size Church
- Synagogue, Mosque
- Metro Station
- Oriented Monument
- Crossing
- Highway around Paris
- Metro + Crossing
- Important plaza

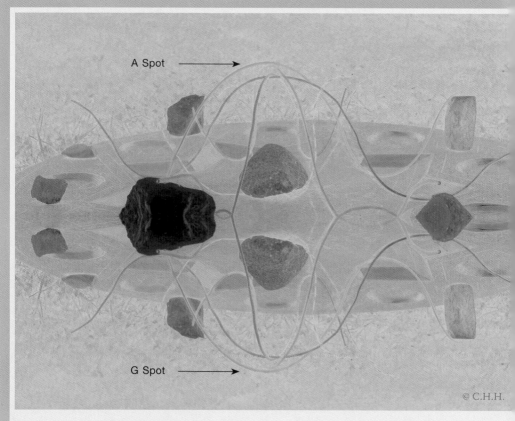

A Spot ⟶

G Spot ⟶

© C.H.H.

Plate 2. A Spot and G Spot at two crossings of cosmo-telluric lines

Ascending Spot: crossing above ground
Grounding Spot: crossing below ground

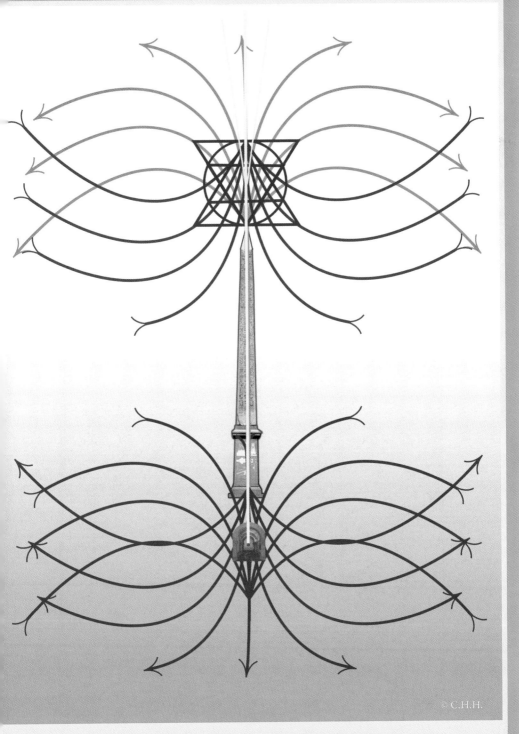

Plate 3. Flow of sacred lines around an obelisk and a cave

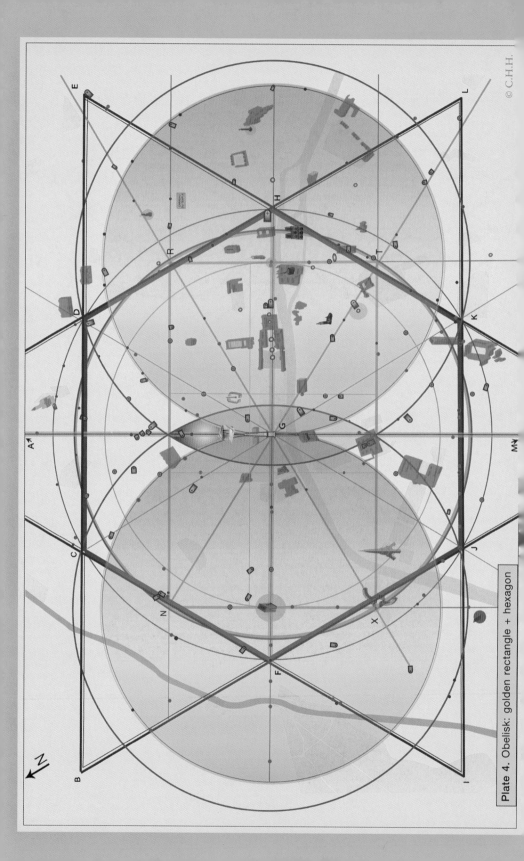

Plate 4. Obelisk: golden rectangle + hexagon

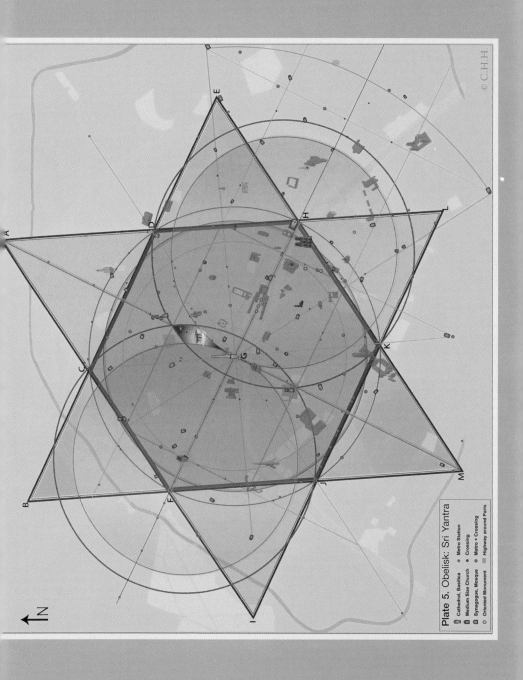

N

Plate 5. Obelisk: Sri Yantra

- Cathedral, Basilica ● Metro Station
- Medium Size Church ● Crossing
- Synagogue, Mosque ◆ Metro + Crossing
- Oriented Monument ▨ Highway around Paris

© C.H.H

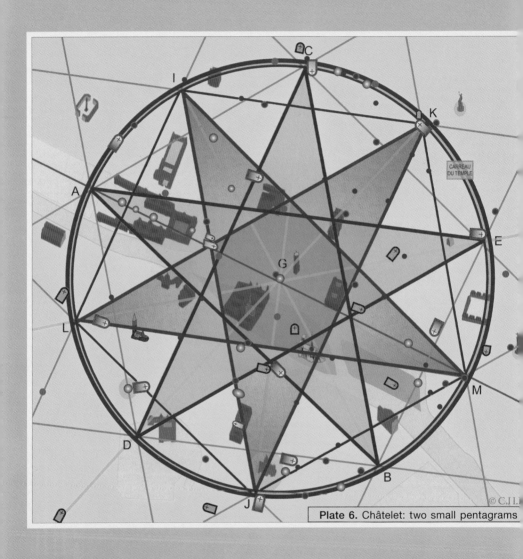

CARREAU
DU TEMPLE

Plate 6. Châtelet: two small pentagrams

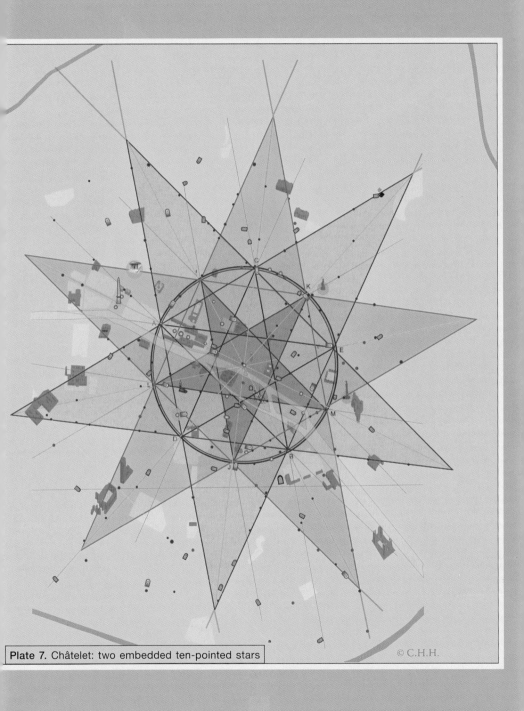

Plate 7. Châtelet: two embedded ten-pointed stars

© C.H.H.

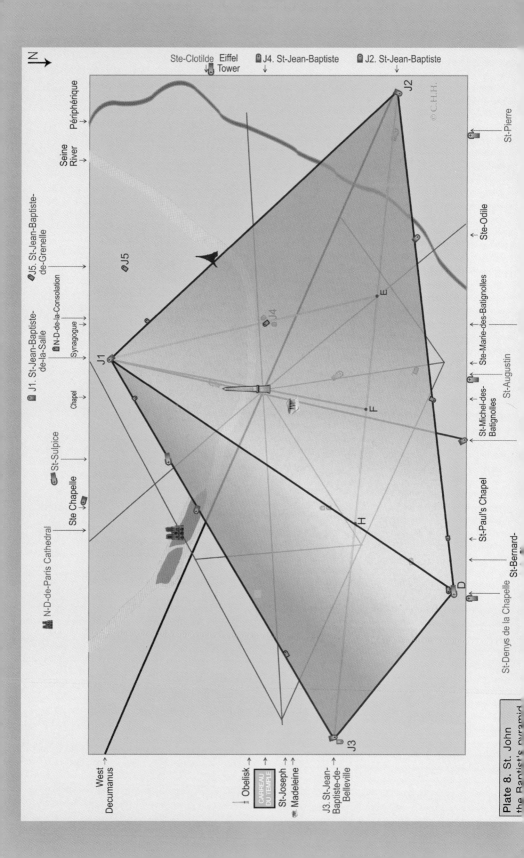

N →

Ste-Clotilde Eiffel
↓ 🏛 Tower

🏛 J4. St-Jean-Baptiste 🏛 J2. St-Jean-Baptiste
↓   ↓

Périphérique →

Seine River →

🏛 J5. St-Jean-Baptiste-de-Grenelle

J5

🏛 N-D-de-la-Consolation →

Synagogue →

🏛 J1. St-Jean-Baptiste-de-la-Salle

Chapel →

St-Sulpice →

J1

E

St-Pierre

Ste-Odile ←

Ste-Marie-des-Batignolles ←

St-Augustin →

St-Michel-des-Batignolles →

Ste Chapelle →

F

© C.H.H.

J4

🏛 N-D-de-Paris Cathedral

J2

H

St-Paul's Chapel ←

West Decumanus →

St-Bernard-

D

Obelisk →

CARREAU DU TEMPLE →

St-Joseph →

Madeleine →

J3. St-Jean-Baptiste-de-Belleville →

J3

St-Denys de la Chapelle

St-Pierre

Plate 8. St. John the Baptist's pyramid

Another mystery to consider involves where this novel architectural expertise originated. Klug traces this sudden surge of architectural know-how to the discovery of a collection of books by the Egyptian Thoth, known in Greece as Hermes Trismegistus, whose forty-plus works were said to cover a vast gamut of scientific disciplines from geometry, mathematics, and astronomy to metaphysics. (We know that prominent Greek philosophers were initiated in Egypt, among them Plato and Pythagoras. The last one that we know for certain went to Egypt is Apollonius of Tyana, who taught his neo-Pythagorean philosophy in Ephesus during the first century CE.) According to Klug, Thoth's books, together with the arcane keys to decode them, were found in Solomon's Temple in Jerusalem. They were carried back by Hughes de Payens to the Cistercian monastery of Cîteaux, founded in 1098, where the head of the monastery, Stéphane de Harding, a friend of de Payens, started the translation with Hebrew and Arab scholars.

De Harding became the mentor of Bernard Fontaine, the future Bernard de Clairvaux, when the latter entered Cîteaux Monastery in 1112. Born in 1090, Bernard was a monk for less than four years when he was given the mission by his mentor to start a new abbey: Clairvaux. Very quickly, he became the most influential person in the Catholic church and, due in part to his family links to great aristocratic lineages, developed relationships with many courts and influential groups.

De Payens was the head of the nine knights who started the Templar Order in 1118 in Jerusalem with the official goal of protecting the pilgrims in the Holy Land. Yet many researchers believe the order started earlier, and that 1118 marks the date that it was officially recognized by Baudouin II, king of Jerusalem. Strangely, 1118 is also the official date of the apparition of the first ogival crossings in Poissy and Morienval (the ogive being the blueprint of the Gothic style).

Klug thinks that because these knights lived in Solomon's Temple, residence of King Baudouin, their real aim was to search the temple (precisely the underground remnants of the first such temple) and then start translating the books uncovered there. He underlines that de Payens's return from the Holy Land happened at about the same time as de Clairvaux's creation of the Cistercian abbey of Clairvaux (1115).

Bernard and the monks of Clairvaux then immediately devoted themselves to the translation from the Hebrew and Arabic languages.

Bernard de Clairvaux is rumored to have had a major influence on the building of the Gothic Chartres, whose head architect, surprisingly, has remained unknown. Traditionally, a head architect was so revered that he was represented in bas-reliefs in the building, together with the bishop and the donators. In the case of such an important cathedral, then, missing the architect image is both uncommon and highly surprising. Does this suggest a link between the translation of Thoth's texts and the Gothic style? Could Bernard de Clairvaux be the architect of Chartres, after having studied the Hermetic science? One thing is quite clear: Bernard de Clairvaux had an immense erudition. De Payens, after accompanying the count of Champagne to the Holy Land in the First Crusade in 1095, must have come back at an unknown date, because we know for certain that he and the count again left France for Jerusalem in 1114 and remained there. Notwithstanding the problem of this date, Klug's thesis about ancient books brought back from the Holy Land and the translations done both at Cîteaux and Clairvaux makes great sense. We know Bernard de Clairvaux had great erudition and that he wrote many influential books. If he was so erudite, it makes sense that he would create a new abbey just for the purpose of translating ancient scrolls and manuscripts, thus centralizing the work started at Cîteaux.

Yet, even in the event that Bernard de Clairvaux had recovered Thoth's books and had them translated, it doesn't follow that the Gothic style could just be derived from them. How could Thoth's principles of sacred geometry and the divine proportion give rise to an architectural style totally different from the Egyptian or Greek models, which were also derived from Thoth's science? Whatever way we look at it, it seems there definitely was a leap, both in terms of consciousness and in terms of sacred architecture.

According to official records, for a few years after 1118, the Templar order consisted only of the original group of nine initiated knights, but they, however, commanded numerous people. In 1126, the count of Champagne joined the order—a tenth knight. That same year, de Payens returned to Europe to find both funding and highly eminent affiliates and to have the Templar Order officially recognized by the pope. This official recognition occurred in 1128 (under Pope Honorius II) at an ecumenical council held in Troyes Cathedral. The pope was represented, rather than present, but attending were the count of Champagne; Etienne Harding, abbot of Cîteaux; and Bernard, abbot of Clairvaux, who, beyond conceiving the new Templar Order's Rule, had also written an eulogy of the order.

To get back to Klug's thesis, Jacques de Molay, before he was burnt in 1314, would have had time to launch the order of Compagnons, who then took over the task of building the cathedrals. The high grades in the corporation of the masons and architects would thus become the Freemasons. Klug's view, however, is somewhat schematic, and the truth is much more complex, because we know that several (not just one) new secret societies were created from 1312 to 1316, and they could very probably have lasted to become some of our modern Freemasonry and Rosicrucian orders. As we will see, the names of some of them suggest they had a bent toward alchemy and Hermeticism.

It is known that two new orders were created in Spain and Portugal just after the dissolution of the Temple: the Order of Montesa in Aragon and the Order of Christ in Portugal. The Templars in these countries had not been persecuted, and most of them joined the new orders. Jean Markale[7] recounts the story that 237 Knights Templar received refuge in the Temple Church in London, then moved toward Scotland, where King Robert the Bruce was a sure ally. There, they joined French Templars who were already settled on Mull Island and had elected a new grand master, Jacques d'Aumont, and established themselves. Among them was a great alchemist, Guidon de Montador, and his disciple, Gaston de la Pierre Phoebus. The latter, following the Templar tradition, created a college of alchemists, which decided to remain a secret society. It adopted the symbol of the pelican in its pity—later used by the Chevaliers de la Rose+Croix et de l'Aigle Noir (Knights of the Rose Cross and Black Eagle). When, in 1316, Jacques d'Euse becomes the new Pope John XXII, well versed in alchemy and Hermetism, de la Pierre Phoebus traveled discreetly with a few trusted men to Avignon to be received by the pope.

The pope gave him the mission to return to Scotland and come back with the elite knights. De la Pierre Phoebus, however, died on the way in an ambush after giving all his secrets to a prior of the Hospital Order who was in charge of conceiving a rule for the new order. Only a handful of de la Pierre Phoebus's comrades reached Scotland. Soon thereafter, the nephew of the pope, Jacques de Via, departed from Scotland to France with a troop of knights. Then, under the supervision of the prior, a college of thirty-three sages was elected to be authorized successors of de la Pierre Phoebus. The successors of this secret college took the name Frères aînés de la Rose+Croix (Elder Brothers of the Rose Cross), and the organization still exists today.

Another tradition, according to Markale,[8] says that a few days before his death, de Molay asked for his nephew, the count of Beaujeu, and requested that Beaujeu fetch a crystal casket from one of the tombs of the ancient grand masters. When Beaujeu returned with the casket, de Molay initiated him, revealed the order's mysteries, and made him swear to be a guardian of the tradition. Soon after, Beaujeu was elected grand master and decided on veiling the order even more. His successor was d'Aumont—the same knight who was elected grand master by the French Templars who settled on Mull Island in Scotland and the 237 knights who had fled France and taken refuge in London's Temple Church on their way to Scotland. Thus, the Templars' tradition seems to have been handed down three times in this period of great turmoil: two currents finally joined with d'Aumont, and the third one became the Elder Brothers of the Rose Cross.

However, to say that some secret societies, heirs of the cathedrals' architects and builders, have played the role of guardians of the traditional knowledge and have been highly competent in preserving as well as enriching the networks of sacred cosmo-telluric sites doesn't mean that they were also (as a group) at the forefront of the tremendous changes happening in the minds of human beings. Even if they had hunches and/ or guidelines about the momentous transformations in the making—or, to go to the extreme, even if they themselves had launched social, political, and economic changes, they wouldn't necessarily be on top of things as far as deep consciousness transformations are concerned. They wouldn't and couldn't, because hardly anybody can fathom where we are heading, that is, if we make it through this desperate End Time.

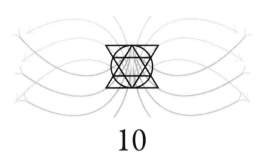

10

ST. JOHN THE BAPTIST'S PYRAMID AND THE CHÂTELET NODE

On realizing that there were no less than four churches dedicated to St. John the Baptist in Paris and its immediate vicinity, I had the idea of drawing lines linking them to check if the similarity in names could hide some meaningful connections. The method was rewarding; I discovered a large structure that had both an interesting geometry and an instructive constellation of interconnected meanings—a true semantic constellation in geo-architecture. Let's remember that John the Baptist is the patron saint of both the Templars and the Priory of Sion.

ST. JOHN THE BAPTIST'S PYRAMID

A large triangle is formed by joining three of the five churches—which I call, respectively, John 1, John 2, and John 3. (See J1, J2, and J3 in plate 8: St. John the Baptist's pyramid. In order for the geometrical structure to be easier to see, the map of Paris in the figure is upside down, so that north is on the bottom.) This triangle is so large that it is spread across three-quarters of Paris.

While I drew these lines, I was dumbfounded by the names of the places that were connected: most of them had, very obviously so, something to do with the Templars or the Priory of Sion. I kept checking alignments with a long ruler, turning around the table to draw lines on the huge map and often climbing the stairs to view it from high up and from a distance to get a global impression. Suddenly, there appeared a structure resembling a pyramid that connected four of the five St. John the Baptist Parisian churches. But let's see these St. John churches in detail.

1. **John 1: St-Jean-Baptiste-de-la-Salle** is the upper and main apex of the St. John's structure. It stands near Metro Pasteur, and is in reality south of Paris. We have seen this church on the circle drawn on the apexes of the Obelisk hexagon (chapter 9). On this same circle are two churches linked to the Knights Templar: Notre-Dame-des-Blancs-Manteaux and St-Gervais-St-Protais (node H of the hexagon, to the east—see plate 4). The name of the first, if you remember, refers to their white tunics, and the name of the second is similar to a church in Gisors, stronghold of the Templars and the Priory. St-Jean-Baptiste-de-la-Salle Church is also integrated in ley 13, Géode-to-*La Gloire* Bas-relief. (See plate 1 and the details about ley 13 itself in the appendix 1.)

2. **John 2: St-Jean-Baptiste Church** is situated on the West Decumanus near Metro Pont de Neuilly on avenue Charles de Gaulle (between la Défense and Porte Maillot—thus outside the limits of the périphérique, or circular highway around the city).

3. **John 3: St-Jean-Baptiste-de-Belleville** is on the plaza of Metro Jourdan, on the northeastern side of Paris (and to the bottom left of the map that is plate 8).

4. **John 4: St-Jean-Baptiste** is near Plaza Francois I, to the east of Metro Alma Marceau, center-west of Paris, not far above the Seine River (on the map that is plate 8, center right, below the Seine).

5. **John 5: St-Jean-Baptiste-de-Grenelle** stands north of Metro Felix Faure (to the right of St-Jean-Baptiste-de-la-Salle on the map). John 5 is part of the large Obelisk golden rectangle (see figure 9.4 on page 219). The southern length of the large golden rectangle runs through five churches and one abbey:

St-Hippolyte, St-Anne-de-la-Maison-Blanche, St-Albert-le-Grand, Notre-Dame-du-Travail, **St-Jean-Baptiste-de-Grenelle** (the line runs through the plaza in front of the choir), and Abbaye Sainte-Marie. The northern length runs through two churches: Notre-Dame-de-Lourdes (the northeast apex of the golden rectangle) and Notre-Dame-de-la-Gare. Surprisingly, however, St-Jean-Baptiste-de-Grenelle is not integrated in the St. John structure. (See plate 8.)

Imagine you have drawn the triangle linking the first three St. John churches (J1, J2, and J3). Now divide the large base (J2 to J3) in two and mark point F, and then draw the median (linking J1 to F): it goes through **the Obelisk**, which thus becomes the inner node of the St. John structure. The faint whitish-blue lines that dart out of the Obelisk like spokes of a wheel are the sacred lines that form the northern half of the Obelisk hexagon, which you can see better if you turn the map upside down (when I drew the St. John structure, I had only this northern half fully drawn, plus a triangle to the east).

The Triangle J1-J2-J3 Is Truly Surprising:
John 3 as well as the Obelisk are on Paris's West Decumanus.

- **The side J1-J3** runs through no less than 6 churches, the crucial one being **Saint-Sulpice**, which was a major seat of the Priory of Sion and which was constructed above an ancient Isis temple. Then it runs in front of **Carreau du Temple**, where the castle-temple of the Knights Templar in Paris was located. Their castle was so large that it's quite probable that this line crossed it. The six churches, starting from the top of the pyramid are: John 1, a chapel, **Saint-Sulpice**, **Sainte-Chapelle** (on La Cité island), **St-Joseph**, and John 3.
- **The side J3-J2** passes through only one church (apart from the St. John churches), that of **St-Pierre** (St. Peter), not far from J2.
- **The side J2-J1** runs through the exact center of **Trocadéro Plaza**, then passes between the two buildings that form the Ellipse of

Trocadéro. It then runs very near to the northwest foot of the **Eiffel Tower** and through a **synagogue**.

- **The line to St-Denys-de-la-Chapelle.** But let's go further. Draw now a straight line connecting J1 and J4, and lengthen it to the base of the triangle (J3-J2): you get point E. If you measure the exact segment FE and draw it on the base toward the left, you get point H. Next, draw the line connecting J1 to H, and extend it: it will run through a major church, **St-Denys-de-la-Chapelle** (or St. Denis Basilica). This church becomes point D. Finally, draw the lines connecting J3 to D, and D to J2. The structure that results looks like a pyramid: one of the possible representations in 2-D of a pyramidal volume.

When I drew this line J1-H and, extended, it fell on **St. Denis Basilica**, I had a real eureka experience: an insight that I was dealing with something even more potent than geo-architecture and sacred geometry. For indeed, if St. John the Baptist is the first, St. Denis is the second patron saint of both the Templars and the Priory of Sion. Furthermore, I had on the main triangle **Saint-Sulpice** (seat of the Priory of Sion, ancient Isis temple) and **Carreau du Temple** (part of the the ancient Templar headquarters in Paris). It definitely looked like I was reading in stone a whole constellation of meaning (a semantic constellation). More to the point, it felt like I was unraveling an *egregore*. This ancient concept (from the Latin *agregare,* to assemble) was referring to the immaterial reality of a spiritual group, its collective soul expressing its quest and values. And indeed, it was showing me, just with the first triangle, that the Priory and the Templars had been deeply interconnected within the same egregore. The semantics of the geo-architecture left no doubt: the Priory had been the secret head of the Templars. Why then wasn't the Priory seat at the center of the structure? As we will see, the secret node of the St. John pyramid is the Obelisk, facing La Madeleine, that is, Egypt and the Magdalene. And that means the Priory was itself perpetuating an initiatic chain going back to Pharaonic Egypt, a chain that, at one point, was headed and illuminated by the Magdalene and St. John the Baptist. And indeed, I had the most evident proof of this **two-center structure** when

I discovered that the distance from La Madeleine to J2 is exactly the same as the distance from La Madeleine to J3, and the same as the distance from the Obelisk to J2.

Before we dive further into the meaning encoded in this stupendous constellation, let's see the lines we have just drawn:

- On the line J1-E, St-Jean-le-Baptiste church (J4) is flanked by two other churches: on the left stands the **Church of Scotland**, and on the right stands **Notre-Dame-de-la-Consolation**. The inclusion of Scotland in the pyramid rings a bell, doesn't it? At the time of King Robert the Bruce, Scotland is where the Templars went when they fled France. There, they took refuge under the king. More important, Scotland is where new secret societies were going to sprout, as substitutes for the banned Templar order, namely, the Rosicrucian and Freemason orders. But this is not all. According to Michael Baigent, Richard Leigh, and Henry Lincoln's *Holy Blood, Holy Grail,* Henry de Saint-Clair, baron of Rosslyn (a few miles south of Edinburgh) accompanied Godfroi de Bouillon on the First Crusade.[1] His descendant, Marie de Saint-Clair, became the second grand master of the Priory of Sion after the cutting of the elm and the schism with the Templars. Rosslyn Chapel is one of the seats of the Priory of Sion and stands quite near a main Templar preceptory. In the choir of the chapel, not far from the two renowned pillars of the master and disciple, high on the side of a window, stands the sculpted head of Robert the Bruce.
- On line D-J2 are five churches: St-Denys, St. Paul's Chapel, St-Michel-des-Batignolles, Sainte-Odile, and John 2.
- The line J1-D runs through five religious buildings: John 1, two **synagogues**, **St-Bernard-de-la-Chapelle**, and St-Denys.

Now we see St. Bernard, that is, Bernard de Clairvaux, inserted in the constellation. He created the rule of the Templars, and his uncle was André de Montbard, one of the nine founding Knights Templar in Jerusalem. As for St-Denys-de-la-Chapelle, also called Basilique St-Denis, the first Carolingian-style church was built over a Gallo-Roman cemetery, and a mausolée existed precisely at the place where the altar stands now. The construction of this original church was ordered by Sainte Geneviève to honor and bury Saint Denis, the first bishop of Paris, in the third century CE. Beyond the connection of the saint with the Priory and the Templars, this church has been linked to the kingship in France. It possesses the remnants of two Merovingian royals: a sarcophagus of Queen Arégonde, spouse of Clotaire I (king of Franks, sixth century CE), and Dagobert I (seventh century CE), and it served as a royal necropolis from the time of Hugues Capet (eighth century CE).

The Three Sacred Women's Ley

Additionally, an interesting ley can be drawn connecting John 1 and **La Madeleine**. It runs tangent to **Sainte-Clotilde Basilica** (touching it at the northeastern corner of the facade) and passes through **Sainte-Geneviève-des-Grandes-Carrières**.

Clotilde was the spouse of Clovis, first king of Franks, and she was the one to prompt Clovis to convert to Catholicism. She also brought him the lily of France, and ancient illuminations show that this emblem was a heavenly gift—extremely holy—and was carried to Clovis by Clotilde and angels.

Sainte Geneviève has been the patron saint of Paris since 451 because, in her late twenties, she saved Paris from the invading Huns led by Attila. She urged the people of Paris to remain in their homes and pray and declared that, if she couldn't ask this of the men, then at least each and every woman should remain in prayer until the danger was over. The story goes that the dreadful hordes of invading Huns never found Paris, despite the fact that they passed quite near the city and then attacked Troyes. Then, when Paris was besieged in 464, Geneviève used the Seine River to pass through the siege lines surrounding the city, sailing with boats loaded with food supplies to rescue the already besieged people of Troyes, who were dying from hunger. She also advocated leniency toward prisoners of war—so much so that Clovis, who held her in high esteem, liberated the captives. It's on her behalf that Clovis built an abbey on top of the hill Montagne Ste-Geneviève (both abbey and hill later took her name). The only remnant of the abbey, the **Clovis Tower**, can still be seen inside what is now the Henri IV College on Panthéon Plaza.

A temple to Mercury (Hermes/Thoth) stood on Ste-Geneviève Hill until at least 360 CE, where now stands the Panthéon, **St-Etienne-du-Mont Church**, and the **Clovis Tower**. The two large pentagons on the Châtelet node run through this high site: the St-Germain pentagon runs through what was the abbey and its (Clovis) tower, and the Louvre pentagon passes through St-Etienne-du-Mont Church. (We will find more information about these embedded pentagons further on.)

The sacred line John 1-to-La Madeleine is thus under the auspices of three very holy women whose impact on France was of crucial importance. The fact that two of them were highly revered saints at a young age and knew each other, and that both had a strong Catholic influence on King Clovis, leads us to wonder about the third: the Magdalene. If the lily of France appears with Clotilde and Clovis (the latter having been the first king crowned by the pope), how does this highlight the magnificent lily petal in which is set La Madeleine Church? The Magdalene presence on a ley with Clotilde and Geneviève definitely can be deciphered as the ancestry of the Merovingian bloodline, the origin and source of the lily of France royal line. According to many authors (following Baigent, Leigh, and Lincoln), the Magdalene's descent was precisely Mérovée and the Merovingian royal line. Now the connection of these three holy women to St. John the Baptist, who was brought up with Jesus, is yet another clue that the Magdalene's family, of royal lineage, may also have come from Egypt.

The St. John pyramid contains a wealth of symbols and highly pertinent connections. It makes reference to Egypt and Isis (the Obelisk, Saint-Sulpice Church) as well as the Knights Templar, whose patron saints were St. John the Baptist and St. Denis (or Denys), and whose rule was written by St. Bernard. Furthermore, it also includes the Priory of Sion, whose headquarters were at Saint-Sulpice Church as well as to ancient Egyptian mystery cults linked to the goddess Isis (since ruins of an Isis temple are buried beneath Saint-Sulpice).

Emergent information in several sources suggests that St. John the Baptist, patron saint and highly revered by both the Templars and the

Priory of Sion, had been an adept of a Gnostic cult that originated in Egypt.[2] Moreover, the St. John pyramid reveals the link existing between the Priory of Sion and the Templar order, which the Priory is said to have created and headed secretly, at least until the dramatic meeting at Gisors during which the elm was cut. We may wonder at this dramatic and spectacular event, which has all the necessary features to stand as an archetypal drama, that is, highly symbolic and meaningful. In my view, it is through the "cutting of the ancestral elm" story that the very secretive Priory of Sion was able to tell of its schism with the Templar order.

Thus, the St. John pyramid and its semantic constellation are astounding—and this is only what I have deciphered so far; there's certainly much more to uncover.

The Priory of Sion, as we know, has kept alive ancient mystical rites that are quite similar to the tantric spiritual path in India and Tibet. In alchemy, the mystical marriage represents the harmonization of the polar opposites of the psyche, which Carl Jung has analyzed and which corresponds to the core initiatic path of all cultures.* Could these rites have originated in Egypt before being enacted in the mysteries of ancient Greece such as in the Eleusinian mysteries? They are also, however, clearly linked to the Druidic tradition and the rites of the stag god—which leads one to think that, in order to be complete, the geometrical structure should include a megalith somewhere beneath one of its monuments, or a megalith should have stood at this node in ancient times. The information on buried megaliths is very sparse, but the overall sacred disposition of the St. John pyramid points to a very likely candidate: the Obelisk, the sacred core of Paris.

In my view, there must have been other megaliths in and around the first city of the Parisii. Apart from under the Obelisk, it is very likely that a menhir stood on top of the hill of l'Etoile (the star, in English), because menhirs were often on sacred hills, and this specific hill had ancient bridle paths leading through the forest and forming a star at its summit. Most of the avenues around l'Etoile today

---

*Carl Jung, in his last major work, *Mysterium Cuniunctionis,* or *Mystery of the Conjunction,* studies the polar opposites of the psyche and the process of *individuation* to harmonize them. See Edinger, *Mysterium Lectures.*

still follow these ancient paths. Other possibilities are the mounds in the Buttes Chaumont park (several small mounds or *buttes,* and one steep hill), the top of Ste-Geneviève Mountain (ancient temple to Mercury/Hermes/Thoth)—all of these hills are imprinted with a very high semantic energy—and in general all seven hills of Paris. Montparnasse, for example, is a candidate since the place is devoted to the light—Mount Parnassus, the residence of Greek solar god Apollo and the Muses.

The potential of sacred geometric structures to bring to light hidden connections between entities and secret societies is thus clearly exemplified by St. John the Baptist's pyramid. It opens a window for decoding the basic reality of these structures in the past and the constant connective dynamics that have made the whole sacred network a living, age-old masterpiece consisting of both spiritual semantic energy and a web of human interrelations.

TWO SMALL PENTAGRAMS ON CHÂTELET

An amazing series of embedded structures, all based on the number 5 and perfectly regular, have as a node the Plaza du Châtelet, which stands on the riverside in front of Pont au Change. The plaza has an interesting, round fountain adorned by four sphinxes looking toward and thus guarding the four cardinal directions, forming a cross. At the center of the fountain is a Napoleonic column topped by a graceful woman angel, her long wings spread, who holds at arm's length two crowns, as if offering them. This symbolism is similar to that of the bas-relief outside of the Louvre's Cour Carrée, called *Glory Distributing Crowns.* (See plate 6, Châtelet: two small pentagrams; Châtelet Plaza is center G.)

Between the two crowns, we can draw a straight line (parallel to the Seine), which happens to be the main sacred axis of the two embedded pentagrams (or five-pointed stars). This axis (AM in plate 6) is no less than the West Decumanus and acts as the median of the blue pentagram, crossing the Louvre and its two main pyramids.

The cathedral Notre-Dame de Paris is a prominent node of two embedded pentagrams. Its choir sits at the crossing between the J branch and the M branch of the red star (at the point where the sides JK and ML meet; see plate 6). Moreover, one more star line crosses on the cathedral's choir: the median BI, perfectly geometrically oriented. Another side (DE) passes the center point (transversally) of the cathedral's facade.* A beautiful axis is the median DK, which runs through the two Gothic jewels of **La Sainte-Chapelle Church** (boulevard du Palais, in bright red on the map) and the alchemical **St-Jacques Tower** (just after point G). Extended toward the south, it runs through **Notre-Dame-des-Champs Church** (boulevard Montparnasse) and **Notre-Dame-du-Rosaire Church** (Porte de Vanves). Toward the north, it passes through **République Plaza** (northwest) and **Cité de la Musique** (Porte de Pantin).

Two Small Pentagrams: Generalities

We see first the two small pentagrams that are embedded in the architecture so as to form a perfect ten-pointed star. We can move through them, following the traditional circuit through such a pentagram, which is reputed to possess a magical power, given that such a star represents the human head plus arms and legs stretched, as Leonardo da Vinci's famous *Vitruvian Man* (also called *Man of Vitruve*). Da Vinci, following *Vitruve,* showed how the human body expresses an array of proportions. Some people claim that several golden proportions are naturally expressed by da Vinci's drawing and that any single mark on it (such as on the arms) must be taken into account.

The first pentagram (ABCDEA in plate 6: Châtelet: two small pentagrams) can be called the **Louvre pentagram**, because its main apex (A) on the West Decumanus incorporates the Louvre Museum. In plate 6, the Louvre pentagram is drawn in dark blue. It faces the Louvre, and its median (AM) is the West Decumanus running westward toward the Obelisk, thus passing the southern tips of the pyramid and the inverted pyramid of the Louvre.

The second pentagram (IJKLMI) can be called **La Bourse pentagram**, because its main node (I) is on the Metro Bourse. It appears in

---

*Of course, there are many more sacred lines crossing at the three nodes of the cathedral: the choir, the facade, and the geometrical center of the cross. The complex analysis of these, however, is still in process.

red in plate 6, and its median (IB) passes through the choir of Notre-Dame Cathedral, at the very node where lines JK and LM of the same Bourse pentagram intersect.

All in all, four apexes of the pentagrams fall on, or very near, churches: apex J falls on **Notre-Dame-du-Liban Church,** apex E falls on **Saint-Denys-du-St-Sacrement Church,** apex K falls on **Sainte-Elisabeth Church**, and apex C falls on **Notre-Dame-de-Bonne-Nouvelle Church**. And two apexes of the inner pentagons fall on churches as well (**Notre Dame Cathedral** and **St-Germain-L'Auxerrois),** and one quite near to **St-Julien-le-Pauvre Church.** (See the following for the exact location of the ten apexes of this pentagram. Refer to plate 6.)

The Louvre Pentagram

The Louvre pentagram (ABCDEA) appears in dark blue in plate 6.

- Side AB runs through **Institut de France** (eastern aisle) and runs parallel to the facade of Hôtel des Monnaies and to the Seine in front of Vert Galand (the west tip of La Cité island). It then runs through Metro and **Plaza St-Michel, St-Julien-le-Pauvre Church**, and Jussieu University. Extended to the northwest, it follows exactly the north wall of **Palais de l'Elysée**, Metro Courcelles, and Metro Porte Champerret. Toward the southeast, it passes through **Bibliothèque Mitterrand**.
- Side BC passes **Hotel de Ville** (the northeast corner) and **Centre Pompidou** (at the geometrical center) and reaches

*The exact apexes of the pentagram: Center G is Châtelet Plaza, specifically the column at the center of the fountain adorned with four sphinxes. Apex A falls near the Carrousel Arc de Triomph, and the two sides with this apex surround the Louvre, touching the eastern tips of both aisles of the museum. Apex L falls not far from **Saint-Vladimir-le-Grand Church**. Apex D falls in the Garden du Luxembourg. Apex J falls on **Notre-Dame-du-Liban Church**, on rue d'Ulm, southwest of the Panthéon. Apex B falls on the inner square of Jussieu University. Apex M falls on boulevard Henri IV. Apex E falls on **Saint-Denys-du-St-Sacrement Church**. Apex K falls very near **Sainte-Elisabeth Church** (rue du Temple), precisely on Crossing Turbigo-Temple (the northern limit of the ancient Templars' property). Apex C falls on **Notre-Dame-de-Bonne-Nouvelle Church**. Apex I falls northwest of the National Library (Bibliothèque Nationale), on rue de Richelieu, and embeds Plaza Des Victoires.

Notre-Dame-de-Bonne-Nouvelle Church (apex C).

- Side CD starts at **Notre-Dame-de-Bonne-Nouvelle Church** and runs through **St-Eustache Church** (at the geometrical center), Les Halles' Forum, and Metro and bridge **Pont-Neuf** (at the south end). Then it follows rue Dauphine, Crossing Dauphine-Porte-de-Lodi, Crossing Mazarine-St-André-des-Arts, and **Palais du Luxembourg**.

- Side DE passes through **Luxembourg Palace** (the north facade), Metro Cluny, **St-Séverin Church**, **Notre Dame Cathedral** (the western front porch), **St-Gervais-St-Protais Church**, **St-Denys-du-St-Sacrement Church** (apex E).

- Side EA runs through the **St-Denys-du-St-Sacrement Church**, Musée Picasso, **Centre Pompidou** (at the geometric center), Metro Les Halles and Les Halles' Forum (at the southeast corner and southern wall), Metro Palais Royal, and the **Louvre Museum** (in the north, Richelieu aisle).

La Bourse Pentagram

The La Bourse pentagram (IJKLMI) appears in bright red in plate 6.

- Side IJ passes through Metro Bourse, **Plaza Des Victoires**, **Bibliothèque Nationale**, Metro Louvre-Rivoli, and the northeast corner of **the Louvre** and of the plaza in front of Cour Carrée. Then, it runs through **St-Germain-L'Auxerrois** (both the cloister and the church), **Pont-Neuf Bridge** (the midpoint), Metro Cluny and Crossing St-Germain-St-Michel, **Thermes de Cluny** (ancient Roman Baths) and its **Cluny Museum** (where the Pilier des Nautes is now kept), and finally the **Sorbonne** (the northwest corner and the east front porch), to reach **Notre-Dame-du-Liban Church** (apex J).

- Side JK starts at **Notre-Dame-du-Liban Church** (apex J), and crosses through the **Panthéon** (the south porch, center, and dome), Plaza Maubert-Mutualité, **Notre Dame Cathedral** (the choir, and the eastern garden—Jean XXIII Square), **Hotel de Ville** (it follows along the west wall) and Metro, and the beginning of rue des Archives. For a while, it meets and follows rue du Temple and runs parallel to the **Art and History of Judaism Museum** and **Sainte-Elisabeth Church** (apex K, rue du Temple).

- Side KL runs through Metro Temple, **Sainte-Elisabeth Church** (apex K), and Les Halles Metro and Forum (southeast). It crosses the lines IJ and KL on **St-Germain-L'Auxerrois Church** (at the geometrical center), the south entry point to **Pont des Arts Bridge**, **Institut de France** (west aisle), and Crossing Université-St-Pères. (Extended to the northeast, it crosses **La République Plaza**.)

- Side LM is extremely initiatic. It passes **St-Vladimir-le-Grand Church**, **St-Germain-des-Prés Church**, **St-Michel Fountain** (with, in an arched vault full of initiatic symbols, a giant statue of St. Michael the archangel vanquishing the devil), and **Notre-Dame Cathedral** (where it meets line JK exactly at the choir). It travels west at the beginning of **Pont St-Louis Bridge** and passes through St-Louis Island and then Sully Morland Metro.

- Side MI runs through the Sorcery Museum (Musée de la Magie), Crossing Rivoli-Vieille-du-Temple, **Beauboug Center**, Plaza Stravinski, and the very arcane **St-Merri Cloister** (revered by alchemists). It then passes Les Halles Metro and Forum (at the northeast corner), **St-Eustache Church**, the **Township** (2nd Arrondissement), and **Bibliothèque Nationale**, before returning to node I. (Extended to the northwest, it passes **Opéra Garnier**.)

Two Small Pentagrams: The Medians

Let's look more closely at the medians of the two stars (in plate 6). Since each line starts on an apex, we can follow the circle on the map counterclockwise from apex A.

- The median AM is the West Decumanus and passes through **Carrousel's Arc de Triomphe**, the southern tip of the **inverted pyramid** (Plaza du Carrousel), the southern tip of the **upward-pointing pyramid**, **St-Germain-L'Auxerrois Church**, node G, **Hôtel de Ville**, **Hôtel de Sens** (Flamboyant Gothic style), and node M.

- Median LE passes through Hôtel des Monnaies, **Palais de Justice** (at the northwest), node G, **Notre-Dame-des-Blancs-Manteaux Church**, Musée Cognac-Jay, and node E. (Extended to the northeast, it runs through **St-Ambroise Church** and Porte de Bagnolet.)
- Median DK passes through **Palais du Luxembourg** (on the northwest aisle), **Odeon Plaza** (the eastern side), **Palais de Justice**, and **Sainte-Chapelle**. It then travels through node G, **St-Jacques Tower**, **Beaubourg Center** (at the geometric center), the **Art and History of Judaism Museum**, **Sainte-Elisabeth Church** (rue du Temple), Crossing Turbigo-Temple (the northern limit of the ancient Templars' property), and on to node K.
- Median JC runs through the **Panthéon** (the western facade), Collège de France, **St-Séverin Church** (at the choir), Metro Cité, Pont-au-Change (the northern entry point, on Châtelet Plaza), node G, Metro Etienne Marcel, then node C.
- Median BI runs through **Notre Dame Cathedral** (the choir and the main node), node G, Forum des Halles (the garden), **Bourse du Commerce**, **Plaza des Victoires**, Bibliothèque Nationale, and node I.

Circle around the Two Embedded Pentagrams

The circle drawn around the apexes of the two small pentagrams (marked in double violet lines in plate 6) runs through very interesting places— notably, the famous **Bibliothèque de l'Arsenal**. The Arsenal Library collected a treasure of books on the Templars and Hermetic sciences, among them many Vatican archives confiscated by Napoleon I, and it is where Charles Nodier (one of the Priory of Sion's grand masters) held his Hermetic and literary circle in the early nineteenth century.

From apex A at the Louvre, the circle, moving counterclockwise, passes through Crossing Université-Bac, **St-Thomas-d'Aquin Church**, node L, boulevard St-Germain, Crossing Sèvres-St-Sulpice, Crossing Vaugirard-Guynemer (northwest corner of Luxemboug Garden), node D, École des Mines, node J, **Notre-Dame-du-Liban Church** (rue d'Ulm), **Plaza de la Contrescarpe**, **Arènes de Lutèce** (Roman arena), Metro Jussieu, node B, **Préfecture de Paris**, **Bibliothèque de l'Arsenal**, Plaza du Père Teilhard de Chardin, node M, Plaza and Metro Sully-Morland, and Sainte-Marie Chapel. It follows the east wall of Plaza des Vosges, and passes through node E, **St-Denys-du-St-Sacrement Church** (touching the choir), Crossing Turenne-Froissard, **Carreau du Temple** (linked to the Templars), node K, **Sainte-Elisabeth Church** (at the exact center of the choir), Crossing Temple-Turbigo, **VertBois Synagogue**, Metro Strasbourg-St-Denis and the ancient **Porte St-Denis**, node C, the crossing at Hauteville-Bonne-Nouvelle, **La Bourse** (the French Stock Exchange), Bibliothèque Nationale (the west wall), Metro Pyramides, **St-Roch Church** (along the median), and back to the Tuileries Garden.

EMBEDDED PENTAGONS

Each five-pointed star (or pentagram) creates a pentagon; thus, node A is an apex of the blue pentagram (ABCDEA) and is also an apex of the red pentagon (ADBECA; refer to plate 6). Thus, the two small pentagrams lead to two embedded pentagons (the sides of which are dark red and blue in plate 6).

The first (ADBECA) is called the Louvre pentagon (in red, not to be confused with the Louvre pentagram) because one of its apexes (node A) incorporates the Louvre Museum. The second is called the St-Germain Pentagon (in blue) because node L is on boulevard St-Germain (and incorporates St-Vladimir Church). It runs through LJMKIL. These two pentagons, when their sides are extended, form the two larger five-pointed stars (mauve and light blue in plate 7).

The Louvre Pentagon (ADBECA, in Red)
A prominent feature of this structure is the perfect embedding of the Louvre, first with the large red pentagon and then with the small blue star. (Refer to plate 6.)

The two sides that run from apex A of the red pentagon delineate the two tips of the horseshoe-shaped Louvre. The southwestern tip falls on AD and the northwestern tip falls on AC. Moreover, the inside blue star (on node A) delineates the two corners of the main buildings (sides AB and AE of the blue pentagram). This is definitely a remarkable embedding!

Let's look at the pentagon from the West Decumanus, moving counterclockwise from the Louvre (apex A).

- Side AD runs through the southwestern tip of **the Louvre's horseshoe**, Crossing Jacob-Saints-Pères, Crossing Sèvres-Four, **Plaza St-Sulpice** (at the center), **Saints-Innocents Fountain**, and Luxembourg Garden.
- Side DB runs through Crossing Médicis-St-Michel, follows the northern side of **St-Etienne-du-Mont Church** (on top of the hill Montagne-Sainte-Geneviève), Metro Cardinal Lemoine, and the node at Jussieu University.
- Side BE runs through the **Institut du Monde Arabe** (at the northeast corner) and the corner where Ile Saint-Louis meets **Pont Sully** (Quai de Béthune). It then runs through the splendid **Hôtel Lambert** (seventeenth century, conceived by the architect Louis Levau), follows rue Saint-Paul, passes slightly on the west of **St-Paul-St-Louis Church**, and then more on the west of St-Denys-du-St-Sacrement Church, situated at apex E.
- Side EC runs through **St-Denys-du-St-Sacrement Church** (obliquely from the front porch), Metro Arts et Métiers and Crossing Réaumur-Turbigo, **Notre-Dame-de Bonne-Nouvelle Church** (eastern side of the choir) at node C.
- Side CA passes through Metro Sentier and Crossing Réaumur-Montmartre, Crossing Petits-Champs-Banque, **Palais Royal Garden** (in the northwest) and Theater, Crossing Rivoli-Pyramides, and the northwestern tip of the **Louvre**'s horseshoe shape.

St-Germain Pentagon (LJMKIL, in Blue)

To trace the pentagon, from node L, we can follow counterclockwise the lines in light blue.

- Side LJ runs through **Saint-Sulpice Church** (in the choir), **Palais du Luxembourg** (at the northeast), Plaza Rostand (main entrance to Luxemboug Garden), **Plaza de l'Estrapade**, and apex J at rue d'Ulm.

- Side JM crosses the southeast corner of **Place du Panthéon**, and then rue Clovis. The Panthéon Plaza is on the top of a hill that, around 360 CE, was the site of a temple to Mercury. At that time, the Parisians were just starting to become Christians under the influence of St. Denis, who was martyred.

The line runs through the gracious **Clovis Tower** and what had been the Sainte-Geneviève Abbey, on top of the Montagne Sainte-Geneviève. (The street leading to the abbey still bears this name.) Remember, Geneviève has been the patron saint of Paris since 451, and while in her late twenties, she saved, with prayer and spiritual power alone, the town from the invading Huns led by Attila.

The JM line then runs through the Crossing Tournelles-Écoles and the **Institut du Monde Arabe** (at the center), parallels the south end of Pont de Sully, crosses the eastern **tip of Ile St-Louis**, follows exactly **Sully Bridge** (on the north) and boulevard Henri IV, and runs through Metro Sully-Morland.

- Side MK passes through Carnavalet Museum, Crossing Bretagne-Archives, **Mairie du 3ème** (Square du Temple), **Sainte-Elisabeth Church** (rue du Temple), and apex K on Crossing Turbigo-Temple (the northern limit of the Templars' property).
- Side KI runs through Conservatoire des Arts et Métiers, Crossing Poissonnières-Réaumur and Metro Sentier, and apex I (rue de Richelieu).
- Side IL follows rue de Richelieu a short while, then crosses the Louvre perfectly perpendicular to the West Decumanus (between Carrousel's Arc de Triomphe and the inverted pyramid). Then it runs parallel (but quite far) to Pont du Carrousel.

GRAND TEN-POINTED STAR ON CHÂTELET NODE

Extending all the sides of the two large embedded pentagons forms a very large ten-pointed star. (See plate 7, Châtelet: two embedded ten-pointed stars.) This star is the exact replica of the smaller ten-pointed star created by the two embedded Châtelet pentagrams: it is isomorphic (has the same form), but is on a different scale. The larger star also contains two pentagrams, which are embedded and centered on the Châtelet node. Let's look at it globally (see appendix 3 for a detailed description). In plate 7, to distinguish between the smaller pentagrams and the larger pentagrams, I have used the same colors at slightly different intensities or with slightly different tones to highlight the isomorphism of the two sets of ten-pointed stars.

Something striking about the blue A branch (see page 348), which has as its median the West Decumanus, is that one of its sides (extended KI) crosses through **La Madeleine**. The other side (extended JL) crosses through **Palais Bourbon** (Assemblée Nationale).

A funny feature is that all of Paris's five train stations fall on the grand ten-pointed star, the lines passing right through the buildings apart from Gare d'Austerlitz, which is only touched on one corner by the east side of the blue B branch.

On the whole, the blue star and its inside pentagon run through 9 churches and 14 monuments; the red star through 13 churches or temples (including 1 synagogue and 1 mosque) and 16 monuments. In total, the grand ten-pointed star connects 22 religious buildings and 30 monuments.

CONCLUSION
Back to Global Consciousness

This second part has taken us through an arcane layer of reality: a deep interconnection between the human spirit, the cosmos, and our living planet, Gaia. The arch-network of megaliths and megalithic constructions worldwide has remained extraordinarily vibrant, with cosmo-telluric and meaningful energy, and later ages and cultures have embedded it in a more extent and complex sacred network. In Paris, its refined symbolism points clearly to the perennial quest of humanity for a harmonized and fully accomplished spirit—a collective and integrated consciousness. The sacred network, vibrant with energy everywhere on Earth, is a magnificent devotion and tribute to our human quest.

PART 3

EXCEPTIONAL TELHAR FIELDS

Space and Time Singularities

Just as geo-architectural networks are like mandalas with sparkling centers, human telhar fields are also organized around one or several nodes. The energetic structures in human fields, however, present as transient forms because they are not anchored to monuments, stones, or places. Yet saying they are transient and modified during the duration of a telhar field doesn't mean they are fuzzy or unstable. To the contrary, in this third section we will explore telhar fields showing structures that are quite extraordinary and complex yet are recurrent and therefore stable. These structures include funnel shapes that appear at very specific moments and trigger a leap into the syg-dimension's strangest properties and processes, such as the annulling of space.

The phenomena I discuss in part 3 take us far beyond the basic semantic fields and telhar fields that we saw in part 1. They are extraordinary in the sense that they defy what we consider at the present to be the laws of physics and of cognitive sciences. Not only are they at odds with our good old Newtonian physics (stating that any electromagnetic [EM] energy travels through space and its speed is limited to the speed of light), but they also run against the bedrock of cognitive sciences, such as the impossibility for consciousness to function autonomously from the brain—a feat clearly exemplified in out-of-body experiences and near-death experiences. For example, people who were clinically dead (and revived later) were nevertheless able to describe what happened in the emergency room and in the hospital, including remarks exchanged among the surgeons. And finally, these phenomena certainly have a resemblance to some processes studied by quantum physics, but because they can be provoked intentionally or else they imply a focused consciousness, they run contrary to the absolute indeterminism of a quantum field. But they perfectly fit a dimension of reality made of syg-energy as I postulate it. Phenomena such as annulling space or annulling time are precisely what can make us understand the strange properties of consciousness-as-energy. They are extreme phenomena in the vast domain of syg-fields and telhar fields, but what they reveal helps us understand the properties and dynamics of telhar fields and of the sacred network that we have encountered in the first two parts.

The out-of-the-ordinary syg-fields and syg phenomena in the following chapters thrust us into a new layer of reality, thereby opening the horizon of a novel physics of consciousness based on a syg–space-time manifold.

11
ANNULLING SPACE

STRIKING EFFECT OF A TELHAR FIELD WITH
A ROD ON GOA BEACH

On several occasions, I was able to observe energetic structures in great detail that resembled well-known patterns of electromagnetic (EM) fields. Indeed, if I hadn't been persuaded (based on several parapsychology experiments) that telhar fields have little or nothing to do with EM fields, I could have recognized the specific pattern of magnetic fields lines created by a *dipole:* a magnetized rod with opposite charges at each end (one positive and one negative). Such bipolar structures of telhar fields still baffle me, but my observations were very clear, and the fact that I experienced them more than once indicates that they're a fundamental pattern. The first instance of such an experience happened in Goa in the seventies, but in order for you to understand fully the psychological impact of this telhar field, let me first describe the context of the time.

In the early seventies, there was only a single guest house on the whole length of Goa beaches. There were no roads or even rickshaws. To get to a few shops, we had to go to the village of Calangute, and from Baga where I lived that was a two-mile walk on a tiny path among palm trees. In 1970 and 1971 (really, the second winter that hippies were in Goa), at the full moon, there was only one party that drew, at maximum, the two hundred or so hippies that lived between Calangute and Anjuna Beach. In those early years of the hippies in India, full-moon gatherings weren't the kind of trance dance parties that have rendered the Goa trance music so famous. The state-of-the-art instruments were the various guitars, flutes, and drums that most hippies carried with them on the road as well as the sound equipment given to us by The Who when they left Goa, which was amorously guarded and attended by a couple of trustees. At that time, we remained in high meditative states throughout the night, sitting quietly on the sand while a handful of musicians gathered around the famous generator and played all night long.

But that night was an exception. For whatever reason, the generator hadn't been produced, and we had no central group of musicians. We were a quiet crowd of about 150 people sitting on the beach at random, either alone or in tiny groups. We naturally formed a sort of giant circle with no center. A new wave of hippies had just arrived from southern Europe, and it was strange to have among us so many people who had not yet adapted to our meditative and highly spiritual state. Usually, we shared a deep and intense state of consciousness, communicating silently through music rather than through words.

It was early in the night, and I was sitting quite far from the center of the huge circle of people and thus had a good view of most of the people gathered on the beach. About six feet from me, his face at a three-quarter angle, sat a mysterious man in his early twenties who seemed to appear at my side at every gathering of this kind, though I had neither seen nor met him on any other occasion. Perpetually in a deep meditative state, he was a heartening sight for me: he wore a calm smile on his face; his long, fair hair fell to his shoulders; and he was very beautiful. We had never talked to each other—and we never would. Our sole mode of communication was eye and soul contact and sharing a deep empathy in meditation. That night, I silently acknowledged his presence as usual. Some musicians, dispersed in the crowd, played deep, soft music in harmony with other players, despite the distance between them. I was in a meditative state, but, after a half hour or so, I had the impression that there was something wrong. It wasn't the usual deep, silent state we had shared in the past—and I opened my eyes.

Something utterly strange and perturbing attracted my attention: it was as if an erotic breeze had been blowing. Wherever I looked, people hugged and *kissed and assumed sexual preludes. It was all so sudden and at the same time so overwhelming that it seemed that in no time our sacred full-moon ritual was about to give way to an orgy, European style. It was akin to having our Oriental temple assaulted by the very kind of Western decadence that we had left behind when we started our mystical quest or "Journey to the East."**

I stared, bewildered, assuming the probable outcome of a giant sex party, when my eyes fell on my singular secret ally. He was staring at the crowd, mouth wide open and eyes bulging with such a look of horror and utter disbelief that it was like seeing in a mirror the very expression I must have had a few seconds before. I burst out laughing, because his expression was so dramatic and strong, like a theater mask. The sound of my laughing moved him from his spellbound state, and then we looked at each other. He remained where he was sitting, but moved around to face me. We exchanged a serious gaze, and a thought seemed to cross our two minds at the same time: we can't let this happen; when we gather on a full-moon night, we—all of us—have something much more important to do than have casual sex. (Needless to say, the situation didn't seem to point to the possibility of any kind of tantric meditative lovemaking.) We both knew that all of us had to enter a heightened state of consciousness and then connect to the cosmos as a group. These were the seeds of a new way of living together: to mutually support and enhance our high state and to sustain it not only day and night, but also specifically while living together and interacting socially. And so far, for months we had been experiencing such a high meditative collective state. Even more surprising, we would interact most of the time in silence. We had been able to attain the unthinkable: to stop and even reverse our Western civilization's craving for petty and mundane chatting, for down-to-earth and incessant automatic thinking. We had brought our thoughts to a stop, and our day-to-day state was inner silence. We were, all of us, the habitués, *on a spiritual quest. We had fled our respective countries to pursue it.*

Some of these thoughts must have crossed both of our minds while we stared at each other, sitting in a lotus posture. Then we seemed to share another

---

* *Journey to the East* is a well-known book by Herman Hesse that inspired a generation of people to go on a quest for spiritual awakening.

thought: "Let's create a perfect harmony between us two; let's put our mind waves in perfect sync." Instantly, we stopped our thoughts and went into inner silence, again with a strong intent. We stared at each other's third eye and in hardly a few dozens seconds, we brought our mental waves into perfect harmony. I saw two vibratory rays emanating from our two forehead chakras, each starting to adjust its frequency with the other.

Suddenly, a unique ray of light was formed and was becoming stable, the two-way flow now passing freely between us. And instantaneously, with the quickness of a flash, a larger telhar field was created that surrounded all of the people gathered there. I felt with my friend that everybody was once again assuming a meditative posture as all our minds were harmonized into a collective field. That telhar field was so stable that it lasted throughout the night, our silent state sustained by the music.

After a few minutes, we knew everything was back on track, and the two of us started to relax our gaze. Once again, each of us entered a "one to all" connection and forgot the rod we had created. When I looked around again, everybody was sitting upright and in inner silence. No couples were kissing anymore. Then, a ring of people started forming on the outside of the giant group, dancing lightly and slowly, making an outside circle similar to that of Sufi dancers. It was as if they were closing the field on itself. I felt this outside circle of slow movement had a very deep meaning regarding the whole telhar field.

The strong ray created between me and my friend while we harmonized our two consciousnesses (thus a syg-energy), definitely resembles a magnetic rod or dipole, similarly creating a large field around it. If you look at the field lines of a dipole on the classical 2-D representation, you will note that they form arcs linking the two ends of the rod and moving farther away from the middle of the rod (on both sides). Inside the rod, the current moves from the negative pole toward the positive one (n to p), while for the flow of the field lines (surrounding the rod) it seems to be the inverse (it moves from p to n) but in fact isn't: you have to imagine that the rod itself is a segment that, still in 2-D, is tangent to the two large circles (one above and one below the rod). Thus, all the lines are in fact turning in large circles, counterclockwise above the rod and the inverse below. In a 3-D representation, the energy turns in circles all around the rod, and the circles flatten upon passing through the rod. As for the equipotential surfaces, they present multiple embedded shapes of a figure eight, each circle of the figure eight around each end of the rod, the central crossing of the figure eight at the midpoint on the rod.

When my friend and I became perfectly synchronized, we became two nodes linked by a strong two-way flow of syg-energy: a structure very similar to the bipolar rod, apart from the fact the energy moves both ways. This synchronization created, quasi-instantaneously, a larger field that showed clear telhar properties (harmony and telepathy among people). This is where the field definitely departed from the usual matterlike magnetic energy.

What came as a total surprise to me was to be able, with a harmonic rod of syg-energy, to create the harmony field and a very large telhar field among 150 people, especially given that this rod was not at the geometrical center of the group. So though this is not EM energy, we have evidence that two consciousnesses in sync can willingly create a very large collective telhar field.

The outside circle of people standing and dancing in slow motion created a "closure" that contained the group energy as if it was surrounded by a round wall—sending this energy back toward the center, forming the well-known vertical rotation flow called *Benard cells,* studied in chaos theory. Benard cells form in boiling water and show that a complex system can change its own dynamics at the global level. When heat increases regularly under a pan of water, at first, bubbles appear at the bottom and rise to the surface, and then, when the water boils, the Benard cells start forming (to see the flow of the cells clearly, add a few tea leaves to the boiling water).

If we imagine all these vertical rotation flows from center to periphery, at the global group level, all the circular flows would form a torus— a round doughnut.

In fact, while writing this, something I had never remarked before just sprang to my mind: as my unknown ally at the full-moon gathering was seated nearer to the center of the group than me, the axis of our rod was perpendicular to the outside circle—that is, it was itself in the axis of a ray drawn from the periphery to the center. Therefore, it was perfectly positioned to start a Benard cell rolling in a doughnut-shaped torus.

The most important feature of this case is how a telhar field, once created, harmonizes the state of consciousness of each and every person within the group. This creates the shared state of the field.

Energetic structures and dynamics still retain an aura of familiarity, which puts us at ease. We have seen syg-energy structures—created willingly by two minds—that resembled magnetic rods. I know this similarity to EM energy is a lure, because syg-energy shows many behaviors that are totally at odds with EM fields. (We will see further on how it also differs fundamentally from quantum fields.)

The upshot: in case what you've read up to now is already too much for you, and your rational self has gone into frantic rejection mode, then you'd better drop this book now, because what's coming next is dealing with downright strangeness and doesn't have any kind of similarity to common EM fields, only to the strangest aspects of quantum physics—those most remote from day-to-day reality. I'm talking about three weird processes: the first one has to do with annulling space, the second with reversing time (what is called in quantum physics *retrocausality*), and the third with annulling time.

ROD STRUCTURE AND DISTANT SPACES JOINED THROUGH A FUNNEL IN BRAZIL

A couple of years ago, I experienced the rod structure again, this time in Brazil and with an even greater clarity than I had years earlier in Goa. On this new occasion, the telhar field in Brazil synchronized itself with another happening in India, thus creating a stupendous spatial disruption, as if the space separating the two telhar fields had collapsed.

It was a weekend in February, the month preceding Carnival, and, in preparation for the event, a group of thirty drummers—a whole school of samba—was playing in a frenzy. The crowd assembled in the large Matriz Square was dancing or marking the beat, enraptured with the powerful energy of the drums. After the show ended around midnight, the atmosphere was still very upbeat, and many people remained in small groups under the trees of the square. A vendor of caipiri *(typical Brazilian cocktails made with natural fruit juices) set on the pavement next to his stall a powerful stereo worthy of a New York rapper, and began spinning full-blast Goa trance music. People started dancing in the streets bordering the square where the drummers had been.*

We can picture the scene: the large street on the side of the square was bordered on one side by Matriz Garden, whose ground was higher, with paths full of people passing under the trees and around flower bushes. The wooden benches and many low stone walls in the garden were also used as seats by numerous people. On the other side of the street was a large paved area, also at a higher level, with some benches under the shade of trees along a block between two small alleys, on one of which was the caipiri stall.

I was among the people dancing in the large street, and I quickly entered a trance—which was certainly enhanced by the caipiri vodka I had drunk earlier. I began a frenzied dance, happy to feel the energy of Goa trance music, but this didn't last long, because after about ninety minutes, I tripped on a paving stone and hurt my knee. After this mishap, I went to sit on a stone wall bordering the square on the garden side, in front of the speakers, which were set on the other side of the street.

I closed my eyes, and very quickly I entered a heightened state of consciousness and felt I was translocalized into another space: a trance dance party in Goa, India. (At this same time of year in Goa, parties could last until noon the next day or even go on for three days in a row.) In my mind, I was trance dancing in a crowd gathered at that very same moment in Goa. After a while, I had the feeling I was back to Brazil, and I opened my eyes. I focused my attention again on Matriz Square—sitting on the stone wall, my body marking the beat. Fewer people were dancing, but there were still many people around where I sat. A man sat on a bench next to the hi-fi equipment, and he seemed in a trance too. The music was enthralling, its beat very rapid. I was totally immersed in the music and focused on its source, the speakers. Now I realized I was connected energetically to this man: I saw a ray of light connecting us, a rod, that created a very strong harmonization between our minds. Then I realized I was in the consciousness of telhar fields and that a large telhar field was created around the rod. I focused my attention to sense how large it was. Beyond the square, it extended to another part of town.

I was in a rare state of consciousness, hyperlucid and hypersensitive to syg-energy. After some twenty minutes, I started to hear the specific energy of Goa again. That's when I saw a huge funnel forming in between the two nodes of the rod (that is, between me and the man next to the speakers). The funnel was vertical but at a slight angle, its large end about three yards above street level and its small end touching the middle of the rod. I felt as though I was sucked into the funnel, toward its small end, at a vertiginous speed, and abruptly I found myself trance dancing at the Goa party. There was a telhar field in Goa too. I sensed it, how it had harmonized the thousands of people gathered and dancing in Goa. (See figure 11.1.)

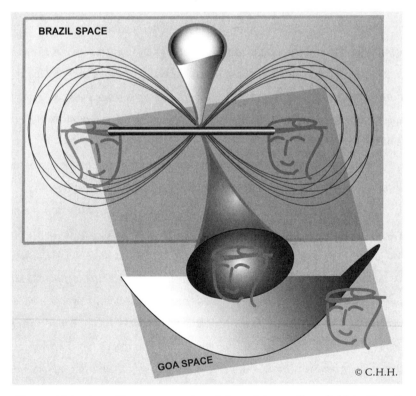

Figure 11.1. Annulling space: rod and funnel in a telhar field in Brazil
Digital artwork by Chris H. Hardy

From this point onward, I alternated between the two places—Brazil and Goa—switching at intervals of about twenty minutes. Each time, I felt the energy of Goa (Goa's ambience and quality of music) becoming more and more present. Then I saw the funnel (its lower, thinner tip at the level of the rod), and suddenly I slid into the funnel and plunged into its sink—zap!—Goa. Then, after some time dancing there (with bodily sensations: feeling the crowd around me, the music, and the large telhar field), I emerged back in Matriz Square.

After about two hours, I began to notice a very strange phenomenon: it was now around 3:30 a.m., and most of the people lingering in the plaza were seated, scattered on the various benches and walls. Some other people exited the dancing bars bordering the plaza—one, or two, or three at a time, and they all came from my left and walked down the street, passing in front of me, toward the parking lot farther away to my right. They were crossing the rod energy midway through the street. While observing their individual energy fields (their auras), I noted something stupendous: at the very moment when they were passing through the rod, their aura was lighted. Before crossing the rod, they already appeared to have a stimulated aura, which everybody had that night after the concert. Yet the rod—the double node of the telhar field—and the space in its vicinity had a still-higher energy. At the moment when these people came into contact with it, they became attuned to this higher energy. They then kept walking, surrounded by an intense aura, which was stable as far as I could see—that is, all the way to the end of the street, where the people were lost to my sight. It was odd to see moderately colored or grayish auras suddenly become ablaze and then remain in that higher state of consciousness. All but one of the people I saw walking by was able to tune in to the energy of the rod.

In this complex experience, the center of the telhar field was again a rod of syg-energy created between two people acting as coupled nodes. And from this high-energy rod, a large telhar field had been formed that covered a whole quarter of town. Though my bodily sensations alternated between a park in Brazil and a party in Goa, I don't believe that my physiological body ever left the low stone wall in Brazil that I sat on with a painful knee. My consciousness, on the contrary, penetrated the no-space of the semantic dimension with its access to all space and time. The connection between the two spaces was first and foremost semantic—that is, drawn by the similarity of consciousness states between the telhar field in Brazil and the telhar field in Goa.

I had several such experiences of mind translocalization, like the shift between Brazil and Goa, before this one. In none of them, however, had I witnessed the funnel structure and been sucked into it at the moment of shifting the location of my consciousness and body sensations. That night, however, I experienced it only after exiting Brazil and entering Goa space. This crucial funnel structure seemed to collapse space where its small end was—that is, midway through the rod structure.

We can consider another strange aspect of telhar fields: the possibility of spaces being enmeshed and embedded in one another through the existence of telhar fields. This reveals a phenomenon that only quantum physics has mentioned: the possibility of annulling space. To consider this, we must detour to see how the semantic dimension can support and explain such a phenomenon.

SEMANTIC PROXIMITY
Annulling Space and Time

Psychologist Carl Jung has proposed understanding all psi experiences as synchronicities—a meaningful coincidence based on an instant relation between two minds, or between a mind and an object. He has recounted many cases of synchronicities in his biography, with the most famous one being that of the golden scarab: a scarab with golden hues flies into the room through the open window at the very moment when his patient is recounting a dream she had about a golden scarab.

Synchronicities, says Jung, happen outside of any chain of events—outside of causality (A is the cause of B is the cause of C). This is why he called them acausal events. In a synchronicity, A can strongly interact with event M, without prior chains of events leading from A to M. Yet because most of science is based on causality (an event causes other events), synchronicity is a totally novel type of phenomenon.

As an example, we can look at precognition. For Jung, precognition—

knowing about a future event—is a synchronicity between a mind in the present and an event in the future. In other words, a strong acausal link is created between a consciousness and a future time, and the decisive factor for this link is based on a similarity of meaning (resonance of concept, name, a thought, and a real event). In the golden scarab example, for instance, there was a strong resonance (in terms of meaning) between the scarab in the dream recounted by the patient and the real bug that flew into the room at that precise moment.

Similarly, in a precognitive dream, there is a strong semantic link between the dreamer and the event that will involve him in the future. (We must remember that precognitive dreams can be precise in minute details; we are not talking about a gross approximation of a future situation.) We can argue that in this case time is annulled: the link between the present mind and the future happens independently of the time dimension. In Newtonian physics, such a link that bridges widely different time frames is deemed impossible, but it is quite possible in quantum physics. This is why Jung worked on these concepts with the physics Nobel laureate Wolfgang Pauli. Only quantum physics can allow such time and space singularities.[1]

For example, in the next chapter, we will see how two consciousnesses belonging to two different time frames can carry on a conversation with an amazingly precise exchange of information—including names, proportions, and other details. This exchange entices an annulling of time (the Newtonian linear time), or, more to the point, it means a break or a fault in the Newtonian time frame. Semantic Fields Theory (SFT), on the contrary, predicts and explains this type of phenomenon by posing that consciousness is nonlocal. Minds influence other minds, and semantic fields influence other semantic fields, without the "barrier" of linear space and time. Semantic fields connect spontaneously, one with another, on the basis of shared values and similarities of feelings, ideas, intent, objectives, and so forth. Semantic fields are called *proximate* when they interact strongly with each other, when they have (through past interactions) formed links and bonds in term of meaning and feelings. This doesn't preclude the links from being negative, as they would be, for example, in situations of competition, opposition, or extreme dislike. As we know, hatred can be a link so powerful that it's among the most difficult to break. At the other end of the feeling spectrum, profound love, admiration, and fascination are extremely conducive to psi occurrences (such as telepathy, clairvoyance, precognition, or healing at a distance). Love feelings easily trigger nonlocal exchanges between two distant semantic fields.

In addition, deep and long-term interactions between two people—between twins, a parent and a child, or the two members of a couple in a relationship—create a strong proximity between the two semantic fields involved. This proximity is so strong, indeed, that many individuals have reported spontaneous psi experiences with their loved ones.

SFT poses that two semantic fields are proximate if they show strong links in terms of meaning—such as similarities, opposition, and inversion—irrespective of space and time. When two fields are proximate, the Newtonian linear distance in space or in time is annulled.

Annulling of time, for example, allows us to literally have an influence on past events or to converse with past geniuses, as happened to me in two instances—a lengthy discussion with Pauli and a therapeutic consultation with Paracelsus, a renowned sixteenth-century physician. In these two discussions, the time distance was annulled through a strong link in terms of preoccupations (how to heal) and in terms of ideas (synchronicity and so forth). (See chapter 12.) In general, the interaction between two consciousnesses allows for a wide range of phenomena: from a telepathic exchange of information to a strong inter-influence, as would be the case in a healing process.

The influence on an event in the past is called *retrocausality*. In other words, a future cause (or causal principle, like the mind) affects a past event. We can call the opposite of this influence on the past a proactive influence—that is, a consciousness that affects the organization of future events.[2]

But what about the interaction between a consciousness and the environment? As we have seen, objects, as well as the environment, are also semantic fields (or eco-fields, in short). It follows that sacred sites and sacred monuments, because they are charged with strong cosmotelluric and semantic energies, are very powerful eco-fields. The Obelisk in Paris, with its crossing of sacred lines, is thus a stunning dynamic eco-field. I have witnessed two impressive interactions with distant semantic fields that entailed an annulation of space. In both instances, a strong harmonization with a distant space resulted in the two spaces being embedded in each other.

In the first instance, the harmonization of the two spaces created a single energetic structure: a concentric spherical embedding. More precisely, a mind focused on a mental task inside a house in Europe (the inner sphere) was surrounded by an event happening outdoors in a far-away land at the exact same time (the outer sphere).

In the second instance, the embedding of the two spaces was quite similar, save for the fact that (1) the protagonists were numerous, and (2) the configuration of the concentric spheres was inverted. A large crowd at an outdoor feast (the outer sphere) was suddenly in sync with another crowd at a similar outdoor feast in a faraway land, and suddenly, a portion of the latter appeared contained in a sphere inside the first space. Further, in the inner sphere, both the present and the distant collective semantic fields were superimposed.

Let's look more closely at the first instance.

DESERT STORM INTRUDES ON THE CHER VALLEY

Just before the first Gulf War, the whole world held its breath while waiting for the final decision of war or no war from the United States and other coalition countries. The wait lasted (as far as I remember) about eight to ten days before the decision was finally revealed. When it was, we were told through the media that no precise date had yet been agreed upon for the start of Desert Storm, but it was known that weather conditions wouldn't allow for a long delay. What transpired from the cryptic comments was that it would most probably start within five to six days.

Just after the decision was made public (after two or three days), I was in my writing house in the Cher Valley, and, as usual, I was spending the whole night writing. (In cases of an exceptional creative state, I would carry on through the night until 7:00 a.m.)

I was in a large room, sitting cross-legged at a low table in front of the fireplace, two candles lighting my writing space and a dim, orange glow falling from above my head. I was fully absorbed in my writing in the space delimited by the candles (one in front and one on my desk, both at about the same height) that shed light on my stack of paper. It's important to note that bending your head to write on a low table creates a spherical field of vision that radiates about a yard around each eye. This field, in my case, included the whole tabletop and the candle on a stand in front of it. As usual, ambient music was playing.

Suddenly, while I was constructing a sentence and writing it, I sensed some movements on the outside of my sphere of vision—a few well-delineated silhouettes, nothing remotely reminiscent of a bug moving around the room. I knew that the peripheral cells of the eye have access to another spectrum of perception, and I had often used this peripheral vision. Not only can these cells see better than the central cells in the dark, but also they can better perceive the semantic energy and the semantic dimension.

Sensing something utterly strange, I stopped writing and froze in the exact same position I had been assuming, my eyes now unfocused on the white page. Immediately, I shifted my vision fully to the peripheral cells. Now I definitely saw a few silhouettes (all around me in my room, from two to a few dozen yards away) and a sandy desert ground. In the first tinge of predawn light, these men moved in the dark with slow, feline movements, crawling and then freezing, noiselessly and with astounding agility. I focused my peripheral gaze (my face and eyes still turned toward the page) on a soldier to my left. Not only did I see him crawling and sensed the desert landscape around him, but even more, I felt his fear that tensed his belly and how he controlled his fear: his constrained breathing.

The vision took place in a sort of sphere that encircled the writing sphere. All around my writing table, starting at about two yards beyond it, lay the desert landscape, as if the walls of my room were nonexistent. As more shadows of soldiers crawled into position further away in the open desert, the first tints of dawn appeared.

"The war has just started," I thought with an absolute confidence in my vision. "For now, it's a surprise attack, kept totally secret. We will get the news later today."

This is indeed what happened much later in the day. When I called my husband later and recounted my strange experience, thus disclosing the news to him, it was still well before the story of the attack came out in the media.

The sensations and perceptions involved in that vision had been unbelievably clear—the men; the landscape; the feeling of the desert floor and open space; the sly, shadowy movements; the darkness receding slowly, the first tinges of dawn.

Even more bewildering for me was the fact that I heard these men's thoughts and felt their sensations: their muscles tense and ready for swift action, the control over their fear. The overall perception lasted for about fifteen or twenty minutes. I was so amazed by both the perceptive phenomenon and the dramatic news that I had no desire to resume my work or to sleep. I remained in front of the fire, meditating, all curtains blocking the light of the day.

In terms of exceptional psi experiences, the most interesting point of this one is the fact that it came with its own proof. Of course, we are dealing here with an empirical proof rather than an experimental one: the fact that I disclosed the information much later that morning but nevertheless well before it came out in the news.

Once I had experiences of that type and was able to confirm their reality, I became more confident that similar experiences for which no proof could be obtained were indeed substantial and not just illusory. Now let's look more closely at the second occurrence.

OUR MINDS AFFECT SOUND SYSTEMS (SYG-ENERGY AND MATTER)

For the turn of the millennium (around New Year's 2000 and New Year's 2001) there were gigantic parties in Goa, India, that gathered between three thousand and eight thousand people from all countries in the world. The actual size of the crowd depended on the number of simultaneous parties, the occasion (full moon, Christmas, etc.), and the size of the place. Similar parties happened just about everywhere on the planet. For New Year's 2000, parties were so gigantic in Australia that they contained about five thousand drums and didgeridoos in one place.

For the great parties in India during these two years, the techno music, especially Goa trance style, was in full force. Many people (myself included) didn't like techno music at first; the beats sound somewhat too simple. Even then, however, I did remark that, in terms of collective consciousness, it possesses an essential quality: it transmits the rhythm very easily. Techno music makes the body move, it speaks directly to the body, and the beat is easy to follow. In a very short time, all people present can harmonize at the bodily level, dancing with the beat. This settles a sort of ground state of harmony. At first, it's neither spiritual nor fluid; on the contrary, it's very physical, though not sexual, as was the hard rock of the seventies and eighties.

From this ground state, when all are physically tuned in, when all bodies are in the same rhythm, anything can happen: all evolves according to the crowd present and the time and place. The party can remain at this mostly physical level, though it's quite rare in Goa; most of the time, especially on very energetic days (such as full moons, solstices, etc.), the trance will evolve into a highly spiritual collective state of consciousness—a telhar field. Then the music becomes aerial and meditative, while the rhythm grows more sophisticated and complex.

In reality, what happens is that the physical and rhythmic harmonization creates at first a crude, unsophisticated telhar field at a low energetic level. This field progressively rises to a high state of consciousness—to a full-blown telhar field—by the force of the people participating in the field. The higher the minds of people present, the higher will be the collective field.

Here is a dialogue I heard between two people in Goa:

"There will be a party at X on day Y."

"Yeah, but I don't like techno music."

"Ah! But once you get there, you make the music!"

I smiled when I heard this last comment, but I soon found it to be true to an unimaginable degree. In intimate gatherings of a handful of people, I had already realized that prerecorded music I knew very well was actually modified by the collective state of consciousness. A tape I used to listen to very often would suddenly become unrecognizable, as if it was a different music. It would express the very quality of what was happening in the collective consciousness field, our feelings and mind state. If, during one of these gatherings, a telhar field was created, the recorded music expressed the source of energy we were connected to, the soul quality of the person who was the node at that moment, and, of course, the evolution of our collective state.

When we first experience such a heightened collective state and realize the music sounds totally different—even unrecognizable—the obvious explanation we come up with (in our left-brain societies) is that this is pure psychological hallucination: we know our internal state is different, and therefore we believe that only our perception is modified. "But not the music of course!" any scientist, especially a psychologist, might exclaim while laughing loudly. That's what I thought until I ran across some strange phenomena.

All my life, I have written nearly every night. Modern society eats so much of our time that, in order to be absolutely sure to give most of mine to my work, I began the habit of writing while everybody sleeps. At this time, I experience no interruption, no distraction, and minimal noise and EM pollution. (Problems can spoil and enslave my days, but my nights are for me, a time when I can reach pure freedom.) To enter a creative state, I use music with specific rhythms and frequencies that I feel put my mind into a higher gear. I have my preferred pieces of music whose influence is guaranteed. Just like everybody else, I sometimes exchange music with friends, and it so happened that I lent one of my preferred tapes (at the time we still used tapes) to a close friend.

When the tape was returned to me one or two weeks later, horror! I didn't recognize my music. It was my tape, all right, and my writing appeared on the label, but now, on listening to it, I heard something that expressed the particular sensibility and feeling of my friend. I heard the music in his way. I realized that the fact that he had listened to this tape a few times had left a print on the tape itself! Of course, a professional musician hates to lend his beloved instrument, because when it's returned, the sound has been subtly changed. This is especially true with flutes; each person has their own way of blowing air into a flute, which affects the flute itself. The same is true with guitars and even with cars. Good drivers hate to lend their cars.

The modification of my tape was not uniform, which would have been the case if it had been damaged by a bad tape recorder. What was changed was the psychological atmosphere, as if the musician playing the music was another person with a different personality. Yet that personality was recognizable as that of my friend.

This happened to me on several occasions. Each time, I had to listen to the tape a few times while remembering intensely the musical ambience I loved. After a few days of this intensive re-evocation, I once again added my own imprint to the tape.

I was intrigued by this phenomenon. I had a hard time believing it, but it happened so many times, with different friends, that I eventually accepted it. I also asked some musician friends if they had noted the phenomenon, and some answered that they did. If that's so, then not only how we play the chords of a guitar or blow air in a flute affects the instrument, but the instrument is also affected by the mind-set and feeling of the player.

But let's see how we can understand this phenomenon through SFT. For example, a Bob Marley CD is a semantic field (or in short an eco-field) that first comprises the music itself—a semantic energy: feelings, emotions, meaning. Second, the plastic bears the physical imprint of this music (the engraving), but it is also changed (subtly, invisibly) by the mental quality of the music. Finally, the CD bears the collective imprint of all the people who have listened to this music (these songs in general, this CD in particular).

The material support (the plastic disk) is the physical part of the eco-field (it is modified by the semantic imprint). The consciousness quality of the music is the *semantic constellation* attached to it—the semantic constellation of this music.[3] The collective imprint is the *collective semantic constellation* attached to any renowned art object. The three together form the semantic field (or eco-field) of a cultural object. In this way, SFT distances itself from the old Cartesian dualism: here, we don't have matter on one side and mind on the other with a huge, forever unexplainable gap in between. Here, matter itself is modified by consciousness. The plastic is itself changed and imprinted by the semantic field enclosing it.

A new listener to Bob Marley's CD will generate a new semantic constellation on the CD itself—the semantic constellation of his listening (thoughts, emotions, state of mind, state of the moment, and so forth). In the same manner, we affect all the objects with which we interact. Our houses, furniture, cars, everything that is of great value to us (jewels, loved art objects, and the like)—all are semantic fields that bear our personal mind imprint. Similarly, all cultural objects (especially collective buildings and great artworks) bear the imprints of all people who are interested in them. An object is the expression of intent and purpose (the core of the original semantic constellation). Through interaction with all people connected to it, the semantic constellation of an object is further charged with semantic energy, and then it keeps on evolving, becoming more complex.

Thus the subtle imprinting of objects (and matter) by consciousness creates the eco-fields of objects, and through their eco-fields, the matter reality of these objects is deeply modified.

The eco-field is thus like a trace left by consciousness on matter: it bears the memory of consciousness's intent, its history, usage, and all minds and beings to which it has been strongly connected. This is how the eco-field of an antique ring can bear the psychological imprints of its past owners, which can be decoded by psychics (a capacity called *psychometry*).

Our entire social environment and all man-made modifications of the natural environment are thus predominantly semantic: they bear a strong meaning that can be decoded. Take, for example, a hill: it will be immediately evident to all tourists walking by if the place is a park, or if it is a golf course, a mining site, or in the midst of a totally wild place. We live in a universe of meaning that is deeply embedded in matter. We live in a semantic world.

As the pioneers of quantum physics stated, there is no way for us to know the world as it would be without the interaction brought by human consciousness, because as soon as we observe a phenomenon, the act of observation has already modified it. The only reality that is accessible to us is a reality generated by the interaction of our meaningful sensing and thinking and nature itself.

We must also remember, however, that we are not the only beings to generate semantic fields. All living beings modify their environment. Life on Earth has modified in a very deep way the chemical and universal organization of our planet. Life is a powerful semantic force, and it has been since the beginning—since the age in which, for about four billion years, only bacteria existed, inventing the main processes of life. Life was able to modify our planet to the point of making life sustainable on it. (Refer to the beautiful and exciting books of Lynn Margulis and Dorion Sagan and James Lovelock.[4]) Life, with its raw and forceful intent, rendered the world livable. This is a magnificent semantic energy at work.

TWO DISTANT SPACES EMBEDDED IN A GOA PARTY

Another clear-cut occurrence in which space was annulled took place during one of the exceptional trance dance parties that, for the turn of the century, occurred all over the world on December 31, 1999, and January 1, 2000. (In some places, such as Goa, the parties lasted for three days without interruption.)

*On December 31, 1999, to celebrate the turn of the century, I and several thousand others attended a huge trance dance party in Goa. There were about a half dozen dance floors, each flanked by two walls of speakers. They looked like huge plateaus in the forest. The ground was soil that had been wetted beforehand to keep the dust down while people danced. Branching out of the dance floors, dozens of alleys lead quite far into the forest, with many Indian women—*matadji—*preparing tea and coffee on mats. The deejays were on a separate platform overlooking the highest dance plateaus.*

The collective state of consciousness was so high and so strong that we formed a telhar field very early on that remained whole all through the night while its intensity and the trance state we were in kept deepening. One deejay replaced another every couple of hours, and the music became more and more entranced and cosmic. Soon, our own telhar field started being connected to other telhar fields of parties going on simultaneously in other parts of the world until we reached a planetary telhar field. At that point, we could easily sense the various parties going on in many countries, but with the clear perception that they were at a distance and in various directions, interconnected but still far away from us. In other words, even with a planetary telhar field, the structure of semantic space was not yet altered.

Suddenly, part of another party occurring in Australia materialized itself in a large circle on the dance floor, just below the one on which I was dancing. Our deejay music was immediately transformed into drums and didgeridoos, a frenetic improvisation of the Australians. Along with this, there materialized a crowd of drummers and didgeridoo players, obviously themselves harmonized in a telhar field, as if they were superimposed onto the people dancing in Goa. The two collective spaces—Australia and Goa—were moving through each other, as if each one had the whole space for itself, dancing bodies moving through the musicians' bodies.

The Australian music party took over the node of our Goa telhar field for the duration of its apparition, about fifteen to twenty minutes. Maybe a half hour after the first embedding ended, the same phenomenon happened again, this time with a group of African drummers playing in Nigeria—though they were less numerous, maybe only forty or fifty musicians. They appeared at the same place and took over our node as well as the music. (In telhar fields, the music is always imprinted with the node's semantic energy.) This appearance lasted less time, about a dozen minutes.

Still later, I perceived some sort of energetic disruption on the same dance floor—the kind of fuzzy, undulating waves created by intense heat on an asphalt road. I expected a new materialization, but nothing more happened.

In both cases, it was as if one party happening at a distant locale was superimposed on and embedded within our party in India. The strong similarity in syg-energy, as well as the very high collective states of consciousness in both telhar fields, must have triggered an embedding of two distant spaces via the two telhar fields. In Goa, at the place where the apparitions materialized, people were still dancing; it was a superimposition of collective spaces without one disturbing the other, with a strong influence and modification of the music and ambience. In both cases (Australia and then Nigeria), a sort of encompassing meta-telhar field was created comprising two distinct and superimposed telhar fields. The people belonging to the two telhar fields were perfectly harmonized and synchronized in their minds and bodies through the music, and I believe it is this very synchronization that triggered the embedding of the two telhar fields in the first place.

Thus a harmonized collective field, a telhar field, can trigger a nonlocal phenomenon of great magnitude: the harmonization of two resonant telhar fields to such a degree that one becomes superimposed on the other, thus annulling space. Let's now look at the theoretical facet of this phenomenon.

PONDERING FUNNELS AND ANNULLING SPACE OR TIME

The Funnel Phenomenon

It's only after reviewing this section that the phenomenon of the funnel and its sink in Brazil suddenly struck me as being of tantalizing importance. Even though I have perceived it only once up to this day—while in contrast I saw the rod structure more often—it seems to be a key energetic structure as far as syg-energy and syg-fields are concerned. (Syg-fields refer to all possible fields created from syg-energy—the non-EM spectrum—and thus they include more than telhar fields.)

As I stressed earlier, the fact that we have a rod structure with two nodes should not lead us to assume that this rod is a typical EM field, polarized, with a plus and a minus end. My understanding through years of meditation has been that in the semantic dimension (at the level of the Self and beyond) there is no more duality or polarity.

On the one hand, all ancient Eastern treatises pose that the level of the *purusha,* or Brahman (neutral), or the Tao is beyond duality. This is why the core spiritual philosophy in India is called *advaita philosophy,* meaning "nonduality philosophy." The unity and harmony dimension is attained when the head chakra reaches full activation. On the other hand, accumulated experimental evidence shows that telepathy can occur between two people while the receiver is in a locale shielded from most EM energies, such as a submarine deep in the sea or a Faraday cage. While preparing for my Ph.D. on psi phenomena and altered states of consciousness, I worked as a research assistant at Psychophysical Research Laboratories (PRL) in the Forrestal think tank at Princeton University in New Jersey. In PRL, we were conducting telepathy experiments in a hypnagogic state (between sleep and wakefulness) called *Ganzfeld*. The subjects who participated in these experiments at PRL, just as those who were doing remote viewing (clairvoyance) experiments at Stanford Research Institute, sat in a Faraday cage. And yet the results that were obtained in these two labs did show a strong evidence of psi; in other words, the shielding of most EM waves didn't affect in the least the reception of telepathic or clairvoyant information. Based on these findings, we can be reasonably certain that syg-energy, linked to consciousness and thought, has little to do with the kind of EM fields to which we are accustomed.

Following is a list of the structures at play in telhar fields. I will describe them without making any projection on them of what our actual science knows about EM fields or quantum processes. On the contrary, I will stress the discrepancies they present. (Refer to figure 11.1.)

Node: The two individuals (or nodes) creating a rod are both in heightened consciousness; both willingly initiate the contact/harmonization (a process that is contrary to quantum physics's indetermination).

Rod: The syg-energy between two nodes shows a two-way flow inside the rod (contrary to EM dipole).

Telhar Field: The telhar field created through the rod is quite extended. It has a high energy level, but the rod field is still higher. (When crossing the rod, the auras of humans are boosted and lighted.)

Funnel: In the Brazil experience, first I saw the funnel, and then my consciousness was drawn to the funnel, but only prior to a shift from Brazil to India. I entered via the large opening and was sucked toward the sink, and abruptly, without transition, I found myself in Goa. In contrast, each time I shifted from Goa to Brazil, I didn't see any funnel. Given there were thousands of people at the Goa party and given that I was there in my energetic body (my semantic field), it is possible that there was a funnel that I did not perceive (it may have looked different), or perhaps there was no funnel in Goa. Theoretical considerations point to the first option as being more plausible.

The funnel appearing in Brazil was obviously an energetic structure created by, and specific to, syg-energy and syg-fields. This syg-funnel acted as a gate opening onto the second space—the semantically proximate telhar field of Goa. Its small end, acting as a sink, was located at about midpoint on the rod (M), while its larger end was about one yard higher at a slight angle. My inference is that where the funnel ends at M, an antifunnel begins, penetrating the Goa telhar field. I never actually saw an antifunnel, but I infer that it would have an inverse funnel shape, the two small ends meeting at point M, so that the whole structure would look like an hourglass or an elongated X shape. We can call it an X funnel. (See figure 11.1 on page 274.) Instead of attracting and swallowing syg-energy, the antifunnel makes it spurt out like a geyser right into the spatial coordinates of the coupled syg-field.

Let's now compare Brazil's rod and the rod willingly created by two people acting as nodes during Goa beach's collective meditation.

The Goa beach rod created a large telhar field that harmonized the entire group of about 150 people, modifying their state of consciousness quasi-instantaneously, their minds shifting from a sexual attraction to a meditative state. There was no spatial disruption; only a collective harmonization of minds.

Brazil's rod created a large telhar field, but it also created a funnel (hypothetically, an X funnel), putting into contact two distant telhar fields and their spatial environment. Thus we can infer that it is the syg-funnel, and not the rod itself, that collapses space. Nonetheless, it seems the syg-funnel is either a possible feature of the syg-rod (one among all possible states of the system) or, at the very least, somehow linked to it, since its small end touches precisely the rod's midpoint M.

Let's remember that the semantic dimension is a dimension of deep reality, a layer below quantum fields and processes (matter as energy), which is itself below the level of EM fields (matter). In a way, the funnel gives weight to the basic concept of SFT, namely that semantic proximity connects semantic fields independently of space and time.[5] Semantic proximity, as we have seen, is a function of meaningful connections between two semantic fields, either similarities of feelings, viewpoints, or aims, or a strong dissimilarity, such as opposition or antinomy.

The parameter of semantic proximity describes phenomena that are both energetic and meaningful (thus linked to consciousness). In short, it accounts for physico-semantic phenomena and especially for how consciousness (the process of giving meaning) can collapse time or space by linking or embedding two semantic fields (two mental events with their linked state of consciousness and semantic environment). Thus we have a syg-space-time manifold (or SST manifold).

When the semantic proximity between two semantic fields (or events) reaches a given threshold (i.e., of harmony, resonance, inverse symmetry, etc.), it interconnects spontaneously the fields and consequently collapses the distance between them, either in space or in time.

- If semantic proximity collapses space, it connects the syg-fields at the exact same time.
- If semantic proximity collapses time, it connects the syg-fields within the exact same dimension of space (same planet in the universe).
- If time and space were to be collapsed together, we would most probably lose the source syg-field or event.

Our first conclusion is that when two syg-fields that are distant in space are spontaneously connected through semantic proximity, a syg-energy funnel is created. The source node of the contact is pulled toward the funnel and, passing through it, emerges within the other syg-field.

As far as I can fathom, in Brazil, I was coming and going in consciousness and energetic body (syg-body, dreamtime body, and so forth), but could the semantic dimension also allow for a transfer of matter?

This reminds me of an anomalous event that a venerable scientist recounted to me while I was interviewing him. This scientist, Stéphane Lupasco, was a logician and a philosopher of science who had developed a type of three-term logic.[6]

While helping his wife clear the table after lunch, a silver teaspoon fell from his hands, and his eyes followed the object's fall toward the ground. Suddenly, he perceived a small funnel that appeared halfway to the ground, and he watched in amazement as the teaspoon was literally swallowed by the funnel. After describing the phenomenon to his wife, they decided nevertheless to count the silverware and make a thorough search everywhere . . . but to no avail: one silver teaspoon had disappeared.

The funnel shape is nothing but a curved cone, and the fact that a syg-field (a consciousness) can be attracted and sucked into it evokes an analogy to black holes and light cones. Light cones and their distortion have been modeled in the physics of black holes.* Black holes create an enormous distortion of space-time, and they have such strong gravitational fields that matter and light cannot escape the boundary of the black hole's singularity—called the *event horizon* and thought to be a point without volume (in general relativity's framework).

In his first model of black holes, Stephen Hawking thought that all matter and energy pulled toward the black hole's disk of accretion and then its central cone (now called the event horizon) disappears entirely. Up to this day, black holes have been theorized both in general relativity and in quantum theory, with no harmonization yet possible between the two models. Both, nevertheless, soon started conceiving the event horizon as a point (represented as round) with zero volume—and once matter and energy had passed its boundary, only a specific radiation,

---

*Stephen Hawking and Roger Penrose modeled black holes in 1970, on the basis of Einstein's general theory of relativity. Black holes were postulated as black stars at the end of the eighteenth century by the geologist John Michell and the mathematician Pierre-Simon Laplace. The general theory of relativity predicts that the collapsing of stars creates an enormous distortion of space-time—the black hole—with such an enormous gravitational field that matter and even light cannot escape. It predicts that only gravitational waves (gravitons) are emitted at the speed of light.

called the Hawking radiation, was released, creating a strong luminosity in the case of quasars and thus revealing the possible black hole to astronomers. The point was called the event horizon because once matter or energy had gone inside its boundary, it was crushed by the enormous gravity forces inside. It thus seemed that all information about the stellar systems (and their events) was lost. That proposition raises a paradox (the black hole information paradox), because quantum physics does not allow for information to be entirely lost, and this is still a matter of harsh debate. In 2004, Hawking revised his theory and postulated that some energy could escape the accretion disk.

This is what is said to occur in black holes: space-time bends on itself more and more toward the event horizon, and all worldlines of matter and events are said to end past its boundary. The syg-funnel, however, points to a different hypothesis: what if there was an inverse white hole coupled with the black hole, with a disk of ejection spurting energy into another space-time universe? Then all matter (star systems) and events that had been crushed into the black hole would have escaped our visible space-time universe, only to emerge, as energy and information, in another one.

Here is what physicist Roy Kerr proposes, based on his solution of the equations of general relativity:[7]

- The properties of space-time between the two event horizons allow objects to move only toward the singularity.
- But the properties of space-time within the inner event horizon allow objects to move away from the singularity, pass through another set of inner and outer event horizons, and emerge out of the black hole into another universe or another part of this universe without traveling faster than the speed of light.
- Passing through the ring-shaped singularity may allow entry to a negative-gravity universe.

Yet there is no point in making any analogy, for several reasons. The first and foremost reason is that we are not, with syg-fields, in the same manifold—we are in a syg-space-time manifold (or SST manifold).

The phenomena we are analyzing here (telhar fields annuling space and time) are prominently semantic, linked to consciousness.

Among other discrepancies are these:

1. The syg-funnel is formed spontaneously and instantly.
2. The funnel allows a syg-field (a collective or individual consciousness) to exit a set of SST coordinates and appear in another SST set. In other words, the syg-field doesn't just disappear in the funnel. The two-way X funnel is only a transfer gate.
3. The force driving the process (the control variable) is semantic proximity—that is, a consciousness force. We can recall that despite the fact that the funnel is formed spontaneously (at a certain threshold of proximity or attunement between two semantic fields), it is nevertheless a person (a mind) who decides, or is inclined, to connect with another semantic field (another mind, a collective consciousness field elsewhere, etc.).

Thus, in the SFT framework, semantic proximity can spontaneously link two distant spaces, instantly collapsing the space separating them and creating either an embedding or an attunement.

- **In syg-embedding:** one syg-field appears within the other one—that is, they share the same node and become superimposed. In syg embedding, a consciousness perceives two usually distant semantic fields in *synlocality* (the same locality). The two local universes of the two syg-fields become superimposed. In other words, the node's consciousness remains stable in our own SST coordinates (local universe), while the other local universe is translocalized to the exact same SST coordinates.
- **In syg-attunement:** two syg-fields are strongly interconnected and contiguous. Each, however, may have a different node. One or more minds can transfer themselves instantaneously back and forth from one local universe to the other.

Regarding a collapse of space, we saw syg embedding with a synlo-calization of two distant spaces in two instances: in the Desert Storm case and in the Y2K party in Goa.

There was a syg-attunement in the Brazil case, with a translocaliza-tion of at least one individual consciousness. (In fact, there is a possibil-ity that the second node of the rod, the man sitting next to the speakers, was also translocalized to Goa.)

To answer the question I posed earlier: I don't think there's any-thing precluding a transfer of biological or physical matter as far as attunement is concerned (though embedding would certainly pose a "hard problem" to resolve!). The decisive factor, however, is the control variable that creates the semantic proximity in the first place.

If semantic proximity is affected by a consciousness state (similari-ties between distant states of consciousness), then the synlocalization or the translocalization will affect one or more consciousnesses (their syg-field and their mental environment).

Let's say, however, that semantic proximity is created by a matter field—that is, similarities between distant physical fields, such as iso-morphic EM or magnetic fields, coupled particles with opposite charges, or coupled particles with complementary spins (for example, the ones showing nonlocal correlations or entanglement—the famous EPR para-dox). In that instance, the translocalization (in cases of attunement) or the synlocalization (in cases of embedding) would primarily affect mat-ter and the EM or quantum fields (and the bodies of people within these fields, if any). The synlocalization of matter (physical or biological) is either implausible or else would lead to bodies being partly jammed within matter fields—a kind of Philadelphia experiment nightmare!

Returning to Lupasco's teaspoon: such an anomalous process as a teaspoon disappearing from a local universe through a funnel is indeed permitted by SFT. Yet (and this is a big caveat) SFT predicts that the teaspoon, instead of having simply disappeared, has been in fact trans-localized to another set of SST coordinates, that of an EM or quan-tum field that was somehow strongly linked to Lupasco at that very moment.

12
TIME SINGULARITIES

REVERSING TIME

Precognition (knowledge of the future) and retrocognition (knowledge of the past) are quite frequent psi phenomena, for which there are a great deal of data, both in terms of experimental research and surveys. If the skeptics have denied their reality, it's mainly because they are at odds with good old Newtonian physics; how could a person know about events that have not yet happened? Yet, in general relativity, the time dimension is spread in space, and thus past, present, and future coexist.*

The physicist Olivier Costa de Beauregard has proposed that the unconscious dwells in this spread-time dimension and that this is how the Self (the subject of our personal unconscious) can know about past or future events.[1] I share this viewpoint.

In this light, precognition and retrocognition are already tinkering with the Newtonian dimension of time, which is seen as a line and in which past causes bring effects in the future—in a word, *normal causality*. Thus, our notion of causality relies on a commonsense and basic time arrow: from past toward future.

Our ego is strongly attached to our body (to biological matter) and to our material environment (towns, buildings, objects, and the like). It rebels and enters denial mode whenever it perceives something at odds

---

*More precisely, this is what's happening outside the Einstein-Minkowski light cone.

with gross matter laws. If, for example, a leaf falls from a nearby tree, touches the ground with its tip, and then remains standing still on its tip for thirty seconds (as I once observed), the ego shouts, "I'm hallucinating!" In psychology, this is called a *cognitive dissonance:* what we see doesn't match what we "know" should appear or occur. Yet it is only what we think we know should be happening. As the physicists would say, there is always a possibility, even if incredibly tiny, for such an event to occur. Yet when we become perturbed by such an improbable event, the common healthy reaction is pure and simple denial—which is somewhat better than thinking we are crazy.

Highly psychic individuals, however, those on a spiritual quest and those who experience heightened states of consciousness, generally deal fairly well with cognitive dissonance. When we experience high states of consciousness, we access a dimension of reality in which events are more influenced by our mind and the semantic dimension than by material causes. At times, the syg-energy of a person can be powerful enough to change the natural organization of matter and the basic causality in the physical dimension.

We can consider again the creation of a large telhar field through the shared intent of two people, as happened in the Goa party, when, by creating a rod, my elusive friend and I helped reverse the course of a potential orgy (see chapter 10). The normal biological course (once two people have willingly started sexual preludes) is that the sexual drive takes precedence over everything apart from a catastrophic interruption. How could something as intangible as syg-energy and a telhar field, in the absence of any dramatic event, be strong enough to reverse sexual arousal? Moreover, the fact that it occurred similarly to so many people makes the case even stronger! This definitely was a singularity in terms of biological and instinctual behaviors. (Physicists call a singularity an event that has either an extremely low probability to occure or that infringes on common laws.)

Can We Change Past Psychological Events?
This is of course the first question that springs to mind when we reflect on annulling time. First, let's look at the possibility of influencing past

events with an intent (and mental impulse) that is set in the present. This phenomenon is a strong retrocausal process because it implies more than information (e.g., receiving information from the future, as in prediction or precognition). The possibility of affecting past events implies an organizing mental energy that is activated in the present and affects the past.

Retrocausality has been discussed in depth within quantum physics and has been posed at the theoretical level by several physicists. The brilliant mathematician Henri Poincaré proposed it as early as the nineteenth century.[2] He suggested that retrocausality, associated with a reversal of the time arrow (future to past instead of past to future), was a direct consequence of the temporal symmetry found in most equations of classical physics. The quantum physicist Richard Feynman posed that antiparticles may be considered as normal particles that move backward in time (along a future-to-past axis)—creating what is called a temporal zigzag. Other physicists, such as Costa de Beauregard and Jack Sarfatti, advocate the possibility of information coming from the future and propagating backward in time. In ancient Greece, the philosopher Aristotle had already sorted out four different types of causes, one of which, named *final cause* (or *teleology*), implies a retrocausal force whereby goals and the final state of a system (in the future) influence its evolution in present time.

Therapeutic Techniques for Changing Past Traumatic Events

Precognition—to receive information coming from the future—is a quite common phenomenon. A person has a premonitory dream showing— often with a great detail—a precise situation that will happen in reality a few days later. In precognition, however, only information follows the future-to-present time arrow (or the reversed time arrow), and the scientists studying anomalous and psi phenomena make a great distinction between information and matter. While spontaneous cases of precognition are found by the thousands in diverse collections of scientists, examples about tinkering with past events are quasi-nonexistent—even for somebody hoping to get his or her hands on a good case in the literature.

Of course, a handful of psychotherapists use with great efficiency techniques for curing past trauma based on modifying these past events, but this is more a question of changing how the person reacts to the event than really changing the event itself. Psychotherapists work with viewpoints and psychological perspectives. A person can be cured instantaneously whenever he is able to visualize himself back in the dramatic situation and imagine that he now reacts to the terrifying event with positive and strong emotions. For example, therapists suggest that their patient develop a global perspective on why such an event may have happened. Then, they try to trigger in the patient a healthy anger and an ability to defend himself or laugh derisively in order to retain his own integrity. At the very moment the person "impersonates" a new role in the past situation with strong belief and involvement, he annuls the chain of psychological effects and recovers his psychic energy that was previously lost in this psychological knot. As Carl Jung explained, a trauma is like a cyst in the psyche, attracting energy and then trapping it inside its protective walls. Modifying a psychological stand within that encysted memory is like breaking down the walls and liberating the energy.

Does this kind of therapeutic technique change the past event itself? In a strict sense, no. Yet it's quite baffling to consider that the chain of psychological events dating from the trauma and warping the emotional life of an individual can be obliterated in a session of a few hours.

WORLD EVENTS IN A DEEP THEORY FRAMEWORK

In physics, an event is a complex network of phenomena that happens at the deep level of the organization of matter. It is the behavior of waves and particles (such as a collision or the shooting out of photons) that leads to a material event. Thus, any material event implies the complex interactions of billions of subatomic events. In cognitive science, our thoughts and feelings are similarly interwoven with billions or trillions of infinitesimal events that happen not only at the neuronal level, but also at the subatomic level. Semantic fields theory (SFT) adds that the deepest level of reality is consciousness energy, a mind-matter embedding.

In SFT, I propose that the distinction between mind and matter is blurred when we consider the whole individual (mind-body-psyche) in a holistic way, as an ensemble of *complex dynamical systems* cooperating and coevolving. SFT poses that every biological organism and material system is also a semantic field pertaining to the semantic dimension. In other words, there is a dimension of consciousness (however primitive) in all systems in the universe—animals, plants, rocks, planets, or even man-made objects such as paintings and crafts, buildings, parks, and so forth. Of course, these semantic fields can be wholly projected by creators and users (as in the case of simple man-made objects), but they belong properly to all natural systems, whether biological or crystalline (water, metal, and rock).

In consequence, all events, whether mental, emotional, or apparently material, can interact among themselves through this deep reality, or semantic dimension, which pervades the universe. Indeed, it makes sense to consider events in the world as existing not only at a hard matter level, but also at social, psychological, political, and ideological levels. All these levels of an event are constantly mixing and interacting.

We can use for an example a political event such as a strike. The ensuing battle occurs mostly on a semantic level: rallying supporters, strikers making their case known, discussing and working out a solution. The outcome becomes a question of interpretation and meaning, values, and goals—how the pro-interest and anti-interest groups deal with the situation. Each group interprets and understands the event through a different semantic framework (a different paradigm, a different perspective). Yet the ultimate decision and the ensuing action set up a new event that itself generates material effects. For example, a refusal to negotiate has, in some instances, led to violent rebellion and destruction of goods, which in turn has led to greater repression, setting a spiral of increased violence and turmoil.

When we use the semantic fields' framework, we know from the start that any event has a semantic dimension (a level of meaning). More precisely, any event is a semantic constellation, dynamic and evolving. Hence, the diversified interpretations of this event from various groups, and their subsequent reactions to it, will have much more impact on the course of further events than the material level of the event (in our example, the commotion caused by the strike). In that sense, the reaction of the media and civil groups will be of primary importance on the future development and unfolding of the situation. We can see that the decision makers should consider civil society and the patchwork of non-governmental organizations (NGOs) as major players in world events. The growing impact of such a global force acting as a moderator of otherwise egotistical interest groups and lobbies is quite evident.

If the importance of the semantic dimension is obvious when we consider socio-political events, does it work in the same manner with material and natural events? Let's consider a material event such as the level of carbon dioxide in Earth's atmosphere. It's intuitively clear that this chemical event—the actual ratio of CO_2 in the air—cannot be taken simply by itself, but must instead be understood as the result of political and legal choices: the types of energy used for cars and machines among the vast array of working possibilities (some of which were tested during World War II, to cope with fuel shortages in France), the officially discarded or supported alternative engine fuels, and officially authorized levels of CO_2 pollution. As Brazil has shown, in a matter of a few years, a whole country can develop a swift alternative to using fossil fuels and can master engineering, making, and selling alcohol-based car engines and producing and distributing alcohol from cane.

Thus, in our complex modern societies, events are predominantly semantic—that is, they are meanings, interpretations, and decisions. Only in small part are they hard-core matter. Events mostly reflect past and present political positioning and economic choices. We know already that by making alternative decisions, we can immediately change the course of hard-core matter events.

Let us turn now to an anomalous phenomenon that involved a direct tinkering with a past hard-core matter event.

ANNULLING TIME
Direct Influence on the Past

If it is quite common to get precognitive information or to change our perspective on a traumatic past event, it's something entirely different to change the behavioral and matter level of a past event.

I was fortunate enough to have such an experience and to earn material proof of the influence of my mind over a past event, even if this event involved my own behavior two days earlier.

I was collaborating with my then-husband Mario Varvoglis on the creation of a CD-ROM presenting the wide array of experimental research on psi phenomena as well as its theoretical grounds (in psychology, physics, and science at large). We had prepared the text, and, after some trials, we decided to use my voice for the greatest part of the audio text in French. As a result, at the end of the week, I had gone with him to a recording studio in Paris, where we spent two days with a technician to record the text.

For this psi event to be comprehensible, we must consider a few details about the sound systems of the time and the situation: the recording at the studio was digital, but it was still produced on large tapes and then it had been copied onto small tapes for our digital audio tape (DAT) system. Only in a second phase would it be transferred onto the computer so that the soundtrack could be integrated with the video clip.

During the recording in the studio, I was alone in the recording room. On the other side of a soundproof glass panel were my ex-husband and the studio technician. My ex-husband gave me feedback and told me when a sentence or a paragraph had to be rerecorded, though sometimes, if I had made a clear-cut mistake, I would redo the sentence immediately. To talk to me, my ex-husband used a microphone whose channel was not recorded on the tape, but that I could hear through my headset.

Two days after the recording in the studio, I sat at my desk, where I listened to the DAT recording. I had to choose the best version of all the paragraphs I had done twice in the studio. I marked down each good paragraph with its place on the tape (in minutes and seconds). In front of me were sheets to write on, and the DAT was at arm's length on my left so that I could stop the tape and rewind when needed. The sound came from two speakers set on both sides of the DAT recorder. I had been working for two or three hours already, and everything was going well, when I reached a part of the text that was of utmost importance to me, because it dealt with states of consciousness and techniques of self-development (my preferred area of expertise, in which I have done considerable research).

I listened to my voice delivering the paragraph that introduced the whole subject, and I found that my tone did not have the quality and enthusiasm I would have liked to express for this domain. Next, I heard my voice saying, with an informal tone, "What do you think, Mario [my ex-husband], should I redo that paragraph?"

Then there was a blank space on the tape, because my ex-husband's answer was not recorded. My voice spoke again, saying, "Okay then, I'll move on." (Obviously, he had said it was fine, and I had agreed with him.)

At this point in listening to the tape, I was very upset. I turned to the DAT recorder and literally shouted at myself, "No, redo it, redo it!"

Immediately after, I heard on the tape, with practically no blank space, my voice saying, "In fact, I'll redo it." And I went on, repeating the whole paragraph.

On hearing that, I uttered a big sigh, and listened to my voice as it spoke with the kind of lively tone I wanted.

Three things strike me about this incident. First, the words "I'll redo it" came right after I had finished shouting my command in my office—as if it was a response to my directive. Second, at the moment I shouted and while gazing at the DAT recorder, I was also looking at an image of myself in the studio and shouting the order to this person. I had the impression that I was connected directly to my mind in the past when I gave the order. Third, strangely, when I answered my ex-husband with *"Okay then, I'll move on,"* my voice sounded perfectly casual, as if in total acceptance of his feedback. In contrast, when the second recorded utterance came, "In fact, I'll redo it," (in my command, I was quite forceful, and I gave the order twice), my tone of voice was totally different: a rapid muttering, however clear, as if I was talking to myself, and immediately, I began again with the text, not waiting for any comment from my ex-husband.

While I was sitting at my desk, listening, I had the impression of seeing a person standing in the studio (myself two days earlier), and it was to this person that I gave a forceful, compelling order. I used this imperative mode as if I was talking to someone in front of me. Without this direct connection, I would have just sworn aloud or expressed a strong wish—anything but given an order. And in fact, the tone of the voice on the tape was exactly that of an answer to this command. The tone, the grammatical form, the exact timing of the utterances—all were perfectly coherent, as if they illustrated a real-time exchange between me at my desk and me in the studio two days earlier. In stark contrast, this tone didn't fit at all with an exchange I might have had with someone (my ex-husband, for instance) who had a different idea on the subject.

All these elements were sufficient for me to be certain that I had, in effect, been able to give an order to myself in the past and that I in the past had indeed heard the order coming from the future and acted accordingly.

Let me note that, while working for hours before this happened, listening to the tape and hearing my voice uttering the text and occasional one-way dialogues with my ex-husband, I constantly saw in images what had happened and relived the whole scene at the studio sequentially, so that I had progressively built up a strong connection to that past time and with my past self. This surely had an influence on the phenomenon.

CONSCIOUSNESS AS A DIMENSION OF REALITY

I agree that if a witness had been in my office at that precise moment, the scene would not have lacked a certain humor: somebody shouting and rolling her eyes in anger at a tape recorder, ordering the voice that came out of it!

In the semantic dimension, however, the only part that has any reality is the consciousness aspect—that is, thoughts and feelings, all that which is meaningful. Viewed from this dimension, an object is only a dense network of meanings, feelings, and thoughts as well as the links and paths between them. In other words, in the semantic dimension any thing (a building, a jewel, or a village) appears as a semantic field that is more or less complex: the eco-field.

Thus, all objects, buidings, and the environment as well have an eco-field, interacting with larger eco-fields—for example, the eco-field of a painting in the larger eco-field of a room. In fact, if we look more closely, objects created by humans are no more and no less than a specific embodiment of a constellation of meanings, such as their usage, their intended beauty, the gestures and behaviors linked to their handling, or the feelings attached to them. Objects are thoughts reified: they are concepts, feelings, and intents embodied and expressed through matter. Take, for example, notebooks and pens: they express intent—the use for which they were created. Yet no object is nearer to the semantic dimension than a cultural object: a book, a movie, a CD of music . . . SFT posits that in the semantic dimension—that is, consciousness-as-energy—all semantic fields of people and eco-fields of objects interact and interinfluence each other. Moreover, this dynamic influence happens spontaneously, triggered by links and similarities in terms of meaning.

How can consciousness be defined through SFT? Let's narrow down our definition of human consciousness: human consciousness is a semantic field, that is, an extremely complex, multilevel system of intertwined semantic events and processes constantly interacting with other semantic fields and in a dynamic flow. In other words, our consciousness is in constant interaction with other consciousnesses and with the eco-fields of man-made objects (tools, monuments, towns, and so forth) or of natural systems (trees, lakes, etc.).

SFT thus views consciousness in a chaos theory framework, as global interactions in an ensemble of complex, dynamic systems—here, cognitive and semantic systems. Yet the specificity of SFT goes beyond this complex dynamic framework. Its revolutionary concept is to attribute nonlocal properties to consciousness, due to the fact that syg-energy is not bound by the space-time of Newtonian physics. In short, consciousnesses (and semantic fields) may interact with each other over great distances in both space and time.

A NONLOCAL CONSCIOUSNESS

Let's consider the semantic dimension: imagine that consciousness doesn't dwell in our usual time and space, that it is constrained neither by matter nor by space-time. Visualize that consciousness and the semantic dimension pervade all matter and the whole universe.

From this perspective, consciousness is immortal. It's not that an individual consciousness remains eternally; rather, it exists beyond time, in a no-time that is accessible from any space-time frame. (More precisely, part of an individual consciousness is bound to the space-time of its brain and body, while another part—the Self—extends to, and is rooted in, the no-time.)

Consequently, the individual consciousnesses of Plato or Leonardo da Vinci still exist in the semantic dimension and are accessible for contact. Moreover, if an individual consciousness keeps on existing, then it must keep on evolving and learning, which, being the fundamental processes of the living, are certainly even more essential to an intelligent individual being. If, then, the individual consciousness of da Vinci has relentlessly kept on evolving, and given that the semantic dimension is accessible from all limited time frames, a sensitive could theoretically discuss something either with da Vinci as he was in Renaissance Italy or with the even more sophisticated consciousness he has become.

Indeed, to say that individual consciousness is immortal doesn't mean it is fixed and forever identical to itself. Just as we grow in knowledge on Earth, we must grow in knowledge within a spiritual dimension. To live means to acquire knowledge and, it is hoped, to turn that knowledge into wisdom. What besides understanding and discovering infinite new possibilities would make existence worth living? All living beings acquire experience and therefore knowledge. Minds cannot dwell in a fixed dimension, but only in a dimension in which consciousness opens a path of knowledge and wisdom.

Let's therefore imagine this semantic dimension more deeply. Imagine the consciousness of da Vinci, who, in the fifteenth century, was already a paragon of the kind of left brain–right brain harmonization that instantiates the path of spiritual development laid before humans of the twenty-first century. We can picture cosmic and individual consciousnesses spread in a dimension that's reminiscent of space, having access to any time of Earth: past, present, and future.

In this way, the consciousness of da Vinci, dwelling in the semantic dimension, can have access to any person on Earth living in any time. Similarly, we humans have our own permanent branching into the semantic dimension, either unconsciously or consciously, through our Self. Thus da Vinci's mind can be contacted from any point of our planetary time and space.

Of course, our own consciousness—our Self—is of the same spiritual essence as any other human Self. Our Self has thus, in principle, the capacity to connect to any moment of Earth time, from the most ancient past to the far future. This is a possibility despite the fact that a part of our being (mainly, our ego) is intertwined more tightly with biological and physical matter (brain, body, environment, objects) in a given space-time. This possible cross-time connection means our consciousness will be inclined to connect with consciousnesses with which it has shared values, interests, and spiritual or artistic sensibility. Our Self, mainly living in the semantic dimension, will tune in to, and connect with, many resourceful souls and cosmic guides, looking to deepen its knowledge and improve its talents. Our Self, able to access so many sources of inspiration and wisdom, would thereby have in this semantic dimension many connections and many friends who may remain totally unknown to our conscious mind.

Some of these connections, however, may surface to our conscious self inadvertently, through dreams or a vivid vision or psi phenomenon. While in an altered or heightened state, we may be able to record consciously some of these connections, exchanges of information, or contacts with unknown friends. These anomalous phenomena are not rare in lucid dreams (dreams in which we become conscious and can intentionally modify the dream's development) or in visionary, mythical, or meditative states or peak experiences. There are a number of cases in the literature that deal with dreams and psi, showing that a person can have a conversation with a guide or a deceased person who gives some advice or clear information.

DIRECT CONTACT WITH PAST GENIUSES
Annulling Time

The semantic fields of artistic and cultural objects are particularly strong, because they are complex and multilayered systems, and furthermore, they have been highly charged by their creators and by subsequent art lovers. Paintings, sculptures, and books of great masters are gigantic collective semantic constellations that remain dynamic and keep on evolving through collective input. They are open, and they act as a gate that leads into the semantic dimension. In this way, even a book, a film, or music can become the medium of a conscious connection with the semantic dimension, both creating the connection and rendering us aware of it.

Paracelsus Extends a Healing Hand through Time

Several times I have experienced a spontaneous connection to the author of a book, but on this specific occurrence, I felt a deep connection to Paracelsus while I read about him in a book by Jung.[3] Paracelsus was a renowned Swiss physician and alchemist who, at the beginning of the sixteenth century, traveled and practiced medicine everywhere in Europe, treating the poor with dedication equal to how he treated those who were royal or imperial. The *magus monstruosus,* as he was called by his enemies (who were as numerous as his followers), transformed the field of medicine, which was still stuck in the decrepit precepts of Galen and Avicenna. He was also the herald of a new current of liberty and of spiritual renewal attached to the Rosicrucian movement.[4]

Paracelsus held that quaternary structures were particularly sacred. Already, in the Pythagorean tradition, some geometrical structures were held sacred—for example, a circle that passed the four vertices of a square. The inner circle was said to be the "squaring of the circle"—that is, the circumference of the circle was equal to the perimeter of a square that had the same center.

A square within or outside a circle is the fundamental structure of the mandalas used by Tibetans to enhance concentration and meditation. Each mandala is drawn around a central Buddha or divinity and shows the symbolic attributes of this cosmic being. There can be larger circles or arcs of buddhas, divinities, and gurus surrounding the central being.

We also must consider the magnificent geometrical quaternary structures created in stone: the crossing of four (or eight) arcs at the keystone to support the global architecture of sacred buildings in the Gothic and Roman styles as well as in Muslim architecture. See, for example, the splendid ogival crossings in Notre-Dame-de-Bourg.[5] In terms of mandalas made in stone, there are also magnificent geodesic domes such as the one in Ispahan in Iran. Also, there is the extraordinary complexity of mandalas in the Muslim and Catholic religions (e.g., cathedrals' rose windows), many of which are based on the number 4, meaning that they are constructed on multiples of the number 4. An exquisite example is the south rose window of Notre-Dame de Paris, with its twelve grand petals and its twenty-four small, ogival arcs touching the outer circle, the core of which is the fundamental four-petaled rose designed within a small circle.[6] According to the tradition, this knowledge about sacred numbers and sacred geometry, expressed so superbly by the cathedral builders, was handed down from Pythagoras, who developed the basic principles of sacred geometry in ancient Greece, and further back, from Hiram, the architect of Solomon's Temple in Jerusalem. In Chartres, therefore, there are the famous sculptures representing Pythagoras and Aristotle. Still further back, this knowledge is said to have been revealed by the Egyptian god Thoth (the Greek god Hermes and the Roman god Mercury), whose books, if you remember, may have been found by the Templars in the ruins of Solomon's Temple. Also, sacred geometry and knowledge about sacred numbers is the core of the Judaic Kabbalah and of diverse tantric traditions in India, China, and Tibet.

I was reading Jung's account about Paracelsus and how the physician thought quaternaries were highly sacred. Suddenly, I felt my mind was connected to that of Paracelsus. For two or three days, I had been very sick. The illness had been getting worse for a few months, and it culminated that day in an acute crisis. It was Sunday, so I was unable to find a physician. To try to take my mind off of my distressing situation and to enter a higher state of consciousness (which I thought was the best path toward self-healing), I searched for a thought-provoking book in my library. I chose one of Jung's works on alchemy, knowing there was a wealth of inspiring symbolic drawings in it. I opened it at random to a section describing Paracelsus's work and how he used quaternaries in his medical practice.[7] Yet there was no mention in what I read about specific quaternaries—that of plants or magical mandalas related to both planets and angels.

Suddenly and unexpectedly, I experienced a deep connection to Paracelsus's consciousness and felt it was strong enough to allow for an exchange. I spontaneously had the idea to plead for his help regarding my illness, and I asked him for a cure, which he gave me with explicit details. He spelled out the importance of using four different herbs (a quaternary), three of which were not only rare, but also extremely unusual in the context of herbal therapy. I had no idea, for example, that ivy and hops from which beer is made could be used as medicines, and I doubted that I could even find them in a chemist's shop specializing in herbal drugs. Paracelsus then went on to explain their dosages and the technique of preparation, which included something as exotic as leaving the concoction under the light of the moon for a few hours.

After thanking him, I decided to try to find these rare plants right away. Because it was a Sunday, pharmacies, apart from rare ones, were closed, and, to top it all, I was in the countryside. I intuitively decided to take a road I did not know well. After ten miles or so, not only did I find a pharmacy that was open, but, to my great surprise, it specialized in herbal therapy. As I handed her the list of plants, I told the pharmacist that a physician of alternative therapy had given me the list over the phone. Astonishingly, she had all four herbs, but she was so surprised by the list that she told me she wanted to check them in her handbook. I answered that I myself would be very interested in knowing more about these herbs. So we both read the entries. I couldn't believe it. My illness was linked to the matrix: two of the herbs were natural hormones, the third was specifically for gynecological illnesses, and the fourth was a general tonic.

The moon was quite large that night, and I left the opened, nonmetallic container of the mixture outside on a table, feeling a bit nonsensical (yes, even me!), but I was determined to follow the instructions to the letter. Late in the night, I started drinking the potion. After twenty-four hours, the symptoms started to decrease, and I felt much better in a matter of days.

A Conversation with Wolfgang Pauli

Another time, I had a totally unexpected connection to the physicist and Nobel laureate Wolfgang Pauli while reading an article about his work with Jung on synchronicities.[8] For about an hour, we had a lengthy dialogue full of detailed information, including background on quantum physics.

When I realized Pauli was, from the start, addressing me with a direct "you" and referring matter-of-factly to some ideas I had developed, as if he knew me and my work inside out, I thought to ask his advice. At the time, I was at a crucial stage in the development of my theory and was facing a particularly intricate problem. Not only did he give me highly pertinent advice, but he also went as far as predicting that I would at some later time work out a whole new level of this theory. He then prodded me to adopt a strategic perspective in view of what I would later develop.

My specific question had to do with how to draw the difference (theoretically) between the semantic fields of humans (their consciousness) and the semantic fields in natural systems. I asked, "Should I qualify the first ones as active and the second ones as passive?"

"You saw the sea, didn't you?" came the cryptic and slightly amused voice of Pauli.

On hearing this, after an instant of absolute bewilderment, wondering what he was talking about, my mind suddenly jumped back to a spiritual experience I had so long ago that it seemed to belong to another cycle of my life.

During my crossing of the Sahara Desert, in the far south of Morocco, a truck driver driving alone with his young son gave me a lift. Crossing that stretch of desert happened to be an unforgettable experience. The driver, who had gotten off the desert piste early on, drove all night with no road. He guided himself with the stars and through an amazing, hyperlucid state that the three of us shared for twelve hours in perfect silence, as if we were one single mind. The driver and his son had taken me into a magnificent telhar field with a direct connection to his Self, which allowed him to drive intuitively, guided by the knowledge of his Self.

At dawn, we reached a completely deserted beach, where the desert met the Atlantic Ocean at the southern end of Morocco. While the driver and his son used desert scrub to prepare a fire to cook some camel meat for breakfast, I climbed down the cliff toward an immaculate sand beach—just one place along a thousand-mile stretch of deserted land bordering the coast. It was immaculate, devoid of any human trace. I took my clothes off and walked toward the sea delicately, conscious I was the first human to leave an imprint on the sand. The waves were a murmur, the seawater so flat it glistened in the sun like a lake, but the instant my feet touched the water, I was entirely splashed with seawater, all the way to my face! Bewildered, I retreated a bit: I was looking at a perfectly flat sea. Still perplexed as to what had happened, I walked again toward the sea. And again I was splashed all over! I then understood the sea was playing with me. When I entered the water and started swimming, it was as if I were playing with a dolphin.

In this perfectly wild state of nature, the ocean played with me with convincing humor and intelligence. I experienced the living consciousness of the ocean, eternally young, joyful, and free.

After recalling this, I realized that I had to make more room in my theory for an actively sentient and autonomous consciousness in complex natural systems. There was a concept I could use. After a moment of pondering, I said to Pauli: "Self-organizing natural systems, then?"

To which he replied, with more than a touch of humor: "If that's the foremost concept, why not?"

Soon after this conversation, I came up with the term *eco-fields,* which resolved the issue. But let's consider the intuitive process that Pauli triggered in me. Though the questions I asked Pauli were mostly intellectual, he prodded me to bridge the gap in my life between a scientific cycle and a previous cycle, one in which I had mostly explored reality through meditation and expanded consciousness. At that earlier time, I had recurrently communicated with the consciousnesses of not only the wild sea, but also trees, rivers, and sacred mountains. Mine was a type of experience widely acknowledged in many civilizations—in the East and in shamanism all over the world. In the West it is recognized not only in Hermetism and esoterica, but also by many sensitive individuals—indeed, so much so that it's only in the narrow mindset of the materialistic science of the past two centuries that natural systems have been deemed inert and without consciousness. Not only do meditators and shamans see the energy field around sacred trees and rocks, but in addition, they can communicate with these beings: they definitely know they are endowed with consciousness.

EMPIRICAL PROOFS

The dialogue with Paracelsus, which had given me detailed information about a cure for my illness, lead to several empirical proofs.

First, three out of four plants were indeed linked to a gynecological illness. Second, the cure worked beyond my wildest expectations. Third, save one of them, I had never heard about these plants being used as medicines. Last, synchronicities happened to be linked to communication: driving intuitively, I stumbled on a pharmacist who carried those uncommon plants and who prodded me to check them in a handbook, thus providing a sound proof.

The dialogue with Pauli similarly carried empirical proofs. First, I later checked on the time information he gave me about quantum physics developments (he had stressed I was wrong on that point), and it turned out that the date he gave me was correct. Second, for days I had been pondering the problem with my theory, unable to find a better solution than the active-passive description; and yet I didn't feel satisfied with it. Third, Pauli took my mind back to an experience I would never have imagined was linked to the subject at hand yet that perfectly answered my question. In doing so, he helped me to merge intellect and spiritual experience. Fourth, his biting humor was refreshing and was not the kind of self-gratifying nonsense that a deluded person would create out of pure imagination.

CAN WE ACCESS THE SEMANTIC DIMENSION?

As we can see from the above examples, it's possible to move beyond symbolic dreams that convey a message from our Self into a full-fledged conversation with inspiring minds of the past (not just a reception of vague ideas from them). Drawing on these two occurrences (my discussions with Paracelsus and Pauli), let's sort out what they suggest about the capacities of human consciousness.

Access to the semantic dimension occurs in a heightened state of consciousness in which the individual is in the consciousness of his or her Self. It presupposes much more than a telepathic ability. Outside of extraordinary occurrences, it is based on a stable connection with our own Self and the capacity to fuse with it—at first during transcendental states (meditation, creativity, and so forth) and then on a regular basis.

All paths of inner knowledge in all cultures lead to this identification and eventually to the fusion with our Self (soul, spirit, solar angel, etc.). When, on this path, we begin connecting to our Self, and we also start accessing the semantic dimension of consciousness. When harmony and fusion with our Self is reached, many possibilities open to us, including the cocreation of telhar fields and accessing what Hindus call the Akashic Records (or Akasha)—which contain the meaningful information impregnating the entire semantic dimension. Any further path of knowledge, based on our own responsible quest, can be explored. This is why the best guidance for our spiritual quest, from the start, is to develop our own access gate to our Self, which will lead us without fail to accessing the semantic dimension.

13

TOWARD A PLANETARY CONSCIOUSNESS

Our planet is now embarked on a major collective transformation in terms of consciousness, and this is already triggering sea changes. Yet to understand the evolution of this transformation, we must watch it happening at the level of individuals, at least during this entire period of transition, which may last three or four generations—but in the time frame of the species, it constitutes an abrupt change. The consciousness mutation started in 1967 and 1968, and it is my intuition that it will have swept the world by the late 2020s. With an exponential pace, the change is already reaching most sectors and levels of societies all over Earth. In the diverse cultures of the planet, numerous individuals have gone through an awakening of their consciousness, whatever their social, scientific, political, religious, or philosophical backgrounds. The best course of action, since we will all be involved sooner or later in this sea change, is to decipher and understand the kind of phenomena we are bound to be confronted with in our daily lives. Let's review, then, what information the new sciences of consciousness have already gathered.

EMERGENT MIND POTENTIALS

The development of greater mind potentials appears at first glance to be linked to the development of our right brain (right hemisphere), whose main qualities are global thinking and artistic sense. To my understanding, however, the mental potentials emerging at the present are more specifically triggered by building a smooth cooperating network between our two brain hemispheres. The left brain (mathematical, logical, analytical) has been oversized during the last four centuries of near-exclusive exploration of matter through an analytical and materialistic science. The deeper interconnection and cooperation between left and right hemispheres can happen only after the right brain has been stimulated to the point of gaining a new preeminence in our life. (Contrary to the current supposition, age is not a hindrance to mind growth—not even in terms of neuronal connectivity: I know people in their forties or fifties who have gone through major leaps in mental capacities or in psi.) Thus, the individuals who tend to be too rigid and conservative (instead of open-minded and creative), too analytical and judgmental (at the expense of intuition and empathy), or who stick to the rules and dogma (instead of searching for their inner realization as free beings) will have more difficulties opening up to a new consciousness. They will tend to resist undergoing the necessary changes and will fear rocking through the uncertainties and instabilities that always accompany inner transformation.

We may infer that the psychological factors that have been shown to enhance psi phenomena in laboratory experimentations are also conducive to the mental awakening of individuals, if only because psi is primarily an array of mental processes.

Among the factors that have been shown to enhance psi in laboratory experiments are: self-confidence, openness of mind, creativity, sensitivity to others (extroversion), artistic sense (artists show greater psi results in experiments), practice of self-development techniques, and an expectation of success (positive autosuggestion).[1]

In addition, Myers-Briggs Type Indicator (MBTI) tests developed according to Carl Jung's psychological types and routinely performed on subjects prior to experiments show that psi results are stronger for people who are bent toward feeling (as opposed to perceiving) and toward sensing (as opposed to judging).[2]

Regarding spiritual evolution and transformation, I would add to these enhancing factors: a fecund inner life, intuition, a capacity to enter heightened consciousness (or trance), a richness of feeling (high emotional quotient, or EQ),[3] empathy, high values, a visionary mind, and the capacity to sense subtle systemic interactions.[4]

How, then, can we set this transformation in motion in our life?

There are very easy techniques capable of triggering the emergence of our latent potentials. We all possess these potentials, undeveloped and dormant in our deep unconscious—yet they do exist, waiting only for a trigger to emerge. This fact has been shown clearly in many experiments in parapsychology that were done with individuals who were neither psi subjects nor professionals and reflected the normal population—such as the series done in the Psychophysical Research Laboratories (PRL) at Princeton University. Each experiment generally lasted a few months and comprised between fifty and one hundred subjects. Meta-analysis (statistics done on a group of similar experiments) was positive and showed an evidence of psi, and this result means that psi capacities are latent in the normal population.[5] In this period of great change, with stupendous creative genius and much information being exchanged, it's often enough simply to put ourselves to the task to see these potentials emerge. Indeed, it has been my experience all along that we are now at a most favorable time for mental and spiritual growth. Whatever capacity we try to develop, we will easily reach encouraging results with minimum effort, and even with a playful mindset. This was not at all the case in the seventies or the eighties. The reason for the easier and faster development of our spiritual potentials is that we have already initiated the transformation of the mind that is occurring in humanity.

REGRESS OR MOVE FORWARD?

The field of cultural anthropology shows that practically all traditional cultures had some form of trance, whether shamanic trance or possession trance.[6] The difference between the two is that shamans remain conscious of their own Self throughout the trance, and they control their shamanic journey in the dimension of the spirit, while initiates of possession trance (such as the Brazilian Umbanda or Haitian Voodoo) typically welcome the *orishas* (spirits) to take possession of their minds and bodies and to talk through them. Because of this, they generally have no recollection of what happens during their trance. There exist some cultures, though—such as those of the Zulu and Swazi of southeast Africa—in which the two forms of trance are mixed. According to this classification, shamanism is quite extended over the entire planet: in the cultures of Native Siberians, North American Indians, Australian Aborigines, and cultures in Southeast Asia, Canada, Tibet, and of course all over Africa. Ancient religions and trance cultures agree that, over time, initiates develop stupendous psychic capacities: the gift of healing, the capacity to see and travel through the dimension of the spirit, and the main psi capacities (precognition, clairvoyance, clairaudience, and telepathy). These psi gifts, far from being contained and repressed, as they have been in Judeo-Christian religions, were held in high esteem in ancient cultures. Thus they were naturally nurtured and supported by the society and could blossom in individuals without being blocked.

However widespread and respected psi capacities were in traditional cultures, though, it seems quite certain that what we are now witnessing has nothing to do with a resurgence of magical thinking and superstition.

Let me explain why I think this by using an argument based on the understanding of civilizations. Notwithstanding their deep knowledge of nature and of the interaction of all living beings, from which stemmed their respect for life, many traditional cultures were plagued by obscure and hair-splitting rules for dealing with the spirit world. A number of superstitions were handed down from one generation to the next, rendering life and social relations absurdly complicated. A few centuries of hard science has triggered a reorganization of the neural networks of our brain. Even if the left, logical, hemisphere has been hyperstimulated in the process, it has nevertheless brought about a change in our entire brain. This ever-growing complexity of the neural networks of our brains—fortunately—cannot be undone. In fact, greater activation of our right hemisphere, and the emergence of new talents in global thinking, intuition, psi, and so forth, will trigger two decisive leaps in the complexity of our neural systems, which will propel these very talents to new heights. The first leap will see a rapid development of the right hemisphere, and the second will consist of an astounding level of connectivity with the left hemisphere (and the whole neuronal system)—so much so, in fact, that we cannot predict the novel possibilities it will entail.

In the process, science has helped us free our minds and take the helm of our own lives. Our actual civilization's difficulties lie not in the return of superstition, but rather in the necessity to free ourselves, once again, from yet another set of rigid rules defining reality: rules of the paradigm of materialistic science. Times are changing. Our task now is to maneuver around an oversized and shortsighted logical brain in order to access and activate a pool of totally different mind capacities: the whole domain of intuition and psi capacities, symbolic and global thinking, collective intelligence, and the understanding of ecological interactions between natural systems.

A second line of thought, which shows that we are moving forward, is that this transformation is worldwide. The 1968 revolution in France was the crest of a wave that moved all around Earth, and many countries entered the movement of revolt, whatever their political system at the time: countries in Europe and Asia, the United States, and countries in South America (where the movement was felt in several nations, including Brazil). The fact that the revolt was a grassroots movement—that it sprang from the collective unconscious as a surge for change and for the recognition of new values—is evident because it took so many different forms in different countries and contexts.

The 1968 revolution was the first emergence of a planetary consciousness in the sense that all sensitive people felt the need for change—and even if their messages and demands were different from one country to another, the same values were shared: a need for a more spiritual and creative perspective, and a craving for freedom and the free expression of their collective personality. Since then, several such waves of change have swept the planet. It seems quite clear that the two old systems—communism and capitalism—are both headed for sweeping changes, because both have been rooted in a materialistic ideology and a science driven by the will to control. Neither humanity nor our planet can afford such a blind outlook anymore. If we want to save our world from ecological disaster, each person must develop a new sensitivity to our natural environment. We must become the new shamans in renewing our deep connection to the living—plants and animals. We will have to turn into *les voyants* (the seers) that the French poet Arthur Rimbaud envisioned: humans gifted with a novel sensitivity to the subtle energy of consciousness pervading nature.

QUANTUM PHYSICS, PSI, AND SPACE-TIME SINGULARITIES

Many scientists still refuse to acknowledge laboratory research on psi capacities, because it is at odds with classical physics. Yet the phenomena involved in psi, such as retrocausality and nonlocal correlations, are bedrock processes for quantum scientists.

In terms of scientific proof, precognition is the least questionable phenomenon. In a typical psi experiment, the lab first creates a pool of images (or target pool). In telepathy experiments, an image is chosen randomly out of the pool by a computer (through a sophisticated random number generator) and is automatically displayed on the sender's screen. The sender then proceeds to mentally send this image (called the target) to the receiver (or subject). The receiver (after a relaxation period) then describes aloud any and every image that passes through his or her mind, and all he or she says is recorded; at the end, four randomly selected images (one of which is the target) are displayed on the receiver's screen, and he or she has to choose the target. At the end of an experiment, the statistics of hits and misses from all subjects are calculated.

In PRL, sometimes the descriptions were so precise that a subject, for example, would describe a tiger or cheetah running, while the target showed exactly that. The protocol is called double-blind because both the subject (receiver) and the experimenter don't know the target. Nevertheless, the skeptics will try to argue that subtle cues could have been given to the subject; that is, they will invoke fraud and leaks in the lab to explain the positive results. In contrast, precognition experiments (perceiving a future target) do not allow the skeptics to invoke information leaks to the subject (whatever the manner), because the target is randomly selected only *after* the subject has described what he thought was the target. So that during the experimentation per se, nobody and not even a computer possesses the information (this is called triple-blind). This is why researchers consider precognition as the least questionable psi capacity: whenever an experiment obtains positive results, it can't be easily explained away.

In precognition, it seems the mind can access a future time in great detail, as if the mind either annuls space or travels along a reverse time axis, from the future toward the present. This amounts to a kind of tinkering with time. As for clairvoyance (acquiring information about distant events without the medium of the physical senses or technology), it shows a clear-cut tinkering with space.

While the space-time dimension of the physics of Newton (and the electromagnetic, or EM, spectrum) clearly fails to support psi, quantum physics, on the contrary, has laid the ground for its theoretical possibility, at least in terms of space and time singularities. Processes such as particles moving from the future to the past, or a particle being informed about the state of another one at a distance through "nonlocal correlations" (also called entanglement) are central in quantum physics. These processes can account for precognition (information from the future) and telepathy (information between two systems).

Because a particle has a statistical probability to be anywhere in the universe, quantum physics could account for space anomalies (and psi researchers have thus proposed several theories of psi based on quantum physics). Yet, the great pitfall is meaning. Quantum events are purely indeterministic, and despite the fact that quantum physics posits nonlocal processes, in no way can it explain how such a nonlocal process could be directed according to the intention or the will of a person—that is, it would be *responding* to a deep and meaningful psychological process. (At the very moment when I finished typing *responding,* following the text I had written a month and a half ago, a strange psi phenomenon occurred, which we will analyze further on.)

Quantum events follow statistical rules; they are perfectly indeterministic. In such a framework, meaning—what makes sense for an individual (mind-body-psyche)—cannot be accounted for, because meaning is the absolute antithesis to randomness and indetermination.

If, as quantum physics shows, the influence of consciousness on the physical world can be neither ignored nor evaluated within the quantum physics framework, then in order for a theory of the universe to be complete, it must include a theory of consciousness. Therefore, we are in need of a global theory that would account not only for the organization of matter at a deep level, but also for consciousness and its most important feat: the constant creation of new meaning—creativity, invention, psi capacities, understanding and learning, and the constant transformation of our intellectual and artistic life. Bearing this in mind, I elaborated Semantic Field Theory (SFT) and hoped to achieve a theory that would fill the gap.

POSTULATING A DEEP LAYER OF MIND-MATTER INTERCONNECTION

To say that quantum physics cannot account for meaning while meaning is deeply connected to psi does not take us backward into negating quantum physics. Due to the fact that only quantum physics can support the kind of space-time anomalies shown by psi events, the way backward is blocked. The only possibility is to move forward, farther into layers where consciousness and energy and matter must be deeply interconnected to the point of merging or fusing. Indeed, if meaning cannot be explained at the quantum physics level (of particles), then we must assume a deeper layer of reality in which mind and matter are so fundamentally intermingled and fused as to become a single substance: consciousness-energy. This deep level of reality, the dimension of consciousness-as-energy, is the semantic dimension, and syg-energy (semantic energy) is the energy of this dimension, having the characteristics of both consciousness and very subtle energy.

The semantic dimension presents a totally new set of properties pertaining both to consciousness and energy. It's at least a 5-D manifold, with one (or more) dimension of consciousness, one dimension of time, and three dimensions of space (normal 3-D). The semantic dimension is thus as much of a metadimension to space-time as 3-D is to 2-D.

Thus syg-energy is organized by consciousness itself; it is steered by meaning and intention or, more precisely, by the act of creating meaning. This consciousness-energy has nothing whatsoever to do with energy waves carrying information. Here, the syg-energy itself *is* the embodied meaning.

HIDDEN VARIABLES?

At this point, a question arises: does adding a dimension of deep reality mean endorsing some sort of hidden variables? The assumption of Albert Einstein, in proposing hidden variables, was that some hidden causal factors are at work in what appear as random events at the quantum level, bending them toward specific effects, and that these factors, presently impossible to assess, could nevertheless be unraveled one day.

Hidden variables were supposed to be sets of causes leading to deterministic effects. The idea of Einstein, in proposing hidden variables, was to save the concept of a deterministic universe: "God doesn't play dice," he said against the new and formidable concept of pure indetermination proposed by Werner Heisenberg, Niels Bohr, and the "orthodox," or Copenhagen, school of quantum physics. Physicist David Bohm, in his *implicate order* theory, is in accordance with the concept of hidden variables.[7] This implicate order posits a deeper layer, annulling space. Bohm, however, saw physical reality (the *explicate order*) as totally determined by the implicate order: no free interactions or two-way influences, but rather a deep level of causes from which the physical reality itself unfolds in a deterministic way.

Let's consider the question anew: does, then, a dimension of deep reality endorse hidden variables? The answer is no. The deep reality layer, as we will see, is neither deterministic nor indeterministic. Its reality lies in a novel framework nearer to synchronistic acausal events proposed by Jung and Pauli than to either of the two schools of quantum physics (the orthodox, pure indetermination and the hidden variables deterministic framework).

AN OUTSTANDING PK EVENT IN
SYNCHRONICITY WITH THOUGHTS

Let's turn to the highly meaningful psychokinetic (PK) event that occurred while I was typing a version of this chapter. Psychokinesis is the capacity to influence matter, either physical or biological, and thus includes a wide range of phenomena from bending spoons to psychic healing.

At the 2004 Psi Meeting in Curitiba, Brazil, I gave a paper on synchronicity. I had reread this paper just before writing and editing this very chapter you are reading now. I believe that having freshly reviewed the ideas from that earlier article incited a PK phenomenon during the writing of this chapter that happened in synchronicity with my thoughts. Before I tell you about that phenomenon, let me first present the important points from my 2004 paper on synchronicity:

> . . . I thus propose to consider that a meaningful coincidence is a synchronicity IF:
>
> (1) There is a low probability that the event would occur by chance alone;
>
> (2) There are numerous significant links between the interfering event and the subject's activated Semantic Constellation (SeCo); and
>
> (3) The meaning of the external event clearly influences the person, to the point of drastically modifying the SeCo.
>
> I believe synchronicity is deeply connected to the unconscious; not expressly to archetypes but rather to the Self (the subject of both the unconscious and the conscious) willing to influence the ego in a specific way.
>
> Synchronicity, thus,
>
> (1) expresses the will of the Self to influence the ego toward a certain mindset, decision, or action. And
>
> (2) shows the capacity of the Self (when the person is engaged in a process of spiritual evolution, or individuation) to succeed in organizing physical reality and events according to its own semantic energy (higher spiritual values, goals, and orientations).[8]

With those statements in mind, what follows below is the sentence I was writing for this current chapter, when, after typing the word *responding,* the psi phenomenon occurred:

Because a particle has a statistical probability to be anywhere in the universe, quantum physics could account for space anomalies (and psi researchers have thus proposed several theories of psi based on quantum physics). Yet, the great pitfall is meaning. Quantum events are purely indeterministic, and despite the fact that quantum physics posits nonlocal processes, in no way can it explain how such a nonlocal process could be directed according to the intention or the will of a person—that is, it would be *responding* . . . [I hear a chime.]

On the spot, I started typing a description of this event. Here is an excerpt of what I typed:

Time: 1.10 am. Psi phenomenon on the spot with chime suddenly ringing out strongly. I look up: the chime's weight—a vertical moon crescent in wood of 4.5 inches—turns on itself at least 10 times, extremely rapidly, like a gyroscope. (This motion cannot possibly be triggered by a gust of wind or an animal. . . . It can only be done by intentionally turning the weight on itself. Anyway, all windows are closed here and downstairs, it's cold, it's been raining, and the door is locked. Furthermore, all curtains are closed, as every night.)

Then the tensed thread brings it back to normal by making it turn the other way around, as quickly.

The moon weight, suspended by a nylon thread, is one yard from the wooden floor, 1.5 yard from the ceiling, 8 inches from the window and wood frame, and curtain covering the window. I'm sitting cross-legged at my table, about 3.5 yards away from the chime. Nothing else moved in the room. Physical reaction: as if my whole body was frying and was electrified, especially at the level of the belly and chest, the whole front of my torso.

In any case, the spinning movement (rotation on itself), moreover about ten times one way, and very quickly, is impossible as a natural movement.

As I was able to verify the next day, even with the window open and the wind coming in, the weight tends to move very slowly, mostly in a lateral motion (and more rarely in a spinning way), because the moon crescent, in the shape of the letter *C*, gives only little surface against the wind.

Analysis: this phenomenon is quite remarkable in the sense that I was emphasizing both the meaning and the intentional aspects of syg-energy as the most important facets of consciousness (as far as theory is concerned), since neither orthodox quantum physics nor the hidden variables school can explain such creation of meaning from their own frameworks. Further, the phenomenon produced cannot in any way be produced by random natural causes. Only a human hand can turn a thread on itself many times, building such tension in it that, on releasing it, it unrolls itself at great speed.

Not only is the event paranormal, it's also synchronistic. It corresponds perfectly to the first definition I gave in my paper on synchronicity: *"Synchronicity . . . (1) expresses the will of the Self to influence the ego toward a certain mindset, decision, or action."*

The PK event also expresses the second part of the definition I gave in the same paper: *"Synchronicity . . . (2) shows the capacity of the Self . . . to succeed in organizing physical reality and events according to its own semantic energy. . . ."*

My semantic energy was strong (since I was in a creative process, not only typing, but also enlarging my text), and through this psi event reality was *reorganized* in such a way that it adapted and conformed itself to the meaning being (re)created. That is, my Self, through the PK event, organized physical reality and events according to its own semantic energy.

We can also note two meaningful coincidences: I had just typed: *"[psi] would be responding. . . ."* Indeed, it responded! And then I was about to type the end of the sentence: *"[psi] would be responding . . . to a deep and meaningful psychological process."* I was involved in a strong creative and meaningful process while I was pondering these ideas about synchronicity, and psi responded to it!

The second coincidence is that of words and action between the chime's "spin" and the "spin" in quantum physics, which is one of the parameters used to describe particles and the one used to test nonlocal correlations between distant particles. (The experiments of Alain Aspect and other physicists have proved the reality of these nonlocal correlations.)

This psi event certainly comprised all three requirements I cited in my paper for defining an event as synchronicity versus mere coincidence. I could even say that it was a strong voice irrupting from deep reality and making its case known.

This "psi spin" points to another possibility: in nonlocal correlation experiments, when the experimenter physically changes the spin of particle A, the spin of particle B is instantly modified. In the chime PK, obviously my mind (rather my Self) produced the PK effect. The psychokinetic action on the chime thus shows that my semantic state (my thoughts) can have an effect on the state of a distant system (and even the spin of a particle). In other words, this PK event implies that consciousness and semantic energy have a powerful effect on material systems—a bedrock concept of SFT, because the embedding of consciousness-energy-matter allows for continuous, if subtle, two-way influences between mind and matter.[9] Additionnally, this PK event gives weight to another postulate of SFT—that the greater the semantic intensity and proximity (two factors linked respectively to creativity and meaning correlation), the greater the strength of the syg-energy (and its influence on linked systems).

For me, what could be both more meaningful and more intense than working in a creative way on my theory? The fact is, the effect was strong: PK on objects is one of the rarest psi phenomena and the hardest to produce.

SYSTEMS, CHAOS, AND THE CHANGE PROCESS

Several great scholars have underlined that universal themes can be found in the diverse cultures, religions, myths, and cosmologies of

Earth. Mircea Eliade has highlighted that a basic pattern of initiation existed in many cultures.[10] Similarly, Jung brought to light the foundational symbols of the collective unconscious—archetypes—showing that they were present across different systems of knowledge.

The cultures on Earth are as many terrains of experience for the human mind: they are knowledge systems about reality and consciousness. More important, each group of people has developed particular capacities in terms of consciousness. The West, up to now, focused on the understanding of matter, while the East explored consciousness relentlessly. Together, all Earth cultures form the giant tapestry of the collective mind, expressing some of its boundless possibilities. We are now living in a most extraordinary time in the sense that we have access to the knowledge systems of most traditional cultures, at a time when they are still not yet drastically modified by their interaction with world-dominant cultures. Despite the fact that some people and cultures—such as Native American, Australian Aborigine, and many African cultures—have been decimated by colonization from Western powers, their message has nevertheless been carried on and sustained. Though we can block neither the building of an interactive world nor the trend toward globalization, the very way we understand these processes and attend to them can make a crucial difference.

The interaction between systems that have their own specificity leads to an increase of complexity, as complexity theory has shown.[11] In highly complex systems, however, (such as human groups or cultures), great connectivity triggers self-organization, the ability for a system to reach a novel global order from its own spontaneous momentum, as chaos theory has shown.[12] Self-organization is thus at the antipodes of disorder and entropy. The progressive rise in interconnection among people through information and communication technologies (and especially the Internet) will lead to a self-organized global system that is several orders of freedom higher than the disconnected cultures and of much greater complexity. Moreover, the dynamics of creativity triggered by the interconnection and mutual influences will keep increasing (in strength and pace of change) within the novel global system. This wouldn't be the case if the change process was driven from the top and commanded, as in a hierarchical society or a planned economy. The creative dynamics of change have to be an emergence from the bottom—a grassroots spontaneous sprouting—in order for this change to be creative and lasting.

Yet some may ask why it is so important to give free rein to creativity. Why not tighten society in order to implement rational decisions to deal more efficiently with global problems? There are several shortcomings with such a perspective.

First, decisions—rational, it is hoped—are always based on analysis and understanding of past situations using a logic grounded in already-formalized modes of reasoning. In contrast, a spontaneous emergence of collective intelligence comes up with truly innovative solutions.

Second, the so-called rational decision process is one of the main forces that contributed to the building of a civilization heading toward its own destruction, so its potency in saving the same entity is doubtful at best.

Third, we must bear in mind that humanity is confronting a worldwide situation that has never existed in the past. The possibility of destroying our home planet has to be considered in the wider context of nearby worlds and intelligent life in the universe, which might be affected in many different ways from the collapse of an ecological and intelligent system—ways that may include space-time disruption in case we would destroy Earth through, among other scenarios, a nuclear Armageddon or an antimatter disaster. From this perspective, again, only a drastically innovative stand could allow us to extricate ourselves from the deadlock situation we are in.

Fourth, collective intelligence may come up with a solution through a wealth of emergences taking place quasi-simultaneously within many individuals—similar to an array of adaptive mutations in an endangered species that offer as many survival chances as are being tested ad hoc. Mental and cognitive emergences thrive on such survival necessity, and the most marked among these are collective consciousness and the harmonization of minds.

To insure the building of a dynamic and creative society able to come up with innovative solutions and technologies, exchanges and mutual influences in the context of freedom must be favored without being tampered with or monitored. In such a flow state, connectivity among people will rise, and at the same time, groups will organize themselves naturally according to their semantic interests. As we can already observe on the Internet, individuals connect through keywords and search actions according to their own interests, and thus groups of similar focus, values, and objectives start self-organizing. This is exactly the process at work with the innumerable communities of interest and international groups, whether scientific societies or other kinds of associations. The same is also true with the numerous NGOs at work in the world: each one is like a semantic node and a lighthouse for all people sensitive to the specific area of problems that it tackles. What we are seeing now is the rise of a multinodal society—the rhizomatic organization dear to Gilles Deleuze and Felix Guattari.[13]

In this multinodal society, the interrelations based on cooperation and harmonic resonance that we have seen at play in telhar fields and expressed through the sacred network can be an inspiration for launching our next step in evolution as a humanity coupled with its natural environment.

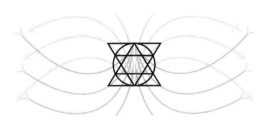

CONCLUSION

Within Paris, we have seen the magnificent mandalas and global structures designed in edifices and constructions as diverse as churches, palaces, plazas, fountains, and bridges. Geo-architecture is a masterpiece in space that establishes meaningful and symbolic connections at great distances. As we've seen, its designs are so complex and intricate that a single monument can be part of several geometric structures embedded within one another or superimposed upon one another.

At a minimal level, a single edifice presents a wealth of mandalas and symbols on its global architecture, facades, tympana, rose windows, and abundant internal decorations. At the city level, there exist global geometrical structures such as the golden rectangles, hexagons, Sri Yantras, and pentagons we have explored in depth. These global structures are themselves embedded in still larger ones that link towns and countries. Finally, at the planetary level, circle routes that turn around Earth interconnect sacred sites.

Yet we would have remained trapped in a 2-D map of a 3-D Great Work if we hadn't tackled the greater mysteries found in these arcs of light bouncing in and out of monuments, gracefully distributed by geniuses and angels overlooking the city from the tips of columns illuminating the metropolis's purple sky. Indeed, as we have seen, the sacred network doesn't dwell solely in stone artwork: it exists largely within the collective dimension of consciousness.

It is highly probable that the progressive building of the sacred network over centuries followed a visionary plan—and the fact that the network extends worldwide suggests that its aim has been global. Could the inspiring vision have been to achieve one day a network of interconnected minds encompassing the whole of humanity? Could the purpose of the sacred network be to prepare the planet for its next stage: harmonizing at the collective level?

Bringing to light such numerous marvels in the diverse cultures of Earth demands many dedicated individuals to tackle different parts of the giant tapestry. My own task in this book has been to highlight the interconnection between the sacred network, as embodied in cosmotelluric lines and geo-architecture, and the aspect of its collective consciousness—that is, telhar fields.

Telhar fields are like the blueprint of a novel type of human interaction. Because all of us can be the node and steer the group-mind whenever we are connected to our inner Self, telhar fields point to a multinodal society organized in cooperative networks and efficiently teaching us how to harmonize with others in spirit. The crucial point, however, is for this harmonization process to occur at the highest energy level of the group, thus triggering a collective uplifting of consciousness. From this perspective, telhar fields inspire the cocreation of a vibrant collective spirit, one that can best make use of the geo-architectural grid of links.

Decoding the sacred network has thus given us a unique perspective into a fifth dimension of geo-architecture: the consciousness or semantic dimension. The interconnection of sacred sites to form impressive worldwide mandalas prods spiritually awakened individuals into weaving no less fascinating mandalas with telhar fields.

Through the sacred network, the torch of consciousness is handed down from one sacred site to another, turning around Earth in undulations punctuated by fountains and arcs of light.

The network is already there, sculpted in stone and light, just waiting for us to become sensitive and to sail on it in the collective consciousness dimension.

SACRED LINES IN PARIS

Major Axes and Leys

In my previous description of the major axes and of some leys in chapters 9 and 10, I highlighted the most important features of the lines, the ones pregnant with symbolism and meaning and that best revealed the overall design of the builders. But the discovery I made of geo-architectural structures came after a long study to bring the leys and axes to light. This book wouldn't be complete without me giving the full and thorough description of all the significant landmarks that are located along the axes and leys, which I present to you in the text below. Please see plate 1 (Main axes and leys in Paris) for an overview of the location and convergence of these lines, as well as some of the major landmarks.

MAJOR AXES IN PARIS

Following is a detailed description of the five most prominent axes in Paris. Refer to plate 1, Main axes and leys in Paris.

All axes and leys have their beginning called point A and their endpoint called B, with the axes labeled by their most prominent feature and the leys labeled numerically (1–17). The points A and B on the périphérique (the highway around Paris) are given approximately.

West Decumanus (Axis 1): Etoile-to-Concorde-to-Louvre

Starts A: Porte Maillot; **Ends B:** near Porte Dorée (northern side); **Global:** 2 churches, 9 Metros, 6 plazas, 13 monuments (9 centers of main porches).

Description: Paris's prominent alignment, crossing through the Grande Arche at La Défense, the Arc de Triomphe of L'étoile, the Obelisk at Concorde Plaza, the Arc de Triomphe of Carrousel, the Louvre, and the Châtelet Plaza.

This axis follows the central line of **La Défense Esplanade** (monument 1, the line running through its center) and Metro Esplanade, then goes through the exact center of the **Grande Arche of La Défense** (the center of monument 2), follows the Pont de Neuilly (the center of monument 3) and Metro Pont de Neuilly, avenue Charles de Gaulle (and Metro Les Sablons), Plaza and Metro Porte Maillot, avenue de la Grande Armée (and Metro Argentine), Arc de Triomphe (center of monument 4) at Plaza de L'Étoile, avenue des Champs-Elysées (and Metro George V, Metro Franklin-Roosevelt), Plaza Rond-Point des Champs Elysées (meets ley 11 and ley 1), Plaza Clémenceau (and Metro Champs Elysées-Clémenceau), Plaza Concorde, the Obelisk (center of monument 5), and the central line of the Tuileries (center of monument 6). It then runs though Arc de Triomphe of Carrousel (center of monument 7), which is the starting point of the East Decumanus, or axis 2, then the Louvre Palace (center of monument 8), the inverted pyramid (southern side of monument 9), and the Louvre's pyramid (southern side of monument 10). It follows the southern wall of Cour Carrée, the southern wall of St-Germain-l'Auxerrois Church, and Plaza and Metro Pont-Neuf. It follows the Seine from Pont-Neuf to Pont d'Arcole, crosses Plaza du Châtelet and its fountain with sphinxes (the center of monument 11), follows the Cité Internationale des Arts, Hôtel de Sens (monument 12, a masterpiece of the Flamboyant Gothic style), Quinze-Vingts Hospital (southern side of monument 13), St-Antoine des Quinze-Vingts Church (southern wall), Marché St-Antoine, Plaza de Reuilly (northern side), Saint-Mandé Cemetery (aligned with southern wall), and ends above Porte Dorée. Extended to the west, it runs just below Vincennes Castle, near the circle drawn in the garden.

East Decumanus (Axis 2): Louvre's Pyramids-to-Bastille

Starts A: near Porte Maillot (south end); **Ends B:** near Porte de St-Mandé (southern side); **Global:** 3 churches, 3 Metros, 3 plazas, 13 monuments (8 exact centers or front porches).

Description: Starts at Arc de Triomphe of Carrousel (center of monument 1); runs through Plaza du Carrousel with its inverted pyramid (exact center of monument 3); follows the central line of the Louvre Museum (center of monument 2) and the grand pyramid (exact center of monument 4), the fountain (center of monument 5) at the center of Cour Carrée, and finally the Louvre's eastern facade and the porch adorned with *La Gloire* bas-relief (center of monument 6). This porch is aligned with the Cloister's Tower of St-Germain-l'Auxerrois. The axis then runs through St-Germain-l'Auxerrois Church (north of the choir) and St-Jacques Tower (along the southern facade of monument 7). It follows rue de Rivoli, Hôtel de Ville (northern wall of monument 8, Paris's townhall), Metro Hôtel de Ville, Plaza Baudoyer, Mairie du 4th arrondissement (northern wall of monument 9), Metro St-Paul, St-Paul–St-Louis Church, Plaza de la Bastille, Bastille's column (center of monument 10 with angel Hermes). There, it meets ley 10 and continues parallel to rue du Faubourg St-Antoine, Metro Ledru-Rollin (northern side), and Plaza de Picpus (northern side).

Extended to the west, the axis from Arc du Carrousel meets Petit Palais (center of the western front porch of monument 11), leys 1 and 6 at the geometrical center between Grand Palais and Petit Palais, Grand Palais (northeast of monument 12), and crosses Marceau-Bassano and Jardin d'Acclimatation and its Musée National des Arts (monument 13).

Obelisk Cardo (Axis 3): Obelisk-to-Madeleine

Starts A: Porte de Clignancourt; **Ends B:** near Porte de la Plaine; **Global:** 3 churches and 2 chapels, 4 Metros, 5 plazas, 5 monuments (4 main porches).

Description: The line begins at Metro and Porte de Clignancourt (center). It runs on to Metro Lamarck-Caulaincourt, rue Blanche's Chapel (meets ley 7), St-Louis-d'Antin, and Haussmann-Tronchet Crossing. It follows rue Tronchet, Sainte-Marie-Madeleine (called

La Madeleine; central axis in length from north facade to the choir to south facade), rue Royale, Metro Concorde, the median (north to south) of L'Etoile Plaza, running through the two fountains (centers of monuments 1 and 2) and the Obelisk (center of monument 3). It runs through Pont de la Concorde (center of monument 4), Assemblée Nationale (nearly parallel to the eastern wall, near the southern end of the front porch of monument 5), Invalides (SE, meets ley 17), Plaza Vauban (southern end, meets ley 6), Villa de Saxe's chapel, Metro Ségur, and St-Seraphin de Sarov (meets ley 12). Runs through Crossing Lefebvre-Dantzig (center, meets ley 13), Théatre Paris-Plaine, and ends at Porte de la Plaine (eastern side).

Eiffel Tower-to-École Militaire (Axis 4)

Starts A: Défense, Porte Dauphine (south side); **Ends B:** Porte d'Italie (center); **Global:** 1 church, 2 Metros, 10 plazas, 7 monuments (6 main porches).

   Description: This grand axis runs through La Défense Esplanade (center of monument 1), Porte Dauphine (southern side), Crossing Longchamp-Sablons, Trocadéro Plaza, Palais de Chaillot (center of monument 2), Plaza de Varsovie, Pont d'Iéna (center of monument 3), Eiffel Tower (center of monument 4), the elliptical and diamond garden mandala within Champ de Mars (center of monument 5), École Militaire (center of monument 6), Plaza de Fontenoy (major node), Plaza de Breteuil (minor node), Metro Gare Montparnasse (runs exactly on the plaza between the tower and the station), Metro and Plaza Denfert-Rochereau (major node), St-Dominique Church, and Sainte-Anne Hospital (monument 7). It runs south of St-Albert-le-Grand Church (rue de la Glacière) and Crossing Kellermann-Peupliers, and ends on Porte d'Italie (center on the périphérique, which circles Paris).

Etoile Cardo: Etoile-to-Trocadéro (Axis 5)

Starts A: near Porte de Clichy; **Ends B:** near Quai d'Issy/Porte St-Cloud; **Global:** Zero churches, 6 Metros, 8 plazas, 4 monuments (3 geometrical points), 2 avenues.

   Description: Starting at Porte de Clichy, it runs from Crossing

Malesherbes-Péreire to follow avenue de Wagram, Plaza du Brésil (Crossing Villiers-Wagram), Crossing Wagram-Courcelles, Metro and Plaza des Ternes, and L'Etoile Plaza with its Arc de Triomphe (central line on the length of monument 1). It follows avenue Kléber and Metro Kléber, Metro Boissière, Place du Trocadéro (geometrical center and Metro), and Metro avenue Président Kennedy. It runs exactly tangent to Maison de Radio-France (eastern side of the building of monument 2), Plaza Clément Ader (eastern side tangent). It crosses Pont Mirabeau (mid-point of monument 3), Pont de Garigliano (eastern entry point of monument 4), Quai d'Issy, and Plaza and Metro Issy-Plaine/Val de Seine.

Let's now look at leys in Paris: they are numbered clockwise from the west, starting at the West Decumanus, the main axis from La Défense to Etoile; follow the sequence based on their beginning points. A ley's beginning is called point *a,* and its endpoint is called *b.* Refer to plate 1, Main axes and leys in Paris.

MAJOR LEYS IN PARIS

Ley 1—Franklin-Roosevelt-to-Bibliothèque Mitterrand

Starts A: proximate to Porte Maillot; **Ends B:** proximate to Quai D'Ivry; **Global:** 3 churches and 1 mosque, 4 Metros, 4 plazas, 4 monuments (3 porches).

Description: It begins at Plaza T. Bernard (Ternes-Guersant Crossing), then runs through St. Joseph Church (avenue Hoche), Metro Franklin-Roosevelt, Plaza and Metro Rond-Point des Champs-Elysées (meets ley 11). The ley then crosses transversally the Grand Palais and Petit Palais (front porch) and runs through the center of the space between these two palaces, where it meets the East Decumanus and ley 6; then through St-Germain-des-Prés Church (boulevard St-Germain, northern wall), Plaza d'Acadie (proximate to Metro Mabillon), where it meets meridian 0 (MD 0 in plate 1) at the exact center, the Sorbonne University (the main east and west porches), St-Etienne-du-Mont Church, Plaza Monge (north side), the Mosque of Paris, Metro St-Marcel, Pitié-Salpêtrière Hospital, Metro Chevaleret, and Metro

Bibliothèque Mitterrand. Extended to the northwest, it reaches the Pont de Courbevoie (northern entry point).

Ley 2—Arc du Carrousel-to-Notre-Dame de Paris

Starts A: proximate to Porte Champerret; **Ends B:** south of Porte de Charenton; **Global:** 2 cathedrals, 2 churches, 2 plazas, 7 monuments.

Description: From Plaza Bineau, the ley runs through Newsky Cathedral (proximate to Salle Pleyel), St-Philippe-du-Roule Church (facade), Palais de l'Elysée (southern side), Plaza Concorde (northern side, two hostels), Jeu de Paume Museum (northeast corner), Arc de Triomphe du Carrousel (meets ley 12), inverted pyramid (southwest apex, meets East and West Decumani), the Louvre (southern side, aisle Denon), Sainte-Chapelle Church (northern wall), Notre-Dame de Paris Cathedral (runs transversely), Institut du Monde Arabe (meets ley 14 on the western porch), and Palais Omnisports de Bercy (center).

Ley 3—Vendôme Column-to-Sainte-Chapelle

Starts A: proximate to Porte d'Asnières; **Ends B:** proximate to Porte de Bercy; **Global:** 3 churches and 1 chapel, 2 Metros, 2 plazas and 2 squares (center), 5 monuments (four centers), 2 bridges (one at center), 1 sculpture, 1 fountain (center), 1 garden.

Description: The ley begins at Plaza de Wagram. It follows the northern side of boulevard Malesherbes and passes through Crossing Malesherbes-Constantinople, St-Augustin Church (center choir and runs the length), Metro St-Augustin, Plaza de La Madeleine (northern side), Vendôme Column (exact center), St-Roch Church (choir), and the Louvre (northern side, aisle Richelieu). At Cour Carrée of the Louvre, the ley goes through the round basin at the exact center of the square and also through the sculptures of Isis and Osiris, which adorn the wall on the left side of Sully Pavillon's porch. It then passes through Pont-Neuf (center of the bridge, north of Ile de la Cité), Sainte-Chapelle Church (runs transversely west to southeast), Pont au Double, Chapelle des Bernardins, Jussieu University (exact center of the inner square), Jardin des Plantes: Muséum d'Histoire Naturelle (main porch of the central south building), and the Metro Bibliothèque Mitterrand (meets ley 1).

Ley 4—Obelisk-to-Plaza Denfert Rochereau

Starts A: Porte de Clichy (center); **Ends B:** proximate to Porte de Gentilly; **Global:** 1 church, 3 Metros, 4 plazas (4 centers), 1 monument (center), 1 sculpture.

Description: The ley runs from Porte de Clichy (center of the plaza) through Plaza Goubaux (center) and Metro Villiers, Obelisk (Plaza Concorde), St-Ignace Church (proximate to Metro Sèvres-Babylone), and Metro Notre-Dame-des Champs. It follows the center line of boulevard Raspail, Metro Raspail, Plaza Denfert-Rochereau (center, Lion de Belfort sculpture, major node, meets leys 8 and 9), and Metro Denfert-Rochereau. It then follows avenue Président Coty on the west side, Montsouris Park, and runs to Cité Internationale Universitaire.

Ley 5—Blanche-to-Carreau du Temple

Starts A: north of Porte de Clichy; **Ends B:** proximate to Porte Dorée; **Global:** 1 church, 4 Metros, 4 plazas and 5 crossings, and 2 monuments.

Description: The ley begins at Batignolles Cemetery (follows the western wall) and crosses the southern corner of Montmartre Cemetery. It runs through Plaza Blanche (center, meets ley 8), Metro Blanche, Crossing Lafayette-Rochechouard (northern side), Crossing Richer–Faubourg Poissonnière, L'Evantail Museum, Crossing St-Martin–St-Denis, Sainte-Elisabeth Church (southern wall), Carreau du Temple (meets ley 10), Metro Sébastien Froissart, Crossing Lenoir-Chemin Vert (eastern side), Théatre de la Bastille, Crossing Trousseau-Charonne, Metro and Plaza Faidherbe-Chaligny (center), Plaza Reuilly-Picpus (center), Porte Dorée (center), Metro Porte Dorée, and Lac Daumesnil (Vincennes Forest).

Ley 6—Les Invalides Axis

Starts A: proximate to Porte de Clichy; **Ends B:** proximate to Porte de Châtillon; **Global:** 2 churches (2 central axes), 1 Metro, 6 plazas (6 exact centers), 4 monuments (2 porches, northern and southern), 1 bridge, 3 avenues (center).

Description: The ley runs through Metro Villiers, Plaza Clémenceau (center, proximate to Metro Champs-Elysées–Clémenceau), avenue Winston Churchill (center, between the Grand Palais and Petit

Palais), bridge Alexandre III (center), avenue M. Galiéni (center, central north-south axis of the Invalides Gardens), Plaza des Invalides, Hôtel des Invalides (central axis), St-Louis Church and Eglise du Dôme Church (median in length), Plaza Vauban (center, meets the Obelisk Cardo), avenue de Breteuil, and Plaza de Breteuil (center, meets École Militaire and axis 4). It then runs through Plaza Henri Queuille (eastern side, proximate to Metro Sèvres-Lecourbe), Pasteur Institute, Plaza Falguière (center), St-Joseph Hospital (western side), and Didot Stadium (eastern side).

Ley 7—Trinité Church-to-St-Sulpice Church

Starts A: Porte de St-Ouen (center); **Ends B:** proximate to Porte de Gentilly; **Global:** 4 churches and 1 chapel, 2 Metros, 3 plazas (2 at center), 3 parks, 6 monuments (3 porches).

Description: From Porte de St-Ouen (center), the ley runs through Montmartre Cemetery (cutting through in a north-south direction, then marking the cemetery's exact southwest corner, on rue Caulaincourt), the chapel of rue Blanche (meets the Obelisk Cardo), Sainte-Trinité Church (northern porch to southwest corner), Park d'Estienne d'Orves (center), Plaza d'Estienne d'Orves, Opéra Garnier (central dome, northeast corner, southern front porch), Plaza de l'Opéra (center), Metro Opéra, St-Roch Church (choir), Arc du Carrousel, the Louvre (front porch of Denon aisle; in front of Carrousel Bridge), St-Germain-des-Prés Church (main tower and steeple, western front porch), Saint-Sulpice Church (geometrical center), Luxembourg Garden, and Paris Observatory (crosses the building on the west, then runs through the southern wall [center] of the garden). It runs through Metro St-Jacques (meets meridian zero), then Montsouris Park (meets ley 4).

Ley 8—St-Roch-to-Denfert Meridian

Starts A: proximate to Porte de St-Ouen; **Ends B:** proximate to Porte d'Orléans; **Global:** 1 church, 3 Metros, 4 plazas, 5 monuments (including 1 plaza statue and 1 bridge).

Description: The ley runs through Bichat Hospital (center), Crossing Caulaincourt-DeMaistre (eastern side), the western corner of Montmartre

Cemetery, Plaza Blanche (western side, meets ley 5), Metro Blanche, Metro Trinité, Plaza d'Estienne D'Orves (eastern side), Opéra Garnier (southeast corner), Metro Opéra, Plaza de l'Opéra, St-Roch (transversal, geometrical center), and the northwest tip of the Louvre's horseshoe. It then passes to the west of Arc du Carrousel, Pont du Carrousel (southwest corner), town hall Mairie du 6ième (facade), and Crossing Vaugirard-Guynemer. It follows the western wall of Luxembourg Garden, St-Vincent Hospital, and Plaza Denfert-Rochereau (center), and meets leys 9 and 4 on the Lion de Belfort statue. This plaza embeds a perfect double cross, with ley 8 perfectly perpendicular to ley 16 and axis 4 perfectly perpendicular to ley 14. Moreover, all angles between these 4 lines are 45 degrees. The ley then runs through Crossing Tombe-Issoire-Alésia.

Ley 9—Montmartre-to-St-Sulpice
Starts A: proximate to Porte de Clignancourt; **Ends B:** proximate to Porte d'Orléans; **Global:** 3 churches (2 center), 4 Metros, 4 plazas (2 center), 4 monuments (1 main porch), 1 significant sculpture, 1 flea market.

   Description: From the flea market (Marché aux Puces), the ley passes Crossing Championnet-Letort (center), Metro Lamarck Caulaincourt (tangent to Montmartre Hill), Abbesses Church (center on facade, eastern side) and Metro Abbesses. It passes Plaza Pigalle (eastern side), Metro St-Georges, Palais Royal (southwest corner), Plaza André Malraux, the Louvre (northwest corner of the Pavillon Richelieu), the pyramid (southwest apex), the Louvre aisle Denon (central inner porch facing the pyramid), St-Germain des Prés Church (geometric center, meets ley 1), Saint-Sulpice Church (nave), Luxembourg Garden (nearly parallel to the western wall), Plaza Denfert-Rochereau (center of the Lion de Belfort sculpture; center of the plaza), and Metro Denfert-Rochereau.

Ley 10—Templars' Carreau-to-Bastille Column's Hermes/Angel
Starts A: proximate to Porte de Clignancourt; **Ends B:** Quai d'Ivry (southwest); **Global:** 1 church and 1 chapel, 3 Metros, 4 plazas, 5 monuments (3 main porches), 1 bridge (midpoint).

Description: The ley runs from Porte de Clignancourt (exact, on périphérique) through St-Paul Chapel, Metro Marcadet-Poissonniers (tangent), Crossing Doudeauville-Poissonniers, Crossing Maubeuge-Paré (northeast corner of St-Lazare station), St-Lazare station (main front porch), Metro Gare de l'Est (tangent), St-Laurent Church (follows the western facade), Carreau du Temple (place of the ancient Templar castle in Paris; meets ley 5), and then Plaza de la Bastille, where it runs at the exact center, where stands the Bastille Column, featuring, on top of an obelisk, an angel that symbolizes Hermes/Mercury (and where it meets the East Decumanus. Then it runs through Opéra Paris-Bastille (follows the western wall all the way), Metro Gare de Lyon, Lyon station (main entrance, northwest tower), the small bridge in front of Bibliothèque Mitterrand (midpoint), Crossing Tolbiac-Mauriac (northern side), and Quai d'Ivry.

Ley 11—Eiffel Tower-to-Porte de la Chapelle (at Right Angle to École Militaire Axis)

Starts A: proximate to Porte de la Chapelle; **Ends B:** proximate to Porte de St-Cloud; **Global:** 0 churches, 2 Metros, 4 plazas, 4 crossings, 3 monuments (including 1 bridge and 1 center).

Description: The ley begins at Porte de la Chapelle (northern side, highway) and runs through Notre-Dame-de-Clignancourt Church (southeast corner), Metro and Plaza Jules Joffrin (center), Mairie du 18ème (northwest corner), Crossing DeMaistre-Lepic, Plaza St-Augustin (meets ley 3), Crossing LaBoétie-d'Argenson, Crossing Matignon–Faubourg-St-Honoré, Plaza Rond-Point des Champs-Elysées (crossing of 3 leys), and Pont de l'Alma (midpoint, Eiffel Tower; precise center and 90-degree angle to the grand axis École Militaire). From there it crosses in front of Bir-Hakeim Bridge (Quai de Grenelle), and follows the Seine from Bir-Hakeim Bridge to Mirabeau Bridge, then to Metro Javel.

Ley 12—Plaza de Breteuil Perpendicular to Axis 4 (École Militaire)

Starts A: Porte de la Villette (center); **Ends B:** proximate to Porte de Versailles; **Global:** 1 church, 2 Metros, 3 plazas and 5 crossings, 4 monuments (including 1 bridge).

Description: The ley passes from Plaza and Metro Porte de la Villette to Crossing Aqueduc-Louis-Blanc, Crossing Alsace-LaFayette, Crossing Hauteville-Petites-Ecuries, Palais Royal (perfect diagonal of the garden from the northeast corner to the southwest corner), Comédie Française (Theater), Arc du Carrousel (meets ley 2), Pont Royal (southern entry point), Plaza de Breteuil (major node, perfect perpendicular to axis 4 and meets ley 6), Crossing Volontaires-Lecourbe, St-Seraphin de Sarov Church (meets the Obelisk Cardo), Crossing Vaugirard-Convention and Metro Convention (tangent to eastern side), and Porte de Versailles (eastern side).

Ley 13—*Géode-to-La Gloire Bas-relief*
Starts A: proximate to Porte de la Villette; **Ends B:** Porte de la Plaine; **Global:** 3 churches, 2 Metros, 2 plazas and 5 crossings, 7 monuments (including 2 bridges, 3 centers/porches), 1 sculpture.

Description: The ley passes through Géode (center), Cité des Sciences, Crossing Ourcq-Quai-de-L'Oise, Metro Jaurès, bridge Louis-Blanc (midpoint of canal St-Martin), Crossing rue and boulevard St-Denis, Porte de Paris (ancient gate of Paris), Bourse du Commerce (center), and Forum des Halles (western side). The ley then runs through the Louvre, especially the Cour Carrée at the level of the eastern porch, where there stands the marvelous bas-relief *La Gloire distribuant des Couronnes* (sculpted by Pierre Cartellier) and where it meets the East Decumanus. It then runs through Pont des Arts (northern entry point), St-Vladimir-le-Grand Church, Plaza Le Corbusier, St-Ignace Church (inside the triangle formed by leys 17 and 4), and Metro Sèvres-Babylone. It follows rue Dr. Roux (2 crossings), St-Jean-Baptiste-de-la-Salle Church (facade), Crossing Lefebvre-Dantzig (meets the Obelisk Cardo), and Porte de la Plaine (center).

Ley 14—*Place des Vosges-to-Observatory*
Starts A: proximate to Porte du Pré St-Gervais; **Ends B:** Porte de Châtillon; **Global:** 0 churches, 4 Metros, 5 plazas and 4 crossings, 4 monuments (2 centers), and follows 2 streets.

Description: The ley passes from Robert Debré Hospital to Plaza

Notre-Dame-de-Fatima, Crossing Belleville-Ribière, Parc de Belleville (eastern corner and crossing), Metro rue St-Maur, Metro Richard Lenoir, Metro Chemin Vert, Plaza des Vosges (diagonal northeast to southwest), Crossing Quai Hôtel de Ville-St-Paul, Hôtel Lambert, Plaza Tournelle, and Institut du Monde Arabe (western facade). It then follows rue des Fossés St-Bernard and rue du Cardinal Lemoine and passes through Metro Cardinal Lemoine, Val-de-Grâce Hospital (dome, center), Crossing Port-Royal-St-Jacques, Paris Observatory (geometrical center), Plaza Denfert-Rochereau (center, right angle with the École Militaire axis; meets many leys), and Porte de Châtillon (center).

Ley 15—Eglise du Dôme-to-Sainte-Chapelle's Parallel
Starts A: proximate to Porte de Montreuil (southern end); **Ends B:** south of Porte de Passy; **Global:** 6 churches and 2 synagogues, 1 Metro, 2 plazas and 7 crossings, 8 monuments.

Description: From Crossing Vignoles-Réunion, the ley passes through St-Jean-Bosco Church, Synagogue Basfroi (southern end), Crossing Lenoir-Sedaine, Synagogue Tournelles (center), the magnificent Plaza des Vosges (southwest corner, meets ley 14), and Plaza Marché Sainte-Catherine. The ley then runs through St-Gervais–St-Protais Church on the center of the choir, where it meets many leys, including the perfect St-Gervais–St-Protais Church meridian, heading north toward St-Bernard de la Chapelle Church. This is a geo-architectural reminder of the relation St. Bernard (Bernard de Clairvaux) had with the Templars and consequently with the Priory of Sion. The ley then runs through Hôtel Dieu (Paris's most ancient hospital, with its initial building erected in 651 CE; northwest corner), Sainte Chapelle Church inside the Palais de Justice, Crossing Quai and rue des Grands Augustins, Crossing Dauphine-Lodi, Crossing Mazarine-Guénégaud, Jussieu University (runs transversely, center), Crossing Varenne-Jouy, and Musée Rodin (center). The ley then passes through the Invalides and, astonishingly, between its two enclosed churches (Saint-Louis and Eglise du Dôme), which are aligned north-south, with their choirs facing each other. The ley then runs through Champ de Mars (transversely, under the central ellipse). On the Seine River, the ley passes a crossing between the bridge Bir Hakeim and the island des Cygnes. Then it runs through the historical House of Balzac, Metro Ranelagh, and finally Notre-Dame-de-l'Assomption-de-Passy Church (choir, center).

Ley 16—*Bibliothèque Mitterrand-to-Denfert-Rochereau's Parallel*

Starts A: Porte Dorée; **Ends B:** Porte de Sèvres; **Global:** 0 churches, 2 Metros, 3 plazas and 5 crossings, 1 monument (center).

Description: The ley passes through Crossing Daumesnil-Ceinture (Bois de Vincennes) and Crossing Poniatowski-Decaen. There is a crossing of three leys on Quai Mauriac (our ley 16 with 17 and 10) in front of Bibliothèque Mitterrand (geometrical center). Then the ley runs through Crossing Jeanne-d'Arc-Auriol and Plaza Denfert-Rochereau (center), where it is perfectly perpendicular to ley 8 (Denfert's meridian). It passes through Metro Pernety, Crossing Vouillé-Castanary (meets ley 6), Crossing Dantzig-Morillons, Porte de Sèvres (center on the périphérique), and Plaza and Metro Marcel Sambat (Boulogne).

Ley 17—*Bibliothèque Mitterrand-to-Trocadéro*

Starts A: Porte de Bercy; **Ends B:** proximate to Porte Dauphine; **Global:** 4 churches, 1 Metro, 3 plazas and 3 crossings, 2 monuments.

Description: The ley runs from St-Pierre Church (Charenton) to Porte de Bercy (eastern side), Pont de Tolbiac (midpoint), crossing 3 leys on Quai Mauriac (16, 10, and of course 17), Bibliothèque Mitterrand (transversal and northern porch), Crossing Auriol-France, and Notre-Dame-du-Liban Church (choir). It then follows rue Royer Collar, Luxembourg Garden's central basin (northern side) and the northwest corner (exact), Crossing Vaugirard-Bonaparte, Plaza Deville (center), St-Ignace Church (front porch), tangent to Metro Sèvres-Babylone, Eglise du Dôme Church (front porch) Crossing Université-Bourdonnais (meets ley 11), Plaza du Trocadéro (center, crossing axis 4 and Etoile Cardo), and ends south of Puteaux Bridge.

CIRCLE DRAWN ON THE APEXES OF THE OBELISK HEXAGON

In appendix 2, we'll see in detail the circle drawn on the apexes of the Obelisk hexagon. This circle, while interesting in itself, is of minor importance to our general discussion, and it would have slowed down the discussion in chapter 9, hence its inclusion here as an appendix. In chapter 9, we discussed only the prominent features and the generalities; here is the detailed and sequential information.

Please refer to plate 4: moving clockwise around the circle from the West Decumanus, after crossing apex F, the circle meets Plaza and Metro Pereire (and follows boulevard Pereire for a bit). Then it crosses apex C, Metro Brochant, the upper tip of Cimetière Montmartre, and St-Pierre-de-Montmartre Church. The next marker is the crossing between the long steps down the Sacré-Coeur Basilica (and extending the staircase's central line) and rue du Cardinal Dubois. At apex D, the circle is tangent to boulevard Magenta. It then runs through Mairie du 12ème (town hall of the 12th arrondissement), Hunting and Nature Museum, Archives of France (Hôtel de Soubise, 1704), and Notre-Dame-des-Blancs-Manteaux Church. The western apex of the hexagon and the circle are marked by St-Gervais–St-Protais Church (Flamboyant Gothic style, fifteenth century, save for its seventeenth-century facade). Next on the circle is St-Nicolas-du-Chardonnet, then the Panthéon (dome), Mairie du 5ème (town hall), St-Jacques-du-haut-Pas (rue St-Jacques), Metro Edgar Quinet, then apex K of the hexagon at Bobino Theater. The circle then diagonally crosses Montparnasse station, Crossing Pasteur-Vaugirard, St-Jean-Baptiste-de-la-Salle Church, Metro and Crossing Emile Zola, hexagon apex J, Metro Passy, Crossing Passy-Franklin (center), Crossing Longchamp-Sablons, and Crossing Foch-Poincaré. It then returns to hexagon apex F on avenue de la Grande Armée.

APPENDIX 3

GRAND TEN-POINTED STAR ON CHÂTELET NODE

THE INSIDE LINES OF THE GRAND TEN-POINTED STAR

We can check in turn each apex of the ten-pointed star to describe the two sides of this apex (northern and southern, eastern or western) and then its median. Refer to plate 7: we'll move counterclockwise from the West Decumanus (see the Obelisk in the northwest point of the star).

The smaller ten-pointed star is exactly fitted inside the larger one; each larger branch envelops a smaller one, and their apexes are in a straight line with the central node (Châtelet Fountain). Thus we can call each branch of the grand ten-pointed star by the letter marking the apex of the smaller ten-pointed star. For example, the median of the small branch A is the West Decumanus (AGM extended on both sides). Similarly, the enveloping larger branch has the West Decumanus for a median, and we can call this larger branch the A branch of the grand star.

1. **Blue A branch** (extended around A). The point falls on the northwestern side of the Eiffel Tower golden rectangle, precisely at Plaza George V (Metro) on the Champs-Elysées. The N line (KI extended) passes through La Madeleine (front porch) and Palais de l'Elysée. The S line (JL extended) runs through Grand

348

Palais and Assemblée Nationale (Palais Bourbon). The median is the West Decumanus, running through the Tuileries and the Obelisk and then following the Champs-Elysées (Plaza and Metro Champs-Elysées Clémenceau and Franklin-Roosevelt).

2. **Red L branch.** The point falls on Village Suisse, near St-Léon Church. The N line (CA extended) goes through the entry point to Solférino Bridge, Sainte-Clotilde Basilica, the Invalides (specifically, the small St-Louis Church), then École Militaire (the tower and the porch facing the Eiffel Tower), Metro Charles Michel and Porte de St-Cloud. The S line (BD extended) goes through St-Léon Church. (Extended, it reaches Maison de la Radio.) The median runs through Plaza Vauban (southern side, exact center on the beginning of avenue de Breteuil, thus facing the front porch of the Invalides).

3. **Blue D branch.** The point falls on St-Joseph Hospital, near Metro Plaisance. The N line (IL extended) passes through Metro Sèvres-Babylone, Montparnasse station (two buildings at the back and the southern side), Porte de Vanves (eastern side). The S line (MJ extended) runs through St-Jacques-du-Haut-Pas Church. The median crosses Notre-Dame-des-Champs Church, Plaza Edgar Quinet, and Plaza de Catalogne (eastern side).

4. **Red J branch.** The point falls near St-Albert-le-Grand Church and Crossing Reille-Alésia and Metro Plaisance. The E line (continuation of AD) passes through Metro and Plaza Port-Royal, Paris Observatory (northeast corner), and Porte de Gentilly (center, on the périphérique). The W line (EB extended) runs through the Grand Mosque of Paris, Plaza and Metro Censier Daubenton, and Sainte-Irénée Church. It runs parallel to the east of St-Albert-le-Grand Church. The angle formed by the median and the east line encloses St-Albert-le-Grand Church.

5. **Blue B branch.** The point falls on the center of Crossing Tolbiac-Patay and near Notre-Dame-de-la-Gare Church (Plaza Jeanne d'Arc). The W line (LJ extended) runs through Notre-Dame-du-Liban Church (rue d'Ulm), Plaza and Metro Censier Daubenton, and Metro Campo-Formio, then passes near Metro Nationale,

and runs through the Notre-Dame-de-la-Gare Church. The E line (KM extended) passes through Metro Quai de la Rapée and Austerlitz Bridge. The median runs west of the central building of the Evolution Museum (Jardin des Plantes, on rue Buffon).

6. **Red M branch.** The point falls near St-Eloi Church and Metro Montgallet. The S line (DB extended) runs through Austerlitz Bridge (entry point), Gare de Lyon (train station, facade and geometrical center), and Crossing Daumesnil-Rambouillet. The N line (CE extended) runs through Metro Chemin Vert, St-Antoine Hospital, St-Eloi Church, Plaza and Metro Montgallet, and Plaza Felix Eboué (northeast side). The median runs through St-Antoine-des-Quinze-Vingts.

7. **Blue E branch.** The point falls on Père-Lachaise Cemetery (northeast side), on the entrance facing rue du Père-Lachaise. The W line (JM extended) runs through Metro and Plaza de la Bastille, Bastille Column, Plaza Léon Blum, and Metro Voltaire, near Plaza Gambetta (southern side). The E line (IK extended) passes south of Plaza République, then runs through Plaza and Metro Parmentier. The median runs through Metro Richard Lenoir, St-Amboise Church, and Plaza and Metro Porte de Bagnolet.

8. **Red K branch.** The point falls on Buttes Chaumont Park, at the entrance, in front of the town hall Mairie du 19ème, near St-Serge Church. The E line (BE extended) goes through Metro Froissart and Buttes-Chaumont. The N line (AC extended) runs through Metro Château-d'Eau, Crossing Magenta-St-Martin, Plaza Colonel Fabien (southern side), St-Georges Church, and a synagogue. The median goes through the Crossing St-Maur-Veletaux.

9. **Blue C branch.** The point falls west of Crossing Ordener-Marcadet. The W line (LI extended) runs through Metro Cadet, Crossing Maubeuge-Rochechouart, Metro and Plaza Barbès-Rochechouart, and Metro and Porte de la Chapelle. The E line (MK extended) passes through Crossing Magenta-St-Martin, St-Laurent Church, Gare du Nord (train station, center back),

and Crossing Maubeuge-Chapelle. The median goes through two crossings and follows rue d'Hauteville for a bit.

10. **Red I branch.** The point falls near Metro La Fourche (to the west). The E line (EC extended) is the northeast side of the Eiffel Tower golden rectangle. It passes through Notre-Dame-de-Bonne-Nouvelle (apex C, major node), Metro and Crossing Bonne-Nouvelle, Crossing LaFayette-Drouot, Notre-Dame-de-Lorette Church, and Metro and Plaza de Clichy. The W line (DA extended) runs near Metro Tuileries, through the southwest corner of Plaza Vendôme, Crossing Haussmann-Auber, and St-Lazare train station. Extended, it meets St-Joseph-des-Epinettes Church and Crossing Jonquière-Pouchet. The median goes through St-Trinité church.

THE INSIDE PENTAGONS OF THE TEN-POINTED STAR

• **Inside Blue Pentagon** (LJMKIL): 2 churches and 5 monuments.
• **Inside Red Pentagon** (ADBECA): 1 church and 8 monuments.

NOTES

INTRODUCTION

1. Picknett and Prince, *The Templar Revelation: Secret Guardians of the True Identity of Christ;* and Brown, *The Da Vinci Code.*
2. Philip Thomas is actually writing a book on circular routes. See also the deck of tarot cards he created, *Tarot de Paris* (New York: St. Martin's Press, 2002).
3. Jung, *Answer to Job;* see also Robertson, *Your Shadow.*
4. Bailey, *Treatise on Cosmic Fire.*
5. Will Hart, "2012: End of the 5th Sun," www.diagnosis2012.co.uk/5thsun.htm (accessed June 5, 2010).
6. Teilhard de Chardin, *Phenomenon of Man.*

CHAPTER 1. A QUESTER'S DIRECT PATH

1. See Roger Nelson's Global Consciousness Project (GCP) at http://noosphere .princeton.edu (accessed June 5, 2010). Reported in Nelson, Bradish, Dobyns, Dunne, and Jahn, "FieldREG Anomalies in Group Situations."
2. Dossey, *Recovering the Soul: A Scientific and Spiritual Approach.*
3. Jaulin, *La Mort Sara;* Roumeguère-Eberhardt, *Quand le python se déroule.*
4. Bramly, *Macumba, forces noires du Brésil.*
5. Castaneda, *The Fire from Within;* Castaneda, *The Power of Silence.*
6. Casti, *Lost Paradigms;* Robertson, *Jungian Archetypes;* Dennard, "The New Paradigm in Science and Public Administration."
7. Hardy, *Networks of Meaning: A Bridge between Mind and Matter;* Hardy, "Multilevel Webs Stretched across Time: Retroactive and Proactive Inter-Influences"; Hardy, "Self-organization, Self-reference and Inter-influences in Multilevel Webs: Beyond Causality and Determinism."

CHAPTER 2. MUSIC AND HARMONIC RAPTURE

1. Hardy, *Le vécu de la transe.*
2. Csikszentmihalyi, *Flow: The Psychology of Optimal Experience.*
3. Pritzker, "Does Creative Flow Represent an Altered State?"
4. Penrose, *The Emperor's New Mind;* Zohar and Marshall, *The Quantum Society;* Hameroff, Kaszniak, and Scott, *Toward a Science of Consciousness.*

CHAPTER 3. THE SECRET OF SHARED PRAYER

1. Dossey, *Recovering the Soul: A Scientific and Spiritual Approach.*
2. Redfield, *The Celestine Prophecy.*
3. Jung, *Man and his Symbols;* Jung, *Memories, Dreams, Reflections;* Jung, "Two Essays on Analytical Psychology."
4. Feinstein and Krippner, *The Mythic Path.*
5. Roumeguère-Eberhardt, *Python Uncoils. Baraka,* directed by Ron Fricke (produced by Mark Magidson, 1996).
6. Hardy, *Le vécu de la transe;* Black Elk and Lyon, *The Sacred Ways of a Lakota;* Neihardt, *Black Elk Speaks;* Sapa (Black Elk), *Rites secrets des indiens Sioux.*
7. Ushte and Erdoes, *Lame Deer, Seeker of Visions.*

CHAPTER 6. CONSCIOUSNESS AS ENERGY

1. Bagnall, *The Origin and Properties of the Human Aura;* Bigu, "On the Biophysical Basis of the Human Aura." See also a review of this research in Hardy, *L'Après-vie à l'épreuve de la science.*
2. Black Elk and Lyon, *The Sacred Ways of a Lakota.*
3. On lucid dreams, see Tart, *Altered States of Consciousness;* LaBerge and Rheingold, *Exploring the World of Lucid Dreaming.*
4. See Bagnall, *The Origin and Properties of the Human Aura;* Bigu, "On the Biophysical Basis of the Human Aura."
5. On transpersonal psychology, see Goleman, *Emotional Intelligence;* Tart, *Altered States of Consciousness;* Hardy, *Le vécu de la trance;* Hardy, *La science et les états frontières.*

CHAPTER 7. CATHEDRAL BUILDERS AND MEGALITHS

1. Gimpel, *Les Bâtisseurs de cathédrales,* quoted in Bayard, *La tradition cachée des cathédrales,* 64.
2. Markale, *Chartres et l'énigme des Druides,* 154–55.
3. Le Scouëzec and Court-Payen, "Géosophie des hauts-lieux: Lignes de force terrestres ou instrument d'un pouvoir?"; Le Scouëzec, *Bretagne Terre sacrée;* Le

Scouëzec, *Guide de la Bretagne;* Le Scouëzec and Masson, *Bretagne mégalithique.*

4. Le Scouëzec and Court-Payen, "Géosophie des hauts-lieux: Lignes de force ter-restres ou instrument d'un pouvoir?"

5. Markale, *Chartres et l'énigme des Druides,* 154–55.

6. Court-Payen, "L'Empire Mégalithique."

7. Devereux and Thomson, *The New Ley Hunter's Companion.*

8. Watkins, *The Old Straight Track.*

9. Bayard, *La tradition cachée des cathédrales,* 135.

10. Ibid.

11. Ibid.

12. Guygnard, *Atlantis,* no. 320 (May/June 1982), based on archives of the Guygnard Notaries of Chartres, running for two centuries.

13. Bayard, *La tradition cachée des cathédrales,*132.

14. Watkins, *The Old Straight Track.* See also the online article "Ley Lines" by Chris Witcombe, professor of art history at Sweet Briar College, England, and the rest of his very diversified research on his revisited website, Earth Mysteries, www.britannia.com/wonder/wonder.html (accessed October 11, 2010).

15. Taylor, "Stones as Ley Indicators."

16. See www.leyhunter.com/archives/michigan.htm (accessed June 15, 2010).

17. Markale, *Carnac et l'énigme de l'Atlantide,* 54, 62.

18. Le Scouëzec and Court-Payen, "Géosophie des hauts-lieux: Lignes de force ter-restres ou instrument d'un pouvoir?"

19. Court-Payen, "L'Empire Mégalithique."

20. Devereux and Thomson, *The New Ley Hunter's Companion.*

21. Phaure, *Introduction à la géographie sacrée de Paris Barque d'Isis,* 20–21, illus.

22. Jim Alison, http://home.hiwaay.net/~jalison (accessed June 16, 2010).

23. Picknett and Prince, *The Templar Revelation,* chapter 5.

24. Haagensen and Lincoln, *The Templars' Secret Island.*

25. On Bornholm, see Erling Haagensen's website, www.merling.dk/indeng.html (acccsscd June 16, 2010).

26. Markale, *Carnac,* 52.

27. Ibid.

28. Krippner and Welch, *Spiritual Dimensions of Healing.*

29. Baigent, Leigh, and Lincoln, *Holy Blood, Holy Grail;* Brown, *The Da Vinci Code.*

30. Waters, *The Book of the Hopi;* Mails, *The Hopi Survival Kit: The Prophecies, Instructions and Warnings Revealed by the Last Elders.*

31. Wilson, *From Atlantis to the Sphinx.*

CHAPTER 8. UNVEILING THE
CHRISTIAN-DRUIDIC GRID

1. Phaure, *Introduction à la géographie sacrée de Paris Barque d'Isis,* 90, illus.

CHAPTER 9. THE SACRED NETWORK OF PARIS:
THE OBELISK NODE

1. Lavallée, "Histoire de Paris depuis le temps des Gaulois jusqu'à nos jours."
2. Phaure, *Introduction à la géographie sacrée de Paris Barque d'Isis,* 4, 52–53, 85, illus.
3. Thomas, *Tarot de Paris.*
4. Baigent, Leigh, and Lincoln, *Holy Blood, Holy Grail.*
5. Maestracci, *Géographie secrète de la Provence,* 77–82.
6. Klug, *Kathedrale des kosmos: Die heilige geometrie von Chartres.*
7. Markale, *Gisors et l'énigme des Templiers,* 303–6.
8. Markale, *Gisors,* 307–8.

CHAPTER 10. ST. JOHN THE BAPTIST'S
PYRAMID AND THE CHÂTELET NODE

1. Baigent, Leigh, and Lincoln, *Holy Blood, Holy Grail.*
2. Picknett and Prince, *The Templar Revelation;* Brown, *The Da Vinci Code.*

CHAPTER 11. ANNULLING SPACE

1. On synchronicity, see Combs and Holland, *Synchronicity;* Peat, *Synchronicity: The Bridge between Matter and Mind.*
2. Hardy, "Multilevel Webs Stretched across Time."
3. On Semantic Fields Theory (SFT), see Hardy, *Networks of Meaning: A Bridge between Mind and Matter.*
4. Margulis and Sagan, *Microcosmos: Four Billion Years of Evolution from Our Microbial Ancestors;* Lovelock, *The Ages of Gaia.*
5. For a more detailed argument, see Hardy, *Networks of Meaning,* chapter 8. See also Hardy, "Psi as a Multilevel Process: Semantic Fields Theory."
6. The interview in French in which Stéphane Lupasco recounts this anomalous event was published in Christine Hardy, *La science devant l'inconnu* (Paris: Rocher, 1983), now out of print.
7. Roy P. Kerr, "Gravitational Field of a Spinning Mass as an Example of Algebraically Special Metrics," *Physical Review Letters* 11 (1963): 237.

CHAPTER 12. TIME SINGULARITIES

1. Costa de Beauregard (presentation at the Euro-PA, Melun, France 1992); Costa de Beauregard, "Quantum Paradoxes and Aristotle's Twofold Information Concept."
2. Poincaré, *Science and Method.*
3. Jung, "Alchemical Studies."
4. Waite, *Hermetic and Alchemical Writings of Paracelsus.*
5. Bayard, *La tradition cachée des cathédrales,* 207.
6. Ibid., 348.
7. Jung, "Alchemical Studies."
8. Atmanspacher and Primas, "The Hidden Side of Wolfgang Pauli." On synchronicities, see also Jung and Pauli, *The Interpretation of Nature and the Psyche,* and Jung, "Synchronicity: an Acausal Connecting Principle."

CHAPTER 13. TOWARD A PLANETARY CONSCIOUSNESS

1. Regarding the experiments on which I ground my development and discussion, here is a comprehensive list of books addressing experimental research on psi: Broughton, *The Controversial Science;* Mishlove, *The Roots of Consciousness;* Pigani, *Psi: Enquête sur les phénomènes paranormaux;* Ullman and Krippner, *Dream Telepathy;* Radin, *The Conscious Universe;* Rogo, *Mind beyond the Body;* Schwartz, *The Secret Vaults of Time;* Varvoglis, *La Rationalité de l'Irrationnel.*
2. Broughton, *The Controversial Science;* Radin, *The Conscious Universe.*
3. Goleman, *Emotional Intelligence.*
4. Hardy, "Complex Intuitive Dynamics in a Systemic Cognitive Framework"; Franquemont, *You Already Know What to Do.*
5. Regarding meta-analysis results, see Radin, *The Conscious Universe.*
6. Hardy, *Networks of Meaning;* Hardy, *Le vécu de la trance.*
7. Bohm, *Wholeness and the Implicate Order.*
8. Hardy, "Synchronicity: Interconnection through a Semantic Dimension."
9. Hardy, "Psi as a Multilevel Process."
10. Eliade, *Myth and Reality (Religious Traditions in the World).*
11. Gell-Mann, *The Quark and the Jaguar.*
12. On chaos theory, see Gleick, *Chaos;* Abraham, Abraham, and Shaw, *A Visual Introduction to Dynamical Systems Theory for Psychology;* Guastello, *Chaos, Catastrophe, and Human Affairs.*
13. Deleuze and Guattari, *A Thousand Plateaus.*

BIBLIOGRAPHY

Abraham, F., R. Abraham, and C. Shaw. *A Visual Introduction to Dynamical Systems Theory for Psychology.* Santa Cruz, Calif.: Aerial Press, 1990.

Atmanspacher, H., and H. Primas. "The Hidden Side of Wolfgang Pauli." *Journal of Consciousness Studies* 3, no. 2 (1996).

Bagnall, O. *The Origin and Properties of the Human Aura.* New York: Weiser, 1975.

Baigent, M., R. Leigh, and H. Lincoln. *Holy Blood, Holy Grail.* New York: Arrow Books/Random House, 1982.

Bailey, Alice. *Treatise on Cosmic Fire.* New York: Lucis Publishing Company, 1973.

Bayard, Jean-Pierre. *La tradition cachée des cathédrales.* Paris: Editions Dangles, 1990.

Bigu, J. "On the Biophysical Basis of the Human Aura." *Journal of Research in Psi Phenomena* 1, no. 2 (1976): 8–43.

Black Elk, Wallace, and William Lyon. *The Sacred Ways of a Lakota.* New York: Harper Collins, 1991.

Bohm, David. *Wholeness and the Implicate Order.* London: Routledge and Kegan Paul, 1980.

Boshier, Adrien. "African Apprenticeship." In A. Angoff and D. Barth, eds., *Parapsychology and Anthropology.* New York: Parapsychology Foundation, 1973.

Bramly, Serge. *Macumba, forces noires du Brésil.* Paris: Albin Michel, 1975.

Broughton, Richard. *The Controversial Science.* New York: Ballantine, 1991.

Brown, Dan. *The Da Vinci Code.* New York: Doubleday/Random House, 2003.

Castaneda, Carlos. *The Fire from Within.* New York: Pocket Books, 1991.

———. *The Power of Silence.* New York: Pocket Books, 1991.

Casti, J. *Lost Paradigms.* New York: William Morrow, 1989.

Combs, A. and M. Holland. *Synchronicity: Science, Myth, and the Trickster.* New York: Marlowe, 1995.

Costa de Beauregard, Olivier. "Quantum Paradoxes and Aristotle's Twofold Information Concept." In *Quantum Physics and Parapsychology.* New York: Parapsychology Foundation, 1975.

Court-Payen, Philippe. "L'Empire Mégalithique." In Gwen Le Scouëzec and Philippe Court-Payen, eds.,"Géosophie des hauts-lieux: Lignes de force terrestres ou instrument d'un pouvoir?" *Bulletin du Corps à vivre* 19 (March 1979).

Csikszentmihalyi, Mihaly. *Flow: The Psychology of Optimal Experience.* New York: Harper and Row, 1990.

Deleuze, Gilles, and Felix Guattari. *A Thousand Plateaus.* New York: Continuum P. G., 2004.

Dennard, L. "The New Paradigm in Science and Public Administration." *Public Administration Review* 56, no. 15 (1996): 495–99.

Devereux, Paul, and Ian Thomson. *The New Ley Hunter's Companion.* Glastonbury, England: Gothic Image Publications, 1994.

Dossey, Larry. *Recovering the Soul: A Scientific and Spiritual Approach.* New York: Bantam New Age Books, 1989.

Edinger, Edward F. *The Mysterium Lectures: A Journey Through C. G. Jung's Mysterium Conjunctions.* Toronto, Ont.: Inner City Books, 1995.

Eliade, Mircea. *Myth and Reality (Religious Traditions in the World).* Long Grove, Ill.: Waveland Press, 1998.

Feinstein, David, and Stanley Krippner. *The Mythic Path.* New York: Tarcher/Putnam, 1997.

Franquemont, Sharon. *You Already Know What to Do.* New York: Tarcher/Putnam, 1999.

Gell-Mann, Murray. *The Quark and the Jaguar.* New York: W. H. Freeman and Co., 1994.

Gimpel, Jean. *Les Bâtisseurs de cathédrales.* Paris: Le Seuil, 1959.

Gleick, James. *Chaos.* New York: Viking Press, 1987.

Goleman, Daniel. *Emotional Intelligence.* New York: Bantam, 1995.

Guastello, Stephen. *Chaos, Catastrophe, and Human Affairs.* Mahwah, N.J.: Lawrence Erlbaum As., 1995.

Haagensen, Erling, and Henry Lincoln. *The Templars' Secret Island.* New York: Barnes and Noble Books, 2004.

Hameroff, S., A. W. Kaszniak, and A. C. Scott, eds. *Toward a Science of Consciousness.* Cambridge, Mass.: MIT Press/Bradford Books, 1996.

Hardy, Christine. "Complex Intuitive Dynamics in a Systemic Cognitive Framework." *Proceedings* (CD-ROM) of the annual meeting of the International Society for the Systems Sciences, Crete, Greece, 2003.

———. *Diverging Views. On Our Way to the Galactic Club.* Delhi, India: Terra Futura, 2008.

———. *L'Après-vie à l'épreuve de la science.* Paris: Rocher, 1986.

———. *La science devant l'inconnu.* Paris: Rocher, 1983.

———. *La science et les états frontières.* Paris: Rocher, 1988.

———. *Le vécu de la transe.* Paris: Editions du Dauphin, 1995.

———. "Multilevel Webs Stretched across Time: Retroactive and Proactive Inter-influences." *Systems Research and Behavioral Science* 20, no. 2 (2003): 201–15.

———. *Networks of Meaning: A Bridge between Mind and Matter.* Westport, Conn.: Praeger, 1998.

———. "Psi as a Multilevel Process: Semantic Fields Theory." *Journal of Parapsychology* 64 (March 2000).

———. "Self-organization, Self-reference and Inter-influences in Multilevel Webs: Beyond Causality and Determinism." *Journal of Cybernetics and Human Knowing* 8, no. 3 (July 2001): 35–59.

———. "Synchronicity: Interconnection through a Semantic Dimension." Presentation at Second Psi Meeting, April 21–26, 2004, Curitiba, Brazil.

Jaulin, Robert. *La Mort Sara.* Paris: Plon, 1991.

Jung, Carl. "Alchemical Studies." In *The Collected Works of C.G. Jung,* Bollingen Series, vol 13. Adler, G., and R. F. Hull, eds. Princeton, N.J.: Princeton University Press, 1968.

———. *Answer to Job.* New York: Routledge and Kegan Paul, 1954.

———. *Man and his Symbols.* Garden City, N.Y.: Windfall Books/DoubleDay, 1964.

———. *Memories, Dreams, Reflections.* New York: Vintage Books/Random House, 1965.

———. "Psychology and Alchemy." In *The Collected Works of C. G. Jung,* Bollingen Series, vol. 12. Adler, G., and R. F. Hull, eds. Princeton, N.J.: Princeton University Press, 1968.

———. "Synchronicity: an Acausal Connecting Principle." In *The Collected Works of C. G. Jung,* Bollingen Series, vol. 8. Adler, G., and R. F. Hull, eds. Princeton, N.J.: Princeton University Press, 1960.

———. "Two Essays on Analytical Psychology." In *The Collected Works of C. G. Jung,* Bollingen Series, vol. 7. Adler, G., and R. F. Hull, eds. Princeton, N.J.: Princeton University Press, 1966.

Jung, Carl, and Wolfgang Pauli. *The Interpretation of Nature and the Psyche.* New York: Pantheon Books, 1955.

Klug, Sonja Ulrike. *Kathedrale des kosmos: Die heilige geometrie von Chartres.* Hugendubel, Germany: Verlag Heinrich, 2001.

Krippner, Stanley, and P. Welch. *Spiritual Dimensions of Healing.* New York: Irvington, 1992.

LaBerge, Stephen, and H. Rheingold. *Exploring the World of Lucid Dreaming.* New York: Ballantine Books, 1990.

Lavallée, Théophile. "Histoire de Paris depuis le temps des Gaulois jusqu'à nos jours" (originally published in 1857). At www.gutenberg.org. Accessed June 28, 2010.

Le Scouëzec, Gwenc'hlan. *Bretagne Terre sacrée.* Brasparts, France: Éd. Beltan, 1977.

———. *Guide de la Bretagne.* Paris: René Alleau/Tchou, 1966.

Le Scouëzec, Gwen, and Philippe Court-Payen. "Géosophie des hauts-lieux: Lignes de force terrestres ou instrument d'un pouvoir?" *Bulletin du Corps à vivre* 19 (March 1979).

Le Scouëzec, Gwenc'hlan, and Jean Robert Masson. *Bretagne mégalithique.* Paris: Éd. Seuil, 1987.

Lovelock, James. *The Ages of Gaia.* New York: Bantam books, 1990.

Maestracci, Robert. *Géographie secrète de la Provence.* Bron, France: Cheminements, 2005.

Mails, Thomas E. *The Hopi Survival Kit: The Prophecies, Instructions and Warnings Revealed by the Last Elders.* New York: Penguin, 1997.

Margulis, Lynn, and Dorion Sagan. *Microcosmos. Four Billion Years of Evolution from Our Microbial Ancestors.* New York: Simon and Shuster/Summit Books, 1986.

Markale, Jean. *Carnac et l'énigme de l'Atlantide.* Paris: Pygmalion/Watelet, 1987.

———. *Chartres et l'énigme des Druides.* Paris: Pygmalion/Watelet, 1988.

———. *Gisors et l'énigme des Templiers.* Paris: Pygmalion/Watelet, 1986.

Mishlove, Jeffrey. *The Roots of Consciousness.* New York: Marlowe and Co, 1997.

Neihardt, John G. *Black Elk Speaks.* New York: Harper Collins, 2004.

Nelson, R. D., G. J. Bradish, Y. H. Dobyns, et al. "FieldREG Anomalies in Group Situations." *Journal of Scientific Exploration* 10, no.1 (1996), 111–41.

Peat, F. D. *Synchronicity: The Bridge between Matter and Mind.* New York: Bantam Books, 1987.

Penrose, Roger. *The Emperor's New Mind.* Oxford, England: Oxford University Press, 1989.

Phaure, Jean. *Introduction à la géographie sacrée de Paris Barque d'Isis.* Etival le Mans, France: Borrégo, 1993.

Picknett, Lynn, and Clive Prince. *The Templar Revelation: Secret Guardians of the True Identity of Christ.* New York: Touchstone, 1998.

Pigani, Erik. *Psi: Enquête sur les phénomènes paranormaux.* Paris: Presses du Châtelet, 1999.

Poincaré, Henri. *Science and Method.* New York: Dover Publications, 1952.

Pritzker, Steven. "Does Creative Flow Represent an Altered State?" Presentation at Third Psi Meeting, April 21–23, 2006, Curitiba, Brazil.

Radin, Dean. *The Conscious Universe.* New York: Ballantine, 1997.

Redfield, James. *The Celestine Prophecy.* New York: Warner Books, 1993.

Robertson, R. *Your Shadow.* Virginia Beach: A.R.E. Press, 1997.

———. *Jungian Archetypes: Jung, Gödel, and the History of Archetypes.* York Beach, Me.: Nicholas-Hays, 1995.

Rogo, Scott. *Mind beyond the Body.* New York: Penguin, 1978.

Roumeguère-Eberhardt, Jacqueline. *Quand le python se déroule.* Paris: Laffont, 1991. Film: *Python Uncoils.* Paris, France: CNRS-AV, 1982.

Sapa, Héhaka (Black Elk). *Rites secrets des indiens Sioux.* Paris: Petite Bibliothèque Payot, 1975.

Schwartz, Stephan. *The Secret Vaults of Time.* Charlottesville, Va.: Hampton Roads Publishing, 2005.

Tart, Charles, ed. *Altered States of Consciousness.* New York: John Wiley and Sons, 1969.

———. *States of Consciousness.* New York: Dutton, 1975.

Taylor, Ian. "Stones as Ley Indicators." www.leyhunter.com/archives/arch13.htm. Accessed June 28, 2010.

Teilhard de Chardin, Pierre. *Phenomenon of Man.* New York: Harper Torch Book, 1965.

Ullman, Montague, and Stanley Krippner. *Dream Telepathy.* New York: Macmillan, 1973.

Ushte, Taca, and Richard Erdoes. *Lame Deer, Seeker of Visions.* New York: Simon and Schuster, 1972.

Varvoglis, Mario. *La Rationalité de l'Irrationnel.* Paris: InterEditions, 1992.

Waite, Arthur E., ed. *Hermetic and Alchemical Writings of Paracelsus.* Boston: Shambhala, 1976.

Waters, Frank. *The Book of the Hopi.* New York: Viking/Penguin, 1963.

Watkins, Alfred. *The Old Straight Track.* Boothbay Harbor, Maine: Abacus, 1994.

Wilson, Colin. *From Atlantis to the Sphinx.* New York: Virgin Books, 1997.

Zohar, Danah, and Ian Marshall. *The Quantum Society.* New York: William Morrow, 1994.

INDEX

A Spots and G Spots, 165–73,
    188–89, 172, 209, Plate 2
alchemy, 5, 14, 29–31, 152, 245, 254–56,
    309, 355
alignment, 141–49, 154–55, 163–64,
    167, 169, 176
    in Paris, 199, 202, 207–13, 217–18,
    227, 234, 247, 333–35, 344
anchor (verb), 20, 25, 39, 109, 132, 161–
    62, 183, 187, 189–92, 194, 265
    point, 45–47, 190
annul(ling) (space), 3, 64, 116,
    267–95, 274 (fig. 11.1), 323, 354
    time, 3, 307, 296–314,
anomalous, 29, 38, 41, 86, 292, 295, 298,
    301, 307, 355
antenna, 4, 69, 100, 103, 162,
    169 70, 188–89, 237
Apocalypse. See Armageddon;
    Revelation (John's Book of the
    Apocalypse)
arc. See ogival; Roman (Empire)
Arc de Triomphe, 199–350
arch, 39, 45, 48, 147, 151, 188, 190, 192,
    195, 201, 259
    arch-mandorle, 231

arch-network, 4, 5, 241, 264
arch-telhar field, 42–43
archetype, 42, 70–72, 104, 106, 113, 119,
    121–22, 231, 254, 324, 328. See also
    Jung, Carl G.
Aristotle, 298, 309, 355
Armageddon, 8–12, 329
Asclepios, 170–72
attractor, 9–10, 12, 44
attunement, 1–2, 19–20, 39, 68, 76, 78,
    185, 188, 294–95

Baigent, Michael, 179, 237, 251, 253, 354
Bayard, Jean (-Pierre), 137–39,
    352–53, 355
Bernard (St., de Clairvaux), 150, 153,
    243–45, 251, 253, 344
Black Elk, Wallace, 106, 352
black hole, 292–93. See also funnel
black virgin, 138, 171
blazon, 6, 34, 168, 234
Bohm, David, 323, 356
Bornholm, 154, 156–67, 353
Brahman, 11, 288
Bramly, Serge, 32, 351
Brown, Dan, 179, 197, 241

Buddha, 22, 108, 308
builder(s), 39, 40, 74, 134–41, 149–53, 164, 216–17, 242, 246, 309, 352

cardo, 148, 153, 200, 203, 206, 211–13, 216–64
Carnac, 136, 138, 141, 143–51, 163–64, 166, 169, 196, 353–54
Castaneda, Carlos, 32, 155, 351
Cathar(s), 36, 175, 181, 183
cathedral, 4–5, 39–40, 46, 74, 124, 134–39, 143–55, 186, 200, 207, 214, 216, 255–60, 337–38
Celtic, 17, 69, 73–74, 124, 135–38, 145–46, 148, 153, 161, 166, 170–71, 178, 180, 183, 195–96, 208, 217, 242
chakra, 21, 57–58, 66–68, 100, 104, 118–19, 121–22, 126–31, 176, 185–88, 203–6, 270
    head, 16, 18, 21–22, 28, 30, 45, 67, 107–8, 112–13, 186, 195–96, 288
    navel, 127–30
chaos, 42, 44, 271, 305, 328, 356
Chartres, 4, 73, 135–38, 148–53, 169–75, 190–94, 201, 231, 236, 238, 241–46, 309, 352–60
Christian-Druidic, 124, 185
circle route, 7, 154, 210, 331, 351
collective mind, 2, 36, 53, 55, 328
collective unconscious, 28, 48, 70, 107, 319, 328
Compagnon, 149–52, 245
consciousness energy, 2, 3, 5, 13–16, 85, 100, 112, 266, 305, 320, 322
cosmic, 10–12, 27, 29, 45, 169, 185
cosmo-telluric, 5, 40, 74, 133, 139, 154–60, 164–75, 181, 187–94, 201–3, 241, 246, 264

Court-Payen, Philippe, 137, 146, 353
Cross, Maltese (St-John), 143, 206–7 (fig. 9.2, 207)
crypt, 139, 150, 170, 242

deep reality, 300, 323, 327
Deleuze, Gilles, 330, 356
de Molay, Jacques, 151–53, 245–46
Devereux, Paul, 137, 142, 353
Dogon, 33–35
dolmen, 34, 73–74, 124, 144, 167–69, 172, 173, 242
Dossey, Larry, 61, 351–52
dream, 12, 32, 41, 70, 104–7, 117–18, 121, 277
dreamtime, 36, 117, 291
Druidic, 4–5, 40–41, 73–74, 124, 138, 144, 154, 170, 193–95, 200, 242, 254, 354

eco-field (eco-semantic field), 5, 278–79, 284–85, 304–5, 312
Egypt/ian 6–7, 154, 167, 170, 214, 235–56, 243–44, 250, 253–54, 309
    network, 4, 135, 138, 151, 182, 184, 209–11, 227, 235
Einstein, Albert, 41, 106, 292, 296, 323
Eliade, Mircea, 327, 356
elm, 239–40, 251, 254
embedding, 47, 218, 222, 234, 238, 261, 279, 287–88, 291, 294–95, 299, 327
End of Time (End time), 8, 11, 246
energy field, 3, 45, 58–59, 67, 78, 85, 101–3, 117, 126, 128, 132, 186, 312
    structure, 20, 58–59, 67, 85–87, 184

Fibonacci, 216–18, 222

Freemason/ry, 152, 199, 230, 235, 245, 251

funnel, 265, 272–76, 288–95 (fig. 11.1, 274)

syg-, 290–93, 294

fusion (state), 2–3, 22–23, 27–28, 45, 64–65, 110, 130, 314

Gallo-Roman, 4–5, 74, 135–36, 193, 200, 252

Gaul (Gallic) 73, 136, 148–49, 166, 170, 195, 200, 248, 334, 354

geo-architecture, 6, 154, 157, 233–34, 236–37, 238

principles of, 6, 205, 208–9, 211, 216, 218, 223, 233, 237

geomagnetic (GM), 4, 124–25, 141, 154, 158–60, 162, 183

geometry, sacred, 6, 149–54, 199, 207, 309

principles of, 40, 46, 133, 151, 187, 193, 202, 207–21, 230, 237, 241–46, 250, 309

Gisors, 239–40, 248, 254, 354

Global Consciousness Project (GCP), 24, 351

golden proportion (*phi*), 39–40, 46, 124, 149, 151, 214–18, 219 (fig. 9.4), 216n, 222, 237, 256

Gothic 5, 171, 186, 188, 190, 210, 226–27, 231, 236

style, 5, 134, 149–53, 239, 241–44, 259, 308, 334, 346

Grail (Holy), 178–81, 251, 354

Grand Master, 106, 151, 240, 245–51, 260

Great Work, 5, 7–8, 38, 126, 149, 198, 200, 206, 331

grid in the sky, 19, 77, 80, 82

Haagensen, Erling, 156–57, 353

harmonization, 2, 21, 27–30, 58, 64–65, 96–98, 113, 133, 174, 188, 273, 282, 288–90, 292, 329, 332

at a distance, 279, 288

future, 12, 28, 42–43

inner, 27, 30, 44, 203, 254, 306

harmony field, 3, 20–22, 24, 26, 36, 40, 42, 44–45, 57–59, 61, 64, 69, 78–79, 81, 82–83, 92, 96, 131

Hermes (Thoth/Mercury), 29, 109, 135, 147, 170, 195–96, 209, 220, 235, 243–45, 253, 255, 258, 260, 263, 309, 335, 341, 355

high site, 41, 141, 146, 154, 175, 179, 253

improvisation. *See* jam

intention, 29, 40, 44, 55, 102, 106, 113, 131–32, 177, 187, 321–22, 325

interconnected/ness, 8, 19, 37–38, 40, 44, 55–58, 70–71, 78–79, 81, 88, 95, 133, 154, 193, 247, 250, 287, 294, 322, 332

interconnection, 28, 42–43, 46, 55, 86, 98, 152, 154, 241, 264, 316, 322, 328, 332, 356

inverted, 40, 215, 203

pyramid, 173, 175, 198–99, 203, 206, 209–10, 212, 221, 256, 259, 263, 334, 337

Isis, 7, 136, 236, 249–50, 253, 338

jam, 26, 36–38, 52–57, 69, 80, 90–97

Jung, Carl G., 10, 41, 70–71, 88, 106–7, 254, 276–77, 299, 308, 310, 323, 328, 355

Krippner, Stanley, xiv, 70, 352, 354–55
Kumb(a) Mela, 19, 21, 25, 77, 197
kundalini, 16, 21, 28, 120–21, 122, 131,
    186, 188, 196–97

Leigh, Richard, 179, 237, 251, 253, 354
Leonardo da Vinci, 195, 256, 306
Le Scouëzec, Gwen (Gwenc'hlan), 136,
    144–46, 164, 353
ley (ley line), 4, 47, 74, 137, 141, 147n,
    148, 154–56, 161, 163, 166, 187,
    199, 333–45, 353
  in Great Britain, 141–43
  in Paris, 202, 205, 207–8, 211,
    217–18, 220–21, 227, 239, 248
  sacred women's, 252–53
liberation, 22, 27–29,
lily, 6, 212, 233–35, 252–53
Lincoln, Henry, 156, 179, 237, 251, 253,
    353–54
Living Creatures (Four), 231, 236
local universe, 294–95
Louvre (and leys), 147, 198–202, 206,
    209–13, 221, 253–63, 333–43. *See
    also* pyramid (structure)

Madeleine Church (La), 6, 208–9,
    212, 217–18, 221, 226–28, 231,
    233–36, 250–53, 264, 335, 338,
    347
Magdalene (Mary), 6, 140, 179–80 (fig.
    7.4), 230, 233–37, 250, 253
mandorle, 6, 212, 219 (fig. 9.4), 230–36,
    238
Margulis, Lynn, 286, 354
Markale, Jean, 136, 139, 144, 163–64,
    171, 245–46, 353–54
Maya, 10–11, 165

megalith(s), 3–5, 34, 36, 44, 73–74,
    124, 133–55, 162–78, 181, 192–96,
    200–201, 208, 254, 264, 352–53
  people, 4, 34, 73–74, 138, 141–42,
    147, 161, 164, 169
menhir, 4, 73–74, 124, 137–39, 144, 147,
    163–64, 166–74, 181, 242, 254
Mercury (god). *See* Thoth; Hermes
Meridian, 197–98, 205, 227, 340,
    344–45
mind (potentials), 10, 29–31, 88,
    315–17, 319
  and matter, 5n, 299, 322, 327, 351,
    354
  one mind, 59, 65, 68
Mitterrand, 47, 199, 203, 205–6, 238,
    257, 337–38, 342, 344–45
monastery, 2, 17–18, 33, 74–77, 80–81,
    114, 141, 150–53, 181, 243–45
Montségur, 36, 40, 42, 44, 50, 52,
    122, 133, 175–84. *See also* seat
    (headquarters)

Napoleon, 47, 148, 153, 208–10, 217,
    234, 260
Nasik, 2, 19–21, 25–26, 38, 74, 77,
    79–81, 85, 87, 89
Nautes, 135, 148–49, 195, 201, 258
Nelson, Roger. *See* Global Consciousness
    Project (GCP)
node (role), 3, 6–7, 13, 23, 26, 59–60,
    65, 67–72, 81–86, 90–96, 113
  network, 13, 23–24, 146, 148, 156,
    163, 165, 167, 171, 176, 182, 186,
    191, 194, 197–265
nonduality, 288
nonlocal/ity, 102, 277–78, 288, 295,
    305, 320–22, 325, 327

Notre-Dame de Paris (cathedral), 4, 135–36, 190, 195, 200, 223, 226, 229, 255, 309, 337

Obelisk, 6–7, 46, 147–48, 156, 189, 197–98, 203, 208–12, 216–40
ogival, 6, 61, 134, 188, 191, 195, 231, 233, 243, 309
OM (AUM), 14–15, 185–86, 191
Omega (Point), 6, 11, 38, 42–43
oneness, 3, 24, 27, 64, 66, 131
Order, 150–51, 153, 240, 243–45, 251, 253–54. *See also* Templar (Knights)
oriented, 47, 60, 133, 135, 157, 159, 187, 190, 193, 199, 201, 207, 210, 232, 234, 241, 256, 351

Paracelsus, 11, 278, 308–10, 313, 355
Pauli, Wolfgang, 277–78, 310–13, 323, 355
Phaure, Jean, 190, 201, 353–54
phi. See golden proportion
Physics, 3, 87, 102, 265–66, 272, 276, 285, 292–93, 296, 298–99, 302, 305, 311, 313, 320–27
prayer, 2, 19, 25, 27, 33, 61–65, 75, 89, 93, 252, 263
prediction, 10, 15, 42–43, 87, 298
Picknett and Prince, 156, 179, 351, 353–54
Priory, of Sion, 7, 157, 240, 247–54
properties (semantic), 13, 58, 88–89, 100, 124–31, 265, 293, 305, 322
network, 144, 163, 172, 214
proximity (semantic), 276, 278, 291, 294–95, 327
psi, 296, 298, 302, 307, 316–27, 355–56
psyche, 5, 9, 29–30, 36, 70, 88, 93,

101–2, 106–7, 125, 185, 196, 203, 254, 299, 321, 355
purusha, 19, 27, 30, 288
pyramid (structure), 1, 173–75, 209
Louvre's, 198–99, 203, 206, 209, 212, 221, 256, 259, 263, 334–41
See also St. John the Baptist's pyramid
Pythagoras, 170, 214, 243, 252, 309

quantum, 113, 295, 208, 311, 313, 320–27, 352, 355

Radin, Dean, 355
ray (syg-), 16, 34, 45, 63, 110–11, 119–24, 157, 167, 178, 182, 186, 189, 205, 270, 272–73
Redfield, James, 67, 352
resonance, 9, 36, 39, 45, 51, 63, 185–87, 241, 277, 291, 330
retrocausality, 272, 278, 298, 320
Revelation (John's Book of, The Apocalypse), 9, 231, 236
Robert (The) Bruce, 245, 251
rod, 3, 48, 180, 267–76, 288–97
Roman (Empire), 4, 5, 73–74, 138, 140, 147–49, 166, 183, 196, 200
style, 4, 5, 48, 74, 134–37, 142, 150, 188, 191, 193, 200, 209, 233–34, 242, 252, 258, 260, 308
rose window, 135, 151, 160, 238, 309, 331
Rosicrucian, 245, 251
Rosslyn Chapel, 251
royal/ty, 140, 179–80, 193, 195–96, 197, 213, 233–37, 252–53

samadhi, 24, 67, 104, 108. *See also* transcendental

Scotland, 141, 245–46, 251
seat (headquarters), 7, 249–51, 253
  of power, 40, 42, 44, 133, 175–84
  See also Montségur
Self. *See* Jung, Carl G.
semantic (syg) energy, 5, 13–14, 48, 52,
    58, 87, 91, 100–03, 107, 109–17,
    123–27, 130–33, 162–63, 177,
    186–89, 206, 255, 270–72, 275,
    280–91, 297, 305, 322–27
  dimension, 14–15, 28, 36, 42, 51, 81,
    101, 112–13, 276, 280, 288, 291,
    297, 300–301, 304–8, 313–14,
    322, 332, 356
  field, 100, 103, 125, 265, 277–79,
    285–86, 291–94, 300, 305–07,
    311. *See also* eco-field
  manifold, 266, 291, 293, 322
Semantic Fields Theory (SFT), 5, 9, 42,
    101, 277–78, 284, 291, 294–95,
    299–300, 305, 322, 327, 354–55
Shakti, 131, 196
singularity, 265, 277, 292–93, 296–97,
    320–21, 355
snake, 35, 71, 164, 196, 200
Solomon, 235, 243, 309
soul, 5, 19, 22–29, 39–40, 42–43,
    52, 107, 110, 112, 132, 174, 185,
    203, 250, 268, 283, 307, 314,
    351–52
spacetime (space and time), 3, 52, 265,
    276–78, 291, 294, 305, 307, 321
sphinx, 7, 46, 221, 255, 257n, 334
spin, 68, 87, 295, 325–27, 355
spot (network), 5, 16–17, 20–21, 48,
    156–58, 161, 168–73, 176, 181–83,
    187, 192–94, 234. *See also* seat of
    power; A Spot

Sri Yantra, 173–75 (fig. 7.3, 174), 203–7
    (fig. 9.1, 204), 224 (fig. 9.5), 226,
    229–30, 235–36, 238, 331
St-Michel, 145–47 (fig. 7.1, 145), 164
stag (god), 135, 195–96, 254
standing stones, 4–5, 27, 34, 74, 114,
    137–38, 141–44, 148, 155,
    161–64, 168, 181, 241. *See also*
    megalith
state, collective, 1, 11, 15–19, 59
  of harmony, 1–3, 13, 36–37, 53–56,
    63, 71, 81, 282
  of unity, 28, 44
  See also fusion (state); transcendental
St-Gervais-St-Protais Church, 217,
    226–27, 239, 248, 258, 343–44
St. John the Baptist's Pyramid, 7, 208,
    224, 239, 247–55
St-Sulpice Church, 4, 7, 136, 198, 222,
    249–50, 253, 260, 262, 340–41
Sufi, 10, 19, 32–33, 61–65, 123, 270
Syg. *See* semantic
symbol, 6, 70–72, 151, 180, 203
symbolism, 34, 149, 151–53, 168, 180,
    188, 230, 233–35, 242, 255, 264,
    333
synchronicity, 276–78, 323–26,
    355–56
synlocalization, 295

tantrism, 14, 37, 254, 269, 309
Tao, 11, 288
Tart, Charles, 352
Taylor, Ian, 141–43, 163, 353
Teilhard de Chardin, 11, 42–43, 351
telepathy, 3, 9, 17–18, 20, 26, 64, 66, 75,
    77, 80, 180, 237, 271, 278, 288, 318,
    320–21, 355

field, 2, 13, 17–20, 24, 26, 66, 68,
    76–82, 90
    See also telhar field
telhar field, 2, 8, 9, 13, 23–30, 36–45,
    50, 59, 61, 64, 67–74, 79–99, 113,
    125, 131, 133, 265–267, 270–76,
    282, 283, 286–90, 294, 297, 311,
    314, 330, 332
    boundary of, 2, 13, 18–20, 38, 44,
    74–89, 136, 292–93
    properties, 88–89
telluric, 4, 51, 158–69, 190, 192
    current, 74, 157–58, 171, 188–90
    energy, 50, 156, 159, 188–89, 192, 264
    See also cosmo-telluric
Templar (Knights), 7, 150, 239, 245, 251,
    351, 353–54
    Order, 150–51, 153, 240, 243–45, 251,
    253–54
    See also Bornholm
temple (and network), 3–7, 40, 73–74,
    107–14, 135–39, 151–56, 161–62,
    167–72, 181–84, 187–93, 200,
    227–35, 241–42, 263
    and India, 19–27, 77–82, 114, 183, 203
    See also Madeleine Church (La);
    Gallo-Roman; Egyptian
Temple (Templars) 7, 239, 245–46, 249,
    257–63
theosophy (and Bailey, Alice), 10, 30, 43,
    152, 351
therapy/therapeutic, 278, 298–99,
    310

Thoth, 170n, 235, 243–34, 243–44,
    253–55, 309. *See also* Hermes
torus, 2–3, 13, 26, 41, 66–69, 87,
    103–8, 112–13, 133, 196, 271
tradition, 74, 137, 152, 170, 207, 216,
    237, 245–46, 254, 308–9, 352–53,
    355
trance, 27, 29–30, 36, 50–57, 60, 63–65,
    69, 90–96, 128, 273–74, 282, 286,
    316–18, 352, 356
    -dance, 26, 29, 42, 51, 119, 268, 273,
    286
transcendental, 15, 16, 18, 28, 67, 81–82,
    98, 104, 108, 112, 121, 314
transformation, 27, 29–31, 315–17,
    319, 322
translocalized, 273, 276, 294–95
transmission, 31–34, 116, 156, 192,
    241–46

unconscious. *See* collective
    unconscious
underground, 4, 47–48, 73, 88, 133,
    137–39, 143, 168, 170–75,
    183–84, 186, 190, 199, 243

Watkins, Alfred, 4, 137, 141, 208, 353
Wilson, Colin, 184

yoga, 28, 98, 103, 121, 127, 169, 188,
    196
    harmonic resonance, 187, 241
    infinite space, 22–23, 42

ABOUT THE AUTHOR

A scientist and seer, Chris H. Hardy has completed extensive research on consciousness and has evolved a theory of mind about which she has given or published more than fifty papers. A Ph.D. in cultural anthropology and former researcher at Psychophysical Research Laboratories in Princeton, she has addressed such various areas as cognitive science, system theory, chaos theory, consciousness studies, artificial intelligence, and parapsychology. A persistent traveler, she has spent considerable time exploring various knowledge systems and cultures, maintaining a keen interest in Eastern religions, shamanism, and esoterica. Author of a dozen books on consciousness, she has developed original techniques of visualization and meditation. She is also an author of science fiction, novels, and a body of poetry.

Visit the sacred network website at
www.sacrednetwork.net

BOOKS OF RELATED INTEREST

The Mayan Code
Time Acceleration and Awakening the World Mind
by Barbara Hand Clow

How the World Is Made
The Story of Creation according to Sacred Geometry
by John Michell with Allan Brown

The Akashic Experience
Science and the Cosmic Memory Field
by Ervin Laszlo

Science and the Akashic Field
An Integral Theory of Everything
by Ervin Laszlo

Quantum Shift in the Global Brain
How the New Scientific Reality Is Changing Us and Our World
by Ervin Laszlo

Science and the Reenchantment of the Cosmos
The Rise of the Integral Vision of Reality
by Ervin Laszlo

WorldShift 2012
Making Green Business, New Politics, and Higher
Consciousness Work Together
by Ervin Laszlo

The Healing Energy of Shared Consciousness
A Taoist Approach to Entering the Universal Mind
by Mantak Chia

INNER TRADITIONS • BEAR & COMPANY
P.O. Box 388
Rochester, VT 05767
1-800-246-8648
www.InnerTraditions.com

Or contact your local bookseller